Civil Society and the Political Imagination in Africa

Civil Society and the Political Imagination in Africa

Critical Perspectives

EDITED BY

JOHN L. AND JEAN COMAROFF

THE UNIVERSITY OF CHICAGO PRESS
Chicago & London

The University of Chicago Press, Chicago 60637
The University of Chicago Press, Ltd., London

Printed in the United States of America
08 07 06 05 04 03 02 01 00 99 1 2 3 4 5

Library of Congress Cataloging-in-Publication Data

Civil society and the political imagination in Africa : critical perspectives / edited by John L. and Jean Comaroff.
p. cm.
Includes bibliographical references and index.
ISBN 0-226-11413-9 (cloth : alk. paper). — ISBN 0-226-11414-7 (paper: alk. paper)
1. Civil society—Africa. I. Comaroff, John L., 1945–
II. Comaroff, Jean.
JQ1879.A15C583 1999
320.96-dc21 99–23280
CIP

♾ The paper used in this publication meets the minimum requirements of the American National Standard for Information Sciences-Permanence of Paper for Printed Library Materials, ANSI Z39.48–1992.

CONTENTS

PREFACE

THE INCREASINGLY GLOBAL preoccupation with civil society, one of the big ideas of the millennial moment, is shot through with ironies. Also with ambiguities and impossibilities. As a quest for panacea in the post-everything age, it is at once productive and fraught with problems. At once a new beginning and, maybe, a dead end.

Martin Krygier[1] reminds us, after Michael Walzer,[2] that the recent revival of the concept of civil society in Europe was propelled, in the first instance, by anticommunist dissidents in the East, which "lacked it but wanted it." Then it moved toward the West, which was believed to have "had it but hadn't thought much about it." Not, at least, until a few years ago, when it began to evoke a markedly evangelical interest in some quarters—and to raise concomitant qualms in others. For, and here is one of the ironies, the more that occidental ethicists reflected on civil society—the more convinced they were that it should be championed on a planetary scale—the less sure they became of what it actually is. And whether they *do* actually have it. Witness the *Call to Civil Society* issued in 1998 in a *Report to the Nation*[3] by the Institute for American Values (jointly with the august University of Chicago Divinity School). It is addressed to a United States in the throes of crisis: to a country fast "using up, but not replenishing, [its] civic and moral resources."

Civil society, it appears, is known principally by its absence or incompleteness. More aspiration than accomplishment, and an ill-defined one at that, it recedes rapidly before the scrutinizing gaze. Indeed, for all those who, like Václav Havel, would write a road map *Toward a Civil Society,*[4] there are others who deny the utility of so doing. Why? Because, as Michael Hardt argues, we have already entered the age of "postcivil society," an age incapable of producing the conditions of its possibility.[5] Even for Havel, mind you, it is an age marked by the danger of a "new totalitarianism of consumption, commerce, and money." An age in which, for many—especially those who live in the postrevolutionary vacuum of freedoms won—social life "seems to have lost its purpose." In which states, like the Czech Republic, think that they no longer have ideologies.[6] Another, resounding irony.

In spite of this, civil society has served as a remarkably fertile call-to-arms across the world. In inhospitable times, the very idea reanimates the civilizing mission of modernity, both Christian and secular: its specter, to parody Marx, rises as the prodigal spirit of a spiritless age. Which, in and of itself, has raised suspicions in scholarly circles—left, right, and center—as John Keane already noted a decade ago, and Chris Hann reaffirms in a more recent anthropological take on the subject.[7] To be sure, its appeal has been dismissed as overrated, its substance as underspecified. Those who have deployed it find themselves accused of conflating an analytic construct with an ideological trope, thus rendering the former promiscuous and the latter impotent. Worse still, the term itself is said to offer a new alibi for old-style "humane" imperialism, its Eurocentric liberalism promoted by such latter-day evangelists as nongovernmental organizations and development agencies.

But even in the academy, even with all the criticism it has attracted, the idea—the fetish?—of civil society has worked some magic. For in the process of arguing about it, many scholars—like politicians and poets and ordinary people—have rediscovered a language in which to talk about the utopian ideals of democracy and moral community. Amid fin de siècle cynicism and retrospection, in a universe beset by the collapse of grand systems and old certainties, advocates of civil society look bravely toward a new world. True, their idyll has been downsized, localized, tailored to a neoliberal age. It has become, say Cohen and Areto,[8] "self-limiting": purged, in short, of large historical visions and stately transformative schemes—and left to the parochial enterprise of self-constituting, self-identifying actors. Still, while it may lack the grandeur of Enlightenment emancipation, the idea of civil society has kindled a reformist spirit. As we shall see, for some at least, it promises a prospect of rescue from the gaping abyss, the political void, of postmodern nihilism.

What is it, then, about "civil society" that so fires the moral imagination, that makes it a trope for these uncertain times? What, if anything, links the present moment to the one in which the idea first arose? To the post-Enlightenment epoch in Europe, that is, which also gave rise to the nation-state, to the rights-bearing subject, to the concept of culture, the civil, civility, civilization? To the distinction, as John Keane notes,[9] between "the state" and something that came to know itself as "society"? To an assertive, self-constructed bourgeoisie, whose triumphal rise would effect a cultural revolution? To the notion of a public sphere, separate from church or government, perceived as an impersonal, self-regulating site for the pursuit of voluntarist civic action?

Clearly, the preoccupation with civil society at the close of the twentieth century owes much to the transformation of these very things: to forces reconfiguring the sovereignty of the nation-state, the meaning of citizenship, the identity of the modernist subject, the nature of the bourgeoisie and the public sphere, the experience of moral community—indeed, the various coordinates of our apprehension of "society" and "culture." As this suggests, "civil society" is a relational term, one of a set of interdependent constructs. But what exactly *is* the relationship among these terms now? How has it changed over time? And what may a historical anthropology, with its focus upon the evanescent intersections of the cultural and the material, have to bring to the problem?

Finally, where does Africa figure in the equation?

Africa, it goes almost without saying, has long been held to lack any trace of civil society; even more, to lack those things associated with its achievement in Enlightenment Europe—not least, a developed, modern bourgeoisie. Nowhere, wrote Adam Ferguson in 1767, had the torrid zones "matured the more important projects of political wisdom, [or] inspired the virtues which are connected with freedom, and required in the conduct of civil affairs."[10] Two hundred and thirty years later—after almost two centuries as the object of a concerted civilizing mission on the part of Europeans—Africa is home to diverse, determined struggles for popular democracy and moral community. And its aspirations are fueled, in many places, by the kinds of bourgeoisies and bourgeois cultures whose rise was severely restricted under colonialism. Yet, in the eyes of a watching world, it remains more likely to produce civil war than civil society. Why? How are we to make sense of new social movements, new political orders, new cultural coordinates here? And, perhaps most importantly for us, what lessons does Africa have for our understanding of the quest for civil society, sui generis?

It was these concerns, these questions, that prompted the collection of essays presented here; *not* a desire to discuss, yet again, the salience for Africa of civil society as an analytic construct—or to offer ideological prescriptions in scholarly (dis)guise. The small conference for which they were written, held in May 1996, was one of a series convened over the past few years by the Committee on African and African-American Studies at the University of Chicago; the first, in the early 1990s, gave rise to the publication of *Modernity and Its Malcontents* (1993).[11] The committee is bureaucratically lean: its major activity is to facilitate the research and teaching of the Africanist circle at the university. This diverse group spans the campus, from the medical school through the social sciences to the English department. For more than a decade, the engine of its enterprise has been a workshop, one of many interdisciplinary faculty-student forums sponsored by the Council for Advanced Study—which, under the genial guidance of John Boyer, Dean of the College, has enriched and expanded our own academic public sphere.

The term "workshop" is often fatuous, a strained effort to give artful concreteness to insubstantial intellectual exchanges. Yet it aptly describes the African Studies circle at Chicago, to which scholars of varying ages, nationalities, and theoretical proclivities continue to bring their works in progress, confident that they will receive close, constructive reading and engaged critique. While it is the home of passionately held positions, this forum is the province of no single department or discipline. It permits apprentices and senior professors to learn from each other in an atmosphere of affable collegiality. Successive cohorts of graduates have honed their professional skills here, returning to try out new ideas and to participate in symposia like the one that produced this volume.

At a moment when support for area studies is wavering, and sponsorship for Africanist research is more precarious still, such resources should be nurtured. We offer this collection, most of it authored by advanced graduate students and young faculty, as a tribute to those who have sustained our collaborative endeavors over the years. Its ultimate objective—the interrogation of a provocative, planetary issue through a set of geopolitically related cases—is to consider the indispensability of regional perspectives on global processes. For "civil society," however it may be defined or lived, turns out to be protean; simultaneously one thing and many, absolute and refractory, actual and chimerical. Its very plasticity allows an ostensibly universal term, Eurocentrically founded, to take on distinctive local forms. And to become the subject of distinctly local struggles. The essays in this book attest in rich detail to the diverse and unexpected deployment of the concept in, and in respect of, Africa. The authors' concerns range from the impact of colonial ideology and development practice on discourses of civility, through popular movements for reform of the public sphere and the substance of politics, to everyday attempts to conjure up new modes of selfhood and moral community. Together, they raise urgent questions about the location of these African phenomena, dialectically, in larger forces of history; in particular, in the radical reconfiguration of the modernist world order. They also offer evidence of the bold reach of a historical anthropology, broadly conceived, laboring to come to grips with just such forces.

We wish to thank John Boyer, who has given unstinting moral and material support for African Studies at the University of Chicago. So, too, has Richard Saller, Dean of the Social Sciences. Both are remarkably encouraging of the enthusiasms of their faculty. Both have made a great deal of difference. Anne-Maria Makhulu organized the conference with admirable efficiency and good humor, often in adversity. And Jesse Shipley and Maureen Anderson served as insightful, diligent, long-suffering research assistants; each played a major part in bringing this volume to realization. We express our warm gratitude to them—indeed, to all our students, past and present, whose creativity, humor, and vital sense of purpose have been the wellspring of African Studies at Chicago.

John L. and Jean Comaroff

Notes

1. Martin Krygier, *Between Fear and Hope: Hybrid Thoughts on Public Values* (Sydney: ABC Books, 1997), 55.

2. Michael Walzer, "The Civil Society Argument," in *Dimensions of Radical Democracy: Pluralism, Citizenship, Community,* ed. C. Mouffe (New York: Verso, 1992), 90.

3. Council on Civil Society, *A Call to Civil Society: Why Democracy Needs Moral Truths, A Report to the Nation* (New York: Institute for American Values, 1998), 4.

4. Václav Havel, *Toward a Civil Society: Selected Speeches and Writings 1990–1994,* translated by Paul Wilson et al. (Prague: Lidové Noviny, n.d.).

5. Michael Hardt, "The Withering of Civil Society," *Social Text* 45, 14 (4): 27–44, 27.

6. Havel, *Toward a Civil Society,* 95, 77.

7. John Keane, Introduction to *Civil Society and the State: New European Perspectives,* ed. J. Keane (New York: Verso, 1988), 13; Chris Hann, Introduction to *Civil Society: Challenging Western Models,* ed. C. Hann and E. Dunn (London: Routledge, 1996), 2–3.

8. Jean Cohen and Andrew Arato, *Civil Society and Political Theory* (Cambridge: MIT Press, 1994), xii.

9. *Civil Society and the State,* 15.

10. Adam Ferguson, *An Essay on the History of Civil Society,* ed. F. Oz-Salzberger (Cambridge: Cambridge University Press, 1995), 108.

11. Jean and John L. Comaroff, eds., *Modernity and Its Malcontents: Ritual and Power in Africa* (Chicago: University of Chicago Press, 1993).

1

Introduction

John L. and Jean Comaroff

It returned again and again, each time with a different meaning, and all the meanings flowed through [it] . . . like water through a riverbed.

—Milan Kundera, *The Unbearable Lightness of Being*

THE *IDÉE* OF CIVIL society has stirred social imaginations across the globe in recent years. Political aspirations, too. We have yet to see, of course, whether it actually turns out to be a Big Idea—the uppercase here being in deference to Hegel.[1] And to History in the making. In the meantime, however, its discrete charms equip it well to serve as a courtly call to arms in a world often dubbed *post*revolutionary; a late-twentieth-century world weary of grand reformist schemes of the kind fashioned, all over the ideological map, during the high age of modernity.

Not least in, and in respect of, Africa.

Many Africans have embraced the Idea with almost millennial fervor. So, too, have many Africanists. Perhaps the enthusiasm of the latter is whetted by a belief, a provocation really, that goes back at least to the time of Adam; the time, that is, of the enlightened Adams, Ferguson and Smith. It persists today: that the "dark" continent has always been especially hostile, inimical even, to civic development. Africa, wrote Ferguson in 1767, suffers a "weakness in the genius of its people" (1995, 108). Like the "torrid" zones in general, it has not "inspired the virtues which are connected with freedom, and required in the conduct of civil affairs" (above, p. ix). More than two hundred years later, Robert McNamara, erstwhile president of the World Bank, proclaimed its problems in this regard still to be "far more severe than those of other regions" (quoted in Haynes 1997, 17). Even in the "new" South Africa, there are those who suggest that "the continent is in a state of *permanent* crisis," that all the recent talk of an African Renaissance is chimerical.[2] The very different narrative offered by more optimistic, less dismissive Africanist scholars seeks to counter this unremittingly bleak, often racist portraiture. The pursuit of civil society throughout the continent, says Crawford Young, is a "drama of redemption whose potential nobility commands our admiration" (1994, 48).[3] For Harbeson, it—the concept of civil society—is the "hitherto missing key" to understanding and, more importantly, to addressing Africa's current crises, both political and socioeconomic (1994, 1–2).

Others, while not reiterating tired archetypes of African impossibility, have been more prosaic, less persuaded by visions of salvation. Current Africanist discourses on civil society, notes Mamdani (1996, 13–14), resemble earlier debates about socialism: they are more programmatic than analytic, more rhetorical than historical, typically ill defined and unduly abstract. The parallel is suggestive, disturbing. But what makes it thinkable? How *has* such an imprecise, unspecified idea become the metaphor of the moment, standing in, here as elsewhere, for more coherent social visions, more commanding political ideologies? And why do those who join the argument so frequently wax polemical, rooting earnest appeals for reform in assumptions of absence—in a manner unnervingly reminiscent of earlier colonial evangelists, who deemed the Dark Continent incapable of kindling bourgeois civility? Could this have something to do with the fact that Europeans who impute to Africa a lack of anything qualified by the adjective "civil" seldom ground their claims in empirical observation; in the interrogation, "on the ground," of existing forms of association and aspiration, of participatory politics and public life, past and present (cf. Blaney and Pasha 1993, 5)?

This volume was designed as an exercise in just such close-up observation. We seek to interrogate the paradoxes, problems, and emancipatory possibilities presented by the idea of civil society in various African contexts; also, to explore the diverse meanings and deployments of that idea through a series of carefully situated ethnographic cases. But we have another agenda as well: to locate the term itself, critically, within a lexicon of cognate and closely related constructs—among them, moral community, the public sphere, bourgeois society, the nation-state, citizenship, civility. For these terms, in their various modernist guises—legal, secular, ethical, cultural, evolutionary—have a highly charged history in a continent still struggling to extricate itself from a century of European rule; from a cultural imperialism styled, literally, as a *civil*izing mission, whose telos lingers on in the paternalism of both the "charity business in Africa" (Monga 1996, 156) and the ideologically saturated "development" industry (see chapter 3; cf. Ferguson 1994; Escobar 1994).

As all this suggests, the rapid circulation of the Idea in contemporary Africa—as an analytic construct, a political cliché, a Utopian idyll, a grassroots cry for change, an article of faith—has a slippery, equivocal quality to it. Even as an analytic construct, it has come to signify many, sometimes incommensurate, things. Besides now commonplace, often nebulous allusions to "society against the state," to "voluntaristic association," and to the "bourgeois public sphere," civil society has been characterized as a "democracy" that sets publicly accountable limits to governmental power (Molutsi and Holm 1990); a domain of popular opinion, or moral sentiment, that cuts across ethnicity, locality, and class (Woods 1992, 88–89); a space of novel structures and communicative media that channel "the people's" wrath into political ferment (Monga 1996, 145–46); and, most expansively, a "new cultural fabric" capable of restructuring identities, of challenging existing monopolies of wealth and power, perhaps even of reinventing the terms of modernity itself (Bayart 1986, 120).

In short, in Africa as in other places, "civil society" evokes a polythetic clutch of signs. An all-purpose placeholder, it captures otherwise inchoate—as yet unnamed and unnameable—popular aspirations, moral concerns, sites and spaces of practice; likewise, it bespeaks a scholarly effort to recalibrate worn-out methodological tools, and to find a positive politics, amid conceptual confusion. Herein lies the larger object of this book: to explore some of the many exercises in social revisioning that have been licensed by the Idea of civil society—and the broad cluster of values for which it has come to stand—in intellectual debate, academic discourse, political critique, and social activism. Also in life "on the street." The latter, as Stambach stresses in chapter 9, is the pedestrian locale of much ordinary imagining, of talk and embodied practice, about cultural identities, moral communities, and the relation of the citizen to the state in late-twentieth-century Africa.

Ours, then, is a modest effort to reverse the priorities of much recent academic work on civil society; in particular, work that locates its renaissance in broader processes of globalization and the impact of the "new" world order on "local" populations.[4] We set out to ask what a specific set of African cases might tell us about the planetary appeal of the Idea on the eve of the millennium; about populist strivings for moral *community* and *social* being at a time when a triumphal neoliberalism calls into question the very existence of society,[5] trumpeting instead the uncompromising autonomy of the individual, rights-bearing, physically discrete, monied, market-driven, materially inviolate human subject. What, to borrow a phrase, is the elective affinity between this neocommunal ethic and the spirit of late capitalism? How might its versatile appeal, its diverse deployments, yield insight into the forces refiguring the geopolitical shape of our world? How successful is it in giving fresh substance to ever more eviscerated modernist concepts—society, citizenship, democracy, nationhood, the public, moral economy—in what are, for many purposes, postmodern times?

The Archaeology of an Idea, Briefly

[T]he creation of civil society is the achievement of the modern world. . . . [I]t is the territory of mediation [between the family and the state] where there is free play for every idiosyncrasy, every talent, every accident of birth and fortune, and where waves of passion gush forth, regulated only by reason glinting through them. . . .

—Hegel's Philosophy of Right

We have already noted in the preface that the metamorphosis of civil society from anachronistic ideal to global axiom has been laced with irony. Its latter-day advent has already acquired the hardening outlines of neomodern myth:[6] consider the extent to which a diverse body of works—some of them analytic, some pragmatic and prescriptive, some purely philosophical—have begun to tell a very similar story about the genesis and genealogy of the concept, even as they argue over its interpretation, its telos, its theoretical and sociomoral virtues.[7] These archaeologies, alike save for the quantity and content of their surface details, are usually told, layer upon layer, as a chronological epic of ideas and authors. With some notable exceptions,[8] they tend to be remarkably thin in recounting the material, political, and social dimensions of the *production* of those ideas.

They open with an origin story. It begins with the "modern" formulation of the concept, by contrast to its "traditional" precursors, in the mid-late 1700s—the time, as we said, of the Adams, Ferguson and Smith. In this myth, as in so many others, the traditional and the modern are sharply counterposed, the new taking root at the times and places of their intersection. Provoked partly by a philosophical conversation across the English Channel, partly by contemporary historical conditions, the Idea came to dominate the discourses of the Scottish Enlightenment,[9] where it was given its first systematic formulation (often attributed to Adam Ferguson).[10] Before then, the term, still in its "traditional" guise, is said to have been equated with political order, hence with the state. It was defined, implicitly, with reference to the Athenian or Roman polity, to Cicero and Aristotle, to citizenship and liberty. And, explicitly, by contrast to what it was not: the uncivil, "prehistoric"[11] condition of mankind living "in nature" (i.e., without any rational government), under the domination of divine authority, or in thrall to savage despotism (cf. Keane 1988c, 35; Kumar 1993, 376–77; Bobbio 1988, 73; Hardt 1995, 28). Two hundred years later, Lawrence Krader was to put this formula into a dialect of anthropologese: "Civil society," he said, is the "opposite" of "primitive society" (1976, 22). His formulation echoed Marx and Hegel; both, notes C. J. Arthur, editor of *The German Ideology*, contrasted civil(ized) society to "natural" or "primitive" society (1970, 5).[12] At its modern genesis, in sum, civil society was regarded as an accomplishment born out of an awareness of what was required, politically, to secure "a distinctively societal and human life . . . [and] to separate order and freedom from chaos and compulsion" (Tester 1992, 11).

The myth then proceeds through a cycle of four movements. In the first, the concept, now an Idea,[13] is transported from enlightened Scotland to Europe, where it acquires a genealogy of theoretico-philosophical positions, animated in the nineteenth and early twentieth centuries by a few heroic figures, from Hegel by way of Marx through Tocqueville to Gramsci and (usually) Habermas[14]—perhaps including other lesser lights, depending on theoretical preferences. Thereafter, second, it falls into a period of quiescence,[15] to be revitalized, third, during the late 1970s and 1980s by dissident intellectuals in the struggle against totalitarianism in eastern and central Europe, initially in Poland (see, for example, Rupnik 1979, 60; Arato 1981; Kumar 1993, 386; Krygier 1997a, 59). From here, fourth, it is borne back to its original home in the West, where the Enlightenment values it enshrined, those of uncoerced human association, had long been part of the unremarked fabric of society itself (Walzer 1992, 89; Krygier 1997b, 55); hence the notion that we Occidentals have lived in "it" without being aware of the fact (see the preface, vii; cf. Taylor 1990, 96). Finally, to close the circle, Western thinkers, prompted by world-historical events to reflect on the foundations of their own civic culture, set about a self-conscious process of re-membering: of rooting its genealogy in a "lost treasure" of writings by those eighteenth-century social theorists and moral philosophers with whom the story began. And so a heritage obscured by the subsequent rise and fall of grand systemic sociologies and ideologies is recuperated (Kumar 1993, 376; Keane 1988a, 33, 64).

The schematic events recounted in this ur-narrative did not occur in a historical vacuum, of course. Nor has the act of their recounting—a matter to which we shall return. But first, another point, or two.

Paradoxes from the Past, Memories of the Future

The objective in laying out this archaeology is *not* to recapitulate the "career of the concept," to engage in a further "act of recovery,"[16] or to preface our own history of the Idea. Others, more qualified than we, have already done these things to impressive effect. Our goal is, rather, to underscore a pair of observations. Neither is entirely new; both are important. One is that the retrieval of the concept, the final phase of the narrative cycle, has itself become an enthusiastic exercise in the making of "future-oriented memory" (Keane 1988a, 33, 64; Kumar 1993, 376): in contriving a past to conceptualize the continuous present; to bring order to its unruliness, its tendency to fracture familiar boundaries, transgress conventional limits, hybridize and compromise identities; to put into flux and movement what was considered stable, normative. Not that this is difficult to understand. As scholars and public intellectuals like to tell us, we inhabit an epoch marked by a "crisis of representation"; an epoch for which we lack a comprehensive theory, an epoch in which modernist sociological and anthropological constructs appear painfully incomplete, distorting, refractory.

The other observation, which is closely related, is that, for all the efforts to recuperate it, to assign to it a genealogy and a telos, the Idea of civil society has proven impossibly difficult to pin down. The more its advocates have sought to make it a mantra of sociomoral regeneration and social analysis, the more elusive and ambiguous it has become. Part of its attraction, perhaps, lies in the fact that, having lain dormant and invisible for so long, it does not carry the same baggage as other modernist constructs—like, say, culture or society, which have fallen into a state of critical turpitude in recent times. But it *is* a modernist conceit and is no better equipped to grasp the world after 1989—or whenever the postrevolutionary age might be said to have had its new dawn.

Here, then, is the paradox in the search for civil society at the century's end. The very fertility of the Idea—its broad, transnational appeal as a trope of moral imagining—stems from its polyvalence: its capacity to condense distinct doctrines and ethical strains in a fan of pliable associations that can be variously distilled and infinitely elaborated (Kumar 1993, 376). The more inchoate and polymorphous, the more appealing; the more appealing, the less attainable in any substantive, meaningful form. Alchemy of this kind is intrinsic to the work of political revisioning at all times and places. As Durkheim (1947) said long ago, the ritual of conjuring with resonant signs is a condition of the very possibility of imagining society, sui generis.

But, we stress, this process of alchemic imagining has to be understood in its own terms. It belongs to the poetics of ideology, not to the prosaic exercise of social analysis, which seeks precisely the opposite: to reduce ambiguity and delimit meaning. Indeed, in spite of the efforts of highly skilled scholars, East and West, to develop systematic theories of civil society (Rupnik 1979; Keane 1988c; Cohen and Arato 1994), or to give it content as a "necessary *practico-indicative* concept" (Anderson 1976–77, 35; cf. Kumar 1993), even its ontological status remains unclear. Is it a social domain? A type of institution or practice? A normative condition? A moral ideal? The question, in our view, points to its own answer. Or, more accurately, to the impossibility of an answer.

The substance of civil society as sign will always be as various as are the visions of its protagonists, its prophets, its political theorists. As it has always been. Nor can the problem of its specification, its conceptual definition, be decided for once and for all by rational debate, forensic analysis, or empirical investigation. For "it"—again, the irony of rendering singular an obdurate plural—is not a concrete entity waiting to be identified. Intrinsically protean, it is an immanent construct whose manifest materiality exists only to the extent that it is named, objectified, and sought after. To neoconservatives, it describes a depoliticized world in which market forces reign free from government control, free to construct a habitable social order; to post-Marxists, it conjures up a space, forged by "new" social movements, in which the will of "the people"—especially what was once the proletariat—is liberated from the repressive machinations of both economy and the state; to the "postideological," it speaks of moral community and an unfettered, self-sustaining public sphere. And this covers only an abbreviated range of Eurocentric perspectives.

Beyond the confines of the West, the term has spawned palpably different imaginings, many of them distrustful of Euro-modernity.[17] In eastern Europe, for example, it has prompted the quest for a distinctly local social order predating communism (see Rupnik 1988). In India, it has come to connote long-standing communitarian alternatives for those disillusioned with the nation-state (Kothari 1988; Gupta n.d.). In Africa—where, as we have seen, many outside observers have declared it to be at worst impossible, at best "embryonic" or "marginal" (Mamdani 1996, 3)—it has sometimes been given an indigenous identity; one that survives from earlier times in diverse technologies of "invisible governance," in "styles, attitudes, secrets" and in the "aspirations of individuals and groups" (Hecht and Simone 1994, 14–15). More tangibly, perhaps, it might also be seen to have precursors in such precolonial political forms as the Tswana *kgotla* (Comaroff and Comaroff 1997b).

Even by the standard of omnibus sociological categories, patently, the scope of civil society is uncannily wide. So much so that Walzer (1992, 107) describes it as a metaconstruct, a "project of projects." It is this breadth of scope that has led to a further species of question among those who would theorize it: What precisely does it, should it, include? Everything that occupies the space between the state and the individual, or the state and the household? Relations of production, family, and kinship? The market? Are religious organizations, the media, expressive culture, and the politics of consumption in or out? Does civil society exist as the antithesis of the state, in struggle with it, or as a condition of its possibility? Is it coterminous with, or distinct from, the public sphere?[18] What about those legal-jural apparatuses that regulate interpersonal conflict? And the diffuse aesthetics, norms, and sensibilities that constitute "civility"? Finally, how might all this be addressed in non-Western contexts, with their very different social histories and political cultures?

For all the frequency with which they are posed, these problems are not resolvable either. Except, of course, tautologically, by defining "the" concept in such a way as to privilege one or another answer. Which is why, in the face of more exacting efforts to pin down its habitations, civil society often melts into air, or dissolves into more conventional accounts of social and political organization, of the public sector, of the production of goods, values, and desires, of the formation of social movements and voluntary associations; into the business as usual, that is, of the social sciences under one or another of its familiar theoretical paradigms, old and new (Kumar 1993, 392).[19] For, again, civil society, in itself, refers to an empty abstraction, not to a specifiable, principled mode of analysis. It contains no theory to account for itself, and cannot yield one of itself. Neither, as Bayart (1986, 118) insists, does it imply a particular telos, progressive or otherwise; put another way, "civil society is not capable of satisfying manifold claims for social and economic justice" (Becker 1994, xxi). Unless we acknowledge these things, we run the risk of taking its idealizations, exclusions, and obfuscations at face value. Also, of misrecognizing the complex historical forces of which the Idea is a by-product—notwithstanding its capacity to provoke action, argument, and affect.

To bemoan the lack of coherence and specificity of the concept of civil society, in other words, seems rather to miss the point. So too does the effort to pin it down, to wrestle away its inherent ambiguities. For the key to its promise—its power as a sign that is as good to think and feel with as it is to act upon—lies in its very promiscuity, its polyvalence and protean incoherence. Perhaps it has always been so. This may leave its status as an *analytic* term fatally compromised. But it does give it "a strong claim [for] anthropological attention" (Hann 1996, 10):[20] for the effort to fathom why and how civil society serves as a tool of the social imagination, as a cultural construct and an ideological trope, in particular times and places; how those imaginings interact, ever so fitfully, with the logico-philosophical traditions of Western intellectual endeavor; why it has come to dominate recent social discourse within and about Africa—and elsewhere. In respect of Africa, an anthropological optic of this kind must, of necessity, focus on a number of interrelated themes: how the Idea has manifested itself in colonial and postcolonial visions of history and modernity; how it folds into local conceptions of the emerging global order; how it has infused understandings of moral being, citizenship, community, and polity in a world in which liberalizing forces, both political and economic, bear an uneven relationship to formal authority and to everyday life; how it resonates with identities, desires, and fantasy futures fed, among other things, by media images of an increasingly transnational scale; in whose dreams it is an alibi, in whose interests—or disinterest—it is invoked.

First, however, a quick detour back into the past. For in it lies a revealing parallel with the present and an answer to our Big Question:

Why now?

Of Revolutions, Now and Then

"Civil society," wrote Marx and Engels, "is the true source and theater of all history" (1970, 57).[21] What exactly they meant is not clear, especially in light of other things they had to say on the topic.[22] But it certainly *is* true that the term has taken center stage in post-Enlightenment Europe at moments when history itself, when the passage of humankind from the past through the present to the future, has come under radical scrutiny; most notably when, during the late eighteenth and twentieth centuries—at the dawn and the dusk of modernity, some would say (e.g., Tester 1992, 25; but cf. Hardt 1995, 40)—the very fabric of *social* being has been cast into doubt.[23] Such moments of putative crisis, of peril and possibility, are often associated with the opening and closing of epochs, imaginary or real. Typically, they call forth deep ontological reflection, ritual hyperactivity, and, in recent times, a tendency to conjure up the "then" in the "now," the ancient in the contemporary. As if, for a moment at least, the familiar telos of modernity has turned back on itself. Or been set on rewind. Or even stopped forever. Thus we are said to live in an age of "new medievalism," of "neoliberal" capitalism, at the "end of history";

an age in which everything is entirely familiar—and, yet, read from another standpoint, is witness to transformations so revolutionary that they are knowable only by a prefix *(post-)* that describes them by what they are not (see below).

It is, in sum, upon this Janus-faced perception of the history of here-and-now that the late-twentieth-century concern with civil society has entered. What is striking about the contemporary concern with the Idea is how it, too, appears to evoke a simultaneous sense of familiarity and freshness, of the old in the new. And how at once similar and different are the world-historical circumstances to which it harks back.

But why, exactly, *did* civil society become a matter of such concern, beginning in Scotland and England, in the second half of the eighteenth century?

A range of different answers have been given to this question, of course. Woods, like many others, looks for one in the arbitrary, increasingly absolutist, increasingly extractive nature of patrimonial rule in Europe at the time. "Monarchical and semifeudal institutions that [treated] the political arena as the private domain of the king and princely estates," he claims (1992, 79), spawned a potent antithesis: the emergence of a public—"with its own opinion[s]" and "interests" (Taylor 1990, 108; cf. Habermas 1989)—to which government might be held accountable; also of a public sphere in which those opinions and interests might express themselves. Similarly, Keane (1988c, 65) attributes the rise of the early modern discourse of civil society to "the fear of state despotism" stimulated by political processes set in motion by the defeat of Britain in the American colonies and by events in fin de siècle France; although, to complicate matters a little, Ferguson's *Essay on the History of Civil Society* preceded both. Such political explanations—there are a large number of them[24]—differ in their details. But they find a shared cause in the mounting repressiveness of the ancien régime; this, we are told, had the effect of focusing critical attention on the proper relationship between society and authority, between rulers and the rights of their subjects. Which, perhaps, accounts for the strong tendency today among liberal political scientists and philosophers to define the concept, as they recuperate and re-*present* it—the temporal pun here is intended—either "against the state [or] in partial independence from it" (Taylor 1990, 95).

Others, by contrast, look to historical transformations of a more thoroughgoing sort. Gellner (1996, 61) expresses a common viewpoint with startling simplicity. This, he says, was the age of "transition from aristocratic to commercial society." A more nuanced perspective owes its provenance to the Marxian tradition: it finds an explanation for the obsession with the Idea in the troubled history of private property in particular, and the emergence of industrial capitalism in general (Kumar 1993, 377). For Marx and Engels, recall, "civil society as such only develop[ed] with the bourgeoisie" (1970, 57)—as its "hideous embodiment" (Young 1994, 35). This thesis has been disputed, perhaps most forcefully by Keane (1988c, 64), on the empirical ground that, historically, the Idea of civil society antedated the bourgeoisie. In our reading, the objection is not so much right or wrong as it is based on a misconception.[25] The relevant passage in *The German Ideology*—Marx pays little explicit attention to civil society in his later work (cf. Young 1994, 35; Kumar 1993, 377)—suggests that the object was not to find a proximate cause for the genesis of the modern term. It was to argue that the ideological formation of which that term was an integral part *developed,* over time and in tandem, with the advent of the bourgeoisie and new class antinomies; as a result, that is, of broad social and material forces (cf. Tester 1992, 4; Cohen 1982). Those forces, deeply unsettling of the received order of things, embraced, but were not exhausted by, the destruction of patrimonial power and feudal political arrangements. In this respect, the Marxian vantage, to which we shall return again later, does not deny the political instance addressed by Woods and Keane; nor does it downplay the transition summarily stated by Gellner. It encompasses them in a process of more comprehensive historical scope. And it emphasizes the fact that this was truly an age of momentous, troubling transformation.

It is no coincidence that the mise-en-scène of the late eighteenth century engendered in philosophers and poets and everypersons alike—if not in like manner or in like measure—a sense of unease;[26] a phenomenology of uncertainty, if you will, occasioned by the intersection of epochs, at which the generic nature of humanity, of social connectedness, of persons and their abstraction in labor and property, of the value of things, of received means and ends, were all under ontological reconstruction. Even though they might not have fully realized it, they were living at the cusp of an Age of Revolution (cf. Hobsbawm 1962), an age that posed profound questions of practical epistemology. In light of the contemporary malaise of governance, of the rapid development of capitalism and commodity relations, of the birth of the rights-bearing citizen-subject, of the empowerment of the bourgeoisie, of the dawn of the modernist nation-state, of the rise of what Macpherson (1962) was famously to dub "possessive individualism," the problem of "the social" presented itself with particular force. How, given the erosion of old ways of being and knowing, not to mention a transfigured landscape, were the present and future of "society" to be grasped? Wherein lay its foundations? And its appropriate moral, material, and regulatory moorings? Yet more fundamentally, notes Tester (1992, 7), it became imperative to "explain how society was [even] possible" in a world in which "time-honoured answers were collapsing through mixtures of political crisis, intellectual enlightenment, technological development and the . . . rapid urbanization of social life"; in which the "modern self," an increasingly autonomous individual (see Taylor 1989), was taking root amid a new division of labor and the "encroachment on everything of finance";[27] in which the sanctity of the family was seen to be at risk; in which both people and things were being objectified in an altogether unprecedented manner.

Marvin Becker (1994, xii–xiii) reflects on the anxieties expressed by British literati of the period in rather prosaic terms. Many, he says, were perturbed by the onset of economic specialization and the imminent threat of anomie; by the prospect of Adam Smith's fearful, faceless "society of strangers" (cf. Krygier 1997a, 65)—which, they believed, would be the "numbing, . . . stunting" impact of commodity production, of "mechanization and routinization," and of new forms of commerce. Here, however, Becker makes an important point: their doubts notwithstanding, these British intellectuals "acknowledged the necessity for," indeed the inevitability of, "agricultural and commercial improvement, . . . consumerism . . . [and] a type of market for the more efficient satisfaction of human wants" (xiii). Likewise, Oz-Salzberger (1995, xii) observes that Adam Ferguson, neither a romantic recidivist nor a political reactionary, "was willing to condone . . . assembly-line economics." But the "necessity" of "improved" consumerism, and an efficient market—an alarming prequel to our own epoch—forced a contradiction "between [social] benevolence and self-interest [that] became a staple of moral inquiry" (xiv); even more, of the pursuit of a new moral order and a solution to the conundrum of social existence sui generis.

Understood thus, it is not difficult to see why, in the late eighteenth century, discourses of civil society, in both their philosophical-analytic and their utopic registers, should have focused on the issues and imaginings that they did: on the contested relationship between the state (or, more generally, political authority) and society; on the posited existence, in the space between the citizen and the sovereign polity, of a public with a will and interests of its own; on the role of nongovernmental, voluntary associations in providing alternative loci for the achievement of the commonweal; on a democratizing image of self-generating moral community, whose elemental atom was the Christian family; on the significance of the free market in underwriting both that community and its well-being; on the capacity of commerce to inscribe civility in a new civics. Foreshadowings here, in various proportions, of Hegel, Simmel, Durkheim, Habermas. Nor is it surprising that these discourses should have prefigured the neoliberal tenor of our own times. This, after all, was the context that produced Adam Smith and the doctrine of laissez-faire (Knox 1952a, 354), which influenced many early theorists of the Idea.[28]

But it did not produce a monolithic, nor an immaculate, conception of civil society. Quite the contrary. As Charles Taylor (1990) explains, the Idea had two quite different, inimical points of origin in early modern times, each of which gave rise to its own understanding of the beast—and to its own "stream" of philosophical thought (see note 9). One may be traced back to Locke, the other to Montesquieu. Locke, argues Taylor, saw society, itself based on an inviolable social contract, as prior to and independent of the state—and therefore as existing "beyond" and/or "against" it. Montesquieu, in contrast, held society to be defined by, coeval with, and inseparable from its political organization. In his view, however, the polity contained within it various autonomous sources of power, vested in associations, that ruptured and diversified state authority—which is why, from this perspective, civil society is so closely tied to voluntary organizations. Over time, these two "streams" have flowed into each other, hybridized, reformed. To be sure, the epistemic conditions that produced and counterposed them have long since mutated, making the original distinction impossible to sustain. But, taken together, they continue to underline a fundamental point: that civil society becomes especially "good to think," and to signify with, at moments when conventional connections between the political and the social, state and public, are perceived to be unraveling.

Which brings us to the late twentieth century.

As we have already intimated, this epoch has direct parallels to the late eighteenth century. Ours too is an Age of Revolution: if the earlier one is associated symbolically with 1789, the present one has its metonymic moment in 1989, exactly two hundred years later—although both began long before their manifest dates.[29] Of course, "revolution" is very much in the eye of the beholder. Every generation, it is often said, believes itself to be caught up in one; and every generation spawns countervisionaries who deny all evidence of significant change. In our view, however, the indications are undeniable.

Now, as in the second half of the eighteenth century, the discourse of civil society rises—like a Hobbesian horse?—amid a strong tendency to read the history of the present in largely *political* terms (see, e.g., Keane 1988b, 1). Now, as then, the growing obsession with the Idea is frequently explained as a response to processes set in motion by a "deepening separation between state and society" (Young 1994, 34); or, more broadly, by the putative subversion of the nation-state (see below). Now, as then, it is seen as an autonomic reaction to a familiar doubling: (1) to the greater opacity, intrusiveness, and monopolistic tendencies of government; and (2) to its decreasing capacity "to satisfy even minimally the political and economic aspirations" of its component publics (Haynes 1997, 16), or to guarantee the welfare of its citizenry. Now, as then, it is closely related to the perception that the workings of the market have outrun the functional capacities of the state. All of which is held to spark efforts, as it did two centuries ago, to build "independent forms of social life from below, free of state tutelage" (Taylor 1990, 95). The content of those efforts might have varied by historical circumstance. But, again, political contingencies are almost always crucial to their narration. In Central Europe, as we have noted, the populist pursuit of civil society is said to have arisen as a reaction against increasingly repressive communist rule—and, in postcolonial times, to be sustained by the memory of Soviet excesses. In the West, a cause for it has been found in burgeoning state corporatism (Taylor 1990, 95–96). And, in what was once known as the "Third World," it is attributed to the rise of antistatist, promarket populism occasioned by the collapse of totalitarian regimes (Young 1994, 36); by the dramatic debilitation of the state at the hands of small elites, whose "politics of the belly" (Bayart 1993) and vulgar spectacles of power (Mbembe 1992) persuade citizens that governments no longer "champion society's collective interests" (Haynes 1997, 2).

All this, however important it may be, speaks to surfaces and symptoms. It does not reach into the interiors, to the animating force, of the present Age of Revolution. This age has been described in many, diverse ways.[30] In our view, it is, first and foremost, a product of the rise of a newly globalized, neoliberal form of capitalism; this *pace* those who would disclaim the very existence of a "globalized economy" (e.g., Hirst and Thompson 1992, 357; 1996). Note that we do *not* attribute the transformations of the late twentieth century to globalization per se. Having become a trope for our times, "globalism" has, like all clichés and catchwords, been cheapened by overuse and underspecification, by the confusion of an expansive metaphor for an explanatory term (Comaroff and Comaroff 1999). Broadly defined, in any case, "it" has existed, in one or another manifestation, for centuries; not least as a condition of the very possibility of modernity, of colonialism, of the Age of Empire (Hobsbawm 1987).

To cut a very long story short—we have dealt with the matter in extenso elsewhere (J. L. Comaroff 1996; J. Comaroff 1997a, 1997b; Comaroff and Comaroff n.d.)—the present Age of Revolution is the ongoing product of a complex dialectic; a dialectic whose outcome is as yet unknowable. (Which is why the present is so often described by what it is not, by labeling it as *neo-* or *post-*, lately even as "postnative" and "posthuman";[31] as if we comprehend the contemporary only when an adjectival label [a Post-it?] is attached to mark its slippage into the netherworld of anachronism.) Especially salient among these processes are thoroughgoing, worldwide metamorphoses in patterns of production, in the movement and accumulation of capital, in modes of consumption and commodification, and in the deployment of labor (cf. Mandel 1975; Harvey 1982)—all underpinned by the emergence of an electronic economy, a virtual "commons" (Kurtzman 1993) in which time and space are compressed along new coordinates, in which transactions are instantaneous and anonymous, in which unassailable frontiers are few and centers and peripheries are constantly shifting. "Global," here, does not simply mean "international" anymore—although a transformed international "system" certainly remains significant. Nor, in its present guise, does it describe stable linkages among discrete polities, economies, communities, or whatever. It refers to the nonlinear temporality, the four-dimensional geography, of an inherently evanescent world order. Of an order whose impulse, if not always its achievement, is to displace political sovereignty with the sovereignty of the market, to replace the primacy of community with the metaphor of the network, to give free reign to the "forces" of hyper-rationalization, to parse human beings into free-floating labor units, consumers, commodities, clients. Stakeholders, strangers.

Indeed, this is an economy that, like its eighteenth-century precursor, celebrates the mechanisms of "*the* market" as if they had an entirely unmediated capacity to determine the course of history for the good. It also obscures its own ideological imperatives by referring them to the abstract demands of technocratic necessity—which, in turn, becomes the final arbiter of "public" policy and the politics of the commonweal—and it assumes government to be intrusive and undesirable, except insofar as it deregulates and/or protects "market forces." Concomitantly, "the law" is fetishized as *the* mode of monitoring relations among individuals and corporations. This economy, moreover, encourages the rapid movement of bodies, goods, and value—and of the sites of their fabrication—to the extent of calling any form of stable community or locality into question. Indeed, in its social aspect, it seems to reduce personhood and subjectivity to an ever more atomized, objectified, desocialized ensemble of interests, rights, appetites, desires, purchasing "power," satisfiable wants; and, alike in the domain of politics and economics, it equates freedom with choice, especially to consume, to fashion the self, to conjure with identities. And so on and on.

Neoliberal capitalism as economy has not emerged in a vacuum, of course; nor is it to be understood in purely material terms. It depends for its existence on another, ontologically entailed, process: the translocalization of cultural production, distribution, and consumption—and of its worldwide mass mediation through television, radio, print, and the Internet. Again, much has been written about the "global ecumene" (cf. Kopytoff 1987, 10; also Hannerz 1989, 66)—about the planet, that is, as a region of "persistent cultural interaction and exchange" in which old borders dissolve; in which national capitals lose their relevance to new world-cities that arise as pulse-points in labyrinthine pathways of planetary communication and transaction; in which images flow along intricate routes, entering into intricate processes of mediation and appropriation wherever they come to ground; in which, consequently, "the global" and "the local" become conditions of each other's epistemic existence, of each other's imaginings, of each other's continuing presence.

Perhaps the most remarked corollary of all these processes, of the material and cultural dimensions of our Age of Revolution, has been the so-called crisis of the nation-state. Notwithstanding a growing proclivity to do so, it is premature, argues Tölölyan (1991, 5), to write an obituary quite yet. True. But there is nonetheless a widespread perception in many parts of the world—beyond the United States, that is—that the modernist state *is* under acute threat. Lukacs (1993, 157) may or may not be correct in his prognosis that over "the long run, the power of . . . centralized government, will weaken everywhere." In the meantime, however, there is plenty of evidence to support the claim that few regimes exercise much real control anymore over the circulation of information, signs, or ideologies. Few, patently, maintain a regulatory monopoly over the supply of money, the movement of labor, or the means of legitimate violence. And not even the most powerful evince any effective influence on the market or can fend off the capacities of global capital to determine the directions of "national" policy.

The global rise of neoliberal capitalism, in short, seems to be eroding the nation-state in three ways: first, by deconstructing currency and customs boundaries, which formerly gave governments their major means of extracting and redeploying wealth; second, by creating flows of credit and mobile markets across the face of the earth, thus dispersing the production and circulation of value; third, by transnationalizing the division of labor and encouraging large-scale migrations of workers across established political borders. These things have made it progressively more difficult to balance budgets, to reproduce infrastructure, or to support an active public sector—which is measured by investment in social and cultural capital. Taken together, they appear to be leading to the erasure of anything that might be described as a "national economy"; also to undermine sovereignty by establishing supranational political and legal institutions, both formal and informal. As a result, the geographically localized, nationally bounded conception of society and culture, of a homogenous imagined community, is at once compromised, pluralized, problematized. So, concomitantly, is the nature of identity: no longer contained neatly in citizenship, in the modernist subject, it is "free" to redefine itself along any number of axes of being in the world.

Here, then, is our point. As in the late eighteenth century—and in remarkably parallel fashion—the very fabric of the social, the possibility of society, the ontological core of humanity, and the essence of identity are being questioned; this following an epochal metamorphosis in the organization of production and the market, technology and its sociocultural implications, and the constitutive connections between economy and polity. Also under scrutiny, for the same reasons, are the dominant tropes of modernist sociology as lived: community, identity, family, gender, generation. Uniformity is challenged by multiplicity, coherence by polysemy. The threat of the postmodern, the crisis of masculinity, the excesses of identity politics, the demise of family values, the triumph of the commodity over morality, the availability of work and alterations in conditions of employment, the dispersal of community; all of these things have sparked moral panics in many parts of the world. So, too, has the future of the nation-state, the future of the nation and of the state. In some places this has expressed itself in a rise of local occult economies whose object is to solve the mysteries of neoliberal capitalism: the apparent capacity of its masters to garner wealth without work, to control the movement of people and money across space and time (Comaroff and Comaroff 1999). Elsewhere it has sparked an equally millennial pursuit of civil society.

Civil Society in Africa

Received wisdom has it that the concern with civil society in Africa, which became audible in the mid-1980s, followed upon the revival of the Idea in Europe—albeit in response to different local conditions. This might be true of scholarly discourses; also of public spheres that opened up with, or were transformed by, the end of the cold war. Many of the issues at stake, however, have long been part of the legacy of colonialism here, even if the term itself was not employed until a decade or so ago (cf. Young 1994, 38). Nineteenth-century "humanitarian" imperialists, it will be remembered, often framed their mission to Africans in a language of civility that implied universal human rights, norms of citizenship, and legal protections. Some of them, like the radical Reverend John Philip ([1828] 1969, 2, 366–67), superintendent of the London Missionary Society in South Africa, spoke openly in favor of "civil liberties" for colonized peoples; so, too, did the Reverend John Mackenzie (1887, 2, 456–57; see Sillery 1971, 50–51), who saw in "native" customs and modes of governance all the elements of a "rude" civil society. These "liberties" were, for the most part, preached rather than practiced, promised but not delivered. As a result, nationalist resistance to overrule was, from the first, formulated in the argot of rights denied and wrongs perpetrated.[32] And it produced a plethora of political organizations, social movements, and voluntary associations.

As this suggests, civic activism against various forms of government repression, and claims in support of indigenous peoples against the state, long predate the struggle against totalitarianism in Poland (cf. Mamdani 1996, 14). What is more, African intellectuals have reflected provocatively for a good while on questions now very much a part of the worldwide preoccupation with civil society. Witness Ekeh's (1975) thesis that, owing to its colonial experience, Africa may be seen to have "two publics"—the "civil" and the "primordial"—whose uneasy coexistence explains the distinctive political history of the continent in the late twentieth century. His point extends easily to other postcolonial contexts, including central Europe (cf. J. L. Comaroff 1991, 1996).

Out of Europe: Or, How the West Was One

In spite of this, the growing obsession with civil society in Africa during the past fifteen or so years has been phrased largely in the orthodox terms of Western political science; much of it boils down to an effort to evaluate existing institutions of governance against ideal-typical universals (cf. Blaney and Pasha 1993). Mamdani (1996, 3) has already alerted us to the ideological tenor of this exercise. For him, the debate to which it gives rise is locked in an epistemic impasse: while liberal modernists call for civil rights, communitarians decry their Eurocentrism, advocating the reinstatement of marginalized political cultures. Two sides of the same coin, these positions replay the old antinomy between the universal and the particular, between the rationalism and racialism inherent, Wilder reminds us in chapter 2, in Western democracies and the colonial orders created in their name.

In fact, the debate has been more nuanced. The value of Civil Society, in the uppercase, to the normative study of African politics has been the subject of disputes *within* liberal modernist scholarly circles (see, e.g., Harbeson 1994). Some continue to be deeply skeptical of its comparative usefulness. But others—like Azarya (1994, 87), in an influential collection of essays by Western Africanists—express forthright impatience with any such quibbles. Civil society, goes this argument, is no less tangible a concept, nor a more ethnocentric one, than, say, "the bourgeoisie" or "democracy." Writes Bratton (1994, 52), in the same volume:

> Despite . . . formidable obstacles, . . . civil society is a useful formula for analyzing state-society relations in Africa because it embodies a core of universal beliefs and practices about the legitimation of, and limits to, state power.

He goes on, not surprisingly, to conclude that civil society is "underdeveloped" on the continent as a whole. For those who, like him, subscribe to the same "useful formula," and treat it as a universal measure, this deduction is overdetermined.

We shall argue below that there *is* a crucial difference between "the bourgeoisie" and "civil society." For now, we note merely that no amount of normative appeal to universal beliefs and practices can offset what we demonstrated earlier: that the substance of the Idea is inherently elusive, evanescent, opaque; that this is so even in the West, where it is held to be most at home; that, when applied in historical circumstances arising out of different cultural histories, it is liable to have even less purchase on local realities. The implication? That if no heed is paid to these considerations, if civil society is tacitly taken to be a Eurocentric index of accomplishment, Africa's difference once more becomes a deviation, a deficit.

Talk of the "underdevelopment" of the continent in this respect echoes a discourse of older vintage about the "immaturity" of "*the* African state."[33] Which, again, is hardly unexpected: in modernist Western thought, after all, the state and civil society are complementary, mutually constitutive terms. It goes without saying that the nature of both, and hence of their relationship, has varied widely across Africa, past and present; the corollary being that ahistorical generalizations about either lead to some perverse, diametrically opposed inferences. Thus, for example, Dunn (1978, 15) asserts that the "dominance of state power" here is a product of the relative insubstantiality of civil society, while Azarya (1994, 97), from the same epistemic standpoint, holds just the reverse: that the weakness of civil society is a function of the impotence of the state. Suppressed beneath such bland generalities are complex political histories; histories whose momentum seems to have accelerated as our Age of Revolution has unfolded. This has included the refiguration, in divers ways, of the nature of governance, of popular politics, and of the experience of moral community: the very things that have made "civil society" an issue of concern among scholars, activists, and political reformers as the century draws to a close.

So much of an issue, in fact, that in Africa—at least in those parts where the language of liberal political science and international aid has become a lingua franca—the concept of society barely exists alone any more. It is almost always given adjectival qualification. It is almost always *civil.* Or, rather, ought to be. Such things are not happenstance. Among activists and observers who speak this dialect, this dialect without dialectics, it signifies that politics are no longer centered on government. Or, rather, ought not to be. For them, the sine qua non of development and democratization is a discrete civil sphere; a sphere that, ideally, acts in collaboration with the capital but, in view of a recent past of oppressive regimes, actually has to do battle against it (Young 1994, 36). Bayart goes as far as to define civil society as a process whose object is to "'breach' and counteract the 'totalisation' unleashed by the state" (1986, 111).[34] At a time when distrust of sovereign authority across the political spectrum borders on paranoia, the Idea would have to be invented if it did not already exist. In Africa, Asia, Europe. Everywhere.

Bayart's (1986, 109–10) approach to the question of civil society in Africa is, in our view, among the most subtle. For one thing, he does not reduce the continent to adjectivalized stereotypes or to abstract generalities. For another, he situates the circulation of the Idea in specific historical terms. Like the "free individual" entailed in European concepts of democracy and human rights, civil society had no literal counterpart in precolonial times. But, he stresses, this does not mean that African cultures were especially receptive to despotism; nor that, within them, ideals of participatory governance were ill-fitting, foreign imports. Along with other aspects of global modernity, including forms of domination that were the stock-in-trade of colonial rule, these ideals have been thoroughly indigenized. And they have taken on distinctively local forms.

Within the limits of its own logic, this is persuasive. Sensu stricto, civil society and the institutions it presupposes *were* originally a product of the rise of Western liberal democracy. But they were a product also, as Marx and Engels insisted, of the emergence of the international bourgeois order and, more pervasively, of the capitalist relations that sustained it. And, indeed, for many foreign observers, especially political scientists lacking Bayart's sensibilities, the viability of civil society in Africa has little to do with vernacular cultures. Or with anything else indigenous. It hinges on the health of its middle classes, on the presence of conditions that allow "individuals and social groups to develop an independent capacity to accumulate capital" (Bratton 1994, 64). It also, says Woods, demands that a distinction be recognized between public and personal interests. Like many others, he traces the tentative outlines of civility to the self-serving efforts of urban bourgeoisies: efforts to protect their economic status by making arbitrary state authority accountable to "democratic" imperatives and the "needs" of the private sector (1992, 78).

Insofar as civil society in Africa is widely taken to depend on "the triumph of bourgeois-liberal capitalism,"[35] its future is *not* generally perceived to be a mere matter of materialities, of economic interests alone. For Young (1994, 43), something more elevated is at issue: "the embrace of the world historical spirit" that invests civic projects with "immanent purpose." For the less high-minded, the key to civility resides in mundanities; in things like "waiting in line for one's turn" (Azarya 1994, 90). Either way, these formulations are grounded, implicitly or explicitly, in a singular understanding of "*the* world historical spirit." There is no room here for more than one such spirit, one telos. As Hardt says, Euro-American prescriptions for the establishment of civil order elsewhere—whether their provenance be the academy or the state department—turn on an imagined re-creation of the stages of Western civilization, focusing on one in particular: the consolidation of eighteenth- and nineteenth-century capitalist society, with its characteristic social and cultural arrangements, its rights-bearing subjects, its refined manners (1995, 42).

Thus it is that Western-oriented intellectuals, lawyers, entrepreneurs, academics, teachers, and sometimes Christian (never Muslim) leaders are typically seen from outside as the vanguards of civil society in formation. It is they who are thought most likely to commit themselves to the development of an active public sphere, along with its requisite media and voluntary organizations; to create the sites and associations through which bourgeoisies might pursue their interests untrammeled by parochial loyalties, identity politics, or intrusive governments; to equate those interests with the good of society at large, even of "humankind." It is they, moreover, who are portrayed as having the potential to complete a process that began in the nationalist movements prior to independence; movements that shared similar liberal aspirations, but whose urbane, European-educated cadres were crushed by absolutist postcolonial regimes as they suppressed political debate, put paid to unfettered enterprise, and all but dissolved the difference between the private and public sectors (Woods 1992, 86–87; Young 1994, 41). As those regimes have run up against history, as they have been assailed by the forces of neoliberal reform and democratization, this new generation of elites has found itself with a nascent opportunity to build civil order afresh, to push for open electoral politics and a free market, to realize the aborted promise of decolonization. And to usher in the African Renaissance of which we spoke earlier. Or so the story goes.

Conceptualized thus, it is hard to see how the narrative of civil society in

Africa could be anything more than a replay of Euro-capitalist modernity, of its social and moral forms, its conventional ways and mean(ing)s, its economies of desire, selfhood, and subjectivity. Admittedly, some scholars have pushed the limits of this narrative by acknowledging the need to appreciate local "rules of the game": the need to observe, as Bayart does, that liberal democratic forms have been variously domesticated across the continent, laying a basis for the "plural invention of modernity" (Bayart 1986, 120; cf. Owusu 1997). But few go on to identify what African hybrids, Africa*nized* modes of civil society, might actually look like. Or how they might resonate with ideals of sociality and political accountability that differ from those found in the West. Note the plural here too. The West, after all, was never One.

Into Africa, the Uncool: Weaving the Strands of Civility

The essays in this volume attest to the robust debate about democracy taking place in contemporary Africa. In contemporary African terms (Comaroff and Comaroff 1997b). There has also been a good measure of creative experimentation with its forms, some of it at the behest of heads of state, some of it the product of "politics from below" (Makinda 1996; Snyder 1998; Perry 1998). From across the continent come accounts of a widespread suspicion that formal democracy is not always all that it is cracked up to be: that electoral politics, in the words of a Gabonese farmer, is "like a ball-point pen . . . as soon as the ink finishes, you throw it away" (Cinnamon 1998, 5); that multiparty government might well prove to be, as Ugandan leader Yoweri Museveni suspects, "unacceptably confrontational and divisive" (Makinda 1996, 557; Snyder 1998, 2). In addition, critiques of the impact of rampant neoliberalism on local moral orders and modes of social reproduction are everywhere at hand. They express themselves in diverse ways, from direct demands for state intervention in drastically deregulated markets (Perry 1998) to mass-circulation moral tales about the occult appetites, and the cannibalistic imperatives, that sustain new forms of power and wealth (Eaton 1998; Comaroff and Comaroff 1999). Indeed, practical politics at all levels bears testimony to self-conscious reinvention, to a rich dialectic of the here and there, of things local and translocal.

Yet little of this sort of activity is included within the scope of civil society, of its attendant forms of social and political action, as defined by the received literature on Africa. Even Bayart's pioneering, imaginative analysis—drawn, of course, from an earlier moment than the ethnographies cited in the previous paragraph—treats the term in an exacting, restrictive manner:

> In the first instance, it may not be possible to speak of "civil society" where there is no "organisation principle." Civil society exists only in so far as there is a self-consciousness of its existence and of its opposition

> to the state. . . . [M]ost African social formations are characterised by deep cultural, religious, linguistic rifts which prevent the emergence of what Augé refers to as the "idéo-logique." . . . In Africa there are no one-dimensional or homogeneous societies, but rather a collection of time-spaces . . . like so many poles, created by various social actors. (1986, 117–18)

The prospect of unifying these "time-spaces" into an "organisation principle" capable of challenging absolute state control, of building a coherent public sphere, is said to be uncertain at best. In Africa, Bayart concludes, invoking an archaic image, societies "chip at the state from below" (119). What is more, if and when an organized challenge does succeed, it is likely to bear within it the seeds of a "new monopoly."

Several things might be said about this thesis. One is that it renders inexplicable the large number of palpably coherent nationalist and millennial movements that arose to counter colonialism. Another is that, by limiting its definition of political action to initiatives that oppose the state in explicit, organized terms, it excludes modes of mobilization that have been highly significant in African history, from market associations and labor unions to activist churches and reforming Islamic crusades. Also, most recently, populist alliances in pursuit of democracy. Since Bayart's seminal essay was published, this pursuit has become ever more self-conscious, ever more "homogeneous," ever more voluble, even in such formerly strife-torn contexts as Uganda and the Sudan (Makinda 1996; Lesch 1998). Bayart anticipated this last possibility. But he remained skeptical of its consequences: where civil society is able to "capture" (cf. Hydén 1980) political projects, he predicted, it would breed an alternative form of domination. Either that, or it would be condemned to terminal incoherence.

However, Bayart is successful in showing that the dilemmas of civil society in Africa echo the conundrums and contradictions of democratic politics, and of liberal public spheres, everywhere. For much of its modern history, as we have noted, the West has evinced little self-conscious awareness of the existence of civil society in its midst. And, once bidden to reflect on the Idea, Euro-American commentators were quick to decide that they inhabited a world seriously lacking moral or any other kind of homogeneity—in Bayart's terms, a single "time-space." If anything, the forces currently drawing national polities, economies, and cultures ever more tightly into a global capitalist order appear to be further eroding the consensual basis of communities of all kinds—resulting in what Hardt describes as a condition of "hypersegmentation" (1995, 37).

It seems, then, that the notion of "one-dimensional" societies is as chimerical outside Africa as within. At least, in the late twentieth century. Popular coalitions, as Bayart acknowledges (1986, 118), are triumphs over impossibility, complex bridges across diverse orders of difference. As such, they are liable to begin as working compromises; but, if they succeed, the chances, anywhere, are that they will proclaim themselves as new orthodoxies. In the world of practical politics, moreover, all reforms, wherever they take root, carry within them new inequalities, at times less and at times more marked than ones they replaced; that, too, is not an African monopoly. Like other continents, Africa has produced its fair share of reformist movements (Isaacman 1990); as elsewhere, they have not always had the capacity to prevail over dominant state structures; as elsewhere, their means and ends have not always matched the narrow criteria of "civility" laid down in Western ideal-types, in linear narratives of progress, in the conventional categories of Eurocentric political culture.

Perhaps it is this last clause that underlies the continuing uneasiness of normal social science with "uncool" forms of African association; forms dubbed partisan, parochial, fundamentalist (Chazan 1992 in Azarya 1994, 94). Perhaps this is what sustains the tendency to undervalue the role of kin-based and ethnic organizations in forming publics and political pressure groups; the sort Karlström shows in chapter 4 to have been crucial to the democratization of Uganda. Perhaps this also explains the reluctance to recognize the capacity of "tradition" to foster new modes of governance; as in Ferme's account in chapter 6 of the rooting of Sierra Leonean electoral processes in archaic iconography, or Durham's description in chapter 7 of the manner in which "customary" styles of popular critique in Botswana fuel contemporary democratic participation. Neglected, by the same token, is the salience of religious groups in forging new normative orders of universal scope; consider African Islam, which, as Masquelier shows in her analysis of alternative public spheres in Niger (chapter 8), has often been integral to the reconceptualization of citizen and society in a neoliberal milieu. All these things converge in a single conclusion: that, in Europe and North America, there is thoroughgoing prejudice against the "universalizing ambitions" of cultures deemed marginal to the "modern script" (Walker 1994, 689). As a consequence, observes Chatterjee, "the provincialism of the European experience" becomes the "universal history of progress" (1990, 131).

The Eurocentric tendency to limit civil society to a narrowly defined institutional arena—notwithstanding the intrinsic incoherence of the Idea, notwithstanding Bayart's (1986, 112) plea that it be taken to describe a space of diverse kinds of practice—is multiply ironic. Hegel sought the genesis of a civil sphere of relatedness in the historical particularities of capitalist production and exchange; Habermas, Ferme reminds us in chapter 6, traced the conception of the "public" to its bourgeois roots in literary salons and coffeehouses; others have pursued its origins to the codes of conduct and the scientific discourses of Europe in its earlier Age of Revolution (Hunt 1984; Elias 1988; Kuzmics 1988). But there has as yet been little parallel effort to disinter the cultural seedbeds and historical sources of anything that might be regarded as an analogue of civil society in Africa. Few have considered the sorts of public sphere presumed by specifically *African* relations of production and exchange, codes of conduct, or styles of social intercourse; by *African* markets, credit associations, informal economies, collective ritual, modes of aesthetic expression, discourses of magic and reason; by the various strands, in other words, that "weave the fabric" of the civil here beyond the official purview of governance (Hecht and Simone 1994, 14; Azarya 1994, 95).

Until we address such historical and cultural specificities, until we leave behind stereotypic, idealized Euro-concepts, we foreclose the possibility of looking critically at either African *or* European civil society. Or at their complex conjuncture, beginning in colonial times. The history of this conjuncture is distinctly equivocal, distinctly *un*civil (Mamdani 1996, 18–19). Throughout Africa it gave birth, under the midwifery of the imperial state, to a world of difference, discrimination, and doubling: a world in which national, rights-bearing citizenship and primordial, ethnicized subjection—modernist inventions both—were made to exist side by side; a world composed of "civilized" colonists governed by European constitutionalism and "native tribes" ruled by so-called customary law (see Comaroff and Comaroff 1997a, chap. 8). The divisions on which this world was erected—divisions typically represented in stark, manichean binarisms of black and white—might have been transgressed, compromised, hybridized. But, both in the honor and in the breach, they conduced, for colonized peoples, to a deeply conflicted experience of (the promise of) civil society, European-style. And their consequences have endured across the continent in the age of the postcolony, pitting the "cold" language of individual legal rights and protections against the "hot" rhetoric of ethnic entitlement. Add to this the "volatile fuel" of competition for political power and authority, and the outcome, in many contexts, has been various, and variously disagreeable, versions of the patrimonial state (Young 1994, 39). And sometimes genocide.

This African story underscores a more general point: that, even when we set aside its incoherence, the Western conception of civil society, as a *practical* ideology, is riddled with contradictions. Not least in the West. Where it purports to be inclusive and all-embracing, it is founded on exclusion and divisiveness; where it promises equality, it engenders inequity. For the apparently open categories of liberal theory at its core—the nation-state, the individual, civil rights, contract, "the" law, private property, democracy—all presume the separation of citizens from subjects, nationals from immigrants, the propertied from the unpropertied, the franchised from the disenfranchised, the law-abiding from the criminal, the responsible from the irresponsible, the civic from the domestic; distinctions that belie the ambiguities of everyday life and rule out as many from effective participation in the public sphere as are embraced by it. Indeed, some critics have argued that civil being is largely the prerogative of metropolitan white adult males (Tripp 1994; Gal 1997; Pateman 1988). Even more fundamental, perhaps, is another contradiction: that the autonomy of civil society from the state, the very autonomy on which the Idea is predicated, is entirely chimerical. It, too, rests on an a series of idealized separations, starting with that of political authority from private property. But this separation is, de facto, unsustainable; "made opaque," says Samir Amin, "by the generalization of economic relationships," which cut across all the coordinates of the social landscape (1989, 81). As the triumph of global capitalism renders various dialects of liberalism the undisputed vernacular of both the world of politics and the world of business, we are reminded of Foucault's insistence that power dissolves the boundaries between public and private, state and society. And makes any notion of a discrete civil society, normatively and narrowly conceived, a cheerful illusion.

We would do well, in this respect, to return to classic critiques of liberalism. Like Marx and Engels's assertion that, in spite of its ideological representation, civil society was never an independent entity, a thing in itself; that it was merely the "form in which bourgeois society . . . emerged" (Gouldner 1980, 356; cf. Kumar 1993, 379); that, from the start, its content and conception were entailed in the social and material relations that gave rise to the modernist capitalist order and differentiated humanity, sui generis, by class, race, gender, and generation. Hence Blaney and Pasha's claim that, whatever is said in its name about universal rights and the equality of persons, civil society is constructed as a hierarchy of unequally valued individuals with unequal capacities for self-realization (1993, 9). These inequities, moreover, seem to become increasingly visible with the corporatization of the public sphere, when consumerism is the primary means of gaining access to it (Yudice 1995, 8)—and when everything appears subject to the market. To be sure, the extension of the logic of capitalist relations to all domains of production and reproduction, under neoliberal conditions, erodes the institutions and mechanisms that made the ideal of civil society conceivable in the first place. Which renders its pursuit ever more nostalgic (Hardt 1995; see also chapter 5).

None of this is to deny that the Idea of civil society is an important presence in the world. Indeed, one of the failings of the Marxian legacy has been to underestimate the extent to which ideologies, even incoherent, contradictory ones, can take on a concrete reality of their own, thence to figure prominently in political struggles. Whatever its entailment in the rise of capitalism—we see its past and present alike less as determined purely by economic relations than by more-embracing sociohistorical processes—increasing numbers of people *presume* the possibility of civil society. The very fact that they do, and act accordingly, gives it real force in the world. But it is a force less self-generating than is often supposed. And nowhere does it define a discrete or wholly autonomous sphere of social action. As we said before, its capacity to mobilize and motivate, to open up discourses of democracy and moral economy, to hold out the promise of property and political engagement lies in its very incoherence, its polysemy, its slippery opacity. If we wish, then, to make sense of the ways in which the Idea has emerged in our present Age of Revolution, or to investigate the degree to which its second coming replays features of revolutions past, it is necessary to situate our inquiry within the presently unfolding chapter of the history of capitalist modernity. It requires also that we read this history off the many sites where global forces engage with local realities, whether these are emblazoned in the banner headlines of nation-states or hidden in the small print of parochial events and everyday lives.

Of Things to Come

It is with just such a wide angle on European history that our essays begin. Gary Wilder's examination of the practical meaning of subject-citizenship in Imperial Paris (chapter 2) frames some of the concerns raised here into a question central to our understanding of civil society in Africa. It is a question that recurs throughout the volume: In what ways, he asks, must we rethink the category of civil society—and its conceptualization as an autonomous space of individual freedom and association inscribed in Western modernity—when we acknowledge that the racialized colony is as intrinsic to that modernity as is the rationalized metropolitan state? By viewing Western self-understandings through a colonial aperture, Wilder suggests, we gain a reproportioned sense of the inherent contradictions, of the complex play of inclusion and disenfranchisement, recognition and exploitation, citizenship and subjection, on which imperial capitalist democracies were founded.

Regarded from this perspective, liberal constructs like civil society and citizenship take on a far more equivocal aspect; they are seen to be the instruments used to effect the very exclusions on which the colonial order rested. Wilder explores the consequences of these ambiguities in the lives of African and Caribbean elites in metropolitan France between the wars. During this period, official policies of colonial humanism proclaimed universal rights but perpetually deferred granting them to "native" subjects, even though those subjects *practiced* civic virtues in the most exquisitely exemplary form (cf. Comaroff and Comaroff 1997a, 365–66). Here the enduring paradox of modern citizenship, and the Janus-faced character of colonial politics, emerge in stark relief. Citizenship is a necessary principle of equivalence within the democratic nation-state. But, in fact, like the commodity form it mirrors, it has always given rise to regimes of inequality and difference. This reality, this "real abstraction," conditioned the politics of the colonized. It defined not a sphere of freedom and civility, but a space from which emanated, and in which occurred, the "contests of power we call democracy."

It is just such contests of power—and, once more, the contradictions that underlie them—that Elizabeth Garland examines in her analysis of the encounter of Ju/'hoan "bushmen" with the transnational development business (chapter 3). This business is peopled by the staff of nongovernmental organizations (NGOs), who see themselves as postcolonial purveyors of global civil society. They are the latter-day missionaries of liberal democratism. And the whole earth, everything beneath the heavens, is their parish. Modeled on a vision of the world as "the state writ large" (Walker 1994), the kind of civil society of which they speak is imagined as an unbounded, planetary sphere of nongovernmental agencies and activities, one of whose objects is ostensibly to counterbalance an increasingly integrated order of national powers and international capital.

Here again, however, liberal humanitarianism is undercut by its simultaneous gestures of incorporation and disavowal; by the neo-evolutionary visions of well-intentioned emissaries of foreign aid, who take ethnocentric ideals of citizenship and civil society as a measure of all that non-Western others lack; by the fact that the racialized colony lives on in the postcolonial era of global rationalization. Western fantasy has long fixed people like the Ju/'hoansi, "typical" hunter-gatherers of southern Africa, in a prepolitical world, a world that predates the "fateful rift between man and citizen" (Walker 1994, 696). This, in turn, justifies the effort to implant Euro-modern civil institutions in what is presumed to be a political void—and concomitantly, ensures that the full humanity of its African inhabitants is endlessly denied. The ensuing paradox is epitomized in a dispute described by Garland between the Ju/'hoansi and the NGO that sought to bring sustainable development to them. For the Ju/'hoansi, interpolated recipients of overseas "help," did indeed seek to seize the potential of civil society as a "real abstraction." They set up an exemplary civic organization and responded with entrepreneurial astuteness to new market opportunities—only to face the censure of their European "mentors," who had an altogether more paternalistic view of the kind of "culturally sensitive" development appropriate to their station. This struggle over civil society presented the Ju/'hoansi with an acute dilemma: despite the indignities it brought upon them, it held out the prospect of access to a host of otherwise unobtainable benefits—and a language in which to frame new horizons of collective striving and personal desire.

But how effective *is* the language of civil society in actually capturing late-twentieth-century African aspirations? Mikael Karlström suggests in chapter 4 that, to answer this question, it is necessary to go far beyond the conventional social scientific preoccupation with voluntary associations; especially beyond those associations that engage with the state in order to render it more democratic. Interrogating the much-heralded "political recovery" in Uganda, he concludes that, measured by abstract Euro-modern standards, it would not qualify as particularly promising. The Ganda kingship, for example, appears a far cry from the ideal of liberal participatory government. Yet its recent restoration was rooted in the populist view that a political order founded on the coexistence of clan-based organizations and royal rule is more stable, more responsive, more representative than a national party system, with its divisive competition for power and its alienation from grassroots concerns. Viewed historically, Karlström adds, clans have long been a central mechanism of articulation between the citizenry and the monarchy, checking excesses of regal power in various ways. In this and other African contexts, kinship must thus be recognized as having both a public and a private face, a political and a domestic dimension—echoes, here, of Meyer Fortes (1953). This underscores the shifting, culturally specific nature of the opposition between the public and the private (cf. J. L. Comaroff 1987), thus negating the European presumption of its universality; also of its constitutive role in the making of civil society. More importantly, it also points to the fact that African sociocultural arrangements provide their own logic of sovereign accountability, their own public spheres, their own forms of nongovernmental organization and association.

Equally unhelpful, Karlström argues, is the effort to distinguish neatly between state and society. Recalling that this opposition stems from a particular juncture in European history, he points out how it misrecognizes official narratives for analytic categories, rhetoric for reality. All the more so in Africa, where efforts to extend bureaucratic control have consistently been undermined as government agencies are "captured" and appropriated at the local level. Significantly, state initiatives, among them the establishment of administrative councils, succeed in Uganda precisely by accepting that the power of the capital is circumscribed. Thus, for instance, these councils delegate to "society"—to nongovernmental personnel, groups, and associations—responsibility for a range of operations and activities usually associated with government. This vitiates any hard cleavage between the interiors of the state and its various exteriors, replacing it with a porous, graduated continuum that stretches out and away from the political center. The state, in short, becomes less a bounded institution than a quantum, an absent presence that disperses itself in varying degrees into the component publics that make up its national constituency.

The conclusion? While the opposition between state and society is becoming ever more part of the political language of Africa in the neoliberal age, the manner of its parsing—like that of the contrast between the public and the private—is very particular here. Such parsings give the invocation of civil society its salience. They also call for an anthropological analysis of its practical meaning.

The corollary? If the impact on African realities of the Idea of civil society is to be fully grasped—recuperated, that is, from a mere play on ideological tropes—its terms must be read against the specificities of local histories;

above all, once more, against the uncivil histories of colonial subjection. The failure to do just this, to historicize the civic public in debates about the restoration of urban Zanzibar, is the focus of William Bissell's essay (chapter 5). Conservationists engaged in "saving" the city of Stone Town, of preserving it as a unique cultural resource, have had difficulty in locating the very "community" they have labored to serve. In the face of ongoing public indifference, they have taken to condemning Zanzibari "ignorance." As in the "bushman" case described by Garland in chapter 3, these expatriates persist in ignoring the ways in which the planning process itself has marginalized and excluded the local populace; in so doing, they manufacture their own ignorance of indigenous communities of practice, of indigenous public spheres.

This impasse, Bissell shows, replays an old theme that reaches back into the era of British colonial rule. During that time, state officials went to great lengths to avoid handing over power to local municipal bodies; they deliberately fragmented the public sphere—sometimes, ironically, by invoking the "public good"—to discourage popular mobilization. This is nicely demonstrated by a dramatic dispute in which the Ismaili community on Zanzibar claimed a tract of land, arguing that it was a sacred cemetery. This claim was rejected as sectarian and self-seeking by the colonial administration, which wished to expropriate the real estate for a golf course. The links would be open to all, went the counterclaim, and would therefore be a "public" resource; the fact that it would only be used by Europeans was beside the point. In arguing thus, the colonizers represented themselves as being above parochial concerns, as being protectors of the commonweal. This recalls Harvey's general point about the state: that, to impose its will, it must always construct a sense of community based on "a definition of public interests over and above the class and sectarian interests . . . contained within its borders" (1989, 108). Thus it is that, in colonial contexts, the most powerful of partisans seized the high ground, rationalizing its actions with reference to universalist liberal values. Thus it is that alternative visions of public space and civil rectitude, promulgated in this instance by a self-consciously international "local" community, were deemed unacceptable. Thus it is that the Euro-modern terms of civil society were made, by appeal to a dialectic of exclusion, to serve as gatekeeper for established regimes of privilege. All of which has primed the postcolonial tendency to experiment with new, indigenously hatched hybrids.

We have already noted several times that modernist orthodoxy has been reluctant to recognize universalist visions of the world originating beyond mainstream Europe. Or to take seriously non-Western models of society and public life. But if African civic experiments—like those building on ties through kin or king, for instance—tend to be judged as personalistic and premodern, Islamic ideals of community and citizenship evoke yet stronger reactions. They are often seen as sinister inversions of modernity: as irrational, imperialist, fundamentalist. And fundamentalism, Adeline Masquelier observes in chapter 8, on Muslim conceptions of moral order in Niger, is widely associated with conservative ideologies of gender, family, and society. This stereotypic view, however, fails to recognize the complex social values promulgated by the *Izala* anti-Sufi reformists she describes. Their efforts to forge a modernity for Muslims in West Africa results in striking—and, to Western eyes, counterintuitive—juxtapositions. Like the coexistent requirement that women be covered in public *and* that they be educated, registered as voters, and so on. Masquelier insists that, far from shoring up "tradition" from the onslaughts of the postcolonial world, these novel interpretations of Islam provide a means for re-forming it at the crossroads of history; for using its protean terms to frame a growing sense of individualization and frugality—and to facilitate an active engagement with capitalist processes. This has withdrawn *'yan Izala* from the ostentatious redistribution of resources that has long integrated local communities in rural Southern Niger. And it has linked them to other neoliberal puritans of rather different ideological disposition, like born-again Pentecostals in Latin America. Advanced capitalism, as this indicates, is quite catholic in its ethical affinities.

Islamic reform movements of this sort are relevant to the issue of civil society in Africa, writes Masquelier, not simply because they promote an alternative moral order. This order also contests many of the legacies of Western colonialism. They serve, says Watts, as "both an alternative political and economic platform to the state and a critical oppositional discourse" (1996, 284). Nor do they speak with one voice. In a country where *décrispation* has, since the late 1980s, promoted a rapid upsurge in the expression of public opinion, Sufi and anti-Sufi factions advance competing visions of gender and morality, citizenship and nationhood, the private and the public. These struggles often seize on the particular signs, objects, and dispositions that come to embody the civil subject; the dress and deportment of women is an especially redolent one. Civility has many habitations, increasingly being indexed, here as elsewhere, through the language of consumption. In all this it might be argued that movements like Izala, by promoting open debate over reigning social and moral orthodoxies, conduce directly to the emergence of civil society in the world of which they are a part. But, like the movements that seek to define it, this form of civil society is frequently a field of argument, "neither homogeneous nor wholly emancipatory" (Fatton 1995, 93). At once democratic and despotic.

The precarious oscillation of democracy and despotism, of civil order and civil war, is the leitmotif of chapter 6, in which Mariane Ferme discusses the vicissitudes of postcolonial politics and the public sphere in Sierra Leone. Ferme explores this oscillation in a very specific context: the electoral process, that archetypical institution in what Habermas terms the "periodic staging" of civic liberalism. Ambiguity and violence may be integral to the story of political life in this part of West Africa, Ferme suggests. But there is a cultural logic to its unfolding. If the nation-state—here the hypostasis is intended—seeks to invent itself by usurping signs with specific local and regional histories, these signs are also always available for redeployment. And redeployed they often are, with semantic value added, in grassroots exercises of the political imagination. The public discourse precipitated by electoral processes is a prime occasion for this kind of social re-vision. More than in most other circumstances, it prompts participants to reach for resonant symbols. For these symbols give old alibis to new practices, bridging the gap between past, present, and future. They also signal the presence of invisible modalities of power whose operation is an "open secret," and whose mobilization is crucial in determining the destinies of people, their purposes and projects.

Ferme's account invites an anthropological reflection on Habermas's (1989) concern with the *principle* of publicity itself. For the acknowledged presence of invisible modalities of power in this most public of processes renders untenable the liberal fiction of the transparency, the shared and stable meanings, of participatory politics. Indeed, the "open secret" here points obliquely, like the palm branches in Mende political symbology, to forces that work beyond the arc lights of formal "democracy"; forces that empower or exclude without being seen to do anything at all. The public sphere, in other words, traffics in virtual realities, and not only of the palm-waving sort. In this regard, too, Ferme shows that shifts in media technology have heightened the experience of global compression and have altered the boundaries of the polity, with marked effect on the nature of publicity and the scope of civil action. The 1996 multiparty elections, for example, occasioned a "feverish exchange" of faxes, telephone calls, and Internet communications from abroad. In so doing, they made visible an immanent constituency of expatriates whose energetic debates found expression in international newsletters and on *Salonenet*, a Habermasian salon in cyberspace. These expatriates gave expression to classic, if radically deterritorialized, ideals of liberal civility. They raised funds, organized development initiatives, even participated in peace talks to end the civil war. Interacting in complex ways with communities "at home," they had a discernible impact on political outcomes, on the shape of the nation, and on the meaning of citizenship.

Deborah Durham is also concerned, in chapter 7, with the practical production of civil life, but in Botswana. A few dissenting voices aside (see, e.g., van Binsbergen 1995; Charlton 1993; Good 1992; Crowder 1988; Picard 1985), this southern African nation-state is usually said to be Africa's model democracy. By most accounts, it possesses a venerable tradition of participatory government, a fine record of multiparty elections, a self-monitoring press, and one of the fastest growing small economies in the world. And yet, despite appearing to be a textbook exemplar of liberal civility, it is rent at all levels by often acrimonious argument. In chiefly courts and "Freedom Squares," at party conventions, in the press, and on the Internet, debate rages about the adequacy of government and the abuse of power on the part of its leaders. What does this betoken? A growing disjuncture between state and populace? A breakdown of civil society?

There has, Durham notes, been no shortage of speculation on the health of civil society in Botswana. Skeptics argue that the surface civility everywhere in evidence masks an absence of "real" civil institutions; that the country is governed both by an elected parliament and hereditary chiefs, by Roman-Dutch and customary law; that its citizenry has a "superficial" commitment to democracy, preferring instead older forms of ascriptive rule and consensual decision making inimical to a vital public sphere. Such assessments rest, Durham responds, on a rigid, abstract conception of civil society and its appropriate institutions. The question, for Durham, is not whether "Batswana think as democrats." What is at stake in their spirited conflicts over the quality of leadership is something more profound. It is an argument of ontological proportions, one that has been ongoing since time immemorial, over the inherent tension between egalitarianism and privilege in all political, all communal life. But it is the very commitment to engage in this argument at all levels—on the streets, in the media, at royal courts, across the World Wide Web—that is the essence of civil society in Botswana. For it establishes the frame in which are negotiated all the concerns of the public sphere: the nature and propriety of sovereign power, the meaning of privilege and opportunity, the formulation of social policy, the scope of citizenship and the nation. It also lays down the terms in which the actions of living politicians, chiefs, and other public figures may be debated, evaluated, and made accountable—a civic practice with a major impact on the limits of their legitimacy.

What has any of this to do with popular debate about curling women's hair by chemical means in postsocialist Tanzania? A good deal, it turns out. During the early 1990s, Amy Stambach tells us in chapter 9, there occurred an expansive argument in the local press over the pros and cons of curling. This argument gave rare insight into competing ideas about civil being in a country undergoing dramatic political and economic liberalization. For the matter of hairstyles has aroused uncommon public passion; the controversy has been joined not only by religious leaders and journalists, but by a host of often silent citizens, like female high school students. Most participants in the argument have urged women not to buy the imported curl kits. They cite a variety of dangers: threats to physical and reproductive health, damage to the domestic economy, the degrading effects of "white aesthetics." Here, as elsewhere (Masquelier in chapter 8, for example), diffuse anxieties about the moral and material health of nations take root in female bodies. And, in the context of rapid commodification, in the politics of consumption. Women's hairstyles, Stambach suggests, have a double character: they are at once icons of corruption and glossy testaments to personal and national growth. Public discourse about them captures the changing political and moral relationship between citizen and state.

This analysis alerts us to the fact that ideas of civility and moral citizenship are complex, resonant historical constructions; that they are grounded not only in political ideals and formal institutions, but also in public manners and personal dispositions, in conventions of taste and style, in carefully attuned sensuous regimes. Francis Bacon wrote in 1626 that hairiness was the key to telling the civil apart from the savage. Barbarism and barbers, for him, were all of a piece: "Beasts are more Hairy than Men," he proclaimed, "and Savage Men more Hairy than Civil" (Tester 1992, 9). In Tanzania in the 1990s, hair seemed likewise to condense crucial questions of civil being: what was the appropriate reaction to the rise of assertive cosmopolitan identities, epitomized on the defiantly curled heads of young women of newly independent means? How to react to the implications of growing disparities in wealth and to the predatory effects of global marketing? As the vocal, impassioned reaction to these questions makes plain, the indulgence of worldly tastes was taken by many to signal a weakening allegiance to "traditional" family values, itself a global preoccupation in the neoliberal age. It was also regarded quite widely as a threat to established modes of reproducing civil order—the populist commitment to which was the underlying principle that sustained the debate in the first place.

The same specter of the dissolution of civil order haunts the last chapter in this volume, Andrew Apter's discussion of the "politics of illusion" in Nigeria. At issue in this essay are the critical currencies of civil exchange: the regimes of trust, representation, and value that—while never perfectly homogeneous or transparent—underpin the collective faith of a nation of citizens in the possibility of sustaining a habitable universe of order, meaning, and transaction; echoes, here, of Simmel. Apter traces the disintegration of civic trust in Nigeria by interrogating the changing nature of value—monetary and truth-value alike—as a once booming economy went bust. During the heady years of the 1970s, the Nigerian currency was backed by oil, and national prosperity was legible in contracts, letters of credit, bridges, highways, and a rising bourgeoisie. If not exactly democratic, the state was at least accountable in dollars and cents, a locus of truth primarily because it was also the locus of distribution.

When, in the early 1980s, the oil economy began to collapse, so too did the civil fabric of the nation and the credibility of its currency. As successive military regimes sought to restore investor confidence, inflation soared and public institutions crumbled. In a climate of frustrated expectations, broken contracts, and dwindling trust, a new kind of crime became epidemic: the 419, named for the section of the Nigerian criminal code that covers confidence tricks involving impersonation and forgery for fraudulent gain. This mode of deception played on a mimesis of capitalist enterprise: raiding bank accounts, building dummy corporations, and the like. It also deployed the prime tokens of public faith in the civil order: money, receipts, licenses, and contracts. By conjuring up a hermetic world of "improper circulation," in which false credentials and counterfeit media created an impenetrable skein of illusion, these scams effected a drastic depreciation in prevailing regimes of truth and value. Even more, they eroded public confidence in the relation of sign to referent; indeed, in representation itself. Small wonder, then, that the national con game stretched into the domain of would-be democratic politics, manifesting itself in corrupt courts, bogus votes, and sham elections. Less a suspension of civil society, this, than its reproduction as a dark, sinister farce.

This parody of liberal democracy and civil order draws attention to the ways in which Euro-modernist forms may be emptied of substance; how they may be turned into a hollow fetish, available for conjuring up the illusion of legitimate authority, for extracting wealth by illegitimate means, for deconstructing moral community and the public sphere. Such are the dangers of forms without content. Easily counterfeited, they set the scene for a dangerous burlesque. At the same time, these very forms may also be mobilized, as they are now in Nigeria and elsewhere, to contest the excesses of the state. And to demystify its magic; or, more accurately, its sorcery. Civil society may be deeply flawed as an analytic construct; in this hydra-headed guise, as we have said, it can only be a placeholder, a transitional term at a moment of paradigmatic revolution in which the social sciences seek to bring an unruly world to conceptual order. But it still serves, almost alone in the age of neoliberal capital, to give shape to reformist, even utopian visions. As we have seen, it is an inherently double-edged weapon: just as it is summoned up in the name of populist empowerment, so it is also invoked to banish those who fall beyond its normative, often restrictive purview. In this aspect, the discourse of civil society is and always will be the subject of both negative and positive dialectics. Insofar as it must, by its very nature, establish limits, it will always negate, exclude, silence, erase, rule out. On the other hand, its positive dimension lies in its capacity to open up spaces of democratizing aspiration; also—once relieved of the burden of its parochial roots in the European Enlightenment—to mandate practical experimentation in the building of new publics, new modes of association, new media of expression, new sorts of moral community, new politics. These are precisely the kinds of experimentation we are currently seeing in postcolonial Africa. They speak volumes, as do the essays in this book, about the emancipatory potential, and the undersides, of the Idea of Civil Society. Once, that is, it is liberated from its own orthodox confines.

Notes

1. See the translator's foreword (Knox 1952b, ix) to Hegel 1952. The capitalized "Idea" is a translation of *Idée,* the concept in its marked form. *Vorstellung* denotes "idea" in the lowercase: "whatsoever is the object of the understanding when a man thinks."

2. "The Intrigue Behind Congo's Agony: Forget the African Renaissance . . . ," Richard Cornwell and Jakkie Potgieter, *The Sunday Independent* [Johannesburg], 9 August 1998, p. 11. The authors run the Africa Early Warning Unit at the Institute for Security Studies, Midrand, South Africa. Members of this institute publish frequently in the national press. Their views are not the only nor the dominant ones expressed in the South African media—but they are influential.

3. This talk of "African redemption" resonates curiously with a remark made in 1929 by Jan Smuts, prime minister of South Africa before, during, and just after World War II. It is quoted by Mamdani (1996, 5, from Smuts 1929, 76–78, 92), which is how we became aware of it: If "Africa has to be redeemed . . . we shall have to proceed on different lines and evolve a policy which will not force her institutions into an alien European mould."

4. We are not alone in this respect, of course. Others cited in this chapter have written in a similar spirit about Africa and elsewhere. See, for example, Mamdani 1996; Monga 1996; Hann 1996; cf. also Chatterjee 1990.

5. "In the late twentieth century," says Tester, an English sociologist, "the possibility of society can no longer be taken for granted" (1992, 8). This seems especially true in Britain, where, since the Thatcherite 1980s, the topic has been famously—sometimes hotly—debated in the media.

6. We mean this in the anthropological sense of the term: as the construction of a coherent story, fashioned—by making imaginative connections between an originary past and the present—in such a way as to address preoccupations, conundrums, and contradictions in the contemporary world. To call something a mythical narrative in this sense is not to deem it fanciful or untrue.

7. It is not our intention here to annotate this large literature. For a small sample, see Keane 1988b; Taylor 1990; Walzer 1992; Woods 1992; Kumar 1993; Young 1994; Harbeson 1994; Cohen and Arato 1994; Hall 1995; and Krygier 1997a, 1997b; also Black 1984 and Castiglione 1994, texts to which we were alerted by Krygier 1997a (see n. 40). All are impressive works that begin with just the kind of archaeology of which we speak.

8. For two examples of different theoretical ilk, see Keane 1988a; and Cohen and Arato 1994—though, by its own lights (83), the latter is chiefly a conceptual history.

9. Taylor (1990) has a singular and more complex version of the genealogy of the modern concept. He identifies two streams of thought in respect of civil society, which he traces back to Locke and Montesquieu (see above, pp. 11–12). As we note later, we find it difficult to sustain the distinction between the two in twentieth-century writings. Over time, they have become intertwined, compromised, and hybridized.

10. See, for example, Walzer 1992 (90); Gellner 1996 (61). Ferguson, says Becker, was "the first writer in the English language employing the term 'civil society' to proffer a systematic account of its genesis" (1994, xi).

11. The allusion again is to Marx and Engels; in particular, to their disdain for the way in which the German intellectual establishment of the time dismissed as "prehistoric" anything that did not fit its preconceptions of history (1970, 49).

12. In one respect, however, Krader, an anthropological Marxist, departs from Marx: since all mankind is alienated from nature, he argues (1976, 22–23), it is an "error" to oppose civil society to "man in the state of nature."

13. See note 1 above.

14. As Keane notes, the history of that Idea between 1750 and 1850 is complex indeed (1988c, 37; cf. Cohen and Arato 1994, 83–84); much more complex, more confused, than is often allowed. The same is true after 1850. Our concern here, however, is not with its history but with the narration of that history as myth.

15. Strictly speaking, there is a time warp here, since Gramsci's work really gained currency in the twentieth-century period of quiescence. So too did Habermas's *Structural Transformation of the Public Sphere* ([1962] 1989); cf. Calhoun 1997.

16. The phrases in quotation marks are topic headings used by Kumar (1993, 375, 376).

17. This was foreshadowed in the writings of some eighteenth- and early nineteenth-century thinkers. Adam Ferguson, for one, saw distinct civic virtue in the "rude" communal world of Scottish Highlanders, whose values were lost with the rise of "modern society" (Oz-Salzberger 1995, xi). Likewise, romantic naturalists—most notably, Wordsworth ([1835] 1948)—would later speak nostalgically of the "pure Commonwealth" of the "lost" yeomanry of northern England.

18. For discussion of the "casual" conflation of the two, and the need to distinguish them, see Calhoun 1993 (269).

19. We share Kumar's (1993, 392) view that "civil society" adds little to more familiar analytic terms; also that, while its recovery "may be an interesting exercise in intellectual history, . . . it evades the real political challenges at the end of the twentieth century." But we do not agree with him that constructs like "constitutionalism, citizenship, and democracy," or the theoretical positions they imply, are sufficient to the task of understanding the contemporary world.

20. In fact, the anthropological concern with civil society is not unprecedented. Geertz (1963), for example, addressed the issue of "civil politics" in newly decolonized nations some thirty-five years ago. And Krader (1976) discussed it from a Marxist perspective before even the earliest of the current wave of writings on the topic; see above.

21. This statement has been cited, if for different ends, by others writing on civil society; see, e.g., Kumar 1993 (377).

22. Most notably, their assertions that "[c]ivil society as such only develops with the bourgeoisie"; also that it "embraces the . . . material intercourse of individuals within *a definite stage* of the development of productive forces" (1970, 57; emphasis added). We return to the first claim again later.

23. See note 5 above.

24. Hence, for example, Hall's (1995, 7) statement that the modern "construction of . . . civil society emerged in very large part for political reasons"—reasons owed, among other things, to "the impact of an enormous jump in fiscal extraction on the part of eighteenth-century states" (after Mann 1986) and to "an elective affinity between commerce and liberty."

25. For an extensive, critical reading of Marx on civil society, see Cohen 1982.

26. Gellner argues that Ferguson was singular in his perplexed anxiety about the kind of civil society emerging at the time (1996, 62). This claim appears ill-considered. Almost every serious intellectual history of the period, which Gellner's is not, suggests otherwise; cf., e.g., Becker (1994, xii–xiii).

27. The phrase is from Balzac ([1847] 1965, 418); although written about France circa 1838–46, his description applies as well to the times and places with which we are concerned here. Interestingly, Balzac also says, of contemporary Paris, that "[t]he family has been destroyed" (117).

28. Hegel allowed considerable significance, in the building of civil society, to the role of entrepreneurs free to pursue their selfish ends; in this he differed from Ferguson, who stressed the salience of political engagement and active citizenship, virtues threatened by the growing prominence of economic activity in modern society (Oz-Salzberger 1995, xvi).

29. It has become commonplace to make this point about the "new world order," whose birth is commonly associated with the events of 1989; see, for example, Bright and Geyer 1987 (77–78); Robertson 1992 (6, 58–59); Harvey 1995 (2); Yergin and Stanislaw 1998; J. L. Comaroff 1996.

30. The literature on the topic has expanded very quickly and on many fronts in the past few years—so much so that it is difficult to annotate a sample of relevant writings without being utterly arbitrary. At the risk of this, see, for a wide range of contrasting examples, Dicken 1986; Harvey 1989; Featherstone 1990; Wallerstein 1991; Robertson 1992; Lukacs 1993; Mazlish and Buultjens 1993; Featherstone, Lash, and Robertson 1995; Waters 1995; Mittelman 1996; Spybey 1996; Hoogvelt 1997; King 1997; Yergin and Stanislaw 1998; and, with Africa specifically in mind, Edoho (1997) and Ashcroft (1997).

31. "Post-native" is used, interestingly, by Geertz (1995, 6) to describe Obeyesekere's "subject position" in his debate with Sahlins over the analysis of Hawaiian history. "Posthuman" appears, for the first time to our knowledge, in Hayles (1999).

32. See, for example, the resolutions of the South African Native National Congress of 1917 (Molema 1920, 304); also Young (1994, 38–39).

33. And, one might add, African economy, law, medicine, philosophy, and religion.

34. The convergence of writings in French and English here is telling. For, as Wilder observes in chapter 2, French republicanism in the past never took civil society to be *opposed* to the state. Rather, it was an order peopled by citizens, not just individuals; and it defined the right of those citizens to participate in government—not their right to remain untouched by state power.

35. The phrase comes from Hobsbawm (1962, 18); he uses it to describe orthodox understandings of the Age of Revolution, 1789–1848. We cite it here to draw ironic attention to the ideological parallels between that age in Europe and the present age in Africa—and elsewhere. See Mamdani 1996 for a different view of the role of new bourgeoisies in the construction of civil society here.

References

Amin, Samir. 1989. *Eurocentrism.* New York: Monthly Review.

Anderson, Perry. 1976–77. "The Antinomies of Antonio Gramsci." *New Left Review* 100 (November–January): 5–78.

Arato, Andrew. 1981. "Civil Society Against the State: Poland 1980–81." *Telos* 47:23–47.

Arthur, C. J. 1970. Editor's introduction to *The German Ideology,* Part One, by Karl Marx and Frederick Engels. New York: International Publishers.

Ashcroft, Bill. 1997. "Globalism, Post-Colonialism and African Studies." In *Post-Colonialism: Culture and Identity in Africa,* ed. D. Pal Ahluwalia and Paul Nursey-Bray. Commack, N.Y.: Nova Science Publishers.

Azarya, Victor. 1994. "Civil Society and Disengagement in Africa." In *Civil Society and the State in Africa,* ed. John W. Harbeson, Donald Rothchild, and Naomi Chazan. Boulder: Lynne Rienner.

Balzac, Honoré de. [1847] 1965. *Cousin Bette; Part One of Poor Relations.* Translated by Marion Ayton Crawford. Reprint, Harmondsworth: Penguin.

Bayart, Jean-François. 1986. "Civil Society in Africa." In *Political Domination in Africa: Reflections on the Limits of Power,* ed. P. Chabal. Cambridge: Cambridge University Press.

———. 1993. *The State in Africa: Politics of the Belly.* New York: Longman.

Becker, Marvin B. 1994. *The Emergence of Civil Society in the Eighteenth Century: A Privileged Moment in the History of England, Scotland, and France.* Bloomington: Indiana University Press.

Black, Anthony. 1984. *Guilds and Civil Society in European Political Thought from the Twelfth Century to the Present.* London: Methuen.

Blaney, David L., and Mustapha Kamal Pasha. 1993. "Civil Society and Democracy in the Third World: Ambiguities and Historical Possibilities." *Studies in Comparative International Development* 28 (1): 3–24.

Bobbio, Norberto. 1988. "Gramsci and the Concept of Civil Society." Translated by C. Mortera. In *Civil Society and the State: New European Perspectives,* ed. J. Keane. New York: Verso.

Bratton, Michael. 1994. "Civil Society and Political Transitions in Africa." In *Civil Society and the State in Africa,* ed. John W. Harbeson, Donald Rothchild, and Naomi Chazan. Boulder: Lynne Rienner.

Bright, Charles, and Michael Geyer. 1987. "For a Unified History of the World in the Twentieth Century." *Radical History Review* 39:69–91.

Calhoun, Craig. 1993. "Civil Society and the Public Sphere." *Public Culture* 5 (2): 267–80.

———. 1997. Introduction to *Habermas and the Public Sphere*, ed. C. Calhoun. Cambridge: MIT Press.

Castiglione, Dario. 1994. "History and Civil Society: Outline of a Contested Paradigm." *Australian Journal of Politics and History* 40:83–103.

Charlton, R. 1993. "The Politics of Elections in Botswana." *Africa* 63:330–70.

Chatterjee, Partha. 1990. "A Response to Taylor's 'Modes of Civil Society.'" *Public Culture* 3 (1): 119–32.

Chazan, Naomi. 1992. "The Dynamics of Civil Society in Africa." Paper read at conference, Civil Society in Africa, Hebrew University, Jerusalem.

Cinnamon, John. 1998. "Visions of State Power in Democratic Gabon." Paper read at the annual meeting of the American Anthropological Association, December, Philadelphia.

Cohen, Jean L. 1982. *Class and Civil Society: The Limits of Marxian Critical Theory*. Oxford: Martin Robertson.

Cohen, Jean L., and Andrew Arato. 1994. *Civil Society and Political Theory*. Cambridge: MIT Press.

Comaroff, Jean. 1997a. "Portrait of an Unknown South African: Identity in a Global Age." *Macalaster International* 4 (spring): 119–43; and *Novos Estudos* 49 (1997): 65–83.

———. 1997b. "Consuming Passions: Nightmares of the Global Village." In *Body and Self in a Post-colonial World*, ed. Ellen Badone. Special issue of *Culture* 17 (1–2): 7–19.

Comaroff, Jean, and John L. Comaroff. 1999. "Occult Economies and the Violence of Abstraction: Notes from the South African Postcolony." *American Ethnologist* 26 (3). Forthcoming.

———. n.d. Introduction to *Public Culture*, special millennial edition, *Millennial Capitalism and the Culture of Neoliberalism*, ed. J. and J. L. Comaroff. Forthcoming.

Comaroff, John L. 1987. "*Sui Genderis:* Feminism, Kinship Theory, and Structural Domains." In *Gender and Kinship*, ed. J. F. Collier and S. J. Yanagisako. Stanford: Stanford University Press.

———. 1991. "Humanity, Ethnicity, Nationality: Conceptual and Comparative Perspectives on the USSR." *Theory and Society*, 20:661–87.

———. 1996. "Ethnicity, Nationalism, and the Politics of Difference in an Age of Revolution." In *The Politics of Difference: Ethnic Premises in a World of Power*, ed. E. Wilmsen and P. MacAllister. Chicago: University of Chicago Press.

Comaroff, John L., and Jean Comaroff. 1997a. *Of Revelation and Revolution*, vol. 2, *The Dialectics of Modernity on an African Frontier*. Chicago: University of Chicago Press.

———. 1997b. "Postcolonial Politics and Discourses of Democracy in Southern Africa: An Anthropological Reflection on African Political Modernities." *Journal of Anthropological Research* 53 (2): 123–46.

Crowder, Michael. 1988. "Botswana and the Survival of Liberal Democracy in Africa." In *Decolonization and African Independence*, ed. P. Gifford and W. R. Louis. New Haven: Yale University Press.

Dicken, Peter. 1986. *Global Shift: Industrial Change in a Turbulent World.* London: Harper and Row.

Dunn, J. 1978. "Comparing West African States." In *West African States: Future and Promise*, ed. J. Dunn. Cambridge: Cambridge University Press.

Durkheim, Emile. 1947. *The Elementary Forms of the Religious Life: A Study in Religious Sociology.* Translated by J. W. Swain. Glencoe, Ill.: Free Press.

Eaton, David. 1998. "Limits of Transparence in Congo." Paper read at the annual meeting of the American Anthropological Association, Philadelphia, December.

Edoho, Felix Moses, ed. 1997. *Globalization and the New World Order: Promises, Problems, and Prospects for Africa in the Twenty-First Century.* Westport, Conn: Praeger.

Ekeh, Peter. 1975. "Colonialism and the Two Publics in Africa: A Theoretical Statement." *Comparative Studies in Society and History* 17 (fall): 91–112.

Elias, Norbert. 1988. "Violence and Civilization." In *Civil Society and the State: New European Perspectives*, ed. J. Keane. New York: Verso.

Escobar, Arturo. 1994. *Encountering Development: The Making and Unmaking of the Third World.* Princeton: Princeton University Press.

Fatton, Robert, Jr. 1995. "Africa in the Age of Democratization: The Civic Limitations of Civil Society." *African Studies Review* 38:67–100.

Featherstone, Mike, ed. 1990. *Global Culture: Nationalism, Globalization, and Modernity.* London: Sage.

Featherstone, Mike, Scott Lash, and Roland Robertson, eds. 1995. *Global Modernities.* London: Sage.

Ferguson, Adam. [1767] 1995. *An Essay on the History of Civil Society*, ed. F. Oz-Salzberger. Cambridge: Cambridge University Press.

Ferguson, James. 1994. *The Anti-Politics Machine: "Development," Depoliticization, and Bureaucratic Power in Lesotho.* Minneapolis: University of Minnesota Press.

Fortes, Meyer. 1953. "The Structure of Unilineal Descent Groups." *American Anthropologist* 55:17–41.

Gal, Susan. 1997. "Feminism and Civil Society." In *Transitions, Environments, Translations*, ed. J. Scott, C. Kaplan, and D. Keats. New York: Routledge.

Geertz, Clifford. 1963. "The Integrative Revolution: Primordial Sentiments and Civil Politics in the New States." In *Old Societies and New States*, ed. C. Geertz. New York: Free Press.

———. 1995. "Culture War," review of *The Apotheosis of Captain Cook: European Mythmaking in the Pacific*, by G. Obeyesekere, and *How "Natives" Think, About Captain Cook, for Example*, by M. Sahlins. *New York Review of Books* 42 (30 November): 4–6.

Gellner, Ernest. 1996. *Conditions of Liberty: Civil Society and Its Rivals.* London: Penguin.

Good, K. 1992. "Interpreting the Exceptionality of Botswana." *Journal of Modern African Studies* 30:69–95.

Gouldner, Alvin. 1980. *The Two Marxisms: Contradictions and Anomalies in the Development of Theory.* New York: Seabury Press.

Gupta, Dipankar. n.d. "Civil Society or the State: What Happened to Citizenship?" Paper read at the Centre for the Study of Social Systems, Jawaharlal Nehru University, New Delhi.

Habermas, Jürgen. 1989. *The Structural Transformation of the Public Sphere.* Translated by T. Burger and F. Lawrence. Cambridge: MIT Press.

Hall, John A. 1995. "In Search of Civil Society." In *Civil Society: Theory, History, Comparison,* ed. J. A. Hall. Cambridge: Polity Press.

Hann, Chris. 1996. "Introduction: Political Society and Civil Anthropology." In *Civil Society: Challenging Western Models,* ed. C. Hann and E. Dunn. New York: Routledge.

Hannerz, Ulf. 1989. "Notes on the Global Ecumene." *Public Culture* 1 (2): 66–75.

Harbeson, John W. 1994. "Civil Society and Political Renaissance in Africa." In *Civil Society and the State in Africa,* ed. John W. Harbeson, Donald Rothchild, and Naomi Chazan. Boulder: Lynne Rienner.

Hardt, Michael. 1995. "The Withering of Civil Society." *Social Text* 45, 14 (4): 27–44.

Harvey, David. 1982. *The Limits to Capital.* Chicago: University of Chicago Press.

———. 1989. *The Condition of Postmodernity: An Enquiry into the Origins of Cultural Change.* Oxford: Blackwell.

———. 1995. "Globalization in Question." *Rethinking Marxism* 8 (4): 1–17.

Hayles, N. Katherine. 1999. *How We Became Posthuman: Virtual Bodies in Cybernetics, Literature, and Informatics.* Chicago: University of Chicago Press.

Haynes, Jeff. 1997. *Democracy and Civil Society in the Third World: Politics and New Political Movements.* Cambridge: Polity Press.

Hegel, G. W. F. 1952. *Hegel's Philosophy of Right.* Translated by T. M. Knox. Oxford: Clarendon Press.

Hecht, David, and Maliqalim Simone. 1994. *Invisible Governance: The Art of African Micropolitics.* New York: Autonomedia.

Hirst, Paul, and Grahame Thompson. 1992. "The Problem of 'Globalization': International Economic Relations, National Economic Management and the Formation of Trading Blocs." *Economy and Society* 21 (4): 357–96.

———. 1996. *Globalization in Question: The International Economy and the Possibilities of Governance.* Cambridge: Polity Press.

Hobsbawm, Eric J. 1962. *The Age of Revolution, 1789–1848.* New York: New American Library (Mentor Book).

———. 1987. *The Age of Empire, 1875–1914.* London: Weidenfeld and Nicolson.

Hoogvelt, Ankie M. M. 1997. *Globalization and the Postcolonial World: The New Political Economy of Development.* Baltimore: Johns Hopkins University Press.

Hunt, Lynn. 1984. *Politics, Culture, and Class in the French Revolution.* Berkeley: University of California Press.

Hydén, Goran. 1980. *Beyond Ujamaa in Tanzania: Underdevelopment and an Uncaptured Peasantry.* Los Angeles: University of California Press.

Isaacman, Allen F. 1990. "Peasants and Rural Social Protest in Africa." *African Studies Review* 33 (2): 1–120.

Keane, John. 1988a. *Democracy and Civil Society.* London: Verso.

———. 1988b. Introduction to *Civil Society and the State: New European Perspectives,* ed. J. Keane. New York: Verso.

———. 1988c. "Despotism and Democracy: The Origins and Development of the Distinction Between Civil Society and the State, 1750–1859." In *Civil Society and the State: New European Perspectives,* ed. J. Keane. New York: Verso.

King, Anthony D., ed. 1997. *Culture, Globalization and the World System: Contemporary Conditions for the Representation of Identity.* Minneapolis: University of Minnesota Press.

Knox, T. M. 1952a. Translator's notes to *Hegel's Philosophy of Right,* G. W. F. Hegel. Oxford: Clarendon Press.

———. 1952b. Translator's foreword to *Hegel's Philosophy of Right,* G.W.F. Hegel. Oxford: Clarendon Press.

Kopytoff, Igor. 1987. "The Internal African Frontier: The Making of African Culture." In *The African Frontier,* ed. I. Kopytoff. Bloomington: Indiana University Press.

Kothari, Rajni. 1988. *State Against Democracy: In Search of Humane Governance.* Delhi: Ajanta.

Krader, Lawrence. 1976. *The Dialectic of Civil Society.* Amsterdam: Van Gorcum, Assen.

Krygier, Martin. 1997a. "Virtuous Circles: Antipodean Reflections on Power, Institutions, and Civil Society." *East European Politics and Societies* 11 (1): 36–88.

———. 1997b. *Between Fear and Hope: Hybrid Thoughts on Public Values.* Sydney: ABC Books.

Kumar, Krishan. 1993. "Civil Society: An Inquiry into the Usefulness of an Historical Term." *British Journal of Sociology* 44 (3): 375–95.

Kurtzman, Joel. 1993. *The Death of Money: How the Electronic Economy Has Destabilized the World's Markets and Created Financial Chaos.* New York: Simon and Schuster.

Kuzmics, Helmut. 1988. "The Civilizing Process." In *Civil Society and the State: New European Perspectives,* ed. J. Keane. New York: Verso.

Lesch, Ann M. 1998. *The Sudan: Contested National Identities.* Bloomington: Indiana University Press.

Lukacs, John. 1993. *The End of the Twentieth Century and the End of the Modern Age.* New York: Ticknor and Fields.

Mackenzie, John. 1887. *Austral Africa: Losing It or Ruling It.* 2 vols. London: Sampson Low, Marston, Searle and Rivington.

Macpherson, Crawford Brough. 1962. *The Political Theory of Possessive Individualism: Hobbes to Locke.* Oxford: Oxford University Press.

Makinda, Samuel. 1996. "Imagining Democracy: Political Culture and Democratisation in Buganda." *Africa* 66 (4): 485–505.

Mamdani, Mahmood. 1996. *Citizen and Subject: Contemporary Africa and the Legacy of Late Colonialism.* Princeton: Princeton University Press; London: James Currey.

Mandel, Ernest. 1975. *Late Capitalism.* Translated by J. De Bres. London: Verso.

Mann, Michael. 1986. *The Sources of Social Power,* vol. 2, *The Rise of Classes and Nation-States, 1760–1914,* Cambridge: Cambridge University Press.

Marx, Karl, and Frederick Engels. 1970. *The German Ideology,* Part One. Edited by C. J. Arthur. New York: International Publishers.

Mazlish, Bruce, and Ralph Buultjens, eds. 1993. *Conceptualizing Global History.* Boulder: Westview Press.

Mbembe, Achille. 1992. "The Banality of Power and the Aesthetics of Vulgarity in the Postcolony." *Public Culture* 4 (2): 1–30.

Mittelman, James H., ed. 1996. *Globalization: Critical Reflections.* Boulder: Lynne Rienner.

Molema, Silas Modiri. 1920. *The Bantu, Past and Present.* Edinburgh: W. Green and Son.

Molutsi, Patrick P., and John D. Holm. 1990. "Developing Democracy When Civil Society Is Weak: The Case of Botswana." *African Affairs* 89 (356): 323–40.

Monga, Célestin. 1996. *The Anthropology of Anger: Civil Society and Democracy in Africa.* Translated by L. L. Fleck and C. Monga. Boulder: Lynne Rienner.

Owusu, Maxwell. 1997. "Domesticating Democracy: Culture, Civil Society, and Constitutionalism in Africa." *Contemporary Studies in Society and History* 39 (1): 120–52.

Oz-Salzberger, Fania. 1995. Introduction to *An Essay on the History of Civil Society,* Adam Ferguson; ed. F. Oz-Salzberger. Cambridge: Cambridge University Press.

Pateman, Carole. 1988. *The Sexual Contract.* Cambridge: Polity Press.

Perry, Donna. 1998. *The Patriarchs Are Crying: Discourses of Authority and Social Change in Rural Senegal.* Ph.D. diss., Yale University.

Philip, John. [1828] 1969. *Researches in South Africa; Illustrating the Civil, Moral, and Religious Condition of the Native Tribes.* 2 vols. Reprint, New York: Negro Universities Press.

Picard, Louis A., ed. 1985. *The Evolution of Modern Botswana.* London: Rex Collings.

Robertson, Roland. 1992. *Globalization: Social Theory and Global Culture.* London: Sage.

Rupnik, Jacques. 1979. "Dissent in Poland, 1968–78: The End of Revisionism and the Rebirth of Civil Society." In *Opposition in Eastern Europe,* ed. R. Tokes. Baltimore: Johns Hopkins University Press.

———. 1988. "Totalitarianism Revisited." In *Civil Society and the State: New European Perspectives,* ed. J. Keane. New York: Verso.

Sillery, Anthony. 1971. *John Mackenzie of Bechuanaland, 1835–1899: A Study in Humanitarian Imperialism.* Cape Town: Balkema.

Smuts, General Jan C. 1929. *Africa and Some World Problems, Including the Rhodes Memorial Lectures Delivered in Michaelmas Term, 1929.* Oxford: Clarendon Press.

Snyder, Katherine. 1998. "'Being of 'One Heart': Local Interpretations and Responses to Democratization among the Iraqw of Tanzania." Paper read at the annual meeting of the American Anthropological Association, December, Philadelphia.

Spybey, Tony [William Anthony]. 1996. *Globalization and World Society.* Cambridge: Polity Press.

Taylor, Charles. 1989. *Sources of the Self: The Making of Modern Identity.* Cambridge: Harvard University Press.

———. 1990. "Modes of Civil Society. *Public Culture* 3 (1): 95–118.

Tester, Keith. 1992. *Civil Society.* London: Routledge.

Tölölyan, Khachig. 1991. "The Nation-State and Its Others: In Lieu of a Preface." *Diaspora,* spring, 3–7.

Tripp, Aili Mari. 1994. "Rethinking Civil Society: Gender Implications in Contemporary Tanzania." In *Civil Society and the State in Africa,* ed. John W. Harbeson, Donald Rothchild, and Naomi Chazan. Boulder: Lynne Rienner.

van Binsbergen, Wim. 1995. "Aspects of Democracy and Democratisation in Zambia and Botswana." *Journal of Contemporary African Studies* 13:3–33.

Walker, R. B. J. 1994. "Social Movements/World Politics." *Millennium: Journal of International Studies* 23 (3): 669–700.

Wallerstein, Immanuel. 1991. *Geopolitics and Geoculture: Essays on the Changing World-System.* Cambridge: Cambridge University Press.

Walzer, Michael. 1992. "The Civil Society Argument." In *Dimensions of Radical Democracy: Pluralism, Citizenship, Community,* ed. C. Mouffe. New York: Verso.

Waters, Malcolm. 1995. *Globalization.* London: Routledge.

Watts, Michael. 1996. "Islamic Modernities? Citizenship, Civil Society and Islamism in a Nigerian City." *Public Culture* 8:251–89.

Woods, Dwayne. 1992."Civil Society in Europe and Africa: Limiting State Power through a Public Sphere." *African Studies Review* 95 (2): 77–100.

Wordsworth, William. [1835] 1948. *A Guide through the District of the Lakes in the North of England, with a Description of the Scenery, &c. for the Use of Tourists and Residents.* Reprint, Malvern: Tantivy Press (facsimile of the 5th ed.).

Yergin, Daniel, and Joseph Stanislaw. 1998. *The Commanding Heights: The Battle between Government and the Marketplace That Is Remaking the Modern World.* New York: Simon and Schuster.

Young, Crawford. 1994. "In Search of Civil Society." In *Civil Society and the State in Africa,* ed. John W. Harbeson, Donald Rothchild, and Naomi Chazan. Boulder: Lynne Rienner.

Yudice, George. 1995. "Civil Society, Consumption, and Governmentality in an Age of Global Reconstruction." *Social Text* 45, 14 (4): 1–25.

2

Practicing Citizenship in Imperial Paris

Gary Wilder

Interrogating Civil Society

"CIVIL SOCIETY"—that supposedly autonomous space of individual freedom and voluntary association distinct from both the state and the market, located between the private and the public, secured by right, protected by law, where citizens can pursue the good life (together). Civil society—a *real abstraction* that cannot and should not be assumed to exist across time and space, as if it could be "discovered" or "instituted" in any social formation. It is a category of democratic self-understanding that corresponds to modern society's differentiation into distinct spheres: the political, the social, the economic. Civil society emerges from within the specific political and philosophical tradition of a Western modernity whose privileged political forms were the rationalized state and the racialized colony. In what ways must we rethink a category like civil society when we recognize both state and colony, reason and race to be intrinsic elements of an irreducibly imperial nation-state, the political form of a colonial modernity?

For early modern Europe, civil society did important work: delimiting a space of popular sovereignty (opposed to the absolutist state), where free and equal citizens could define their interests, constitute a public, and participate

---

This essay is drawn from my Ph.D. dissertation, "Greater France Between the Wars: Negritude, Colonial Humanism, and the Imperial Nation-State" (University of Chicago, 1999). It is based on research supported by the Franco-American Foundation (Fulbright), the Social Science Research Council, and the MacArthur Scholars Fellowship; my writing has been supported by the University of Chicago William Rainer Harper Dissertation Writing Fellowship and a Spencer Foundation Dissertation Fellowship. For their comments on various drafts of this essay, I would like to thank the participants in the original civil society conference (including my commentator, Ralph Austen) as well as Leora Auslander, Jean Comaroff, John Comaroff, Matthew Trachman, and the members of the Red Line Working Group—Bill Bissell, Neil Brenner, Nick De Genova, and Manu Goswami.

in self-government. Today, from within the crisis of postmodernity—the collapse of public life in Western democracies, the social disintegration of postcommunist societies, and the authoritarian state politics of postcolonial nations—civil society once again proffers a salutary promise.[1] The appeal is seductive. Yet, my analysis of the predicament of colonial subjects in metropolitan France between the wars demonstrates that civil society is as inadequate a solution to modern forms of heteronomy as the free market, the liberal state, and primordial community have already proved to be.[2]

We cannot call on postcolonial nations to *turn* to civil society as a legally instituted space of social autonomy without elaborating the category's relationship to an imperial history. The point is not that European categories are inappropriate for non-Western cultures. Rather, the source of the dilemma lies in the fact that because colonial government rationalized *and* racialized native society, civil society could only be an impossible promise: at once the justification for colonial intervention (civilize the natives) and the sign of native exclusion (they are not yet civilized).[3]

My goal is to interrogate this colonial dilemma, produced by the antinomy between a political formation founded at once on republican universality and racial particularity. Specifically, I explore the ways in which elite Francophone African and Caribbean colonial subjects in the democratic metropole engaged with this contradiction of colonial modernity at a crucial turning point in the formation of black nationalist consciousness between the wars. What kind of relationship did, and could, these colonial subjects develop to republican categories, like civil society and citizenship, that themselves enabled the exclusions on which the colonial order depended?

Interwar Colonial Rationality

After World War I, when the transition from military to civilian administration was virtually complete, a new political rationality—colonial humanism—came increasingly to organize, rather than simply legitimize, the French colonial project (Girardet 1972, 253–73; Cohen 1971, 84–142). Colonial authority was no longer understood to depend on immediate forms of physical exploitation and political coercion, but on the art and science of administration: a mediated form of "governmentality" operating through continuous and intimate contact with indigenous populations (cf. Foucault 1988, 1982, 1981, 1978.)[4] Reports and decrees were seen as less effective than knowing natives, identifying their interests, and recognizing their rights. "Native policy" became the instrument and native welfare the objective of this new modality of colonial rule.[5]

Detailed, scientific knowledge of native society was both the prerequisite and the goal of the administrative art (Hardy 1929, 12; Brévié 1935, 41). The very category "native society" became a newly constructed object of colonial knowledge and field of administrative activity. Inspired by as well as promoting the new Africanist ethnology, the colonial administration began to apprehend indigenous society as an autonomous entity with its own structure, customs, and history (Delafosse 1921, 1912). The new strategy was to protect and respect the specificity of native society in order to maximize the natives' own productive abilities. It required an informed and benevolent administrative intervention into the productive and familial, social, and symbolic lives of natives.

The prewar colonial policy of eliminating indigenous social institutions had produced a growing population of deracinated natives. The interwar administration had begun to identify the mass of increasingly urbanized natives as a source of social instability. Reform-minded humanists argued that colonial authority depended on keeping peasants linked to the land, enmeshed in local social networks. New "governmental" practices began to concentrate on rural village welfare, complementing the former emphasis on producing educated urban collaborators. Colonial humanism identified privileged sites of administrative intervention where village life could most effectively be monitored and managed, including native justice, village cooperatives and political groups, health, hygiene, agriculture, and the family. In large part, colonial authority would be secured precisely in those domains of everyday sociability we would identify as civil society.

This then was a contradictory colonial rationality. Native society had to be known and directed, preserved but improved. Colonial humanism worked to transform cultural communities into aggregates of property-owning individuals, yet to reduce educated elites to their racial determinations. The very administrative practices deployed to know and maintain native society were themselves transformative; and the very process of individuation fixed natives as backward, inferior, not yet ready for individual rights. Villagers were normalized as individuals and individual *évolués* were racialized as "behind." This was a colonial rationality for which culture became incompatible with citizenship, yet such "evolved" natives were fixed to the very culture they had been compelled to transcend. Colonial humanism simultaneously required and forbade natives to abandon their culture; they should, but could not, become abstract universal individuals.

Here was a structure of permanent deferral. Natives were seen as essentially equal in their cultural difference, but native society remained in a state of perpetual adolescence. The moment of maturity, when natives would be granted the full rights of either political equality or cultural autonomy, would be permanently delayed. As one reformer reasoned:

> Despite the thesis so dear to those who would assimilate at any price, it is proven that the education of Africans must be progressive, otherwise it will engender disorder that could lead to fatal consequences for the Protector as much as for the Protected [*protégé*]. . . . Without disputing

> the possibility of extending more and more extensive electoral rights to natives in a relatively distant future, we are permitted to think that the hour when we can envisage this situation for such numerous peoples has not yet arrived. (Labouret 1931, 123)

Colonial humanism thus produced native subjects defined by a colonial double bind: destined to become rights-bearing individuals, but always too immature to exercise these rights. Native demands for autonomy were undermined by the administrative claim that they were minor members of the French nation, while their demands for citizenship rights were undermined by the claim that they were still too different to be equal.

Colonial Citizenship and la Cité Noire

We cannot but problematize civil society once we begin to appreciate the way colonial authority was mediated by the very categories democracy deployed to emancipate individuals from governmental constraint: rationality, individuality, humanity, and so on. If civil society's autonomy from the state depended on legally protected individual rights, what could the category mean in a political space defined by juridical inequality, peopled by racialized subjects rather than citizens?

French political culture had long been characterized by deep structural tensions between administrative authoritarianism and parliamentary republicanism (Rosanvallon 1990). This conflict among governing principles was always most evident on the colonial periphery. Territorial expansion, after all, had required the French imperial nation-state to confront the fact that its supposedly self-governing "people" now included legally, politically, and culturally indeterminate overseas populations. The tension between imperialism and republicanism became especially acute after World War I, when the colonial question became a national question, and the proper relationship between continental and overseas France became the object of public debate. In French West Africa, colonial humanism sought to reconcile republican principles with colonial practices. And in the metropole, there developed a new colonial nationalism, preoccupied with the concept of "Greater France," that understood the colonies to be integral parts of an expanded French nation whose precise legal and political character remained ambiguous and contradictory.

For generations, the so-called old colonies of Martinique, Guadeloupe, and Guyana had been subject to the same nationalizing practices that the republican state applied to the French regions. Revolutionary governments in 1794, 1848, and 1870 had recognized these assimilated colonial populations as French-identified nationals and granted them a citizenship that was then repeatedly annulled by successive antirepublican regimes.[6] Even under the

Third Republic, the status of Antillean citizens remained contradictory. On the one hand, they elected their own deputies to the National Assembly, lived under the *Code Civil* (enjoying the protection of French metropolitan laws), and largely ran their own municipal governments. On the other hand, they continued to live in a racially organized colonial society, under the authoritarian rule of an appointed governor and distinguished by restrictive labor regulations and diminished social legislation. They were at once colonial subjects and French citizens, whose political milieu was characterized by power struggles between popularly elected local politicians—mayors and colonial deputies—and unaccountable, Paris-appointed administrators. Theirs was a paradoxical *colonial* citizenship.

A parallel dilemma existed for colonial elites living in the old Senegalese coastal enclaves—or *Quatre Communes*—of French West Africa. They too had been repeatedly granted citizenship by republican governments that was then revoked by interceding authoritarian regimes. Likewise they were colonized citizens confronted with power struggles between elected republicans and appointed administrators.[7] And again, under the Third Republic, attempts were made to empty their citizenship of content: by limiting their voting rights in 1908 and 1910, as well as by excluding them from the jurisdiction of French courts in 1912 (Buell 1928, 946–52). To protect their rights, these colonial citizens turned to paradigmatic nationalizing institutions, thereby linking cultural and political assimilation. They insisted that universal military conscription—a privileged site for national service—be applied to them, which led to the 1916 Citizenship Law. And they fought to prevent their French secondary schools—sites where national citizens were formed—from being replaced by African-oriented substitutes. Yet, these colonial citizens were permitted to retain their so-called personal status, remain governed by customary civil law, and engage in practices prohibited by French law (such as polygamy).

In contrast, natives born outside these zones of juridico-political privilege were colonial subjects, regardless of their education, social status, or place of residence. Despite the fact that their territory was also claimed as part of the Greater French nation, they were denied the legal protections and political rights of citizenship. The administration argued that native masses either did not want or were not ready to become citizens. Alternatively, a concern for social peace compelled the government to address the educated elite's legitimate demand for a greater role in local self-government. But political order finally required that they too be denied full citizenship, lest they become unmanageable.[8] "Greater France" was thus an ambiguous construction that sought to include natives within the national *family,* but exclude them from the national *polity,* even though a republican nation-state is defined by its homogenous juridical space. Colonial politics thus removed the hyphen between nation and state by restricting republican politics to only one piece of the French nation, thereby dissociating nationality and citizenship.

In one sense, these colonial West Africans were recognized as "French." However, they, like "foreigner" and "immigrant" nonnationals, could only acquire citizenship through naturalization. A 1912 decree established the criteria for colonial citizenship: an ability to read and write French, proof of "devotion to French interests" for at least ten years, demonstration of "a good and moral life," and means of financial support. As M. Benga, an African lawyer living in Paris, reports in "Le problème de naturalisation," applicants were also required to formally renounce their attachment to customary practices contrary to the French legal code (*La Dépeche Africaine* no. 2, April 1928).[9] And a 1932 revision extended the requirement that a native's "way of life and social habits . . . be compatible with French civilization" to an applicant's family (the children now had to be French educated).[10]

Because naturalization would require documentary evidence—such as sworn statements, signed oaths, identity papers, and certificates—colonial citizenship also implicitly required natives to be already integrated within the rationalizing administrative order of colonial society. As these demands were submitted to local administrators or mayors, the process was also highly politicized. Not surprisingly, the number of interwar citizenship demands was quite low and the number of naturalizations even lower.[11] In other words, at precisely the moment when colonial reforms sought to improve the social and political condition of natives, citizenship became more restricted. And just when native policy sought to valorize and preserve indigenous society, naturalization became more explicitly linked to assimilation.

This naturalization requirement meant that a sizable number of educated, assimilated, and integrated members of the Greater French nation never became citizens. In his 1928 article for *La Dépeche Africaine,* Benga called this a "paradoxical situation . . . humiliating for the native who is French, but a diminished Frenchman, even less respected than a foreigner." He pointed out that the 1927 nationality law allowed foreigners to become citizens after only three, rather than ten, years of residence. Moreover, while this and the preceding 1889 law had affirmed the principle of jus solis for foreigners by granting citizenship to immigrants' children born in France, children of colonial subjects settled in the metropole did not automatically become citizens.[12]

Yet, Paris between the wars was becoming an imperial space, containing a small but vital and diverse community of African and Caribbean colonial subjects, including sailors, dockworkers, musicians and performers, hotel and restaurant staff, clerks, professionals, and students.[13] They ranged from working class to bourgeois and included indigents and intellectuals, who could be communist, nationalist, or republican. This transnational black community made up a dense network of voluntary associations—political clubs, student organizations, mutual aid societies, workers cooperatives, trade unions—organized according to geography and ethnicity, ideology and profession (Dewitte 1985; Liauzu 1982; and Spiegler 1969). Most of these groups published their own newspapers or journals. Some had fixed meeting places; others met in restaurants and cafés. Together they constituted a complex social and discursive field permeated by class and political conflict.

The educated, elite fraction of this population inhabited contradictory civil, juridical, and political identities, especially regarding the category of citizenship. Many of them were nominal citizens who were effectively subjects—racialized members of Greater France who enjoyed neither full rights nor genuine equality. Conversely, they were also colonial subjects who were effectively citizens insofar as they were located within French civil society, participated in its political public sphere, and practiced civic virtue. A brief inquiry into colonial citizenship may contextualize this fundamental ambiguity.

In the French republican tradition, civil society was conceptualized in terms of a classical idea of the *cité*—a community of citizens who ideally practiced "civic virtue" by participating in public life and devoting themselves to the common good. Within the *cité* sociability and citizenship presupposed each other; civil rights derived from civic practice (Nicolet 1982, 331). They were an effect of political association and participation, not an essential property of prepolitical individuals in society. Nicolet argues that the "basis of all French republican doctrine" is the idea that there is "a perfect and total continuity between civil society and political society" (1992, 397).

This conception of civil society—and its corresponding political culture—thus differed from that developed by Anglo-American liberal tradition. If liberalism sought to maintain a rigid distinction between civil society (as a space of individual freedom) and the self-limiting state (as legal guarantor of that freedom), French republicanism always imagined a more intimate relationship between civil and political society. Focusing on the freedom to participate in democratic self-government rather than freedom from governmental constraint, republicanism always understood the state to be an extension rather than adversary of the people or nation.

Yet, republican thought did recognize the distinct space of civil society. Rousseau writes that the social contract enabled the transition from "natural liberty" to "civil liberty" where "proprietary ownership" (regulated by law) replaces "possession" (secured by force) (Rousseau 1987, 151). By naming liberty, property, and security "natural and imprescriptable rights" the *Declaration of the Rights of Man and Citizen* marked civil society as a space of unencumbered sociability regulated by contracts, secured by law, and peopled by rights-bearing individuals. But in contrast to Anglo-American liberalism, republicanism never understood civil society to be radically distinct from the sphere of politics. Rousseau argues that the civil society created by the social contract was a "public person" that

> formerly took the name *cité* and at present takes the name *republic* or *body politic*, which is called *state* by its members. . . . As to the associ-

> ates, they collectively take the name *people;* individually they are called *citizens,* insofar as participants in the sovereign authority, and *subjects,* insofar as they are subjected to the laws of the state. (Rousseau 1987, 148–49, original emphasis)

In short, republican civil society is peopled by citizens (not individuals) and defined in terms of their right to participate in government (not in terms of their right to remain untouched by state power). It may thus be more accurate to speak of republican *civic,* rather than civil, society (Nicolet 1992, 33; Schnapper 1994, 96). For republicans the "civil" order indexed *that which concerns citizens,* rather than *that space opposed to the state* (Nicolet 1982, 331). Moreover, Nicolet argues that republicanism is not only defined by institutions, and citizenship is not only a matter of juridical status. He suggests that they are characterized above all by a spirit and mental attitude, a type of behavior and form of practice: informed, critical, and participatory (1982, 11, 31; 1992, 53, 71).

Given these considerations, we can see that this metropolitan population of displaced colonials were exemplary civic republicans. Through their network of voluntary associations—as self-identified members of Greater France—they created and influenced public opinion, spoke politics to power, and argued for colonial reform in the name of national values. Protesting, persuading, and voting, they claimed citizens' rights and fulfilled citizens' duties. In other words, this population of displaced colonials was *practicing* citizenship in the imperial metropole—practicing in the sense of behaving according to the protocols of republican citizenship. And practicing in the sense of preparation, not yet doing the real thing. They were *acting* like citizens: doing what citizens do, but also performing, pretending to be that which they could never fully be. They were at once part of French civil society and excluded from it; they exercised civic virtue without enjoying full civil rights; they made claims to abstract universal equality despite their racialized particularity. And far from being caught "between" cultures, they were members of a historically specific imperial political culture, located in the metropole as well as in the colonies, which included both colonizers and colonized.[14]

Debating colonial and cultural politics, grappling with their own metropolitan dilemmas, challenging public authority, these colonial subjects were ambiguously located within French civil society and its political public sphere.[15] Their metropolitan location offered them greater social and political freedom than they would have in their home colonies. But, they were nevertheless subject to ongoing surveillance, harassment, and censorship.[16] Even as they participated in republican political culture, these colonial subjects also constituted an intentional community of cultural difference. They thus created an alternative colonial public sphere within that civil society to which they did not fully, legally belong.[17]

This discussion of the French imperial nation-state thus highlights one of the enduring paradoxes of citizenship. Citizenship is necessarily a universal (and universalizing) juridical and political category within a given nation-state. It provides political actors with the protection of a common law that they themselves help to formulate (by voting, holding public office, serving on juries).[18] Citizenship thus functions as a principle of equivalence within the democratic nation-state as a political formation, just as the commodity functions as a principle of equivalence within capitalism as a social formation. It is the medium of abstract formal equality that enables self-government based on popular or national sovereignty. But, over time and across space, social movements have struggled over the content and scope of citizenship. They have demanded that the category be expanded to include new rights, such as the right to work, and that the status be extended to disenfranchised social groups, such as women or emancipated slaves (Sewell 1980; Scott 1996; Blackburn 1988). Even within nation-states there have been different registers of citizenship—the "passive" citizens created by the French Revolution or nineteenth-century working-class "citizens" across much of democratic Europe, who possessed civil but not political rights (Sewell 1987; Rosanvallon 1992). The disorderly character of colonial politics, especially, suggests that the category "citizen" was never a fixed designation.[19] Rather, "citizenship" indexed a differentiated field whose provisional definition was always the product of political and ideological conflicts.

My general discussion of colonial citizenship in the French Antilles, French West Africa, and the imperial metropole has already indicated certain of these axes of confrontation and sites of contradiction. In the section that follows, I will further specify this problem by exploring three interwar attempts by racialized colonial citizens to grapple with their paradoxical political condition. Although African and Antillean groups in Paris included communists, trade unionists, and black nationalists, I focus on three liberal reformist attempts to engage this tension between colonial and republican political cultures. I refer to them as the patriotic response, the republican response, and the culturalist response.

Practicing Citizenship: Limits and Possibilities

The Patriotic Response

Rather than dismiss native appeals to republican ideals as expressions of a colonized consciousness, we need to grasp the critical possibilities that inhered in these claims. There was in fact a history of colonial elites (among the "citizens" of the Senegalese Communes and the Antillean colonies, for example) subscribing to republican rhetoric in order to express their affirmative relationship to colonial authority (Johnson 1971; Crowder 1967; Burton 1994;

Pluchon 1982; Bangou 1963). Rather than question the structure or legitimacy of French colonial rule, they pursued assimilation in order to access its goods and maintain their social privilege.

René Maran, commonly known as "the father of French African literature," broke with this tradition and marked a turning point of sorts in Francophone black consciousness. Born in Martinique of Guyanese parents and educated in Bordeaux, Maran was by no means an ethnic nationalist. He was a thoroughly assimilated, French-identified colonized elite who, like many of his Antillais compatriots, spent more than a decade (1910–23) serving the colonial project as a mid-level administrator in French Equatorial Africa.[20] But Maran was the *évolué* who said no. In the course of a loyal career as a proper functionary, Maran in 1921 published *Batouala*. This *"véritable roman nègre,"* as it was subtitled, was an ethnographically inflected, realist narrative of village life in Oubangui-Chari, the colony where Maran had served. It was the first novel ever by a black colonial subject to win the *Prix Goncourt,* the most prestigious award in French letters.[21]

Maran became publicly known through his preface, and beyond its iconic status as the "first African novel" the preface remains the primary reason for which the book is remembered. In contrast to the novel, the preface is a denunciation of French colonial inhumanity in Central Africa. Published six years before Gide's influential anticolonial *Voyage au Congo* (1927), this was the most prominent literary attack on the civilizing mission ever addressed to the French public.

Maran's preface is imperative, the voice of a man no longer able to sustain the contradictions of his problematic double subjectivity as colonial administrator and colonial subject. "I have spent six years translating what I had heard and describing what I had seen in Africa into [this novel]. In the course of these years I have not for a moment given in to the temptation to speak for myself" (1938, 9). In a portrait of colonial bad faith, which is difficult not to read as a self-description, he reveals the way colonial society requires a certain colonial silence:

> the generous life of the colonies . . . debases bit by bit. . . . Rare, even among the bureaucrats, are colonials who cultivate their minds. They don't have the strength to resist the atmosphere. They get used to drinking alcohol. (13)

Such excess, according to Maran, led to "the most abject cowardice" among administrators

> because, to advance in rank, they could not make waves. Haunted by that idea, they gave up all pride, they hesitated, procrastinated, lied and embellished their lies. They didn't want to see. They wanted to hear nothing. They didn't have the courage to speak. And, moral debility

> adding itself to their intellectual anemia with no remorse, they betrayed their country. (14)

Significant in this passage is the idea that the administrator's self-protective complicity is not only morally bankrupt but a *patriotic* failure. Maran's colonial critique is a ringing affirmation, never a rejection, of his country—that is, France.

The preface denounces well-known but ignored colonial "abuse . . . embezzlement . . . atrocities" that led to famine, illness, and social dislocation (12, 15–16). Maran seeks to reveal the contradiction between the rhetorical ideal of French civilization and the reality of colonial violence. In language of lyrical protest he points to colonial inhumanity justified in the name of French civilization:

> Civilization, civilization, pride of the Europeans and the mass-grave for innocents. . . . You build your kingdom on corpses. Whatever you may want, whatever you may do, you advance by lies. At your sight, gushing tears and screaming pain. You are the might that exceeds right. You are not a torch, but an inferno. Everything you touch, you consume. . . . (11)

But Maran does not develop the idea that there may be an intrinsic relationship between "civilized" forms and colonial violence. Rather, this is a debunking exercise focused on the hypocrisy of invoking civilization to mask or justify colonial oppression. It is a reformist critique that operates on the level of individuals and implementation.

The problem for Maran is not French civilization as such, but France's frankly uncivilized colonial practices. His goal is not less civilization, but more. In his view, French colonialism itself is not illegitimate, just colonial abuses. Maran calls on France's civilizing promise to demand a genuine colonial humanism.

Appealing to the tradition of literary protest in the public sphere, he calls on his "brothers in spirit, writers of France" to recognize that colonial domination is inconsistent with the authentic national tradition of legality, morality, and justice:

> Let your voice be raised! You must help those who tell things as they are and not as one would want them to be. . . . I incite you in order to redress all that the administration designates under the euphemism of "bad habits." The fight will be difficult . . . Your task is beautiful. To work then, and no more waiting. France wants it so! (12, 14)

By thus addressing the literary community, Maran challenges France to live up to its own democratic heritage and resist a degraded colonialism that "discredits the nation" (12).

If Maran's political standpoint of critique is the genuine French nation (necessarily antithetical to colonial violence), his personal standpoint is that of a true French patriot. He refers to his "French brothers" and to France as "the country that has given [him] everything" (11). His discourse is animated by the moral outrage and political protest of an enlightened colonial administrator. Maran maintains the objective perspective of the ethnographic observer, a social outsider:

> this novel is wholly objective. It does not even attempt to explain: it notes. It does not show indignation: it records. It could not be otherwise. On moonlit evenings on my porch, stretched out in the chaise lounge on my veranda, I listened to the conversations of *those poor people.* (10) [emphasis added]

Rather than identify with the African victims of colonial violence, he empathizes with them. In short, Maran strains to make clear that he is not writing from or about his own subjectivity. Because he protests colonial oppression as a true Frenchman, not as a colonized *nègre,* he reproduces the colonial schema that distinguishes between "savage" Africans and "evolved" Antilleans.[22]

But Maran's identification remains ambiguous. Although his own literary intervention is an exemplary form of civic republicanism, he ultimately identifies "you, writers of France" as the agents of political reform. He speaks neither of *we writers of France* nor of *we French colonial subjects.* Despite his citizenship, his extended residence in France, the years of colonial service, and recognition by the French literary elite, he remained a colonial subject who was forced out of the colonial service after the publication of his preface.[23] His rapid shift from colonial exemplar to pariah brutally indicates the limits of civic practice without civil rights. Maran spent the rest of his professional life as a freelance writer and sometime editor; a colonized public intellectual negotiating his way through the maze of shoestring newspapers, short-lived journals, ideological battles, and police surveillance that characterized the interwar colonial public sphere.

The Republican Response

One of these newspapers was *La Dépeche Africaine,* a Parisian monthly whose contributors included lawyers, journalists, administrators, students, and writers primarily from Guadeloupe and Martinique. The editor, Maurice Satineau, would later be elected as a deputy of Guadeloupe. During its regular run from 1928 to 1932, *La Dèpeche* pushed even further the kind of critique Maran (who contributed articles and attended editorial meetings) developed in his preface.[24]

La Dèpeche set itself up as a watchdog of colonial excess. Focusing on French West and Equatorial Africa, its articles denounced cases of forced labor, punitive taxation, agricultural expropriation, physical brutality, and arbitrary imprisonment. Like Maran's preface, *La Dèpeche* adopted a reformist position. Rather than challenge the legitimacy of the colonial relationship itself, its contributors produced a critique of the contradictions between republican ideology and colonial practices. They pointed to the possibility of change within the system itself.

But unlike Maran's preface, the *Dèpeche* standpoint of critique was political culture rather than national culture. Its writers spoke not as genuine patriots, but as real republicans:

> [Our conceptions] will be republican, that is to say, based on the immortal principles of the glorious French Revolution, which proclaim . . . that "all men are born free and equal under the law," that "the rights of man are sacred and must be respected and defended without distinction of race or color."

Its stated goal was a "rationally conducted colonialism" focused on "the great principles of equality, public liberty and social justice that serve as the foundation of all modern democracies." *La Dèpeche* emphasizes that "this is not a nationalist project" and calls on all republicans to support its desire "to point out and combat the injustices and errors which are still too often committed in the colonies, so that the true face of France can shine forth, generous, maternal and just" (Première année, no. 1, February 1928, 1).

These colonial citizens formulated their arguments in the republican idiom of 1789 and 1848.[25] They identified the abusive colonial apparatus with the ancien régime and their program for reform with the revolutionary creation of a modern republic, composed of free, rights-bearing citizens, equal before the law. They attacked the French African colonies in terms of "the rule of arbitrary power" by local colonial despots, sustained by the hated native legal code *(indigènat)* irrespective of civil, political, or human rights.

I would name this position critical republicanism. Like the generation of *évolués* before them, these writers identified with France and advocated political assimilation. But this was a critical demand insofar as it pointed out France's systematic failure to recognize the legal equality and political rights of colonial subjects. They did not advocate individual assimilation for personal profit; they challenged France to create republican institutions and honor democratic values for colonized populations.

La Dèpeche articulated a reform program that included full citizenship for all colonial subjects, the immediate application in the colonies of metropolitan political rights, individual liberties, social legislation, a fair judiciary, and a separation of powers. In short, its writers demanded a rationalized and differentiated modern democracy. They were especially concerned with those rights of sociability and communication that characterize republican civic society (freedom of the press, speech, assembly, and association).

By taking seriously French universalizing ideology, *La Dèpeche* challenged the legitimacy of the "rule of colonial difference." By accepting the logic of Greater France, this group asked how a modernizing colonialism could be founded on an authoritarian administrative apparatus ("Notre but, notre programme" 1928). It demanded that France extend republican institutions founded on authentic humanist values to its colonial territories, and politically assimilate them into the nation-state. This was a critique of colonial humanism from the standpoint of humanism itself, and a critique of the civilizing mission from the standpoint of republicanism.

Despite the ambiguous legal status of its writers and readers, *La Dèpeche* exemplified civic republicanism in the vitality of its debate about public issues, addressed in part to political power. *La Dèpeche* defined itself as independent of political parties. According to "Notre but, notre programme," an article in its first issue of February 1928, *La Dèpeche* was devoted to "the defense of native populations' material and moral interests," addressing itself to metropolitan and colonial publics (1). The paper was thus located within French civic society *and* sought to constitute an autonomous black public sphere by linking natives of African descent across the empire. But we can also understand it as speaking to and from a properly colonial public sphere.

La Dèpeche existed only because sociopolitical transformations had led a greater number of colonial subjects to settle in metropolitan France and provisionally enter its civil society. But their attempts to fully practice civic virtue and create an autonomous public space were systematically obstructed. In Paris writers for *La Dèpeche* and members of its corresponding civic association, the Committee for the Defense of the Black Race, were thoroughly penetrated by secret police, deployed under the auspices of the paradoxically named committee for the *Controle et assistance des indigènes.* Through the efforts of paid informants—themselves colonial subjects—details of meetings, members, upcoming articles, and methods of distribution were carefully recorded and distributed to the Parisian police, the Ministry of Colonies, and the governors of the respective colonies. Newspapers destined for the colonies were confiscated, and natives who wrote for, subscribed to, and sold the journal were watched, harassed, arrested.[26]

Thus, despite *La Dèpeche*'s profession of republican faith, playing by the rules was not enough. Critical republicanism focused on the contradiction between colonial authoritarianism and metropolitan democracy. But in the metropole these subjects experienced precisely the undemocratic abuses they denounced in the colonies. They sought to turn republicanism against itself. But they could not account for the fact that forms of heteronomy existed not only in the absence of republican institutions, but were intrinsic to them. The effectiveness of this critique was finally limited by its affirmation of republican self-understanding.

Consider the kind of "we" that *La Dèpeche* sought to formulate. In contrast to Maran's preface, this was a *black republicanism* that advocated political, not cultural, assimilation. The journal stated its objective in "Notre but, notre programme" as "to serve as a link between *nègres* of Africa, Madagascar, the Antilles, and America, in order to establish a universal correspondence between men of color." Although *La Dèpeche* did not thematize the question of racial identity, it did contain notices on black cultural events in France, articles on black arts, and in its early issues, an English page devoted to "race pride" combining ideas derived from both Garveyism and the New Negro movement.

The journal attempted to balance its republican disavowal of black nationalism with this commitment to "*la race nègre.*" Contributors sought

> to work to tighten and revivify their natural brotherhood, to examine in common the most favorable means for the evolution of their backward brothers, to permit the elite of the Negro race to bring its spiritual contribution to the common patrimony of humanity, to finally confound its detractors by affirming the personality and originality of its genius.("Notre but, notre programme" 1928, 1)

With this gesture of Pan-African solidarity, *La Dèpeche* located itself within a particular racial community (in contrast to Maran's preface).

But this ethnocultural identification entailed a degree of geopolitical ambiguity. By protesting colonial abuses in French Africa, this group recognized that Africans and Antilleans had shared interests and were engaged in a common struggle. And yet, feeling secure as privileged members of the "old colonies" they maintained a paternalistic relationship to their "backward brothers" in Africa, whose rights they defended and whose interests they defined. (Initially, most of *La Dèpeche*'s colonial protest articles focused on abuses in West and Equatorial Africa.) Such elitism led *La Dèpeche* to reinscribe the colonial logic of racial hierarchy that distinguished between Old and New World blacks and correlated political rights with cultural evolution.

But three events revealed the fictive fragility of this distinction and forced *La Dèpeche*'s writers to confront the fact that they remained subjects of administered colonies rather than citizens of the French nation. Thereafter their focus shifted to the defense of their own rights and interests.

First, in spring 1930 *La Depèche* published (in three parts) an article by M. Cenac-Thaly, a teacher from Martinique, protesting a proposal circulating in the Chamber of Deputies to consolidate the French Caribbean colonies into a single federation under the direction of a governor-general, along the model of the "new" colonies in French Africa. Cenac-Thaly argued that the people of the French Caribbean wanted to participate more closely in French national life, through full territorial and political assimilation to metropolitan France: "We demand, in a word, the full exercise of our rights as citizens, and for our functionaries, the total benefits of republican status." Just as it would be unthinkable for governors-general to rule metropolitan French departments, he argued, so colonial citizens could not be administered like African subjects: "we are all, in the Antilles, citizens. All the important questions which concern us must be resolved by the national parliament not by colonial administrators" (15 March 1930, 4). Real republicans, he insisted, could not accept colonial "tyrants": "it is pure and simple assimilation that we want, the independence of our magistrature; it is the support and control of metropolitan public opinion and not the pleasure of a viceroy and the intrigues of his courtiers"(15 April 1930, 1). Cenac-Thaly later attributed the ultimate defeat of the proposal to natives such as himself practicing "republican morality," in which conscious and organized citizens exercised their democratic rights to discuss, criticize, and protest such legislation (15 May 1930, 1).

The second reorienting event occurred in September 1930. Gaston Monnerville, a Guyanese attorney in Paris, wrote to *La Depèche* to protest the unilateral French decision to carve out the richest piece of Guyana and administer it as a separate colonial territory—by an authority with no public accountability so that it could be more effectively exploited. Monnerville explained that despite recent protests over the creation of a governor-general, despite the fact that Guyana had been a part of France for four centuries and had possessed republican institutions as long as the metropole, it must "watch the amputation of its land for the profit of the governor," who had chosen to ignore the popularly elected "representative of real public opinion in the country, the *Conseil General*" ("Notre politique en Guyane," *La Dèpeche Africaine,* August–September 1930, 1).

Monnerville took this antirepublican disregard for an elected body as proof that the governor had possessed "an excess of authority" and governed Guyana "by 'African' methods" (1). Affirming that Guayana was "one of the oldest flowers of the French nation," Monnerville protested the decrees "which seem to treat the Guyanese as pariahs of the French family" ("Une Erreur ministerielle," *La Dèpeche Africaine,* October–November 1930, 1). He suggested that it was as though the Guyanese, who "are as French in spirit and in heart as the citizens of the metropole," were suddenly treated as if they were Central Africans. ("Notre politique en Guyane," 1).

Third, in its May 1931 issue *La Dèpeche* published the complete text of Monnerville's closing argument on behalf of fourteen Guyanese on trial for crimes committed during public riots in Cayenne after the suspicious death of a populist leader, Jean Galmot. Advocate of the working class and adversary of the colonial administration, Galmot had twice received the majority vote in elections for deputy in both 1924 and 1928. But each time his victory was blocked; the local administration fixed the race and named its own candidate as winner of the parliamentary seat. A first round of mass public demonstrations followed the 1928 election fraud, and more serious street riots followed Galmot's alleged death by poisoning soon after.

As defense attorney for the accused, Monnerville argued that this trial was not about the fourteen rioters (chosen arbitrarily from the tens of thousands). Rather, he insisted, the French colonial administration and French colonial policy were on trial before metropolitan public opinion. It was for the people of France, he suggested, to judge "the anguishing question of respect for colonial populations' rights and liberties. . . . It was France itself that is brought to justice." French public opinion, he argued, must decide whether to accept these violations of suffrage rights in the colonies, rights of those supposed to be French citizens. He challenged, "Is France no longer the land of liberty and justice?" (1–3).

At stake, according to Monnerville, was the conflict between republican and authoritative politics in the colonies. He called on the people of France to decide whether colonial society should be governed by popularly elected legislators or by externally imposed colonial tyrants. Although the prosecutor had denounced the rioters' "uncivilized" behavior as being anti-French, Monnerville reminded the jury that nothing was more civilized, more French than the spontaneous struggle for rights and liberties by oppressed individuals. He argued that by acquitting the accused, the jury would express France's condemnation of pernicious colonial politics, thereby showing their Guyanese brothers "the true face of France: generous and understanding France, idealist France, the France of Justice and Peace" (3). In sum, Monnerville used a republican institution to urge public opinion to confront the contradictions embodied by colonial citizens of *la plus grande France.*

Each of these events revealed the vulnerable status of Antillean political subjects. Despite the premise of colonialism's evolutionary ideology, the assimilated Antilles became indistinguishable from "primitive" Africa in terms of imperial prerogative.

Ultimately, *La Dèpeche*'s republican critique of these contradictions underestimated the "rule of colonial difference" by only engaging one dimension of colonial modernity—the failed universal promise of the civilizing project. It sought to turn French republicanism against French colonialism. But, in affirming republican universalism against colonial exclusions, these critics did not recognize that republicanism actually enabled forms of discrimination and domination.

Although *La Dèpeche* identified with *la race nègre,* racialization was never adequately problematized and incorporated into their colonial critique. Their standpoint of republican universality could not account for the fact that democratic forms have their own racially particularizing effects. Trying to win the game by holding their opponent to its own violated rules proved to be intelligible and partially effective, but it ultimately limited critical response to a colonial domination legitimized by modern democratic categories.

Finally, these black republican claims on and for democracy never grappled with the fact that their own racialization as *nègres* was an irreducible element of the republican tradition they invoked. In response to colonial inequality, they affirmed universality without grasping racism as a feature—not a failure—of democracy. At best they produced a descriptive account of racism, but never offered a structural analysis of the way colonial modernity did not simply exclude difference, but produced it.

The Culturalist Response

In contrast, *La Revue du Monde Noir* communicated a culturalist preoccupation with racial difference. Parallel to *La Dèpeche Africaine,* between 1931 and 1932 there appeared six issues of this bilingual cultural journal strongly influenced by the Harlem Renaissance. *La Revue* was published by a group of Antillean cultural elites of similar social provenance as the members of *La Dèpeche.* Several of its contributors—including one of its founders, Paulette Nardal—also wrote for *La Dèpeche.*

Privileging questions of identity over conventional politics, *La Revue* placed the formulation of a racial "we" at the center of its cultural project. But it would be a mistake to read *La Revue* as a retreat from politics.[27] Rather we need to recognize *La Revue* as undertaking a form of cultural politics that marked out a terrain that postwar Francophone black nationalism would continue to cultivate.

The journal was a product of a black Atlantic cultural salon presided over by Jane and Paulette Nardal. These sisters were students of black American literature and devotees of the Harlem Renaissance, and their home became a prominent meeting place for several generations of cultural elites. Antillean, African, Haitian, and American politicians, intellectuals, and professionals regularly gathered to debate politics and discuss "Negro civilization." These legendary Sunday teas determined the content of *La Revue,* which contained articles on black arts, ethnography, and folklore, African history and politics, as well as black Francophone and American poetry (Claude McKay, Langston Hughes) and notices on the black Parisian cultural scene.[28]

The Nardal salon exemplified the colonial public sphere. Like the classic European literary public sphere, the group addressed itself to "opinion." But it sought to produce a particular form of black, not bourgeois, consciousness (Habermas 1991, 27–56). In the first issue, the Nardals stated the aims of *La Revue:* "To study and to popularize, by means of the press, books, lectures, courses, all that concerns *la* CIVILIZATION NÈGRE ("Our Aim").[29]

Like *La Dèpeche, La Revue* was frankly elitist, straightforward in its desire to be "an official organ" for "the intelligentsia of the black race." Its ambition was

> to create among the Negroes of the entire world, regardless of nationality, an intellectual and moral tie, which will permit them to better know

> each other to love one another, to defend more effectively their collective interests and to glorify their race. ("Our Aim")

La Revue thus went further than *La Dèpeche* in identifying with a Pan-African community.

But this identification was neither immediate nor total. Echoing Du Bois's conception of the Talented Tenth and the New Negro movement's focus on race leaders, this privileged group had a clear conception of its special responsibility as an artistic and intellectual avant-garde (Du Bois [1903] 1971; Locke [1925] 1992). In the sixth issue of *La Revue* in 1932, Paulette Nardal promises in an article titled "Éveil de la conscience de race" that they will "tender to their backward brothers a helping hand" (31). They believed in the effectiveness of discursive practices; and their project was simultaneously to represent and produce the Pan-African racial community.

This catalyzing article traced the direction that black cultural politics would henceforth follow, Nardal calls for of the "awakening of race consciousness" among Francophone colonial subjects (25–31). Wondering why this moment of awakening took so long to arrive among French Caribbeans, she remarks that except for *La Revue,* no black journal "studies the Negro question in itself. . . . None of them expresses faith in the future of the race and the necessity of creating a sentiment of solidarity between different Negro groups spread around the world" (29).

By thematizing culture, inciting "race consciousness," and affirming the existence of a diasporic African civilization, *La Revue* articulated a novel critique of colonial exclusion. If *La Dèpeche Africaine* argued for political equality based on natives being assimilated, modern, and French, *La Revue* argued for cultural recognition because African civilizations were as ancient, complex, and universal as Europe's. *La Dèpeche* had challenged Western universality on the grounds that it refused to recognize native equivalence; *La Revue* challenged its refusal to recognize native difference. This critiques universality from the standpoint of cultural particularity rather than from universality's own unrealized promise.

But *La Revue* sought to recuperate rather than reject universality, by grounding it in rather than opposing it to cultural particularity. Its writers argued that colonized subjects' universal humanity was a function of their different but equal African civilization, not their abstract individuality. Likewise, the review's culturalism did not entail a nativist rejection of the West. In "Éveil de la conscience de race," for example, Nardal insists that Negro "pride in being members of a race which is perhaps the oldest in the world" did not obscure the fact that

> We are fully conscious of our debts to the Latin culture and we have no intention of discarding it in order to promote I don't know what igno-

rance. Without it, we would never have become conscious of our real selves. (31)

This was not an antimodernist retreat into primordial culture; it was a culturalist critique of modernity articulated from the inside, aimed at reformulating—rather than rejecting—its categories. The goal was to secure an African-identified place within modern society, rather than oppose traditional Africa to modern Europe. Thus, as they explained in their first 1931 issue, *La Revue*'s writers hoped to articulate race consciousness with humanism: "the Negro race will contribute, along with thinking minds of other races and with all those who have received the light of truth, beauty and goodness, to the material, the moral and the intellectual improvement of humanity." Their racial particularism even became a condition of possibility for democracy, rather than an obstacle to its development: "Thus, the two hundred million individuals who constitute the Negro race, even though scattered among the various nations, will form over and above the latter a great Brotherhood, the forerunner of universal Democracy" ("Our Aim").

But despite such assertions, *La Revue*'s political imagination remained impoverished. Ultimately, it worked with an undifferentiated conception of assimilation. It was unable to grasp the potentially complementary relationship between its critique of cultural assimilation and *La Dèpeche*'s critical republican demand for political assimilation. And despite its focus on racial difference, it too failed to develop an adequate account of racialization. While *La Revue*'s writers developed a dynamic understanding of race, viewing "African civilization," the Pan-African community, and even a hybrid "Franco-African" culture as historical products of slavery, colonialism, and racial oppression—they also ontologized these entities by rooting them in transhistorical racial essences.

Conclusion: The Double Gesture

In each of these cases of interwar black politics, the attempt to engage the contradictions of colonial politics created political and theoretical dilemmas: What kind of relationship could colonial citizens develop to democratic categories and republican practices when these categories and practices were part of a political culture and colonial apparatus that racialized and excluded colonized populations? What kind of demands could these elites make on and in metropolitan civil society—in which they were precariously located but from which they were essentially excluded—when the space was premised on equality but saturated by race?

Clearly, one-sided responses were not enough. Colonial citizens would have to grapple with racialization in its specificity, by recognizing "the fact of blackness" as a dimension of colonial modernity that could not be transcended by affirmative appeals to republicanism's universalist self-understanding (Fanon 1967). And yet, a categorical rejection of civil society and republican universality from the standpoint of cultural difference would leave colonial citizens unable to make legitimate political claims on the nation. It would also reproduce a colonial logic that fixes natives as different and unequal.

A critique adequate to the doubled character of colonial politics would have to be articulated from the standpoints of *both* difference *and* equivalence, making claims in the language of race *and* rights, identity *and* legality. It could then synthesize the power of critical republicanism—in order to demand liberty and equality—and cultural politics, in order to reveal the limits of republican universality.[30] Such a double critique would also recognize the limits and exploit the possibilities of colonial citizenship.

But, in order to practice citizenship in metropolitan Paris, African and Antillean intellectuals would have to make two kinds of double moves. First, as I suggested, they would have to affirm both cultural difference and republican rights in order to respond to a form of colonial domination that was simultaneously universalizing and particularizing. Second, they would have to deploy republican categories—such as citizenship and civil society—under erasure. This would entail a gesture of simultaneous affirmation and disavowal that could exploit these categories' political potential for resisting oppression while recognizing their complicity in the maintenance of that oppression.

Spivak identifies the logic of this kind of double gesture when she describes "the deconstructive predicament of the postcolonial" who must make political claims "from a space that one cannot not want to inhabit and yet must criticize" (1993, 64). This paradoxical stance becomes intelligible when understood in terms of the political dilemma that confronts postcolonial subjects who demand "regulative political concepts"—nationhood, constitutionality, citizenship, democracy, socialism, and culturalism—that were produced "in the social formations of Western Europe":

> They are being reclaimed, indeed claimed, as concept-metaphors for which no *historically* adequate referent may be advanced from postcolonial space, yet that does not make the claims less important. (1993, 281)

The point here is not simply that democratic categories emerge out of European histories. Rather, in colonial contexts these categories have been entwined with practices of European domination. Chatterjee, for example, describes the impossible place of civil society in a colonial order organized around a racializing "rule of colonial difference":

> a modern regime of power destined never to fulfill its normalizing mission because the premise of its power was the preservation of the alienness of the ruling group. . . . The only civil society the [colonial]

government could recognize was theirs; colonized subjects could never be its equal members. (1993, 18, 24)

In such a situation, colonial populations could not uncritically affirm a fundamentally exclusive civil society.

Yet because democratic categories are part of a globally disseminated political tradition, they remain useful critical fictions. Castoriadis names them "socially imaginary significations" (1991, 135). Ferry and Renaut, invoking Kant, refer to the "republican idea" as a "regulative principle": an idea and ideal to which no objective reality corresponds but which is not an illusion. The republican "idea of a free, rational, just society in which law would reign absolutely," they explain, is empirically empty, but has its own reality. It "continues to impel 'moral beings' . . . serving as both a signpost and a criterion for judging positive (historical reality)" (1992, 124–25).[31]

In short, "civil society" and "citizenship" designate discursive spaces—truth effects of democratic discourse that in turn allow discourses of democracy to be articulated. Cohen and Arato remind us that civil society is two-dimensional: a space of social domination and a vehicle of emancipatory possibility (1992, 1–26).[32] Citizenship, too, is doubled because it is at once imbricated with forms of domination and thick with histories of liberation. It could be neither uncritically embraced nor categorically rejected.

So rather than debate whether colonial citizenship entailed actual political rights or whether it was an empty ideological abstraction, I suggest we understand it, to use Marxian language, as a *real abstraction*. In other words, colonial citizenship may not have ensured liberty and equality for subject populations, but as a juridico-political status and object of struggle it opened a space from which colonial citizens could make historically significant *claims* on liberty and equality. Likewise, I suggest we understand civil society not so much as a space of freedom but as that space from which claims to freedom are made. Not a legally protected, rule-governed space where the game of democracy is freely played in the absence of power, but the agonistic social space where the rules of the game are ever articulated, disarticulated, and rearticulated in those contests of power we call democracy.

Notes

1. For a theoretical genealogy of the category of civil society, see Cohen and Arato 1992.

2. For paradigmatic Marxian critiques of the "autonomous" character of civil society, see Marx 1972; and Gramsci 1971, 12–13, 210–76. For a revision of Marx's ideology critique of democratic categories, see Lefort 1986, 245–59.

3. For analyses of the paradoxical relationship between European democratic categories and colonial societies, see Spivak 1993, 280–81; and Chatterjee 1993, 14–34.

4. In my dissertation I analyze interwar transformations of colonial administration in terms of Foucault's concepts of "political rationality" and "governmentality." For another account of "colonial governmentality" in a different colonial context, see Scott 1995.

5. An exemplary interwar text that formulates this new colonial rationality is Delavignette 1946.

6. For general accounts of colonial politics in the French Antilles, see Blackburn 1988; Pluchon 1982; Burton 1994; and Bangou 1963.

7. For general accounts of colonial politics in French West Africa, see Crowder 1967; Johnson 1971; Suret-Canale 1962; and Buell 1928.

8. I discuss these colonial arguments against extending citizenship and political rights to natives at greater length in the chapter of my dissertation on colonial citizenship.

9. Issues of *La Dépeche Africaine* cited in this chapter can be found in *Archives Nationales, Section d'Outre-Mer* (ANSOM), *Service de Liaison avec les Originaires des Territoires Française d'Outre-Mer* (SLOTFOM), V/ 2.

10. The decree of 21 August 1932 is reprinted in full in *Outre-Mer* 4, no. 3 (December 1932).

11. For example, in 1932 citizenship was granted to seven of the forty-one who applied; in 1933 to nine of the fifty; in 1934, to seven of the fifty-four; in 1935 to six of the forty-seven; in 1936 to three of the twenty-two; and in 1937 to none of the fifty-six who applied. *Rapport politique et administratif annuel* 1932, ANSOM, *Anciens Fonds de l'AOF:* 2G31/7; *Rapport* 1933, 2G33/7; *Rapport* 1934, 2G34/12; *Rapport* 1936 (also includes figures for 1935), 2G36/25; *Rapport* 1937, 2G37/1. Buell reports that between 1914 and 1922, ninety-four West African subjects were naturalized as citizens (1928, 945–46).

12. On the 1889 and 1927 nationality laws, see Brubaker 1992 and Noiriel 1996.

13. Perhaps the best representation of the transnational and diasporic character of the metropole remains *Banjo,* Claude McKay's quasi-ethnographic novel of the Pan-African community of workers and intellectuals in interwar Marseilles (1929). For descriptions of transatlantic black popular culture and social life in interwar Paris, see Stovall 1996; Fabre 1991; Rose 1989; Baker and Bouillon 1988; and the sections on France in Hughes 1940 and McKay 1937.

14. This starting point is thus quite different from Homi Bhabha's decontextualized analysis of colonial elites in terms of mimicry and hybridity (1994, 85–122).

15. On the relationship between civil society and the public sphere, see Habermas 1992, 452–57; and Cohen and Arato 1992, 211–31.

16. This police surveillance is well documented in the files of SLOTFOM (1915–1954), ANSOM/SLOTFOM I-VI.

17. See Fraser 1992, 121–28, for a discussion of alternative public spheres.

18. A burgeoning literature considers citizenship in terms of civil, political, and social rights; in terms of liberal rights and civic obligations; legal protection and political participation; as a function of either territory or genealogy; and as a juridico-

political status that may be ascribed at birth, legally petitioned for, and secured through struggle. Cf. Balibar 1996, 1994, 1991; Bossenga 1997; Brubaker 1992; Dietz 1992; Held 1996; Leca 1992; Marshall 1963; Mouffe 1993; Nicolet 1992, 1982; Passerin d'Entrèves 1992; Rosanvallon 1992; Schnapper 1994; Sewell 1994; Stoler 1992; Turner 1993; Walzer 1970; Young 1989.

19. See, for example, Stoler 1992 for one approach to the study of category-crossing colonial subjects that looks at the way citizenship is saturated with discourses of race, gender, sexuality, and nationality.

20. The Ministry of Colonies heavily recruited cadres for its African Service among educated Antilleans, who, according to colonial common sense, were more socially evolved *(les français noirs)* than their African progenitors (*les nègres*). See Cohen 1971.

21. On Maran's early life, colonial career, and writing, see Dennis 1986; Cameron 1985; and Ojo-Ade 1984.

22. For a discussion of Maran's unstable subject position in the preface and his position as forerunner of African nationalism, see Miller 1993, 62–100.

23. In contrast, Gide's colonial criticism only solidified his literary reputation (even earning him a place on the 1936 governmental commission of inquiry into colonial conditions), while other white, liberal reformist critics of colonial abuses—colonial humanists—such as Delavignette and Labouret continued to advance in their careers through the interwar period.

24. A single comeback issue was published in 1938.

25. Maurice Satineau, a graduate of the *École des Hautes Études,* also wrote a full-length monograph, *Histoire de la Guadeloupe sous l'Ancien Régime (1635–1789)* (1928), in which he addresses the relationship between slavery, colonialism, and freedom.

26. See the extensive CAI files in ANSOM, SLOTFOM V/ 2.

27. As do Dewitte 1985 and Spiegler 1969, for example.

28. For a firsthand account of the Nardal salon and the genesis of *La Revue,* see Achille 1992.

29. The review has been republished as *La Revue du Monde Noir: The Review of the Black World* (1931–1932) (Paris: Jean Michel Place, 1992).

30. Negritude, the hegemonic form of black cultural nationalism to emerge from the milieu I have described, unfolded within the space of precisely this problem and must be read in terms of this double gesture.

31. I find this formulation useful, despite the fact that there is a tension between the transcendental implication of Kant's "regulative ideas" and my own antifoundationalist approach to social categories. I thank Neil Brenner for pushing me on this point.

32. Unlike Cohen and Arato, I do not believe this possibility is a function of the communicative rationality liberated by civil society.

References

Achille, Louis. 1992. Preface to *La Revue du Monde Noir: The Review of the Black World. Collection complète, nos. 1–6, 1931–1932.* Paris: Jean Michel Place.

Arendt, Hannah. 1958. *The Human Condition.* Chicago: University of Chicago Press.

Baker, Josephine, and Jo Bouillon. 1988. *Josephine.* New York: Paragon House.

Balibar, Etienne. 1991. "Citizen Subject." In *Who Comes After the Subject?* ed. Eduardo Cadava, Peter Connor, and Jean-Luc Nancy. New York: Routledge, 33–57.

———. 1994. "'Rights of Man' and 'Rights of the Citizen': The Modern Dialectic of Equality and Freedom." In *Masses, Classes, Ideas: Studies on Politics and Philosophy Before and After Marx.* Translated by James Swenson. New York: Routledge.

———. 1996. "Is European Citizenship Possible?" *Public Culture, Issue on Cities and Citizenship* 8 (2): 355–76.

Bangou, Henri. 1963. *La Guadeloupe 1848–1939, ou les aspects de la colonisation après l'abolition de l'esclavage.* Aurrillac: Editions du Centre.

Bhabha, Homi. 1994. *The Location of Culture.* New York: Routledge.

Blackburn, Robin. 1988. *The Overthrow of Colonial Slavery, 1776–1848.* London: Verso.

Bossenga, Gail. 1997. "Rights and Citizenship in the Old Regime." *French Historical Studies* 20 (2): 217–43.

Brévié, Jules. 1935. *Trois études de M. Le Gouverneur Général Brévié.* Gorée: Imprimerie du Gouvernement Général.

Brubaker, Rogers. 1992. *Citizenship and Nationality in France and Germany.* Cambridge: Harvard University Press.

———. 1996. *Nationalism Reframed: Nationhood and the National Question in the New Europe.* Cambridge: Harvard University Press.

Buell, Raymond Leslie. 1928. *The Native Problem in Africa.* New York: Macmillan.

Burton, Richard D. E. 1994. *La Famille Coloniale. La Martinique et la Mère Patrie, 1789–1992.* Paris: Harmattan.

Cameron, Keith. 1985. *René Maran.* Boston: Twayne.

Castoriadis, Cornelius. 1991. *Philosophy, Politics, Autonomy: Essays in Political Philosophy.* New York: Oxford University Press.

Chatterjee, Partha. 1993. *The Nation and Its Fragments.* Princeton: Princeton University Press.

Cohen, Jean, and Andrew Arato. 1992. *Civil Society and Political Theory.* Cambridge: MIT Press.

Cohen, William B. 1971. *Rulers of Empire: The French Colonial Service in Africa.* Stanford: Hoover Institution Press.

Comaroff, Jean, and John Comaroff. 1991. *Of Revelation and Revolution: Christianity, Colonialism, and Consciousness in South Africa.* Chicago: University of Chicago Press.

Crowder, Michael. 1967. *Senegal: A Study of French Assimilation Policy.* London: Methuen and Co.

Delafosse, Maurice. 1912. *Haut-Sénegal-Niger: Tome 1—Le Pays, Les Peuples, Les Langues.* Paris: Larose.

———. 1921. "Sur l'orientation nouvelle de la politique indigène dans l'Afrique noire." *Renseignements Coloniaux No. 6—Supplément à l'Afrique Francaise.*

Delavignette, Robert. 1946. *Service Africain*. Paris: Gallimard.

Dennis, John Alfred, Jr. 1986. "The René Maran Story: The Life and Times of a Black Frenchman, Colonial Administrator, Novelist and Social Critic, 1887–1960." Ph.D. diss., Stanford University.

Derrida, Jacques. [1967] 1974. *Of Grammatology*. Reprint, Baltimore: Johns Hopkins University Press.

Dewitte, Philippe. 1985. *Les Mouvements Nègres en France, 1919–1939*. Paris: Harmattan.

Dietz, Mary. 1992. "Context Is All: Feminism and Theories of Citizenship." In *Dimensions of Radical Democracy: Pluralism, Citizenship, Community*, ed. Chantal Mouffe. New York: Verso, 33–62.

Du Bois, W. E. B. [1903] 1971. *The Talented Tenth*. In *W. E. B. Du Bois: A Reader*. Reprint, New York: Macmillan.

Fabre, Michel. 1991. *From Harlem to Paris: Black American Writers in France, 1840–1980*. Urbana: University of Illinois Press.

Fanon, Frantz. [1952] 1967. *Black Skin, White Masks*. Reprint, New York: Grove Press.

Ferry, Luc, and Alain Renaut. 1992. *Political Philosophy 3: From the Rights of Man to the Republican Idea*. Chicago: University of Chicago Press.

Foucault, Michel. 1978. "Governmentality." In *The Foucault Effect: Studies in Governmentality*, ed. Grahan Burchell, Colin Gordon, and Peter Miller. Chicago: University of Chicago Press, 1991.

———. 1981. "Omnes et Singulatum: Towards a Criticism of 'Political Reason.'" *The Tanner Lectures on Human Values*, vol. 2. Salt Lake City: University of Utah Press.

———. 1982. "The Subject and Power." In *Michel Foucault: Beyond Structuralism and Hermeneutics*, ed. Hubert Dreyfus and Paul Rabinow. Chicago: University of Chicago Press.

———. 1988. "The Political Technology of Individuals." In *Technologies of the Self*, ed. Luther H. Martin, Huck Gutman, and Patrick Hutton. Amherst: University of Massachusetts Press.

Fraser, Nancy. 1992. "Rethinking the Public Sphere: A Contribution to the Critique of Actually Existing Democracy." In *Habermas and the Public Sphere*, ed. Craig Calhoun. Cambridge: MIT Press, 109–42.

Gide, André. 1927. *Voyage au Congo*. Paris: Gallimard.

Girardet, Raoul. 1972. *L'idée coloniale en France*. Paris: Collections Pluriels, La Table Ronde.

Gramsci, Antonio. 1971. *Selections from the Prison Notebooks*. New York: International Publishers.

Habermas, Jürgen. 1986. *The Theory of Communicative Action*, vol. 2. Boston: Beacon Press.

———. 1991. *The Structural Transformation of the Public Sphere*. Cambridge: MIT Press.

———. 1992. "Further Reflections on the Public Sphere." In *Habermas and the Public Sphere*, ed. Craig Calhoun. Cambridge: MIT Press, 421–61.

Hardy, Georges. 1929. *Nos grands problèmes coloniaux.* Paris: Armand Colin.

Held, David. 1996. *Models of Democracy,* 2d ed. Stanford: Stanford University Press.

Hughes, Langston. 1940. *The Big Sea: An Autobiography.* New York: Knopf.

Hunt, Lynn, ed. 1996. *The French Revolution and Human Rights: A Brief Documentary History.* Boston: St. Martin's Press, Bedford Books.

Johnson, G. Wesley. 1971. *The Emergence of Black Politics in Senegal.* Stanford: Hoover Institution Press.

Labouret, Henri. 1931. *A la recherche d'une politique indigène dans l'ouest africain.* Paris: Éditions du Comité de l'Afrique Française.

La Revue du Monde Noir: The Review of the Black World. Collection complète, nos. 1–6, 1931–1932. 1992. Paris: Jean Michel Place.

Leca, John. 1992. "Questions on Citizenship." In *Dimensions of Radical Democracy: Pluralism, Citizenship, Community,* ed. Chantal Mouffe. New York: Verso, 33–62.

Lefort, Claude. 1986. *The Political Forms of Modern Society: Bureaucracy, Democracy, Totalitarianism.* Cambridge: MIT Press, 245–59.

Liauzu, Claude. 1982. *Aux origines des tiers-mondismes: Colonisés et anticolonialistes en France 1919–1939.* Paris: Harmattan.

Locke, Alain. [1925] 1992. *The New Negro: Voices of the Harlem Renaissance.* Reprint, New York: Athaneum.

Maran, René. [1921] 1938. *Batouala: Véritable roman nègre.* Reprint, Paris: Albin Michel.

Marshall, T. H. 1963. "Citizenship and Social Class." In *Class, Citizenship, and Social Class.* New York: Doubleday.

Marx, Karl. [1843] 1972. "On the Jewish Question." In *The Marx-Engels Reader,* ed. R. Tucker. Reprint, New York: W. W. Norton.

McKay, Claude. 1929. *Banjo.* New York: Harper and Bros.

———. 1937. *A Long Way from Home.* New York: Lee Furman.

Miller, Christopher. 1993. "Nationalism as Resistance and Resistance to Nationalism in the Literature of Francophone Africa." *Yale French Studies* 82:62–100.

Mouffe, Chantal. 1993. "Democratic Citizenship and the Political Community." In *The Return of the Political.* New York: Verso, 60–73.

Nicolet, Claude. 1982. *L'idée républicaine en France 1789–1924.* Paris: Gallimard.

———. 1992. *La République en France: État des lieux.* Paris: Seuil.

Noiriel, Gérard. 1996. *The French Melting Pot: Immigration, Citizenship, and National Identity.* Minneapolis: University of Minneapolis Press.

Ojo-Ade, Femi. 1984. *René Maran: The Black Frenchman: A Bio-Critical Study.* Washington, D.C.: Three Continents Press.

Passerin d'Entrèves, Maurizio. 1992. "Hannah Arendt and the Idea of Citizenship." In *Dimensions of Radical Democracy: Pluralism, Citizenship, Community,* ed. Chantal Mouffe. New York: Verso, 33–62.

Pluchon, Pierre, ed. 1982. *Histoire des Antilles et de la Guyane.* Toulouse: Privat.

Rosanvallon, Pierre. 1992. *Le sacre du citoyen. Histoire du suffrage universel en France.* Paris: Gallimard.

———. 1990. *L'État en France de 1789 à nos jours.* Paris: Éditions de Seuil.

Rose, Phyllis. 1989. *Jazz Cleopatra: Josephine Baker in Her Time.* New York: Vintage.

Rousseau, Jean-Jacques. 1987. *The Basic Political Writings.* Translated and edited by Donald A. Cress. Indianapolis: Hackett.

Schnapper, Dominique. 1994. *La communauté des citoyens: Sur l'idée moderne de la nation.* Paris: Gallimard.

Scott, David. 1995. "Colonial Governmentality." *Social Text* 43:191–220.

Scott, Joan Wallach. 1996. *Only Paradoxes to Offer: French Feminists and the Rights of Man.* Cambridge: Harvard University Press.

Sewell, William H. 1980. *Work and Revolution in France: The Language of Labor from the Old Regime to 1848.* Cambridge: Cambridge University Press.

———. 1987. "Le citoyen/la citoyenne: Activity, Passivity and the Revolutionary Concept of Citizenship." In *Political Culture of the French Revolution,* ed. Colin Lucas. Vol. 2 of *The French Revolution and the Creation of Modern Political Culture.* Oxford: Pergamon Press.

———. 1994. *A Rhetoric of Bourgeois Revolution: The Abbé Sieyes and "What Is the Third Estate?"* Durham: Duke University Press, 1994.

Spiegler, James. 1969. "Aspects of Nationalist Thought Among French-Speaking West Africans, 1921–1939." Ph.D. diss., Oxford University.

Spivak, Gayatri Chakravorty. 1993. *Outside in the Teaching Machine.* New York: Routledge.

Stoler, Ann. 1992. "Sexual Affronts and Racial Frontiers." *Comparative Studies in Society and History* 34 (3): 514–51.

Stovall, Tyler. 1996. *Paris Noir: African Americans in the City of Light.* Boston: Houghton Mifflin.

Suret-Canale, Jean. 1962. *L'Afrique noire l'ère colonial, 1900–1945.* Paris: Éditions Sociales.

Tilly, Charles, ed. 1996. *The Emergence of Citizenship in France and Elsewhere: Citizenship, Identity, and Social History.* Cambridge: Cambridge University Press (International Review of Social History, supplement 3).

Turner, Bryan S. 1993. "Contemporary Problems in the Theory of Citizenship." In *Citizenship and Social Theory,* ed. Turner. London: Sage Publications, 1–18.

———. 1992. "Outline of a Theory of Citizenship." In *Dimensions of Radical Democracy: Pluralism, Citizenship, Community,* ed. Chantal Mouffe. New York: Verso, 1992, 33–62.

Walzer, Michael. 1970. *The Problem of Citizenship. In Obligations: Essays on Disobedience, War, and Citizenship.* Cambridge: Harvard University Press.

Young, Iris Marion. 1989. "Polity and Group Difference: A Critique of the Ideal of Universal Citizenship." *Ethics* 99:250–74.

3

Developing Bushmen: Building Civil(ized) Society in the Kalahari and Beyond

Elizabeth Garland

Introduction

ALTHOUGH OTHER conceptualizations of the term exist,[1] one definition of civil society has predominated in recent debates: that deriving from European liberal philosophy (Hann 1996, 5). Dating to Ferguson and the Scottish Enlightenment, at its most basic this liberal tradition holds civil society to be the process or realm in which society forges the normative basis for its collective political existence.[2] Some theorists in this tradition—Hobbes, Locke, and Rousseau, for example—have emphasized civil society's role in the formation of the social contract; others—notably Montesquieu and Tocqueville—have pointed to the importance of civil society in checking the power of the liberal state. In this century, the work of Jürgen Habermas ([1962] 1989), on the pluralist potential of "communicative action" in the "public sphere," has, for many modern analysts, revitalized the relevance of this liberal conception of civil society as the social arena through which governments are rendered accountable to, and consonant with, the values of the people they represent (e.g., Cohen and Arato 1992; Harbeson, Rothchild and Chazan 1994; Keane 1988).

In recent attempts to theorize the emergence of what is often termed global civil society,[3] this liberal vision has increasingly been applied to the planetary stage. Like civil society, articulated against the formal structures of state and economy, global civil society has largely been conceived of as a sphere of nonstate, noneconomic global practices and institutions that provide

---

For their invaluable help and encouragement as I struggled to find a way to write about this material, my warm thanks go to Judith Frank, Jean Comaroff, John Comaroff, Elizabeth Povinelli, Megan Biesele, Robert Gordon, and the participants of the University of Chicago conference on the struggle for civil society in Africa. For their sensible perspectives and kind support while I was in Namibia, I also thank Shebby and Joyce Mate, Queca Fokkert, Marshall Murphree, Brian Jones, Caroline Ashley, and Jonathan Barnes.

a counterbalance to the increasingly integrated power of a world system ruled by nation-states and transnational capital.[4] The worldwide burgeoning of non-governmental organizations (NGOs) features centrally in nearly all such discussions (see Fisher 1997), for NGOs—mobilized around specific social needs or values, and consciously identified as nonstate and not-for-profit—appear to be almost natural institutional embodiments of the liberal conception of the term.[5]

In spite of the pervasiveness of the liberal idea of civil society in both state and global political discourse, scholars with non-Western sensibilities have often challenged the notion as fundamentally Eurocentric. These critics have argued that rather than being a universally applicable analytic term, civil society is instead an ideologically charged ideal, grounded squarely in the cultural and historical specificity of the European Enlightenment from which it sprang (e.g., Chatterjee 1990; Hann and Dunn 1996). Viewed through such a critical lens, the liberal definition of civil society as occupying the social space between the state and the individual amounts to an assertion that both state-based political organization and Western-style individualism are unproblematic universals. Similar criticisms have also been raised about use of the term in the global context, for as Walker points out, global civil society discourse often tacitly "depends on the assumption that the world itself can be constituted as a bounded political community modeled on the state writ large" (1994, 696).[6]

Surprisingly often, however, scholars who critique the concept of civil society for its Eurocentric underpinnings themselves slip back into Western liberal frameworks in their analyses of the term. Azarya (1994, 93–94), for example, probes the assumption (e.g., Chazan 1992; Ekeh 1975) that associations must be voluntarily chosen, rather than ascriptive, in order to count as legitimate components of civil society. In an African context, he notes, where kinship ties and ethnic affiliations often form the basis for social collectivity, the exclusion of "primordial bases of association" from the definition of civil society is unwarranted:

> [E]ven in a primordial public, one witnesses a transcendence to a larger collectivity that in most cases goes beyond family. Common action is taken and responsibility assumed on that collectivity's behalf; action is directed at achieving a common good even at the risk of individual cost. Hence one may see even in such activities a legitimacy for public action. (93)

For Azarya, common action taken on behalf of the collectivity—and not out of individual or family self-interest—marks the essence of legitimate civil society. His efforts to adapt the concept to an African setting notwithstanding, such a conception not only leaves intact a liberal notion of civil society; it also reaffirms the ideological separation of domestic and public spheres, citizen and state, upon which that notion relies.

One possible reason for the intractability of Western presuppositions (see Karlström, chapter 4 of this volume) in critical analyses of civil society is that scholars frequently slip between discussions of the term as a liberal Western cultural construct—as a reified entity, like "the state"—and usage of the term as an analytic concept. Indeed, even those who are seriously committed to probing the cultural and historical specificity of civil society often seem remarkably determined, at the end of the day, to retain it as a universally applicable theoretical tool.[7] Such a slippage is not surprising, I suggest, because civil society (the construct), like the state, is a central feature of liberal Western political ideology—and liberalism is the dominant ideology of the current global political system (as Basil Davidson [1992] has noted, there is no alternative to the international state system; and as Akhil Gupta [1997] points out, it is difficult even to think about society without employing liberal categories like "nation" and "state"). Given that, in the liberal tradition, civil society has long been conceptualized as *the* legitimate arena for social transformation and resistance, it only makes sense that liberal analysts, motivated by political concern for people who are relatively disadvantaged within the world system, would want to resuscitate the concept's viability within the societies they study. To put it another way, civil society—even when recognized as a normative Western construct—has a way of nevertheless seeming like the only viable option for a progressive politics; under such circumstances, scholars have been understandably ambivalent about debunking the term in contexts like Africa.

For a number of analysts, one way around this dilemma has been to look for non-Western *analogues* to civil society—indigenous features of social life that can be seen as alternatives (different but equivalent) to the ways in which Western people negotiate the legitimacy of their governments (e.g., Harbeson 1994, 26). In the Africanist literature, scholars like Vansina (1990) have looked to vibrant precolonial political traditions for evidence of indigenous civil society, while others (e.g., Young 1994; following Mudimbe 1988; Davidson 1992) have suggested that the systematic refashioning of the political landscape by the colonial regimes destroyed these precolonial African structures and practices for the most part, leaving "only furtive, marginal space for a 'civil' society" in the present era (Young 1994, 38). Still other scholars (e.g., Bayart 1993) have focused on identifying African modes of producing political legitimacy and accountability in a postcolonial context.

While research along these lines may open up some room for optimism (about the future of democracy in Africa, for example), such an approach does not really represent a solution to the problem of Western bias in the concept of civil society. Since what is sought is an analogue to the Western, liberal notion, it is this latter conception that acts as the standard of comparison for indigenous practices or realms. In the quest for indigenous analogues, the liberal conception of civil society is naturalized: non-Western modes of "political" practice and meaning are transformed into social "arenas," "realms," or "spheres"—all implicitly bounded—in which "individuals" or "citizens" produce legitimacy and accountability from their "governments."

In the slip from critiquing civil society as a liberal, Western construct to recuperating the notion as a viable analytic category through recourse to such "solutions" as the quest-for-analogues approach, what is prevented is a sustained critical analysis of the ideological dominance of the Western construct in the first place. Hann comes close to recognizing that the dominance of the liberal idea of civil society itself merits scholarly attention, when he calls for anthropological research into

> analogues to the discourse of civil society in non-European cultural traditions, and [into] the interaction of these specific cultural ideas with the putative universalism of civil society as this idea is exported across the globe. (1996, 2)

Because of his recognition of non-Western "analogues" to civil society, Hann frames the issue of exporting the "putative universalism" of the concept in terms of its interaction with other cultural traditions, stopping short of calling for a focus directly on the nature and consequences of this process itself.[8]

I pick up where Hann leaves off by examining the impact of the liberal discourse of civil society in a specific African context: the region of the Namibian Kalahari known as Nyae Nyae, home to the Ju/'hoan "bushmen."[9] More commonly designated by the broader linguistic term !Kung, the Ju/'hoansi[10] are the iconic hunter-gatherers of southern Africa. Known to anthropology undergraduates everywhere via a series of ethnographic classics—Elizabeth Marshall Thomas's *The Harmless People* (1959), Marshall Sahlins's "The Original Affluent Society" (1972), Lorna Marshall's *The !Kung of Nyae Nyae* (1976), Richard Lee's *The !Kung San: Men, Women, and Work in a Foraging Society* (1979), Marjorie Shostak's *Nisa: The Life and Words of a !Kung Woman* (1981), and John Marshall's films *The Hunters* (1957) and *N!ai, the Story of a !Kung Woman* (1980)—the Ju/'hoansi are also familiar to a wider audience through such popular accounts as those of novelist Laurens van der Post and the blockbuster film *The Gods Must Be Crazy* (1981).

Needless to say, the Ju/'hoansi are not famous for their civil society. On the contrary, the very term "bushman" conjures an image of humanity at its least civilized, and indeed, its least social. Despite forceful scholarly attempts to debunk the "myths" surrounding people called bushmen (Gordon 1992; Wilmsen 1989a), sentimental ethnographies and novels, films, picture books, and travel guides too numerous to count continue to promote the image of them as occupying one extreme end of a continuum of human sociopolitical development (recent examples include Perrott 1992; Fourie 1994). "Bushmen" do not even merit mention in Fortes and Evans-Pritchard's (1940) classic taxonomy of African political systems, so lacking are "kinship-based," "band" societies seen to be in any sort of analogue to Western modes of governance. Questions of ethnographic accuracy aside, depictions of people like the Ju/'hoansi as communal, decentralized, peaceful, egalitarian, and nonmaterialistic have rendered them more an appealing foil for the West than a political society in their own right.

While people like the Ju/'hoansi have generally not been accorded recognition as fully political in the Western imaginary, however, "bushmen" have nevertheless played a crucial role in liberal political discourse. Walker, in an attempt to think through the difficulties of extending the concept of civil society on a global scale, points out that beneath much liberal theorizing lies an implicit fantasy about the nature of originary humanity prior to the advent of a civilizing politics:

> Once ripped out of its specificity in the civil societies of modern states, this line of analysis seems inevitably to dissolve into an ungrounded ethics or philosophy. Indeed much of the impetus for such a reading seems to draw on *a nostalgia for a fancifully imagined prepolitical world,* a world before the fateful rift between man and citizen. (1994, 696, emphasis added)

Although Walker does not develop the point further, his allusion to a "prepolitical" (and pre-Enlightenment) "world" rightly draws attention to the presocial human subject imagined as the point of origin for the transformative mission of civil society.[11] In the modern era, people like the Ju/'hoansi serve as indispensable symbols—nostalgic embodiments of humanity's presocial promise. As such, they are central tropes of the liberal imagination, and of its conception of civil society as well.

The Ju/'hoansi, however, are not merely implicated in discussions of civil society as mythic bushmen; they are also, of course, actual people—people who for the last twenty years have been recipients of substantial efforts on the part of a Western nongovernmental organization devoted to promoting their political and economic development. Thanks largely to the efforts of this NGO, the Ju/'hoansi have become intimately engaged with the liberal discourse of civil society, at both national and international levels. In part as a result of this history of engagement, and in part because their status as "bushmen" frees me from the liberal imperative to look for redeemable cultural "analogues," I submit that the Ju/'hoansi are "good to think with" about the global predominance of liberal conceptions of civil society.

I begin by exploring some of the specific ways in which the Ju/'hoansi have been represented in liberal civil society discourse; I then examine some of the contradictory effects of this discourse on the Ju/'hoan community in Nyae Nyae; and finally, I draw upon a Gramscian conception of hegemony to discuss the relationship that has been and continues to be forged between the

Ju/'hoansi and the liberal apparatus of global civil society. Ultimately, I argue, the sense of civilizedness that underpins the liberal notion of civil society is built on the backs of people like them.

Bushmen on the Brink of Extinction: "How You Can Help"

If bushmen are the canonical markers of premodern humanity, in recent years they have also come to be known as one of modernity's most canonical casualties. Perhaps nowhere are both points more eloquently made than in John Marshall's widely acclaimed film *N!ai, the Story of a !Kung Woman,* produced in 1980 to document the socioeconomic and cultural transformations that had taken place among the Ju/'hoansi in the years since Marshall and his family first conducted fieldwork among them in the 1950s.[12] *N!ai* begins, by way of explanation, with the following ominous lines:

> In 1970, the South African government established a reservation on the Namibia/Botswana border which restricted 800 !Kung to an area one-half the size of their original territory. The reservation lacks sufficient food and water for the !Kung to continue their gathering/hunting life.

The opening shot shows a group of !Kung—familiar to most of us as lovely, harmless people—standing in a ragged line, hungrily waiting for rations of mealie meal to be handed out by a white man in military uniform. A female voice-over confirms the viewer's fears:

> Before the white people came we did what our hearts wanted. We lived in different places, far apart, and when our hearts wanted to travel, we traveled. We were not poor. We had everything we could carry. No one told us what to do. Now the white people tell us to stay in this place. There are too many people. There's no food to gather. Game is far away and people are dying of tuberculosis.

Through the biography of one woman, Marshall's film traces the story of the !Kung's fall from grace at the hands of "the white people," following N!ai from her carefree childhood as a member of an independent !Kung band, to the late 1970s, which found her a melancholic tuberculosis patient, squatting on the outskirts of a grimy South West African administrative post. Contrasting vintage footage of Ju/'hoansi hunting in the 1950s with wrenching scenes of social conflict and despair from the late 1970s, the narrator explains that people like the !Kung have occupied the western Kalahari for at least 20,000 years, but that in recent decades, dispossession and government policies encouraging sedentariness and a cash economy have led to dramatic rises in inequality, jealousy, alcoholism, violence, disease, and dependency. The film ends with the recruitment of Ju/'hoan men by the South African military in the war against the SWAPO independence forces in Namibia, leaving viewers with the sinking feeling that things will only continue to worsen for N!ai and her kin in the years ahead.

Nearly two decades later, more than a dozen sites on the World Wide Web address the plight of the Ju/'hoansi. Often displaying images of bushmen with bows and arrows and loincloths, these hypermodern Web pages reiterate, in large part, the bleak story outlined in *N!ai.* As one page produced by the Cambridge-based organization Cultural Survival puts it,

> Thirty years ago, the Ju/'hoansi . . . represented the last totally self-sufficient hunter-gatherers in southern Africa. Held to the land by ancient and intimate ties, they had always lived autonomously, subject only to the law and custom of their own society. Over just three decades, they have lost both their independence and their land.

Citing South African policies promoting settlement and the establishment of bounded ethnic "homelands," the Cultural Survival page continues:

> Over the years the hunting and gathering-based economy collapsed under the pressure of large numbers of Ju/'hoansi settled into a small area. There were few jobs and nothing to do. Ill health and hunger gave way to anger and despair. The death and infant mortality rates accelerated. . . . [When] the South African Defense Force began recruiting young Ju/'hoansi for their war against the South West African Peoples Organization (SWAPO), now Namibia's democratically elected government, . . . the high salaries and food rations given recruits caused deep divisions in the hitherto equitable Ju/'hoan community. (Cultural Survival 1996)

For some years now, debates have been raging in the scholarly literature over representations like these, which depict people like the Ju/'hoansi as having lived a timeless, autonomous, and stable existence in the Kalahari until relatively recent times.[13] Reacting against decades of research on the ecological adaptation and cultural stability of hunter-gatherer societies (e.g., Thomas 1959; Lee and DeVore 1968, 1976; L. Marshall 1976; Lee 1979, 1984), historically minded scholars like Robert Gordon and Edwin Wilmsen have argued that the people called bushmen have been actively engaged in the economic, political, and cultural dynamics of the region for centuries, and that synchronic models of a cultural-ecological or structural-functionalist sort are no more adequate to the study of their societies than they are for any other African peoples (Gordon 1984, 1992; Wilmsen 1989a, 1989b). For writers like Gordon and Wilmsen, representations that depict bushmen as having been suddenly and recently thrust from a timeless, harmonious existence to "the brink of extinction" render invisible centuries of violent colonial policy toward such peoples (Gordon 1992) and fail to consider wider processes of class formation in the region as a whole (Wilmsen 1989a, 1989b).[14]

Ironically, it is clear that neither Marshall nor Cultural Survival had any intention of erasing history in making their respective representations of the Ju/'hoansi's recent tribulations. On the contrary, both *N!ai* and the Cultural Survival Web page appear to have been produced precisely to draw attention to history's ill effects on such populations. History is less absent from such representations than it is located squarely in the realm of the very recent past (beginning, not coincidentally, around the same time that the Marshall family arrived to begin recording it). This presentist history has a very specific, unidimensional content: it is the tale of the Ju/'hoansi's victimization at the hands of "white people." Indeed, in both representations, the Ju/'hoansi appear to have been ushered into history—and modernity—by virtue of their collective experiences of dispossession and colonization. Without doubting for a moment that many Ju/'hoansi have suffered terribly from such processes over the last several decades (a point amply documented elsewhere), I suggest that their recent emergence in Western discourse as fully historical, modern subjects has been crucially linked to their being portrayed as inherently vulnerable, "on the brink of extinction."

My reasons for making such a suggestion have everything to do with what happened next in the Ju/'hoan story, in the years since the bleak circumstances depicted at the conclusion of *N!ai.* Since 1981, Cultural Survival reports, an organization called the Nyae Nyae Development Foundation of Namibia (NNDFN) has been working to turn the Ju/'hoansi's situation around. Committed to helping them "regain their independence and self-sufficiency and to protect their remaining territories," the NNDFN provides the Ju/'hoansi with "training in cattle management and dry-land gardening"; it "develops water sources," "assists Ju/'hoansi to develop communication and organizational skills," and "provides health-care education, vocational training, and adult and primary education." For those who want to join in these efforts, the Cultural Survival Web page concludes with a section called "How you can help," explaining where to write for further information and how to send money in support of the NNDFN (Cultural Survival 1996).

In describing the work of the NNDFN, Cultural Survival offers a redemptive flip side to Ju/'hoan modernity. In place of the inequality, conflict, and despair brought on by what are framed as the corrupting forces of modernization, the development solutions proffered by the NNDFN are represented in the Web page as the tickets to regained Ju/'hoan "independence and self-sufficiency." More than just their luck has changed in the Ju/'hoansi's transformation from victims of modernization to recipients of modernity's benevolent help. Most significantly, underdevelopment has replaced dispossession and colonization as their primary problem. Rather than regaining their lost land and independence, Cultural Survival's Web page implies that what the Ju/

'hoansi need these days is better "organizational skills," "training in cattle management and . . . gardening," "vocational training," and "health education." Like the World Bank's characterization of Lesotho as a "less-developed country"—rather than a South African labor reserve (Ferguson 1994)—the Ju/'hoansi have emerged in the discourse of Cultural Survival as in need, above all else, of development. As Ferguson argues for the Lesotho context, elided in such constructions of "development subjects" are the many exploitative, racist, and violent historical processes that left them impoverished and disempowered in the first place.

Before I discuss the implications of this "antipolitical," developmentalist reframing of the Ju/'hoansi's problems in the context of Nyae Nyae, I want to consider briefly how such a construction—as well as its dissemination on the World Wide Web—fits together with the emergence of a sense that there is such a thing as civil society on a "worldwide" level. Intrinsic in the notion of global civil society is the fundamental humanist assumption of universality. In order to debate global matters of civility—questions of human rights, for example—the world must first agree that it somehow constitutes one big community, a single "global village," to which all peoples automatically belong. Participation in the universalizing discourse of global civil society, however—like participation in all humanist discourses—never derives in any simple way from a shared, egalitarian humanity. As Althusser (1971, 160–65) has memorably argued, we are always *interpellated* by ideological discourses as we participate in them: we are constituted as *subjects,* as a "we" or an "us." As such, we come automatically to occupy particular, differential vantage points within the whole; and this is true even when—as is the case in the humanist ideology of global civil society—that which the discourse is asserting is the universality of the whole itself.

This process of interpellation, by which different kinds of subjectivities are produced, is one of the main operations at work when people like the Ju/'hoansi appear in the liberal discourse of global civil society. When the U.S.-based organization Cultural Survival, against the narrative backdrop of Ju/'hoan dispossession and colonization, offers visitors to its Web site advice on "How you can help," it hails its readers—"How *you* can help"—as the sort of people who, intrinsically, have help to offer. As Web users, "we" are presumed to belong (indeed are constituted as belonging) to a particular global community of people—a civilized, helpful community, certainly, but clearly not one that is universally inclusive. Excluded, we intuitively understand, are societies like the Ju/'hoansi, people in need of the help that only "we" have to offer: "How you can help (them)."

The process by which such global discourse interpellates some people as aid givers and others as indigent is by no means restricted to this single example. In recent years, innumerable other nongovernmental agencies, government bodies, official multinational organizations, private companies, journalists, academics, artists, activist groups, and cyber-communities have similarly committed themselves to a responsibility for helping people constructed as "in need" (see Fisher 1997). In the Ju/'hoan case, the NNDFN (the NGO described by Cultural Survival) is merely the most obvious instance of an entity built around a mandate to "help" the Ju/'hoansi. The many international donor agencies and advocacy organizations that fund the NNDFN could also be said to define themselves, at least in part, in terms of their commitment to helping these peoples. Add to this the many ministries within the Namibian government that work closely with the NNDFN on the Ju/'hoansi's behalf, as well as international organizations like the United Nations (involved in helping promote Ju/'hoan participation in Namibian democratization), along with several private corporate sponsors (mainly mining operations and ecotourism companies), and the list of institutional players invested in "helping" the Ju/'hoansi begins to grow dizzyingly long. All of which does not even mention the steady stream of individual development workers, journalists, filmmakers, musicians, writers, and academics (myself included), who have framed their identities (and careers) to greater or lesser extents in relation to the Ju/'hoansi's ostensible need for help.

This sort of translocal pastiche of interconnected, well-meaning agents—individual, institutional, and virtual—is just the kind of transnational "web" or "network" invoked in most current imaginings of global civil society.[15] Within such a framework, the Ju/'hoansi emerge as a sort of node for the political action that constitutes civil society in the liberal sense of the term: they have become a locus for the mobilization of a host of actors around a collective social objective. By first fashioning people like the Ju/'hoansi as victims of modernity—as "on the brink of extinction" due to their cultural vulnerability in the face of colonial dispossession—the West has cleared the way for its own redemptive role in their lives. With the liberal rhetorics of development, human rights, democratization, and the like, the West has effectively obscured its own less-than-civilized colonial history, erasing (or at least, claiming to transcend) its own complicity in the Ju/'hoansi's current problems.[16] Emerging from such a revisionist process is an image of a postcolonial global society that has succeeded in resuscitating a sense of its own liberal civility from the still-warm ashes of its colonial past.[17]

Global Civil Society in Action: "Development" in Nyae Nyae

As I have argued, the process by which the liberal discourses of global civil society interpellate the Ju/'hoansi as in need of help is also a process by which they are positioned as external to the world of those able to help them. In this section, I question how this process of discursive interpellation has been experienced by the Ju/'hoansi. Do they, too, perceive themselves as in need of help from a beneficent global community? What forms has this "help" tended to take? Has it ultimately been beneficial to them?

To begin to answer these questions, I first focus directly on the history of global intervention in the lives of the Ju/'hoansi in the years since the production of *N!ai, the Story of a !Kung Woman* (1980). I begin with *N!ai* because the film marks a watershed in the recent history of Ju/'hoan development. Shortly after producing the film, and deeply troubled by the poverty and social decay he had documented in it, John Marshall and a colleague founded the Ju/wa Bushman Development Foundation (JBDF; later to become the NNDFN) in order to help Ju/'hoansi secure claims to land and improve their economic lot.[18] As Marshall understood them, the root of the Ju/'hoansi's problems in the late 1970s and early 1980s lay in their inability to support themselves by hunting and gathering on their diminished land base. In his words,

> In 1970 Ju/'hoansi lost 90 percent of Nyae Nyae and all but one of their permanent waterholes when Bushmanland was established as the "homeland" for all the 30,000 people classified as "Bushmen" in Namibia. . . . About 1,000 survivors of Nyae Nyae were forced to live in Eastern Bushmanland—about 3,500 square miles—where 140 people could support themselves by hunting and gathering. The oldest economy on earth collapsed.

Under the circumstances, the necessary course of action appeared to him to be self-evident:

> Ju/'hoansi faced a stark equation: Complete the agricultural revolution in ten years to become more productive on less land . . . transform their hunting and gathering economy, social rules and values in the pressure cooker of a rural slum and immediately begin farming in Eastern Bushmanland. (Marshall 1996)

The Ju/'hoansi, he believed, urgently needed to be brought up to speed technologically and economically, to be ushered into modernity by completing "the agricultural revolution" and transforming their "social rules and values" to match.[19] Economic development alone, however, was not the only thing on Marshall's mind: he also saw the Ju/'hoansi as lacking the political structures and sophistication necessary to enable them to defend their lands against threats from neighboring African groups and the Namibian state. In the words of Megan Biesele, director of the NNDFN in the years following Marshall,

> Traditionally, the Ju/'hoansi had no political organization larger than localized, kin-based living groups. To meet the challenges of self-sufficiency and form a voice on land rights and development, the Ju/'hoansi [needed to begin] exploring the possibility of broadening their

> tolerant, egalitarian way of self-government into a version of representative democracy for the entire region. (1993, 59–60)

As these passages indicate, the vision that guided the work of Marshall, Biesele, and other staff members of the NNDFN in these early years was premised on several key assumptions. First, in keeping with the analysis offered in *N!ai, the Story of a !Kung Woman,* as "bushmen," the Ju/'hoansi were seen to be culturally ill-equipped for their modern circumstances. Reflecting the pervasiveness of Western representations of them as emissaries from the "Stone Age," they were understood to have been—until recently—living in a state of pristine, primitive isolation, with "the oldest economy on earth" and "no political organization larger than localized, kin-based living groups." While such assumptions certainly resonated with ethnographic descriptions of the !Kung dominant at the time (Lee 1979, 1984; Lee and Devore 1968, 1976; L. Marshall 1976; Shostak 1981; Thomas 1959), they bore at most only a partial relation to the actual situation in Nyae Nyae in the late 1970s and early 1980s, when many Ju/'hoansi were employed as soldiers by the South African Defense Force, and most others had largely abandoned hunting and gathering to settle around the military complex and administrative center of Tjum!kui (J. Marshall and Ritchie 1984; J. Marshall 1993). While it seems likely that many Ju/'hoansi did not experience their embeddedness within the South West African state in particularly empowered terms during these years,[20] assertions that they lacked experience dealing with this larger political economy—that their subsistence was drawn from hunting and gathering rather than wage labor or government rations, and that their only political relations were localized or kin-based—were clearly based on preconceptions about their temporal and spatial isolation as bushmen rather than on their actual circumstances.

In addition to making assumptions about them on the basis of ethnographic characterizations of "bushmen," the founders of the NNDFN also made a second set of assumptions about the eventual type of society that the Ju/'hoansi would need in order to better deal with the challenges confronting them in Nyae Nyae. At an economic level, farming and cattle keeping were considered crucial strategies for development; in the realm of politics, it was representative democracy that was assumed to offer the best way forward. Needless to say, both agendas reflect normative Western notions: in the first instance, of legitimate modes of labor and land use;[21] and in the second, of the liberal ideal for political society.

Taken together, the NNDFN staff's insistence on perceiving the Ju/'hoansi as pre-economic and pre-political "bushmen," and their prescriptions for economic and political "development," effectively cleared the way for the liberal action of "civil society" in Nyae Nyae. In the Ju/'hoansi's situation, the founders of the NNDFN saw an opportunity to forge a new society more or less "from scratch"—to transform people from their (projected) presocial state into a fully modern collectivity, in keeping with the liberal principles of equality and democracy, and with the modernist ethics of hard work, education, and bureaucratic, rational organization. Such an idealistic—not to mention ambitious—project had little trouble sparking the liberal imaginations of people well beyond the NNDFN, and the organization's efforts to "help" the Ju/'hoansi quickly attracted the financial and moral support of people and institutions around the world (see Biesele 1993).

My own involvement with the Ju/'hoansi began in 1994, when I was hired by the NNDFN as a short-term consultant to work on the development of tourism in Nyae Nyae. Although fairly remote by Namibian standards, the region has become increasingly popular as a tourist destination in recent years, as growing numbers of so-called ecotourists have come in search of cultural contact with "authentic" bushmen. My assignment, given my previous experience developing tourist ventures in another part of Africa, was to work with the NNDFN to establish a strategy for controlling the impact of tourism in Nyae Nyae and for maximizing its benefits to the Ju/'hoansi (Garland 1994; Garland and Gordon n.d.).

When I began my consultancy in Namibia, I had seen *N!ai, the Story of a !Kung Woman,* but had not kept track of the Ju/'hoan story in the fifteen years since the film's production. Holed up in the NNDFN office in Windhoek, reading through stacks of NGO documents, I was amazed to learn how much things had changed. By 1994, the development organization reached into nearly every domain of Ju/'hoan life. In addition to ongoing programs in "income generation" and "natural resource management" (the two with which my tourism work was to be affiliated), I learned that the NGO also sponsored comprehensive schemes for Ju/'hoan health care, primary education, agricultural extension, and job skills training. At the time, I remember being struck by how cutting edge these programs all seemed: the natural resource management program used the latest in "community-based" techniques; the education program was rooted in the methodology of Paolo Friere, with primary instruction in Ju/'hoan as a first language; the health program emphasized education and preventive care; the agricultural program was carefully tailored to the dryland ecosystem of the Kalahari; advocacy efforts by the NNDFN were coordinated with a worldwide network of indigenous peoples' organizations. Everything I read stressed the importance of achieving sustainability in the long run.

Things sounded encouraging within the Ju/'hoan communities as well. Around the same time that the NNDFN was formed, a number of Ju/'hoansi—in what was described in the NGO literature as an indigenous "back to the land" movement—had apparently decided to vacate Tjum!kui to reoccupy their abandoned hunting and foraging areas, intending to begin supporting themselves in small, dispersed settlements through a combination of farming, livestock keeping, hunting, and gathering. With NNDFN and donor help, I learned, a number of boreholes had been drilled to provide permanent water sources for these settlements. Anthropologists had helped draw up formal maps of community land-use and tenurial patterns, and the combination of the new settlements and these *n!ore* (traditional tenure) maps had provided crucial evidence of the Ju/'hoansi's claims to Nyae Nyae in debates over land rights during Namibia's transition to independence at the end of the decade.

Perhaps even more importantly, I learned that the Ju/'hoansi had established a civic organization of their own, the Nyae Nyae Farmers Cooperative (NNFC), in 1986. At the NNDFN office in Windhoek, I found written statutes (in both English and Ju/'hoan) enunciating the cultural principles underpinning this new structure, as well as frequent references to the debates and elections that had accompanied its formation (discussed in J. Marshall 1993; Biesele 1993). Over the years, this farming cooperative had sent official Ju/'hoan delegations to a series of national and international conferences on land, water, and indigenous rights policy. In my initial informational meetings with various donor agencies and Namibian government ministries, everyone seemed to recognize this cooperative as the established authority of the Ju/'hoan people. In combination, the NNDFN and NNFC appeared to be a truly model example of an indigenous development project: a dynamic partnership between a progressive, savvy NGO on the one hand, and a vibrant, grassroots, community organization on the other.

Even in those first impressionistic days, however, a few things about the NNDFN-NNFC setup made me wonder whether everything was actually as ideal as it seemed on paper. For one, in spite of the fact that the NNDFN was regularly referred to as an indigenous Namibian NGO, it seemed to be staffed almost entirely by white foreigners, notably Germans, Dutch, white South Africans, Australians, and Americans.[22] No Ju/'hoansi worked directly for the NNDFN; the ones affiliated with the project either worked for the Ju/'hoan Farmers Cooperative or were employed by the various development programs run by the NGO staff. The NNDFN is what in Namibia is called a "white-driven" NGO. Its relationship with the Ju/'hoansi (named in its constitution as its "beneficiaries") was explained to me by an NNDFN staff member as one of "mentoring." While the stated long-term objective was to turn over eventual control of development programs and funds to the Ju/'hoansi through the NNFC, it was clear to me that the expectation of most NNDFN staff members was that their managerial expertise and support would be needed for the foreseeable future. While paternalism of this sort is not altogether unusual in development projects, I found it to be strikingly explicit in official NNDFN discourse.

Further, although my job description had assured me that tourism was an issue of urgent concern to the Ju/'hoansi, and that they had specifically requested assistance developing the tourism industry in Nyae Nyae, when I arrived in June 1994, no one in the community seemed to have any idea who I was, or that a "tourism consultant" was coming to work with them for three months. I had been hired entirely at the initiative of the expatriate staff of the NNDFN, not by "the Ju/'hoan community" as I had been led to believe. Indeed, although it was true that there were a lot of tourists in the area, it soon seemed that tourism was just about the last thing on the minds of most Ju/'hoansi.

Instead, it gradually became apparent that the NNDFN was in a state of real institutional crisis. Shortly before my arrival, clashes over management policies within the organization had resulted in the resignations of a number of key expatriate staff. Baraka, the NNDFN base camp in Nyae Nyae, echoed with the ghosts of these people: houses stood locked and empty, untended gardens were reverting back to bush, and food had been left to rot in the communal kitchen. Moreover, signs of the vibrant grassroots partnership I had read about between the NGO and the Ju/'hoan NNFC were nowhere to be found. Instead, the Ju/'hoansi who lived at Baraka—mainly NNFC employees and their families—seemed to steer clear of the few NGO staffers who remained. The camp was literally segregated into expatriate and bushman sections. I was assigned my own house in the white area, and I cooked my meals in a Western-style kitchen with a Dutch woman who worked for the health program. The Ju/'hoansi, ten people or so to a house, lived in an area some distance away and cooked over fires outside. While solar panels provided electricity and pumped water from a borehole to all the houses, the central bathhouse, with flush toilets and showers, seemed to be the exclusive domain of the expatriates.[23]

The interactions that I did observe between NNDFN staff and Ju/'hoansi in Baraka startled me with their volatility. On one of my first nights, I witnessed a scene in which the manager of the NNFC, clearly intoxicated, entered the expatriate kitchen and demanded the keys to a project vehicle. The Dutch NNDFN camp manager angrily refused to comply, and lectured the man—one of the most powerful Ju/'hoan members of the Nyae Nyae community—on his irresponsibility and drunkenness. In the weeks that followed, interviews in Ju/'hoan villages revealed that such confrontations were almost commonplace. Community frustration with the NNDFN was running so high that I had a hard time getting people to talk about tourism at all, and eventually gave up trying. Instead, people either refused to talk with me (I was, after all, an NNDFN employee), or used me—via my translator—to vent their anger at the organization.

The complaints I heard in Ju/'hoan villages ranged from matters of common courtesy ("The new manager drives by without even stopping to greet us!") to the inadequacy of NGO service provisions ("Our borehole dried up a month ago, and they still haven't done anything to fix it!"). Most often, though, objections centered on two particularly volatile issues: the control of access to vehicle transportation in Nyae Nyae, and the control of revenues generated by the development project. Although staff members within the NNDFN have varied as to their attitudes about these issues, in matters of both vehicles and money, the organization has on the whole pursued policies that have been markedly paternalistic, leaving many Ju/'hoansi feeling a lack of control over important aspects of their lives.[24]

In the first instance, members of the NNDFN staff, concerned about the high costs of operating and maintaining vehicles in the Kalahari, have closely monitored Ju/'hoan access to the keys and fuel supplies for trucks owned by the NNDFN and have similarly sought to supervise the use of vehicles bought by the NNFC (the Ju/'hoansi's "own" organization).[25] As there are very few non-donor-funded vehicles[26] and no public transportation in Nyae Nyae—a sparsely populated area exceeding 3,500 square miles—access to motorized transportation is a constraint on all but the most localized of activities in the region. With shifts in desires toward consumer goods (fed by development-driven flows of money into the economy), and with the increasing involvement of community members in various regional development ventures, Ju/'hoan demand for "lifts" to and from the central town of Tjum!kui and elsewhere in the region has grown steadily since the inception of the NGO project.[27] The expatriate staff members of the NNDFN, in nearly complete control of access to this scarce resource, have drawn continual accusations of mean-spirited stinginess from Ju/'hoansi for refusing to provide transport at requested levels. I witnessed paternalistic clashes over keys and fuel—white expatriates towing the parental line in the face of juvenile "bushman" irresponsibility—on nearly a daily basis during my stay in Namibia.

In the case of revenues from development projects, the NNDFN, citing ethnographic representations of bushmen as fundamentally egalitarian and nonmaterialistic, has frequently emphasized the importance of strictly controlling the distribution of funds to the Ju/'hoan community in Nyae Nyae. In practice, this attempt at "cultural sensitivity" has translated into an institutional policy of resistance to Ju/'hoan efforts to earn income outside the purview of the development project. When I arrived in Nyae Nyae, ostensibly to work on "tourism microenterprise development," NGO staffers told me that I must try to incorporate all existing tourism ventures under NNFC control and discourage individual entrepreneurs from developing new projects without working through this centralized structure so that revenue from tourism could be distributed equally throughout the entire population. Such attempts to contain the local economy within the paternal development apparatus were utterly unenforceable: during the three months I was there, numerous Ju/'hoansi offered their services as translators, guides, and trackers to tourists on a freelance basis, and one of the Ju/'hoan settlements opened its own "community campsite"—an instant success with the ecotourists—in spite of concerted objections to such independent activities by the management of the

NNDFN. Even in the face of such clear evidence of Ju/'hoan entrepreneurship, many NNDFN staff members remained undaunted in their conviction that they knew better than the people themselves what was best for them. When a mining company, for example, opened a new concession in Nyae Nyae and announced that it planned to pay wages higher than those paid by the NNDFN and NNFC, the expatriate director of the NGO—speaking "on behalf" of the people—actually lobbied the company to pay Ju/'hoansi lower wages than other (non-Ju/'hoan) laborers to prevent the development project from losing its most qualified staff! The differential, he suggested, could be pooled and given to the NNFC for "equitable" distribution to all the dispersed Ju/'hoan communities.

By the summer of 1994, many Ju/'hoansi had begun to focus their general frustration with the development project into explicit anger at such controlling behavior by particular members of the NNDFN staff. In July, things reached a boiling point when a semiannual gathering of community representatives called a Rada meeting—itself an NNDFN and NNFC invention designed to provide a regular forum for democratic local representation—was convened by the NGO to discuss the status of the various local development programs and policy issues. Although the NNDFN and NNFC staffs had worked out a prior agenda for the meeting, the seventy or so Rada representatives immediately insisted that it be scrapped and that discussion focus instead on the deteriorating relations between the NNDFN and the Ju/'hoan community. The complaints that I had heard in my village interviews might be characterized as symptomatic, but the criticisms leveled at the NNDFN during this meeting were direct and systemic. One of the NNFC leaders set the tone in his opening speech: "We were taking care of the land; why do outsiders come and tell us what to do?" Others loudly agreed: "The Foundation makes all our decisions for us!" By the end of the first day, a motion had been put forward to dissolve the NNDFN entirely. About two-thirds of the Rada members lined up behind the proponents of this motion, arguing that what they needed was a new foundation that worked for them, not the other way around. The remaining third coalesced around the more moderate suggestion that particularly objectionable NNDFN staff members be "sacked" but that the organization itself be permitted to remain. Citing the importance of consensus-based decision making to the Ju/'hoan people, everybody agreed that the best thing to do was to sleep on it for a night and reconsider the question in the morning.

By the next day, people were resolved: after a few emotional speeches, the Rada members voted unanimously to retain the NNDFN but to expel two of its key expatriate staff members, denouncing them as "fighting people" who must go at once. At this point, one of the sacked expatriates got up and left the compound; the other seemed too shocked to move from his seat. Next, the professional facilitator who had until then been running the meeting (a non-Ju/'hoan Namibian development expert hired by the NNDFN for the occasion) announced he would not continue leading the discussion under such revolutionary circumstances and handed over control—symbolized by a magic marker and a flip chart displaying the meeting's agenda—to one of the Ju/'hoansi who had been translating the debates for the expatriate observers.

As the meeting broke for lunch, two other expatriates and I radioed the Windhoek offices of USAID—the donor agency providing the largest financial support to the NNDFN at the time—to apprise them of the morning's events. The program officers there assured us that their agency's commitment was to the NNDFN as an institution, not to particular individuals within it, and that USAID would continue to honor its pledges of support for Ju/'hoan development programs provided that community-NGO relations could eventually be stabilized. This news brought wide applause from the Rada members when the meeting reconvened in the afternoon. For the next day and a half, the council turned its attention to finding ways to restructure the NNDFN and NNFC so that creative and administrative control would remain in the hands of Ju/'hoansi (and not "outsiders") while also retaining the recognition and support of the Namibian state and international donor community.[28] When word came from Windhoek that the NNDFN director—one of the two men fired in the meeting—had called an emergency session of the NGO's board of trustees,[29] the Rada council decided to send a Ju/'hoan delegation to this session to ensure that the board members were accurately informed of their wishes. The meeting dissolved as people began to focus on arranging the logistics involved in making this trip.

The Hegemony of Civil Society

When this extraordinary Rada meeting took place, I initially had little trouble interpreting its significance. Although at the time I had been in Namibia just six weeks, I had seen enough of the workings of the NNDFN to assume, elatedly, that the Ju/'hoansi had at last had enough and had finally decided to protest their domination by the neocolonial development regime. These Ju/'hoan Rada members clearly did not perceive themselves as requiring help from some outside source; on the contrary, they had stated loudly and clearly in the meeting that their experiences with "outsiders" had been more disempowering than helpful. It seemed obvious to me that what they wanted, rather than more foreign intervention cloaked in the benevolent guise of development "assistance," was to regain control over their political and economic lives.[30]

Many events in the ensuing weeks and months appeared to confirm the relevance of this sort of analysis: the NNDFN staff members who had been sacked, for example, immediately began struggling to keep their jobs by contesting the Rada members' decision. In meeting after meeting, these westerners invoked tropes of bushman vulnerability and immaturity, protesting to the NNDFN board of trustees, donor agencies, and members of Namibian government ministries that the Ju/'hoansi had been manipulated by disruptive factions within the expatriate community, had been confused about the implications of their actions, and, ultimately, hadn't meant what they had done. Surely this was as neocolonial as development could get: European development workers fighting to defend their incomes and authority by infantilizing and discrediting acts of self-determination by the very African people they were pledged to help.

On the other hand, other factors emerged in the meeting's aftermath that suggested the limitations of my blunt critical interpretation. For one, many Ju/'hoansi seemed worried—rather than triumphant—about the actions of the Rada members. While most Ju/'hoansi with whom I spoke agreed that relations between the NNDFN and the Ju/'hoan communities had sunk to an unacceptable level, many expressed concern that resource support for transportation, health, education, and other popular development programs would be disrupted as a result of the scandal surrounding the meeting.[31] As had been characteristic prior to the meeting, the Ju/'hoansi's needs for transportation and cash soon highlighted the issue of their dependence on the development regime. In what was to me a particularly excruciating interaction, for example, the delegates sent by the Rada council to meet with the NNDFN board of trustees, lacking adequate funds, were forced to turn to the former director of the NGO—one of the men they had just fired—for help locating money within the NNFC budget to pay for the costs of their travel to Windhoek from Nyae Nyae. When these funds were not immediately available to cover fuel and lodging expenses, the administrator advanced the Rada delegates the money out of his own project budget—in effect bankrolling their efforts to resist his control over them. Their continued dependence on the NNDFN for access to flows of resources and power, rendered glaringly obvious in transactions like these, quickly led even these Ju/'hoan delegates to soften the strongly critical position that the Rada council as a whole had taken. Without rescinding outright the decision to dismiss the two NNDFN staff members, the delegates made a point of assuring board members, donor agencies, and government ministry representatives that the Ju/'hoansi had been more divided and ambivalent than they had seemed in the Rada meeting, and that, most importantly, the Nyae Nyae communities remained committed to their efforts at "development." If the Rada meeting had, as I had initially assumed, been about resistance to the neocolonialism of development, this resistance had been at most partial; the Ju/'hoansi were well aware of the advantages, and not merely the costs to their self-determination, that "development" had brought to Nyae Nyae.

Another factor that suggested to me the need for a more complicated interpretation of the Rada meeting came in the form of reactions to the meeting by development workers and anthropologists with extensive experience working among the Ju/'hoansi. Several of these observers, I was startled to learn, did not seem even to consider the possibility that the meeting had been a rejection of the neocolonial paternalism of the NNDFN. For them, more significant than the meeting's substantive agenda or outcome were the dynamics between the various categories of Ju/'hoansi who had participated in it. Longtime Ju/'hoan anthropologist and advocate Megan Biesele, for example, has interpreted the meeting in light of ongoing processes of generational conflict, elite formation, and cultural transformation (telephone conversation with the author, 1994). Noting the self-aggrandizing and aggressive actions of several young men who played key roles in the Rada debates, she argues that these younger Ju/'hoansi have lost sight of core traditional values like social harmony, egalitarianism, and sharing, and that their actions directly conflict with what she terms the more "idealistic and community-oriented" views of an older generation (1994, 64). To explain the problems that had precipitated the Rada members' dramatic actions, Biesele points to various "mistakes" made by the NNDFN, inappropriate policies that have inadvertently fostered such divisions within the Nyae Nyae communities (64–65). While an analysis like Biesele's leaves intact the possibility of aid being entirely benevolent (provided the NNDFN could rectify its "mistakes," that is), and hence ultimately fails to engage the politics of the development encounter, her point is well taken that dynamics internal to the Ju/'hoan communities—and not just their relationship to "outside" agents like the NNDFN—were also at play in the Rada confrontation.

Indeed, perhaps the most significant inadequacy of my preliminary interpretation of the meeting was the way in which my understanding of it in terms of resistance to domination by the NNDFN necessitated that I ignore the many other power relations in which the Ju/'hoansi are also embedded. By focusing on the paternalistic oppressiveness of the development regime, I was able to assess the Rada council's actions as resistance (and the meeting itself as revolutionary), but in doing so I came to see the NNDFN as the primary locus of politics—and domination—in the Ju/'hoansi's lives. Such a position reflected my perspective at the time as a staff member within the organization and also mirrored the NGO's own efforts to prescribe the horizons of Ju/'hoan society in other political and economic ways (see above). Although the NNDFN did—and does—play a significant role in people's lives in Nyae Nyae, however, so too do representatives of the Namibian state, missionaries, journalists, researchers, tourists, and many others. As scholars like Wilmsen (1989a, 1989b) and Gordon (1984, 1992) have been at pains to point out, so-called bushmen have been embedded within multiple fields of power for a very long time; the one represented by the current development regime is perhaps best understood as merely the most prominent in recent years.

Importantly, by framing the NNDFN as the main problem in the Ju/'hoansi's lives—and the Rada meeting as a refusal of its dominance—I inadvertently elided the degree to which Ju/'hoansi continued to operate within cultural frames of reference—"symbolic fields," in Bourdieu's (1977) terminology—that reflect their long history of interaction with Western people.[32] Although I failed to take notice of it during the actual meeting, the Ju/'hoansi demonstrated their proficiency in the language of Western political action from the outset, in that their first act of rebellion was to call for the revision of the day's agenda. The fact that a formal agenda—a series of hierarchically and chronologically organized "discussion points" written in English (despite extremely low levels of literacy among all Ju/'hoansi and nearly nonexistent English language skills in the community) on a flip chart controlled by a meeting facilitator—would serve as the medium for focusing a rebellion indicates more about the extent to which Western bureaucratic procedural practices have come to structure Ju/'hoan politics than it does the radicalism of the Rada members' actions. Ju/'hoan dissatisfaction with the NNDFN had been quite widespread prior to the Rada debates, yet it was only when the community acted through a council of elected representatives—deploying a formal protocol of speeches, motions, votes and resolutions, and with expatriates documenting their actions in both writing and film[33]—that their anger drew significant notice from donors, the Namibian state, and the NNDFN itself. Seen in this light, the Rada meeting appears less a rejection of Western domination than an ingenious deployment of the West's own civic conventions for particular political purposes. By framing their resistance to NNDFN paternalism in the bureaucratic format of a "meeting," as well as in their interest in the reaction of donor agencies to their actions and their concern about disrupting flows of resources to Nyae Nyae or undermining the national and international credibility of the Ju/'hoan NNFC, the Rada members demonstrated a sophisticated awareness of the rules of the political game in which they existed.

To offer a more satisfactory explanation of these dynamics than a simple resistance-domination model allows, then, I return to the realm of civil society theory. In his introduction to *Civil Society and the State in Africa,* Harbeson argues that the concept of civil society provides a way of understanding the processes by which "working understandings concerning the basic rules of the political game or structure of the state emerge from within society and the economy at large." As a liberal political scientist, Harbeson conceives these "basic rules" and political "structure" as the result of positive social action: "In substantive terms, civil society typically refers to the points of agreement on what those working rules *should* be" (1994, 3, original emphasis). While I clearly reject the universalism of Harbeson's liberal vision of civil society, I find his notion of "the rules of the political game" suggestive, particularly in light of the Ju/'hoansi's deployment of the conventions of liberal political action in the Rada meeting.

The idea that political "games" are governed by "rules" also appears in another strand of civil society theorizing, this time in the Hegelian-Marxian tradition, in the work of Antonio Gramsci (1971) and Louis Althusser (1971). For Gramsci and Althusser, civil society is indeed highly normative, but unlike the liberal conception, in their framework the "norms" in question emerge not from within society but rather are imposed on society by the state. In Gramsci's famous formulation (1971, 206–76, esp. 242–47), civil society is the arena in which states exercise ideological hegemony over their subjects, manufacturing the active consent and collaboration of those they rule. Whereas states themselves are agents of explicit domination,[34] Gramsci argues that civil society "operates without 'sanctions' or compulsory 'obligations,' but nevertheless exerts a collective pressure and obtains objective results in the form of an evolution of customs, ways of thinking and acting, morality, etc." As a result of state "educative pressure," exerted through the law but also through "non-state" entities like schools, churches, and labor unions,[35] "each single individual . . . [comes to incorporate] himself into the collective man," and "necessity and coercion [are turned] into 'freedom'" (242).

Conceiving of civil society as the realm of ideological hegemony goes a long way toward explaining how Western political ideals and practices have so saturated the political aspirations and actions of people in Nyae Nyae. Influenced by years of "educative pressure" from liberal development workers, teachers, missionaries, and the like, as well as from South African and Namibian government bureaucrats, the Ju/'hoansi have come to share—in some fundamental ways, at least—the *habitus* of the Western liberal political field (see Bourdieu 1977).

Yet there is a problem with applying a Gramscian or Althusserian conception of civil society to the Ju/'hoan case: such a model presupposes that the hegemony in question is that of the state—that people are normalized into "subjects" by civil society in order to conform with the ideological and material needs of the dominant state structure. Such a framework is unsuited to a people like the Ju/'hoansi, for the simple reason that people termed bushmen have notoriously tended to fall outside of the complete control of the state. Indeed, "bushmen" have arguably been so classified precisely because of their situation on the geographical and political margins of nations, and because of the consistent difficulty that states have had transforming them into individuated, documented citizens and workers (see Gordon 1992).[36] In Nyae Nyae, the Ju/'hoansi are permitted to move freely across the Namibia-Bostwana international border that runs through the region, although the crossing is strictly monitored (requiring passports and visas) for expatriates and other (nonbushman) Namibians.

If the dominance of the state over the Ju/'hoansi fails to be hegemonic, then how can we account for the extent to which they have come to appreciate the "rules of the political game" in which they operate? I suggest that the hegemony at issue in this case is not that of the state, but rather of Western liberal ideology itself. The state, in this sense, can be seen as a part and product of ideology, not its underlying structure, as is the case in the Gramscian-Althusserian model. Instead of conceiving of civil society as the realm in which states exercise hegemony, I propose that civil society operates as that component of Western liberalism—at once abstract and pragmatic—through which normative political values and practices are themselves exported as universals. In the course of their interactions with the liberal apparatus of global civil society, incarnated in the persons and practices of development workers, anthropologists, browsers on the World Wide Web, and many others, the Ju/'hoansi have come to orient themselves not just to the Namibian state, but to the liberal West more generally.

Conclusion

Because the Ju/'hoansi have been defined by the West as bushmen, their engagement with the orienting (civilizing, disciplining) process enacted by civil society has proceeded along particularly stylized lines. In that liberalism requires the figure of a presocial human subject on which civil society may act, the Ju/'hoansi have been fashioned repeatedly by the West as authentic sociocultural Others: first as decentralized, kinship-based, hunter-gatherers, and, more recently, as victims of colonialism and underdevelopment. At the same time, though, liberalism bases its moral authority on the promise that its civilized sociality will one day embrace all humanity.[37] And so the Ju/'hoansi have been held up as symbols of liberalism's triumph as well. During Namibia's first democratic elections, a special task force from the United Nations was there to ensure and celebrate Ju/'hoan participation in the voting; the international donor community, pleased to be extending the fruits of development even to "bushmen," has showered organizations like the NNDFN with money; and the Namibian regime, eager to demonstrate its commitment to democracy and equality, has proudly espoused "progressive" policies toward the nation's "indigenous" citizens.

For their part, the Ju/'hoansi can at best be described as ambivalent about bearing the weight of all these liberal projections. At times they have successfully capitalized on, and even relished, certain benefits derived from their status as iconic "bushmen"—as in their ability to make money from tourists and their evident pleasure in the resources brought to Nyae Nyae by "development." The fierce nature of their struggles with the NNDFN over the control of vehicles and development revenues, on the other hand, indicates that they are also concerned that their participation in the liberal project of building "civil society" poses a real threat to whatever vestiges of self-determination they still have.[38] Within a liberal paradigm, after all, people like them are forever frozen in the unenviable position of the not-quite-yet fully modern, perpetually cast as needing the civilizing action of liberal civil society rather than as subjects capable of forging a civilized society in their own right.

Ambivalence or no, what the events of the 1994 Rada meeting make clear is that the Ju/'hoansi have no alternative but to operate within this liberal framework. As a result of nearly fifty years of interaction with liberal Western anthropologists; of almost twenty years of active engagement with the ideologies and practices of international development discourse; of regular contact with Western tourists, journalists, and others; and of their situation within a newly democratic, postcolonial nation, the Ju/'hoansi have come to structure even their resistance to Western domination in terms of liberal political idioms and practices. As their story illustrates, the central drama of liberalism—civil society's rendering of presocial humanity into moral, universal Man—is much more than just an ethical ideal; it is also a powerful mechanism by which Western political hegemony comes to encompass even places like the Kalahari.

Notes

1. Most notably, Marxian versions—such as Gramsci's conception of civil society as the realm in which states exercise ideological hegemony over their subjects—have been influential (see Bobbio 1988). I discuss the Gramscian conception of civil society toward the end of this chapter.

2. See Bratton 1994; Hall 1995; Harbeson 1994; Seligman 1992; and Young 1994 for genealogies of the concept.

3. For a discussion of this term, see Fisher 1997; Korten 1990; Lee 1995; Lipschutz 1992; Macdonald 1994; Shaw 1994; and Walker 1994.

4. Barnet and Cavanagh offer a typical vision at the close of their recent book on multinational corporations: "More and more people who are bypassed by the new world order are crafting their own strategies for survival and development, and in the process are spinning their own transnational webs to embrace and connect people across the world. On dreams of a global civilization that respects human diversity and values people one by one, a global civil society is beginning to take shape" (1994, 429–30).

5. Images of NGOs as organic, "grassroots" entities, in combination with widely publicized efforts by NGOs to reform the policies of global international entities such as the World Bank and the United Nations—including the increasingly institutionalized UN practice of holding "NGO Forums" simultaneously with official policy conferences—have all contributed to the powerful perception that NGOs represent a check on the power of the formal international political and economic system. Unmentioned in most discussions of NGOs, however, is the central dependence of most "nonprofit" and "nongovernmental" organizations on the sponsorship of state aid agencies and corporate donors. As Robbins points out, the increasing willingness of states to channel aid through NGOs indicates a rapprochement, not greater critical distance, between states and such agents of civil society (1995, 105).

6. Liberal international organizations like the United Nations perpetuate such conceptions of the world as a democratic community of nations, in that all states ostensibly

participate as free and equal members, like Western bourgeois subjects writ large (see Lee 1995).

7. Harbeson, for example, suggests "that civil society may have a better claim to universality than other elements of Western political philosophy, [for] by definition it upholds the proposition that to be legitimate and viable, political and socioeconomic structure must be consonant with the value systems of any given people" (1994, 26). See also Young 1994; Bratton 1994; Tripp 1994; Hall 1995; and Perez-Diaz 1995.

8. But see Sampson's (1996) discussion (in the same volume) of the Danish government's effort to promote the development of "civil society" in the Albanian "transition."

9. I use the term "bushmen" throughout this chapter with intentional irony in order to signify the shared history of those southern African people who have historically been categorized as bushmen by others with the power to label them as such.

10. Alternate spellings include Ju/wasi, Zhun/twasi, and Zhu-/wasi. A rough pronunciation (minus the click) in English would be "Zhoon-twa-see."

11. This "fanciful" image of the presocial subject, of course, has a long history in Western liberal thought, from Rousseau's attempts to imagine man prior to entry into the social contract, to John Rawls's famous vision of a radically ethical "original position" behind a mythic, culture-free "veil of ignorance" (see Lee 1995, 562–66).

12. Under the sponsorship of the Peabody Museum of Harvard University, the Marshall family (Lorna and Laurence Marshall, John, and Elizabeth Marshall Thomas) undertook a series of exploratory and ethnographic expeditions to Nyae Nyae in the early 1950s (see Ruby 1993).

13. This debate has spawned a voluminous literature; Wilmsen and Denbow (1990) and Lee (1992) frame the outlines. Alan Barnard's "The Kalahari Debate: A Bibliographic Essay" (1992) provides a fairly comprehensive overview. For a current instantiation, see the forthcoming special edition of *Visual Anthropology,* "Encounters in the Kalahari," guest edited by Keyan Tomaselli.

14. Gordon's careful documentation of colonial efforts to exterminate bushmen as vermin (1992), and Wilmsen's arguments about the proletarianization of bushmen in the regional political economy of the Kalahari (1989a) stand in stark contrast to the assertion of Cultural Survival that bushmen have "always lived autonomously, subject only to the law and custom of their own society."

15. Macdonald (1994, 269 n. 8) notes the ubiquity of "web" metaphors in global civil society discourse. The World Wide Web, with its potential for "networking" among "virtual" or "cyber" communities, has played a key role in the collective imagination of global civil society.

16. For an Australian example of the role of indigenous peoples in this process of liberal redemption, see Povinelli 1998.

17. In the Namibian case, official independence from the Republic of South Africa only came in 1990; the country was organized under apartheid until well into the 1980s.

18. Marshall has sought to describe and explain recent sociocultural transformations among the Ju/'hoansi, as well as his own role in shaping them, in a number of

different forums (see especially Marshall and Ritchie 1984; Marshall 1993). The conflation of his own personal trajectory with that of the Ju/'hoan people is nowhere more evident than in his curriculum vitae, currently available on the World Wide Web, which includes a three-page history of the Ju/'hoansi since 1950 (Marshall 1996).

19. See Ferguson 1994 on the centrality of agricultural intensification in the Western imagination of development.

20. Gordon (1992) has documented the exploitation of Ju/'hoan people by the South African military in some detail. However, when I conducted interviews in 1994, many Ju/'hoansi spoke with evident nostalgia of the days when the SADF provided high salaries, food rations, and regular social services to the region, suggesting that a simple exploitation model may be inadequate to understanding this period in Ju/'hoan history.

21. See Povinelli 1993 for an analysis of the importance of labor—the recognizable transformation of the natural environment—in the liberal politics of land-rights for hunter-gatherers in Australia.

22. I eventually learned that there were two nonwhites on the senior NNDFN staff in 1994, a Zambian agronomist and a Namibian automechanic workshop manager. A handful of black Namibians were also employed as office assistants, messengers, and housekeepers at the NNDFN office in Windhoek.

23. Tsau, the utopian Kalahari setting for Norman Rush's novel *Mating* (1991), sprang to mind more than once in Baraka!

24. Although seldom documented in official NGO reports, the expatriates associated with the NNDFN have clashed frequently among themselves over the issue of paternalism—most often in the context of debates concerning whether to distribute food relief during times of hardship, how to manage the revenues generated by NNDFN projects, and whether the NGO should attempt to control the flow of tourists and researchers to Nyae Nyae. The resignations of NNDFN staff shortly before my arrival in Namibia had resulted from ideological conflicts such as these.

25. A grant from the Ford Foundation to the NNFC enabled the Ju/'hoan organization to purchase several such vehicles of its own.

26. I know of only one Ju/'hoan person—a prominent leader of the NNFC—who actually owns his own car.

27. See Urry 1995 (144–46) for a provocative discussion of the relationship between rapid forms of mobility and modern forms of subjectivity and sociality, particularly with respect to human perception of the natural environment. For a more culturally specific discussion, see also Povinelli on the "productive" nature of "just traveling through the country" within the cosmological and economic context of Aboriginal Australia 1995 (514).

28. By chance, a specialist in local cooperative development from the Namibian Ministry of Agriculture had been asked—again by one of the dismissed NNDFN staff members—to attend the Rada meeting as an advisor to the Ju/'hoan NNFC. As he was knowledgeable about the criteria by which local organizations are judged to be

legitimate local government structures by the Namibian state, he was able to provide useful information to the Rada members as they debated restructuring their relationship to the NNDFN.

29. At the time, the NNDFN Board was composed entirely of NNDFN staff (including both individuals fired by the Rada!), lawyers, businesspeople, and anthropologists with an interest in the welfare of the Ju/'hoansi. One of the outcomes of the 1994 Rada meeting was the incorporation of several Ju/'hoan representatives into this advisory structure.

30. My assessment of the Rada meeting in terms of Ju/'hoan resistance to domination echoed the work of development critics like Amin (1990), Escobar (1995), Ferguson (1994) and Hancock (1989), who have forcefully argued that the international development industry is best understood as a systematic—if at times unwitting—arena in which fundamental relations of domination between the West and "the rest" are reproduced.

31. News of the meeting (and especially of the dismissal of the foundation's white staff members by Ju/'hoansi) made the front pages of Namibian newspapers (Lister 1994).

32. See Adams 1996 for a suggestive discussion of the dynamic mimesis that constitutes interactions between westerners and fetishized cultural Others (in her case, Sherpas) like "bushmen."

33. As has been true for an extraordinary number of public events in Nyae Nyae, the entire Rada meeting was recorded on film by John Marshall. The Rada members seemed quite pleased to have a film "record" of the meeting's events, often uttering their speeches directly into Marshall's camera. As Marshall's films have provided important strategic evidence in debates over land rights and other political issues in the past, the Ju/'hoansi can be presumed to have understood the potential importance of documenting their actions against the NNDFN. See Tomaselli n.d. on the overall performativity of Ju/'hoan life, and Wilmsen n.d. on the politics of representation in Marshall films.

34. Althusser (1971) terms the police, military, and other explicit agents of state force the "Repressive State Apparatus."

35. These compose Althusser's (1971) "Ideological State Apparatuses."

36. Similarly, Sharon Hutchinson (1996) has recently argued that people who move around—in her case the Nuer—are more likely than members of sedentary societies to avoid complete incorporation by the state.

37. The apparent contradictoriness of the simultaneous insistence on the Ju/'hoansi's ethnic particularity as "bushmen," and on their universal humanity as national and world citizens, should come as no surprise, for as Comaroff and Comaroff (1997, chap. 8) have recently noted of the colonial context, the assertion of ethnic difference and the promise of its erasure constitute the characteristic "double gesture" of liberal humanism (see also chapter 2).

38. The fact that conflicts in Nyae Nyae have often flared over issues of transportation and money, I believe, is far from coincidental. Control over the mobility and pro-

ductivity of people called bushmen has long been a key issue in the process of their orientation to the West. For albeit different purposes, Sahlins (1972) has famously noted that the !Kung are devoted mobility maximizers, and Gordon (1992) has documented at length the ways that "bushman" peoples historically used their ability to move around in the bush to resist incorporation into the South West African colonial economy. As the extraordinarily violent measures taken to regulate their movement and appropriate their labor during the colonial era attest, these are precisely the issues around which battles over the incorporation of people like the Ju/'hoansi into the Western political field have historically been organized.

References

Adams, Vincanne. 1996. *Tigers of the Snow and Other Virtual Sherpas.* Princeton: Princeton University Press.

Althusser, Louis. 1971. "Ideology and Ideological State Apparatuses." In *Lenin and Philosophy, and Other Essays. Translated by Ben Brewster.* New York: Monthly Review Press.

Amin, Samir. 1990. *Maldevelopment.* London: Zed Books.

Azarya, Victor. 1994. "Civil Society and Disengagement in Africa." In *Civil Society and the State in Africa,* ed. John Harbeson, Donald Rothchild, and Naomi Chazan. Boulder: Lynne Rienner.

Barnard, Alan. 1992. "The Kalahari Debate: A Bibliographic Essay." Center for African Studies Occasional Paper 35, Edinburgh: Edinburgh University.

Barnet, Richard, and John Cavanagh. 1994. *Global Dreams: Imperial Corporations and the New World Order.* New York: Simon and Schuster.

Bayart, Jean-Francois. 1993. *The State in Africa: Politics of the Belly.* London: Longman.

Biesele, Megan. 1993. "Land, Language, and Leadership." *Cultural Survival Quarterly* (summer): 57–60.

———. 1994. "Human Rights and Democratization in Namibia: Some Grassroots Political Perspectives." *African Rural and Urban Studies* 1 (2): 49–72.

Bobbio, Norberto. 1988. "Gramsci and the Concept of Civil Society." In *Civil Society and the State: New European Perspectives,* ed. John Keane. London: Verso.

Bourdieu, Pierre. 1977. *Outline of a Theory of Practice.* Cambridge: Cambridge University Press.

Bratton, Michael. 1994. "Civil Society and Political Transitions in Africa." In *Civil Society and the State in Africa,* ed. John W. Harbeson, Donald Rothchild, and Naomi Chazan. Boulder: Lynne Rienner.

Chatterjee, Partha. 1990. "A Response to Taylor's 'Modes of Civil Society.'" *Public Culture* 3 (1): 119–32.

Chazan, Naomi. 1992. "The Dynamics of Civil Society in Africa." Paper presented at conference, Civil Society in Africa, Hebrew University, Jerusalem.

Cohen, Jean, and Andrew Arato. 1992. *Civil Society and Political Theory.* Cambridge: MIT Press.

Comaroff, John L., and Jean Comaroff. 1991. *Of Revelation and Revolution,* vol. 1. Chicago: University of Chicago Press.

———. 1997. *Of Revelation and Revolution,* vol. 2. Chicago: University of Chicago Press.

Cultural Survival. 1996. "Cultural Survival Special Projects: The Nyae Nyae Development Foundation." <http://www.cs.org/SP/SPNyae.htm> (5 March).

Davidson, Basil. 1992. *Black Man's Burden: Africa and the Curse of the Nation-State.* New York: Random House.

Ekeh, Peter. 1975. "Colonialism and the Two Publics in Africa." *Comparative Studies in Society and History* 17 (1): 91–111.

Escobar, Arturo. 1995. *Encountering Development: The Making and Unmaking of the Third World.* Princeton: Princeton University Press.

Ferguson, James. 1994. *The Anti-Politics Machine.* Minneapolis: University of Minnesota Press.

Fisher, William. 1997. "Doing Good? The Politics and Antipolitics of NGO Practices." *Annual Review of Anthropology* 26:439–64.

Fortes, M., and E. E. Evans-Pritchard, eds. [1940] 1987. *African Political Systems.* Reprint, London: KPI, in association with the International African Institute.

Fourie, Coral. 1994. *Living Legends of a Dying Culture.* Hartbeespoort, Rep. S. Africa: Ekogilde Press.

Garland, Elizabeth. 1994. *Tourism Development in Eastern Bushmanland.* Final Report to the Nyae Nyae Development Foundation of Namibia.

Garland, Elizabeth, and Robert J. Gordon. n.d. "The Authentic (In)authentic: Bushman Anthro-Tourism." In "Encounters in the Kalahari," special edition of *Visual Anthropology* (guest edited by Keyan Tomaselli). Forthcoming.

Gordon, Robert J. 1984. "The !Kung in the Kalahari Exchange: An Ethnohistorical Perspective." In *Past and Present in Hunter Gatherer Studies,* ed. Carmel Schrire. Orlando: Academic Press.

———. 1992. *The Bushman Myth: the Making of a Namibian Underclass.* Boulder: Westview.

Gramsci, Antonio. 1971. *The Prison Notebooks.* New York: International Publishers.

Gupta, Akhil. 1997. "The Song of the Nonaligned World: Transnational Identities and the Reinscription of Space in Late Capitalism." In *Culture, Power, Place: Explorations in Critical Anthropology,* ed. Akhil Gupta and James Ferguson. Durham: Duke University Press.

Habermas, Jürgen. [1962] 1989. *The Structural Transformation of the Public Sphere.* Reprint, Cambridge: MIT Press.

Hall, John A. 1995. "In Search of Civil Society." In *Civil Society: Theory, History, Comparison,* ed. John A. Hall. Cambridge: Polity Press.

Hancock, Graham. 1989. *Lords of Poverty.* New York: Atlantic Monthly Press.

Hann, Chris. 1996. "Introduction: Political Society and Civil Anthropology." In *Civil*

Society: Challenging Western Models, ed. Chris Hann and Elizabeth Dunn. London: Routledge.

Hann, Chris, and Elizabeth Dunn, eds. 1996. *Civil Society: Challenging Western Models.* London: Routledge.

Harbeson, John. 1994. "Civil Society and Political Renaissance in Africa." In *Civil Society and the State in Africa,* ed. John W. Harbeson, Donald Rothchild, and Naomi Chazan. Boulder: Lynne Rienner.

Hardt, Michael. 1995. "The Withering of Civil Society." *Social Text* 14 (4): 27–44.

Hutchinson, Sharon. 1996. *Nuer Dilemmas: Coping with Money, War, and the State.* Berkeley: University of California Press.

Keane, John. 1988. *Civil Society and the State: New European Perspectives.* London: Verso.

Korten, D.C. 1990. *Getting to the 21st Century: Voluntary Action and the Global Agenda.* West Hartford, Conn.: Kumarian.

Lee, Benjamin. 1995. "Critical Internationalism." *Public Culture* 7:559–92.

Lee, Richard. 1979. *The !Kung San: Men, Women and Work in a Foraging Society.* Cambridge: Cambridge University Press.

———. 1984. *The Dobe !Kung.* New York: Harcourt Brace.

———. 1992. "Science, or Politics? The Crisis in Hunter-Gatherer Studies," *American Anthropologist* 94:31–54.

Lee, Richard B., and Irven Devore, eds. 1968. *Man the Hunter.* Chicago: Aldine.

———. 1976. *Kalahari Hunter-Gatherers: Studies of the !Kung San and Their Neighbors.* Cambridge: Harvard University Press.

Lipschutz, Ronnie D. 1992. "Reconstructing World Politics: The Emergence of Global Civil Society." *Millennium: Journal of International Studies* 21 (3): 389–420.

Lister, Gwen. 1994. "Dispute Sees Four NNDFN Members Quit." *The Namibian* 3 (478): 1.

Macdonald, Laura. 1994. "Globalising Civil Society: Interpreting International NGOs in Central America." *Millennium: Journal of International Studies* 23 (2): 267–85.

Marshall, John. 1980. *N!ai, the Story of a !Kung Woman.* Documentary Educational Resources. Film.

———. 1957. *The Hunters.* Films Inc. Film.

———. 1993. "Filming and Learning." In *The Cinema of John Marshall,* ed. Jay Ruby. Philadelphia: Harwood Academic Publishers.

———. 1996. "DER President and Resident Filmmaker." <http://www.der.org/docued/staff/john-marshall.html> (3 May).

Marshall, John, and Claire Ritchie. 1984. *Where Are the Ju/wasi of Nyae Nyae?* Cape Town: University of Cape Town Press.

Marshall, Lorna. 1976. *The !Kung of Nyae Nyae.* Cambridge: Harvard University Press.

Motzafi-Haller, Pnina. 1994. "When Bushmen Are Known as Basarwa: Gender, Ethnicity, and Differentiation in Rural Botswana." *American Ethnologist* 21 (3): 539–63.

Mudimbe, V. Y. 1988. *The Invention of Africa.* Bloomington: Indiana University Press.

Newbury, Catherine. 1988. *The Cohesion of Oppression: Clientship and Ethnicity in Rwanda, 1860–1960.* New York: Columbia University Press.

Perez-Diaz, Victor. 1995. "The Possibility of Civil Society: Traditions, Character, and Challenges." In *Civil Society: Theory, History, Comparison,* ed. John A. Hall. Cambridge: Polity Press.

Perrott, John. 1992. *Bush for the Bushmen: Need "The Gods Must Be Crazy" Kalahari People Die?* Greenville, Pa.: Beaver Pond Publishing.

Povinelli, Elizabeth A. 1993. *Labor's Lot: The Power, History, and Culture of Aboriginal Action.* Chicago: University of Chicago Press.

———. "Do Rocks Listen?" *American Anthropologist* 97 (3): 505–18.

———. 1998. "State of Shame: Australian Multiculturalism and the Crisis of Indigenous Citizenship." *Critical Inquiry* 24 (winter): 575–610.

Robbins, Bruce. 1995. "Some Versions of U.S. Internationalism." *Social Text* 14 (4): 97–123.

Ruby, Jay, ed. 1993. *The Cinema of John Marshall.* Philadelphia: Harwood Academic Publishers.

Rush, Norman. 1991. *Mating.* New York: Vintage Books.

Sahlins, Marshall. 1972. "The Original Affluent Society." In *Stone Age Economics.* New York: Aldine de Gruyter.

Sampson, Steven. "The Social Life of Projects: Importing Civil Society to Albania." In *Civil Society: Challenging Western Models,* ed. Chris Hann and Elizabeth Dunn. London: Routledge.

Seligman, Adam B. 1992. *The Idea of Civil Society.* Princeton: Princeton University Press.

Shaw, Martin. 1994. "Civil Society and Global Politics: Beyond a Social Movements Approach." *Millennium: Journal of International Studies* 23 (3): 647–67.

Shostak, Marjorie. 1981. *Nisa: The Life and Words of a !Kung Woman.* Cambridge: Harvard University Press.

Thomas, Elizabeth Marshall. 1959. *The Harmless People.* New York: Alfred A. Knopf.

Tomaselli, Keyan, guest ed. n.d. "Encounters in the Kalahari," special edition of *Visual Anthropology.* Forthcoming.

Tripp, Aili Mari. 1994. "Rethinking Civil Society: Gender Implications in Contemporary Tanzania." In *Civil Society and the State in Africa,* ed. John W. Harbeson, Donald Rothchild, and Naomi Chazan. Boulder: Lynne Rienner.

Urry, John. 1995. *Consuming Places.* London: Routledge.

Vansina, Jan. 1990. *Paths in the Rainforest: Toward a History of Political Tradition in Equatorial Africa.* Madison: University of Wisconsin Press.

Walker, R. B. J. 1994. "Social Movements/World Politics." *Millennium: Journal of International Studies.* 23 (3): 669–700.

Wilmsen, Edwin. 1989a. *Land Filled with Flies.* Chicago: University of Chicago Press.

———, ed. 1989b. *We Are Here: The Politics of Aboriginal Land Tenure.* Berkeley: University of California Press.

———. 1991. "Pastoro-Foragers to 'Bushmen': Transformations in Kalahari Relations of Property, Production and Labor." In *Herders, Warriors, and Traders*, ed. John Galaty and Pierre Bonte. Boulder: Westview Press.

———. n.d. "Knowledge as a Source of Progress: The Marshall Family Testament to the 'Bushmen.'" In "Encounters in the Kalahari," special edition of *Visual Anthropology* (guest edited by Keyan Tomaselli). Forthcoming.

Wilmsen, Edwin, and James Denbow. 1990. "Paradigmatic History of San-speaking Peoples and Current Attempts at Revision." *Current Anthropology* 31 (5): 489–524.

Young, Crawford. 1994. "In Search of Civil Society." In *Civil Society and the State in Africa*, ed. John W. Harbeson, Donald Rothchild, and Naomi Chazan. Boulder: Lynne Rienner.

4

Civil Society and Its Presuppositions: Lessons from Uganda

Mikael Karlström

IS "CIVIL SOCIETY"—in its currently accepted usage as an institutional domain that mediates between the state and society—an analytically useful construct with regard to contemporary Africa?

The term first gained currency in the late eighteenth and early nineteenth centuries, during the period of modern European state formation, when it was employed and elaborated by, among others, Ferguson, Kant, Hegel, Marx, and Tocqueville. Aside from its usage by Gramsci, however, it did not thereafter figure centrally in Western political theory or political rhetoric until quite recently. Its revival arose out of the democratic opposition movements in communist Eastern Europe, where it was used to articulate the prospects for a domain of social and political activity and organization independent of the totalitarian state. The conception has also been employed in the struggle against Latin American dictatorships and occasionally in efforts to formulate a left alternative to the welfare state in western Europe.[1]

What is common to the various contexts in which the concept has reemerged is the sense of an overempowered and excessively penetrative state, and the felt need for a countervailing revival of nonstate social capacities of organization and action. Scholars of postcolonial African politics have also experienced a disillusionment with the centralized state form and a renewed hope for the resurgence of nonstate forces (Bratton 1989). This experience makes the concept of civil society seem relevant to contemporary Africa as well. Yet despite its vigorous scholarly application and a recent wave of democ-

---

This essay was originally presented at the 1995 annual meeting of the African Studies Association in Orlando, Florida. I want to thank Nelson Kasfir, Ronald Kassimir, and David Mandell for comments on earlier drafts, and Jean Comaroff for a careful editorial reading. Relevant research was funded by a Fulbright-Hays Doctoral Dissertation Abroad Fellowship (1991–93) and by the Harry Frank Guggenheim Foundation (1995). The essay was written under a MacArthur Scholar Fellowship from the University of Chicago Council for Advanced Studies in Peace and International Cooperation (CASPIC).

racy movements, it does not (with the notable exception of South Africa) seem to have taken root in African political cultures. This fact should give pause to those who would apply the concept without attending to its historical specificity or examining its presuppositions.

The general definition of civil society as a domain mediating between state and society has generated vibrant and fruitful theoretical debate. Some approaches, for instance, emphasize the role of civil society in enhancing state capacities, while others emphasize its role in containing state power. Some link civil society directly to the domain of capitalist economic activity, while others view capitalism as its undoing. Some analyses have focused on social institutions and others on social movements.

My concern in this chapter, however, is less with such theoretical debates than with the application of the idea of civil society to Africa, mainly by empirically oriented political scientists. On the whole, this literature has been driven less by theoretical issues than by a desire to determine the actual extent and character of civil society in Africa.[2] Such an endeavor requires a definition of the concept that is conducive to quantification, and these analysts have chosen to focus largely on voluntary associations as the privileged institutional form of civil society.

While some political scientists include virtually all voluntary associations in their definition of civil society (e.g., Putnam 1993, 1995), the dominant trend among Africanists has been to narrow the concept, excluding associations that do not engage with the state in ways that enhance either the democratic character of governance or the state's capacity to carry out its policies. Chazan (1991), for instance, excludes the following five forms of voluntary association: parochial ethnic and kinship-based associations that avoid state contact; organizations that have their own designs on state power (e.g., political parties); associations that are directly tied to the state itself; associations whose constituencies are not sufficiently diverse and cross-cutting; and associations that are insufficiently participatory and democratic. These criteria raise certain problems, because they ignore the fact that the relationship of particular associations with the state depends in significant part on the character and actions of the state itself. Thus, the very same association may be parochially evasive when state power is oppressive and constructively engaged when such engagement seems worthwhile. Likewise, state exclusion or persecution of certain groups may transform their associations into vehicles for overthrowing the state.

The ultimate problem, however, lies not with specific definitions of the "civil" voluntary sector but with the prior decision to focus on voluntary associations as the incarnation of civil society. This focus stems, I think, partly from the influence of Tocqueville and partly from the need to identify quantitative measures of civil society in the objective-categorical sense favored by political scientists (Azarya 1994, 93). But recall that for Tocqueville himself, the vibrant voluntary sector in the United States was significant because it mitigated the dangerously atomizing effects of individualism and egalitarianism. In fact, the organizationally discrete voluntary associations upon which the civil society literature tends to focus presuppose not only the sort of individualism that emphasizes freely chosen over ascriptive solidarities but also firmly anchored contractarian and bureaucratic-procedural orientations. If these are not prevalent features of the African societies to which the category is being applied, then one should not expect to find a prevalence of voluntary associations of this sort.

Political scientists generally conclude from the relative absence of voluntary associations in Africa that the continent suffers from a weak civil society. Yet the concept of civil society surely serves no useful analytical purpose if it merely identifies an absence. Its purpose should be to enable us to identify those forces and institutions that *do* have some potential for producing a more productive engagement between state and society, and, ultimately, the sort of stable, legitimate, and democratic state forms that have proven so difficult to achieve in postcolonial Africa.

In order to show more precisely how the currently influential equation of civil society with voluntary associations falls short as an analytical tool for this purpose, I propose to reverse the usual analytical direction. Instead of applying the objective-categorical conception of civil society to an empirical case, I will apply elements of an empirical case to the conception. Starting from an account of past and present mechanisms of articulation between state and society in Buganda and Uganda, and particularly the contemporary forces for democratization there, I will assess the analytical capacity of the objective-categorical conception of civil society to comprehend them.

State and Society in Uganda

The National Resistance Movement (NRM) led by Yoweri Museveni came to power in Uganda in 1986 following a five-year guerrilla war, putting an end—for the most part—to the cycles of state oppression and violence that Uganda had suffered since independence in 1962.[3] Two of the most notable developments underpinning this political recovery have been the creation of a new form of democratic local government through elective Local Councils; and the restoration of the Buganda kingship, accompanied by a resurgence of ethnic political aspirations and clan associations among Baganda.[4] Both of these developments stem from the NRM's efforts to find new mechanisms of articulation between state and society to replace those that had previously failed so disastrously in postcolonial Uganda. Under the objective-categorical conception of civil society, however, neither of them would qualify as particularly promising in this regard. The Local Council system is a creation of the state and would therefore seem to be insufficiently independent of it, while the revival of kingship and clanship would be judged irredeemably parochial by virtue of its anchorage in ethnicity and kinship.

Kinship

I begin with the least likely candidate for inclusion in the category of civil society: kinship. By virtue of its core position in a domain of "private life"—which stands in categorical opposition to the "public" domain of state and civil society in Western thought—kinship as an axis of solidarity and association is automatically excluded from the objective-categorical conception of civil society.[5]

Does this exclusion of kinship-based associational forms from civil society accord with Ugandan realities? Many contemporary Baganda view the system of sociopolitical organization based on clans under royal rule as a perfectly viable model of social order and integration; in fact, they actually consider it the best of all possible models. They argue that the orderly ascending hierarchy of ranked lineages and clan heads *(bataka)*, which culminates in the king as "head of all the clan heads" *(Ssaabataka)*, produces the most stable, cohesive, and responsive political order possible (Karlström 1996). They contrast this with the divisive and destructive competition for power associated with the system of political parties that developed in the late colonial period and became prominent with independence. The system of clans and king is not conceived as a static stratified structure; on the contrary, it is thought to permit a form of regulated competition that is far more sustainable and conducive to social solidarity than the unregulated competition that arises among political parties. The unity and inclusiveness of the system is guaranteed by the orientation of all competition toward the stable figure of the king, who stands above it and regulates it, and whose own position is beyond contestation. The political party system, by contrast, is deemed partisan and divisive because a party leader is responsive only to the demands of his own followers and not to those of society as a whole. Far from promoting parochial factionalism, then, the clan system is felt by Baganda to be precisely what holds them together as a people, cutting across divisions of geography, status, and interest, and, by virtue of mandatory exogamy, constantly creating localized interclan affiliations as well. This unifying function of clans is so deeply felt that it is frequently projected by analogy onto Uganda as a whole, whose ethnic groups are urged to unite under the national government as the clans of Buganda unite under their king.

This rosy picture of the clans-and-king system is based partially on nostalgia for the colonial era of political stability and Buganda's dominant position within Uganda prior to the abolition of the kingship and the administrative dismemberment of the kingdom. Yet, looking back at the precolonial Buganda polity with an eye to identifying mediating institutions of the civil society type, it is not difficult to argue that clans were indeed the central locus of organizational articulation between the general population and the monarchy, with its administrative apparatus of royally appointed chiefs. The role of clan heads in checking the excesses of royal power was ritually marked in numerous ways. The king's mother and her clan were viewed as a safe and privileged route of access to the king for the commoner population. Many clan heads were immune (at least in theory, if not always in practice) from royal persecution, and could therefore voice complaints that others could not risk. Many clan and subclan lineage heads held courtly ritual offices that served as charters of incorporation into the kingdom for their clans. The Kibaale of the Oribi Antelope clan was, for instance, the only person in the realm who could legitimately stand in judgment over the king in a court case. Royal succession choices were engineered in part through alliances between clans, and clan leaders sometimes orchestrated efforts to overthrow oppressive kings. Although clans were formally hierarchical, they were conceived as substantively much more fraternal and solidary than the hierarchy of chiefs.[6]

In late precolonial Buganda, and even more so under colonial rule, the clan heads and the clans as corporate entities were significantly weakened. Yet well into the twentieth century, commoners continued to voice their political and economic grievances to the king via the clan system, bypassing the new landowning chiefs who had become the real governing elite and against whom most of these grievances were directed. The first organized political interest group in the kingdom was the Federation of Clan Heads *(Bataka)*, which arose in the 1920s to press land claims against the chiefs. This group subsequently evolved into the populist Bataka Party of the 1940s, in which clan heads themselves played only a small role, but for which the principle remained central that it was as clan members that Baganda could most legitimately make claims upon the political system.[7] More recently, the association of clan heads was first and most insistent in giving voice to popular aspirations for the restoration of the kingship after the NRM came to power in 1986, and the restoration itself has been articulated as a project of moral and civil regeneration through the revival of clan structures and activities (Karlström 1999, chap. 6).

In Buganda, then, kinship cannot be viewed as a strictly "private" domain. A similar argument could be made for numerous other sub-Saharan African societies and could probably be generalized to the region as a whole.[8] At the very minimum, kinship in Africa must be conceived as having both a public and a private face. If the application of what I have been calling the objective-categorical conception of civil society to African contexts obscures this public or political dimension of kinship, as I think it tends to do, it is not particularly helpful. The objective-categorical conception carries with it an unexamined presupposition about the division of social life into public-political and private-familial domains. But this distinction is arguably itself a historically and culturally specific construct. The ancient Greek and Roman usage of the public/private distinction, which virtually disappeared during the European Middle Ages, was revived in the early modern period in conjunction with the emergence of new conceptions of the relationship between state and society and the parallel consolidation of a bourgeois domestic sphere centered on the nuclear family.[9]

From such a perspective, it could still be argued that Africa's "modernization" would eventually lead, as did Europe's, to a relegation of kinship to the domain of "private life" and its elimination from the public domain. But the difference between Europe and Africa with regard to the role of kinship may go much deeper. Goody (1976) argues, for instance, that the pattern of unilateral descent-reckoning that is common to most African societies as far back as evidence is available systematically creates more extensive kinship structures than does the equally ancient Eurasian one, where descent is reckoned bilaterally, the conjugal couple tends to dominate over lineages, and clanship has rarely been a prominent institution. Ekeh (1990) proposes a more historical explanation for the enduring centrality of kinship in Africa, invoking the slave trade and colonialism as the causes of a prevalent kinship ideology throughout the continent. In any case, the enduring centrality of kinship relations in contemporary African social life renders the direct application of the modern Western conception of civil society highly problematic. If, as seems likely, kinship in Africa is not simply going to wither away with the advent of "modernity," we may have to consider whether the public/private distinction is relevant there at all—and if so, whether it can be expected to take the same forms as it does in the West.

Ethnicity and Monarchy

Associations based on ethnic identities and solidarities are, like those based on kinship, definitionally excluded from most objective-categorical specifications of the civil society concept. This is not so much because they fall outside the public domain as because their mode of engagement with the state is not considered constructive and because they are held to promote parochial rather than cross-cutting social solidarities (Chazan 1991, 290). An ethnic subnational monarchy like that of Buganda would seem to be an even more unlikely candidate for inclusion in "civil society," because it poses a potential direct challenge to the legitimacy of the national state, and because monarchy itself is generally presumed to be an entirely undemocratic institution.

I will not dispute these characterizations directly; the undemocratic and divisive potential of ethnicity and royalism are real enough. Yet the a priori exclusion of these axes of solidarity from efforts to imagine a more fruitful relationship between state and society in Africa seems to stem from another problematic assumption, ultimately traceable to modernization theory.[10] Just as the domain of kinship was narrowed to the nuclear family with the transition to capitalism and liberal democracy in western Europe, so regional loyalties were replaced during this same period with national affinities, rendering hereditary forms of status and authority anachronistic or marginal.[11] The standard applications of the civil society concept seem to presume a comparable simultaneity, virtually a logical entailment, of all of these transformations in a "modernizing" Africa.

Let me start from a different assumption. Due to the intentional entrenchment of ethnic identities by the colonial powers, as well as the failure of most postcolonial African states to win the stable affective allegiance of their subjects, it seems likely that the salience of ethnic bonds and solidarities is not going to disappear or even weaken significantly in Africa in the foreseeable culture.[12] Under this assumption, it becomes entirely unenlightening to simply relegate ethnic solidarities to an "uncivil," and therefore unanalyzed, domain. If ethnicity-based solidarities and associations are likely to remain a central element of the organizational sector that articulates state and society in Africa, then the analytical task will be to try and understand the conditions under which they can perform this mediating role constructively and the circumstances under which they become divisive and destructive.[13]

At the level of practical politics, this is the task with which the current Ugandan government, faced with inconveniently persistent Ganda ethnopolitical aspirations, has been wrestling since 1986. Whatever the demerits of the semifederal system under which the relationship between Buganda and Uganda was framed at independence in 1962, subsequent attempts to fragment and disempower the kingdom, beginning with its abolition by Obote in 1966–67, had by the 1980s proven disastrously destabilizing. Upon coming to power in 1986, Museveni and the NRM found themselves in a quandary. Having fought a protracted guerrilla war in north-central Buganda with the help of rural Baganda, they owed a considerable debt to this population and relied upon its support for their continued legitimacy. Yet, embracing an uncompromisingly modernist Marxist ideology, they took a sharply derisive view of such "feudal" survivals as monarchy.

After freezing the issue long enough to determine that there did exist an enduring popular royalism in Buganda, the NRM moved toward a policy of strategic accommodation with the royalists in the early 1990s, culminating in the restoration of the kingship in 1993. The political forces and calculations underlying this process have been complex, but one significant strand has been the government's effort to locate and cultivate those elements of the Baganda political and cultural elite capable of channeling Ganda ethnopolitical identity and aspirations toward a stable alliance with the state—to find or create, as it were, "civil" interlocutors among the champions of Ganda ethnicity and monarchy. They chose at first to conduct their dialogue primarily with the association of clan heads, later engaging the heir to the royal throne, Ronald Mutebi. With his coronation came the unofficial reconstitution of the

Buganda parliament *(Lukiiko)*, which has emerged as an influential political force in Buganda and a focus for the articulation of ethno-national demands.[14]

The ultimate outcome of the NRM's strategy of ethnic accommodation is not yet clear, but what is significant in this context is that the regime has placed its faith in a hereditary ruler as the most promising candidate to help consolidate a more productive relationship with a major ethnic group long alienated from the Ugandan state. The immediate effect was to consolidate the NRM-Buganda alliance. In the March 1994 elections for the Constituent Assembly to create Uganda's new constitution, the NRM won a solid majority of seats in Buganda.[15] Despite subsequent attempts by Ganda nationalists to mobilize ethnic and royalist sentiment against the NRM in connection with the failure to achieve a restoration of Buganda's federal status in the new constitution, a surprisingly large majority of Baganda voted for President Museveni in the presidential election of May 1996. Since then, the alliance has deteriorated as a result of intransigence on both sides over the administrative coordination of the Buganda districts and a government-sponsored land reform program. Nonetheless, Buganda remains engaged in Ugandan politics in a way that it was not during much of the earlier postcolonial period.

If it is thus empirically the case that traditional, ethnically based political institutions provide at least the potential for a positive articulation of state and society, then the exclusion of such institutions from the definition of civil society does not seem particularly helpful. What we need instead is a better understanding of their constructive potential.[16]

Local Government

Like associations and solidarities based on kinship and ethnicity, the system of local government by elective Local Councils (LCs) introduced in Uganda since 1986 would fail to qualify for inclusion under the prevailing conceptions of civil society. This is because the definition explicitly excludes associations linked to or dependent upon the state, and the LC system is an institutional creation of the Ugandan state. Any inquiry into the prospects for democracy and political renewal derived from the civil society paradigm would therefore tend to downplay or ignore the LCs, even though they now constitute the most important associational arena outside the religious sphere in much of rural Uganda, and, potentially, the strongest institutional impetus toward democratization and the reconstruction of state-society relations.

The LCs (known until 1995 as Resistance Councils) were initially a structure of governance improvised during the 1981–86 guerrilla war in rural areas controlled by the NRM. The basic unit is the village council composed of all adult residents, who elect an executive committee (LC1) consisting of nine specified posts: chair, vice chair, general secretary, and secretaries for finance, information, women, youth, mass mobilization, and security. With the NRM victory the system was instituted throughout Uganda and elaborated into an indirectly elected hierarchy of councils and committees. All of the LC1 executive committees in a parish thus form a parish (LC2) council to elect an LC2 executive committee, the LC2 executives in a subcounty join to elect a subcounty (LC3) executive committee, and so on through the county and district levels.[17] The LC executives have taken over many of the functions, including dispute resolution, of the local chiefs, who were appointed and controlled through the civil service. Executive committees and their chairs are also subject to recall by their constituents. By comparison with any previous system of local government in Uganda, as well as with most others in postcolonial Africa, the LC system constitutes a major qualitative shift toward popular political participation and democratization.[18]

Although the LCs are undeniably part of the structure of local government, it would be misleading to categorize them without further qualification as either belonging to or dominated by the state. Villagers themselves, at least in Buganda, do not generally view them this way.[19] In speaking of the LC1 and LC2 executive committees, they do not refer to them as "government" *(gavumenti)*, nor do they spontaneously use the verb "to rule" *(kufuga)* in relation to them. LC chairs are not usually referred to as chiefs *(baami)*, despite the chieflike functions they perform. These lower-level LCs are quite explicitly conceived as a form of local self-rule, by contrast with the rule of chiefs who, since the abolition of the kingdom in 1967, have been imposed from above.[20]

These local conceptions of the LCs can be confirmed in some measure by examining the actual functioning of the lower-level (LC1-LC3) committees. Despite the standard form ostensibly imposed on them by the legislation under which they were created, lower-level LCs are highly variable in form and content. For instance, out of the seven LC1s constituting an LC2 in Nangabo subcounty in Mpigi District, which I surveyed in August 1995, only one was described by the LC2 chair as "very active." Another had been reduced by attrition to the chair and general secretary, who recruited local "elders" to help them resolve court cases when necessary. A third had been defunct for some time following a major land dispute and was reconstituted through a by-election while I was there. All of this despite the best efforts of a very active, well-educated, and well-organized LC2 executive, who seemed to be doing as much as could be expected to mobilize the LC1s below them. A similar unevenness characterized the lower-level LCs at the two field sites where I conducted research in 1992–93.[21]

While these findings are somewhat disheartening in one respect, they also disprove the assumption that the lower-level LCs function as organs of the state. In fact, where they are not locally legitimate they virtually cease to exist. Where they are active, moreover, it is not because they are executing state directives or have access to central resources. In fact, I found that virtually none of the LC1 activities in this area consisted of the implementation of directives from above, and that where such directives did exist, their implementation was extremely inconsistent. The one "very active" LC1 in this parish, for instance, oriented its activities around the operation of a bore-hole (the only one in the parish) and the management of proceeds from the sale of water to neighboring villages.

Among the achievements most often cited by members of the LCs I surveyed were the improvement and construction of roads on a private contract basis, the construction of a medical dispensary and a communal pit latrine at the local trading center, the resolution of long-standing village disputes, and the provision of local security. While the enhancement of their security function was perhaps the closest thing to the implementation of a state directive I came across, it is a rather ambiguous case in this regard. Beginning in late 1994, small rebel groups emerged in Buganda in response to a growing perception of government intransigence vis-à-vis demands for a restoration of the kingdom's federal status under the new constitution that was being drafted by the elected Constituent Assembly. In early 1995 several rural police posts in Buganda were raided, a regional police commander was killed, and a government minister was kidnapped and held hostage for several days by a group of army defectors who proclaimed themselves federalist rebels. These events resulted in an acute sense of national emergency. The government, however, decided not to deploy the national army in Buganda in response to this threat, fearing that such an action would be perceived as a return to the oppressive practices of past regimes. Instead, the government chose to enhance the already existing system of local security maintenance, the Local Defense Units (LDUs), under the control of lower-level LCs. The LDUs had been administratively mandated several years earlier, but, like most state mandates, this one had been very unevenly instituted. According to the minister of internal affairs, quoted in the state-owned *New Vision* newspaper, the government now distributed some 5,000 automatic weapons to the previously underarmed LDUs in Buganda and facilitated their coordination with the understaffed and inefficient rural police (20 June 1995, 28).

This rather courageous policy—an attempt to stem an incipient regional insurrection by arming the very population upon whom the rebels relied to support their cause—succeeded remarkably well. By June 1995, virtually no further rebel activities in Buganda were reported. The LC members I interviewed also spoke of this effort as one of their unqualified successes. But the extent to which this process should be viewed as an incorporation of local organizations into the state—as opposed to a virtual cession by the government of a primary state function to local organs essentially beyond its control—remains an open question. It might be inferred from their closer coordination with the police that the LDUs were brought under tighter state management through this process; yet in the view of my rural contacts, it was, on the contrary, the LDUs that brought some measure of accountability and task-orientation to the notoriously corrupt local police. The LDUs, moreover, are neither recruited nor paid by the state; they are recruited by the LCs and are supported largely by contracting their security services to local traders and shopkeepers. Like the lower-level LCs, they tend to be viewed by local residents as organs of the local community rather than organs of the state.

Analytically, what is at stake here is the boundary between state and society. The difficulties I have highlighted in attempting to categorize the lower-level LCs according to this dichotomy indicate that the objective-categorical conception of civil society provides an inadequate framework, in this context, for drawing such a boundary. The civil society conception seems to presuppose that state and society are, or at least should be, distinct and clearly bounded institutional domains. Yet a recently influential Foucauldian approach to this issue (Mitchell 1991) argues that the clarity of the state-society boundary is itself an ideological effect produced by the state; that, indeed, it is one of the primary ideological projects of the modern state to produce this illusion of separation and boundedness. In fact, the origins of the very conception of "society" can be seen as historically bound up with the European transition from absolutist monarchies to liberal nation-states (Habermas [1962] 1989; Wolf 1988; Gordon 1994). Prior to this transition, little if any room existed for a distinction between state and society under the complex system of graded and personalized feudal sovereignty in medieval Europe (Skinner 1989). By the same token, despite the high degree of administrative centralization achieved in precolonial Buganda, the delegation of power from the king had no clear boundaries, shading through chains of descending clientage into the broader sphere of local authority relations at its lower reaches.

There is certainly some truth to the claim that the European nation-state form has been imposed upon Africa during the past century, first through colonial rule and then through a process of decolonization governed by a global order in which nation-statehood is mandatory (Davidson 1992). But colonial attempts to bureaucratize and rationalize (i.e., depersonalize) chiefly authority were uneven in both their implementation and their effects.[22] And if postcolonial African states sought initially to consolidate and enlarge a distinct institutional domain of state operation on something like a modern European model, they have not generally succeeded. The centralization of authority has been systematically misconstrued as a deepening of state power (Wunsch and Olowu 1990), and efforts to extend state control and manufacture clearer boundaries between state and society have been consistently subverted by the "capture" of state agents by local social forces, and the noncooperation of local populations.[23] Institutions like the LCs in Uganda therefore mark a partial return to an earlier model of relations between state and society, where little effort is made to enforce a distinct boundary between them, and there is a pragmatic acceptance of graded levels of power radiating outward from the state.[24]

The Ugandan state has had to confront, perhaps even more dramatically than other African counterparts, its inability to perform many of the functions that an earlier generation of leaders had expected of independent African states. The LC system has provided the NRM with a means of transferring many of these functions and responsibilities back to local populations in a moderately coordinated and coherent manner.[25] It has also made it possible, to some degree, to disguise this abandonment of state functions as a democratic reform of local government and decentralization of state power. For the NRM's commitment to the LC system and its democratizing potential has undeniably been less vigorous than many observers were initially inclined to hope (e.g., Burkey 1991).[26] Whatever the level of their genuine democratic intent, it has been combined, in this context at least, with the urge to rationalize their own relative powerlessness, and with the pragmatic need to develop less ambitious strategies of state power, involving a graded rather than a bounded relationship between state and society.

Thus, what I have been calling the objective-categorical conception of civil society relies upon an excessively sharp distinction between state and society derived from a particular phase of European history—a distinction that parallels the public/private dichotomy that derives, as I noted earlier, from the same historical source. These weaknesses underline the fact that the conception is generally used in a radically ahistorical sense in Africanist academic discourse. Lack of attention to the particular temporal and cultural context in which the concept first emerged has led to insufficient caution in generalizing it beyond that context and to a corresponding disregard of the particularities of the new contexts to which it is applied.

Prospects for an Anthropology of Civil Society

Despite my concerns about the applicability of the European-derived concept of civil society to Africa, I would stop short of denying the concept any generalizability on the basis of its European derivation. Rather, I would insist that when concepts derived from Western historical experience are extended to other contexts, a rigorous and ongoing vigilance must be exercised with regard to their limitations. Such vigilance has been lacking in much of the recent literature that applies the idea of civil society to issues of African state formation and democracy.

What might a more careful and context-sensitive application of the civil society problematic to the African context look like? The effort could fruitfully begin with a return to the context of the concept's emergence in early modern Europe, and more specifically with a focus on the lexical shift from "civility" to "civil society."

The concept of civil society was not a direct product of the discourse of civility in the European eighteenth century. On the contrary, the new term was one of many signs and consequences of the declining prominence of that earlier discourse as a locus of sociopolitical conception and debate. Civility, per se, as Elias ([1939] 1978, 53–70) has shown, had its heyday during the ascendancy of absolutist monarchy in Europe in the sixteenth to eighteenth centuries. It referred inseparably both to standards of personal conduct (manners, good breeding) and to modes of polity and governance (citizenship, political order). Its salience declined in the eighteenth century in tandem with the emergence of a new set of sociopolitical polarities: between state and society, between public and private domains, and between collective and individual goods. In its place arose new terms such as "civilization" (Elias [1939] 1978, 40–50), "society" (Gordon 1994), "the public sphere" (Habermas [1962] 1989), and "civil society," each of which gained prominence in connection with the efforts of the bourgeoisie to assert greater autonomy from the state. Seligman (1992) has argued that the modern concept of civil society arose in the late eighteenth century as part of an attempt within the Scottish Enlightenment by Adam Ferguson and Adam Smith to resolve the tensions emerging out of this new set of sociopolitical polarities.

Thus, whereas civility was founded on a unitary conception of political society as equally encompassing governance and manners, state and society, civil society was based precisely on a presumed division between these two domains. Despite borrowing some of the connotational resonance of civility, the civil society concept could only be formed on the basis of the dissolution of the conceptual unity implied by its predecessor.

If civility is implicit in the civil society conception, it is a residual form. No longer a master term uniting a wide range of social and political virtues and behavioral standards, it is the "mere civility" of modern English usage—the minimum of respect that it is decent to show to one's social interlocutors. The *Oxford English Dictionary* thus lists the political senses of "civility," those "connected with citizenship, and civil polity," as obsolete, and gives as one of its current definitions of "civil,"

> Polite or courteous in behaviour to others; sinking, in recent use, to "decently polite", "up to the ordinary or minimum standard of courtesy", or the merely negative sense of "not (actually) rude"; while courteous and polite denote positive qualities. (1989, 255)

This is the minimal civility of mutual tolerance, the somewhat grudging acceptance of social difference and pluralism—a far cry from the high civility of sociopolitical virtue descended from Erasmus.[27]

The attempt to theorize or locate civil society in Africa might begin, then, by specifying the sense in which, and the extent to which, current African realities correspond to the structure of the concept's European emergence. However different African political cultures may be from those in the European lineage, and whatever the internal contradictions of postcolonial African state formation, the modern state form—with its project of bifurcating and articulating the domains of state and society—is certainly now one of the dominant realities on the continent. Markets and commodities, too, with their construction of persons as individualized owners of property and sellers of labor, are well entrenched, if widely contested, in contemporary Africa. Africans are thus coping with local versions of the bifurcations—between public and private, and collective and individual goods, as well as between state and society—out of which the civil society concept first arose in early modern Europe.

It is the African response—and the variety of African responses—to these bifurcations that should be taken as central to the study of civil society in Africa. Africans are resisting, criticizing, and reinflecting these dichotomies in a variety of idioms—idioms, for instance, of political witchcraft (Geschiere 1997), politics of the belly (Bayart 1993), and presidential patriarchy (Schatzberg 1986, 1993), as well as through local appropriations of "democracy" and electoral practice (Miles 1988; Schaffer 1998). In the case I have examined, the idiom of kingship and an innovative form of local governance are being used and reformulated in an effort to develop new and more satisfactory ways to conceive and enact relations between local populations and the state. The formation of voluntary associations that seek to engage the state without aspiring to capture state power may be *one* societal response to the postcolonial African state—but precisely one among *many*. It is through the ethnographic and historical examination of this range of local discourses and practices of state-society bifurcation and articulation that a genuinely anthropological approach to "civil society" in Africa may become possible.

Notes

1. See Cohen and Arato 1992 (chap. 1) for an account of this reemergence; also Taylor 1990; and Seligman 1992 for analytical overviews of the history of the concept.

2. Two edited collections are particularly significant here: Rothchild and Chazan 1988; and Harbeson, Rothchild, and Chazan 1994. See also Bratton 1989; and Chazan 1991.

3. Rebel movements remain active in the north, due partly to NRM neglect of the region and partly to Sudanese sponsorship; small rebel groups have operated along Uganda's western border in connection with the collapse of the Mobutu regime in Zaïre and the subsequent instability of the renamed Democratic Republic of Congo.

4. Uganda's five old monarchies (Buganda, Bunyoro, Tooro, Busoga, and Ankole) were abolished by Uganda's first independent president, Milton Obote, in 1967 following a confrontation between his central government and that of Buganda. All but Ankole have been resurrected since 1993, but only in Buganda was there mass public support (Doornbos and Mwesigye 1994). It was by virtue of Buganda's geographical and economic centrality, and the fact that its people constitute the largest of Uganda's

ethnic groups (accounting for roughly 18 percent of the national population), that Baganda royalists were able to persuade the NRM government to negotiate on this issue.

5. Even a suggestive attempt by one of the proponents of the dominant civil society conception to complicate some of its central categories holds fast to "the family boundary" in demarcating the lower limits of civil society, a domain situated "between the household and the state" (Azarya 1994, 94–95).

6. Considerable information regarding the role of the clan heads in precolonial Buganda is available in Roscoe 1911; and Kaggwa 1901, 1905; see also Southwold 1961; and Fallers 1964.

7. Apter 1961 remains the best account of the politics of this period.

8. John Comaroff's (1987) analysis of the domestic and public domains in precolonial Tshidi society provides a particularly salient example, because he argues explicitly that each of these domains is structured by a distinct principle of kin relationship: matrilaterality in one case and affinity in the other.

9. See Habermas [1962] 1989, especially chap. 10.

10. What I mean by "modernization theory" here is not so much the canonical postwar theoretical formulation that went under that heading but rather the widespread and tenacious tendency (upon which that formulation is based) to assume that the particular set of institutional transformations that occurred in Europe since the seventeenth century will all take place in roughly the same form and sequence in the rest of the world as (and if) it is successfully incorporated into the capitalist world economy.

11. This characterization of the Western transition to modernity is of course hopelessly simplistic; the actual interconnections between these historic transformations is vastly more complex—but it is precisely the common assumption of modernity's arrival as a monolithic "package" that I am trying to highlight and criticize here.

12. Again, Ekeh's work (1975, 1990) is relevant here; for Ekeh, the abiding ideological power of kinship is central to the continuing significance of ethnicity. Vail adduces mainly economic reasons for the likelihood that ethnicity will remain salient in southern Africa, and argues that rather than "ignoring them as embarrassing epiphenomena that should long ago have disappeared, . . . it will be necessary for the region's politicians and scholars alike to work towards accommodating ethnicity within these nation states" (1989, 17–18).

13. John Lonsdale (1992, 1994) has done much to advance such an understanding in his sustained exploration of the moral and civic dimension of ethnicity among Kikuyu in Kenya.

14. I provide a detailed account of the restoration process and its aftermath to 1996 in Karlström 1999 (chap. 4).

15. I would by no means deny that the timing of the restoration was rather crassly designed to win Buganda for the NRM in these crucial elections (Regan 1995, 180; Mamdani 1995, 236). Cynical political strategizing at this level does not, however, negate my argument that, in a more general sense, Museveni and the NRM have chosen

a path of ethnic accommodation as the best means of reestablishing Ganda allegiance to the Ugandan state.

16. For a wholeheartedly optimistic evaluation of the potential of traditional political institutions for mediating between nation-states and their component ethnic groups, see Sklar 1993; David Apter (1995) has expressed a somewhat more cautiously sanguine view of the constructive potential of the restored Buganda monarchy.

17. Representatives to the Ugandan parliament, the National Resistance Council (NRC), were also elected in this way until the 1996 direct parliamentary elections.

18. For accounts and evaluations of the RC system, see Burkey 1991; Ddungu 1994; Mamdani 1994, 1995; Barya and Oloka-Onyango 1994; Tidemand 1995; and Golooba-Mutebi 1999.

19. Ottemoeller (1998) shows that the situation is different in northern Uganda, where the NRM regime is viewed with hostility.

20. Chiefs prior to 1967 were not, of course, elected; but although they were appointed from above, they were chosen from among local landowners or elders, and therefore not conceived as imposed upon the local population (Karlström 1996).

21. These field sites were also in Mpigi District, which is one of Uganda's largest, stretching from the area around Kampala, the capital, westward nearly 200 kilometers; I worked in Katabi subcounty, near Entebbe town, and in Ngando subcounty, in the western hinterland of the district.

22. Fallers (1956) provides a classic case study of the contradictions of colonial bureaucratization in the Busoga region of Uganda, which borders Buganda and shares with it a range of political and cultural characteristics. In Buganda the British attempted to transform the higher echelons of chiefship into a civil service, but lower-level offices continued to be held by local landowners or their favored clients.

23. The very absence of anything like a civil society concept in local political discourse might be viewed as evidence of this failure, because, as Cohen and Arato (1992; chap. 1) emphasize, the concept has usually become relevant elsewhere in response to growing social penetration by the state. In Uganda the phrase is used sporadically by elites engaged directly with foreign aid and development agencies, but this usage often displays a misunderstanding of the sense in which it is being used by those agencies; it plays no role in domestic political debate.

24. Gupta (1995, 384) points out the similarly "graded" nature of the state-society boundary at the lower levels of the contemporary Indian civil service. My general argument here about state-society relations in Africa should be distinguished from the claim that the state is an irrelevant or vacant category in contemporary Africa. However far the breakdown of the state-society distinction may go (very far in Nigeria, as Andrew Apter shows in chapter 10 of this volume), the nation-state form remains mandatory in the contemporary world order (Mann 1993), and the conception of the state as the primary arena of competition for power and resources remains firmly implanted in African political cultures (Guyer 1992 on Nigeria; Schatzberg 1988 on Zaïre).

25. Tidemand concludes from his study of the LC system that "the rather large

room of manoeuvre left by the NRM to the [LCs] is the outcome of the distinctive impotence of the Ugandan state apparatus as well as the relative strength of . . . the rural communities" (1995, 174).

26. A more recent decentralization program (Regan 1998) may have somewhat revived this impulse, but the results are not yet well documented.

27. John Hall (1995) emphasizes this minimal form of civility specific to "civil society."

References

Apter, David. 1961. *The Political Kingdom in Uganda.* Princeton: Princeton University Press.

———. 1995. "Democracy for Uganda: A Case for Comparison." *Daedalus* 124 (3): 155–90.

Azarya, Victor. 1994. "Civil Society and Disengagement in Africa." In *Civil Society and the State in Africa,* ed. John W. Harbeson, Donald Rothchild, and Naomi Chazan. Boulder: Lynne Rienner.

Barya, John-Jean, and J. Oloka-Onyango. 1994. *Popular Justice and Resistance Committee Courts in Uganda.* Kampala: Friedrich Ebert Foundation.

Bayart, Jean-François. 1993. *The State in Africa: The Politics of the Belly.* London: Longman.

Bratton, Michael. 1989. "Beyond the State: Civil Society and Associational Life in Africa." *World Politics* 41 (3): 407–30.

Burkey, Ingvild. [1991]. "People's Power in Theory and Practice: The Resistance Council System in Uganda." Unpublished manuscript in the author's possession.

Chazan, Naomi. 1991. "Africa's Democratic Challenge." *World Policy Journal* 9 (2): 279–307.

Cohen, Jean L., and Andrew Arato. 1992. *Civil Society and Political Theory.* Cambridge: MIT Press.

Comaroff, John L. 1987. "*Sui Genderis:* Feminism, Kinship Theory, and Structural 'Domains.'" In *Gender and Kinship: Essays toward a Unified Analysis,* ed. J. F. Collier and S. J. Yanagisako. Stanford: Stanford University Press.

Davidson, Basil. 1992. *The Black Man's Burden: Africa and the Curse of the Nation-State.* New York: Random House.

Ddungu, Expedit. 1994. "Popular Forms and the Question of Democracy: The Case of Resistance Councils in Uganda." In *Uganda: Studies in Living Conditions, Popular Movements, and Constitutionalism,* ed. M. Mamdani and J. Oloka-Onyango. Vienna: Journal für Entwicklungspolitik (JEP) Book Series.

Doornbos, Martin, and Frederick Mwesigye. 1994. "The New Politics of Kingmaking." In *From Chaos to Order: The Politics of Constitution-Making in Uganda,* ed. Holger Bernt Hansen and Michael Twaddle. Kampala: Fountain Publishers; London: J. Currey.

Ekeh, Peter. 1975. "Colonialism and the Two Publics in Africa: A Theoretical Statement." *Comparative Studies in Society and History* 17 (1): 91–112.

———. 1990. "Social Anthropology and Two Contrasting Uses of Tribalism in Africa." *Comparative Studies in Society and History* 32 (4): 660–99.

Elias, Norbert. [1939] 1978. *The History of Manners*, vol. 1, *The Civilizing Process*. Translated by E. Jephcott. Reprint, New York: Pantheon.

Fallers, Lloyd A. 1956. *Bantu Bureaucracy*. Chicago: University of Chicago Press.

Fallers, Lloyd A., ed. 1964. *The King's Men: Leadership and Status in Buganda on the Eve of Independence*. London: Oxford University Press.

Geschiere, Peter. 1997 *The Modernity of Witchcraft: Politics and the Occult in Postcolonial Africa*. Charlottesville: University Press of Virginia.

Golooba-Mutebi, F. 1999. "Decentralization, Democracy and Development Administration in Uganda, 1986–1996: Limits to Popular Participation." Ph.D. diss., University of London.

Goody, Jack. 1976. *Production and Reproduction*. Cambridge: Cambridge University Press.

Gordon, Daniel. 1994. *Citizens without Sovereignty: Equality and Sociability in French Thought, 1670–1789*. Princeton: Princeton University Press.

Gupta, Akhil. 1995. "Blurred Boundaries: The Discourse of Corruption, the Culture of Politics, and the Imagined State." *American Ethnologist* 22 (2): 375–402.

Guyer, Jane I. 1992. "Representation without Taxation: An Essay on Democracy in Rural Nigeria, 1952–1990." *African Studies Review* 35 (1): 41–79.

Habermas, Jürgen. [1962] 1989. *The Structural Transformation of the Public Sphere: An Inquiry into a Category of Bourgeois Society*. Translated by Thomas Burger with Frederick Lawrence. Reprint, Cambridge: MIT Press.

Hall, John A. 1995. "In Search of Civil Society." In *Civil Society: Theory, History, Comparison*, ed. John A. Hall. Cambridge: Polity Press.

Harbeson, John W., Donald Rothchild, and Naomi Chazan, eds. 1994. *Civil Society and the State in Africa*. Boulder: Lynne Rienner.

Kaggwa [Kagwa], Apolo. [1901] 1971. *The Kings of Buganda*. Translated by M. S. M. Kiwanuka. Reprint, Nairobi: East African Publishing House.

———. [1905] 1934. *The Customs of the Baganda*. Translated by E. B. Kalibala. Reprint, New York: Columbia University Press.

Karlström, Mikael. 1996. "Imagining Democracy: Political Culture and Democratization in Buganda." *Africa* 66 (4): 485–505.

———. 1999. "The Cultural Kingdom in Uganda: Popular Royalism and the Restoration of the Buganda Kingship." Ph.D. diss., University of Chicago.

Lonsdale, John. 1992. "The Moral Economy of Mau Mau." In *Unhappy Valley: Conflict in Kenya and Africa*, book 2, *Violence and Ethnicity*, Bruce Berman and John Lonsdale. London: J. Currey; Nairobi: Heinemann Kenya.

———. 1994. "Moral Ethnicity and Political Tribalism." In *Inventions and Boundaries: Historical and Anthropological Approaches to the Study of Ethnicity and National-*

ism, ed. Preben Kaarsholm and Jan Hultin. Roskilde, Denmark: International Development Studies, Roskilde University.

Mamdani, Mahmood. 1994. "Pluralism and the Right of Association." In *Uganda: Studies in Living Conditions, Popular Movements, and Constitutionalism,* ed. M. Mamdani and J. Oloka-Onyango. Vienna: Journal für Entwicklungspolitik (JEP) Book Series.

———. 1995. "The Politics of Democratic Reform in Uganda." In *Uganda: Landmarks in Rebuilding a Nation,* ed. P. Langseth, J. Katorobo, E. Brett, and J. Munene. Kampala: Fountain Publishers.

Mann, Michael. 1993. "Nation-States in Europe and Other Continents: Diversifying, Developing, Not Dying." *Daedalus* 122 (2): 115–40.

Miles, William. 1988. *Elections in Nigeria: A Grassroots Perspective.* Boulder: Lynne Rienner.

Mitchell, Timothy. 1991. "The Limits of the State: Beyond Statist Approaches and Their Critics." *American Political Science Review* 85 (1): 77–96.

Ottemoeller, Dan. 1998. "Popular Perceptions of Democracy: Elections and Attitudes in Uganda." *Comparative Political Studies* 31 (1): 98–124.

Oxford English Dictionary (2d ed.). 1989. Oxford: Oxford University Press.

Putnam, Robert. 1993. *Making Democracy Work: Civic Traditions in Modern Italy.* Princeton: Princeton University Press.

———. 1995. "Bowling Alone: America's Declining Social Capital." *Journal of Democracy* 6 (1): 65–78.

Regan, Anthony J. 1995. "Constitutional Reform and the Politics of the Constitution in Uganda: A New Path to Constitutionalism?" In *Uganda: Landmarks in Rebuilding a Nation,* ed. P. Langseth, J. Katorobo, E. Brett, and J. Munene. Kampala: Fountain Publishers.

———. 1998. "Decentralization Policy: Reshaping State and Society." In *Developing Uganda,* ed. Holger Bernt Hansen and Michael Twaddle. Athens: Ohio University Press; Oxford: James Curry; Kampala: Fountain Publishers; Nairobi: East African Educational Publishers.

Roscoe, John. 1911. *The Baganda: An Account of Their Native Customs and Beliefs.* London: Macmillan.

Rothchild, Donald, and Naomi Chazan, eds. 1988. *The Precarious Balance: State and Society in Africa.* Boulder: Westview Press.

Schaffer, Frederic C. 1998. *Democracy in Translation: Understanding Politics in an Unfamiliar Culture.* Ithaca: Cornell University Press.

Schatzberg, Michael G. 1986. "The Metaphors of Father and Family." In *The Political Economy of Cameroon,* ed. Michael G. Schatzberg and I. William Zartman. New York: Praeger.

———. 1988. *The Dialectics of Oppression in Zaire.* Bloomington: Indiana University Press.

———. 1993. "Power, Legitimacy and 'Democratisation' in Africa." *Africa* 63 (4): 445–61.

Seligman, Adam B. 1992. *The Idea of Civil Society.* Princeton: Princeton University Press.

Skinner, Quentin. 1989. "The State." In *Political Innovation and Conceptual Change,* ed. T. Ball, J. Farr, and R. L. Hanson. Cambridge: Cambridge University Press.

Sklar, Richard L. 1993. "African Frontier for Political Science." In *Africa and the Disciplines: The Contributions of Research in Africa to the Social Sciences and Humanities,* ed. R. H. Bates, V. Y. Mudimbe, and J. O'Barr. Chicago: University of Chicago Press.

Southwold, Martin. 1961. *Bureaucracy and Chiefship in Buganda* (East African Studies, no. 14). Kampala: East African Institute of Social Research.

Taylor, Charles. 1990. "Modes of Civil Society." *Public Culture* 3 (1): 95–118.

Tidemand, Per. 1995. "The Resistance Councils in Uganda: A Study of Rural Politics and Popular Democracy in Africa." Ph.D. diss., Roskilde University, Denmark.

Vail, Leroy. 1989. "Introduction: Ethnicity in Southern African History." In *The Creation of Tribalism in Southern Africa,* ed. Leroy Vail. London: Currey; Berkeley: University of California Press.

Wolf, Eric R. 1988. "Inventing Society." *American Ethnologist* 15 (4): 752–61.

Wunsch, James S., and Dele Olowu, eds. 1990. *The Failure of the Centralized State: Institutions and Self-Governance in Africa.* Boulder: Westview Press.

5

Colonial Constructions: Historicizing Debates on Civil Society in Africa

William Cunningham Bissell

IN THE WAKE OF the democratization movements of the early 1990s, civil society was suddenly rediscovered as the "missing link" in the analysis of African politics. As one commentator claimed, theoretical inattention to civil society "has been reflected in less-than-successful policy formation by African governments and donor development assistance agencies" (Harbeson 1994, 3). A renewed focus on this critical domain, it was argued, could go a long way toward explaining African problems of political and socioeconomic development. Whether such a move might occlude more than it explains is precisely the problem that concerns me here. For what happens when civil society becomes unmoored from its very specific history in the West and gets recast as the "essential feature of any democracy" (Hardt 1995, 27)? Deployed in this normative manner, the concept becomes a universal condition of possibility, promoting a neo-evolutionary ranking of polities according to their degree of "civic development." Once established, this framework makes it all too easy to condemn African "cultures" and "societies" for their failure to measure up. Such an approach precludes any consideration of the fact that civil society in the West was only made possible by numerous practices of exclusion (Fraser 1992; Ryan 1992; Eley 1992). It also ignores considerable evidence that the restructurings of late capital in its globalized dimension have undermined the analytic foundations and political forms of liberal democracy, rendering the concept of civil society "empty and ineffectual" (Hardt 1995, 27; Yúdice 1995). Furthermore, in regard to Africa, it forecloses the question of history

The research and writing of this essay was made possible by generous grants from the Fulbright-I.I.E. program and the National Science Foundation, which I gratefully acknowledge. Earlier versions were presented both in Chicago (1996) and at the 40th Annual Meetings of the African Studies Association, as part of the panel "Histories in the Present: Memory and the Remaking of the Past on Zanzibar and Mafia" (1997). I am indebted to the panelists and participants in both sessions, and especially want to thank John Comaroff, Ralph Austen, Laura Fair, and Jonathon Glassman for their insightful comments and criticisms.

itself: what shape might civil society assume in social formations that have been produced, to a greater or lesser extent, within the context of colonialism?

This normative understanding of civil society has been echoed in recent debates over the restoration of urban Zanzibar, which dehistoricize the problem of a civic public in strikingly similar ways. Conservationists engaged in reviving the city stressed the need to "save" it as a unique cultural repository and historical resource for all Zanzibaris. Yet they had great difficulty in locating the "community" that they labored to serve, complaining often about the lack of popular participation in their efforts. In the face of public indifference or worse, planners and officials blamed Zanzibari culture rather than confront the ways in which the planning process worked to marginalize and exclude the local populace. They depicted the issue as one of ignorance, speaking of the need to "educate" Zanzibaris to value and preserve "their" heritage. This patronizing idiom will be all too familiar to students of African colonial history. Above all, it underscores the necessity of historicizing current debates on civil society and the public sphere.

Conservation is merely the latest incarnation in a long history of urban interventions dating back to the early years of the century. British colonial officials labored over many years to create "the City Perfect" (Pearce 1920, 212), capping off their efforts with ambitious master plans in 1922 and 1958. But colonial designs were not simply imposed by the state on the space of the city, reworking the whole in its own image. Although successive administrations claimed that they had such power, their urban plans were more remarkable for their failures rather than successes. Often they remained little more than projections on paper, consuming huge amounts of bureaucratic time and resources as authorities repeatedly failed to rationalize and reorder the urban milieu.[1] Rather than critically scrutinizing their own top-down, exclusionary, and statist approach, colonial officials typically attributed their difficulties to the intransigence of local cultures. Much like contemporary conservationists, they alleged that ingrained "native" practices were the cause of continuing urban problems, especially in regard to matters of petty hygiene. This was at once ironic and hypocritical, as the colonial state went to great lengths to *avoid* handing over any power to locally controlled municipal bodies; in pursuing a classic policy of divide and rule, British officials fragmented the public sphere, seizing upon existing lines of difference to discourage popular mobilizations.

By focusing here on a singular example drawn from colonial Zanzibar—the struggle for control of Mnazi Mmoja, a large plot of land on the edge of Stone Town—I seek to show how the "public" served as a complex figure for colonial authorities to deploy as a means of maintaining control over the distribution of resources, access, and power to communities they assiduously worked to shape as fragmented entities. Invocations of the "public" served to disempower these communities, portraying them as particularistic and self-seeking in their demands, while allowing the colonial government to present itself as standing above the fray, as interested in the common good, and as representative of the whole. It is this political archaeology, this history, that lies behind the current moment, the postcolonial "crisis" of civil society. By analyzing how recent debates are, in a sense, colonial constructs, I hope to demonstrate the futility of thinking about civil society and the public sphere in an ahistorical vein.

Ceremonies, Sites, and the Colonial Public: From Pearce Pavilion to the Peace Museum

In February 1919, at a convocation presided over by the British resident, Major Francis Barrow Pearce, the local Representative Sports Committee (RSC) on Zanzibar requested a grant of government land in Recreation Park on which to construct a sports pavilion ("Pearce Pavilion"), paid for by community subscription. The resident initially embraced the proposal, promising to grant the land, some official funds, and a personal contribution. But his enthusiasm for the project waned somewhat as its public character came into question: complaints arose that the Representative Sports Committee was hardly representative at all, consisting of the heads of "Asiatic" (i.e., Indian) sports clubs. The idea of providing government land and funds to support a "public" project that would be controlled by private interests struck some lower-level officials as neither politic nor sporting. As the supervisor of sport later opined, the "originators of the scheme" were devoid of public spirit, interested solely in promoting an "Indian club on the lines of the European 'Mnazi Moja' [Sports Club]."[2]

Colonial officials attempted to salvage the scheme by modifying it in two ways. First, they sought to enlarge the membership of the committee so that it might seem more representative. Even so, their conception of a broader "public" only went so far as to include elite members of various "communities" religiously and racially conceived: they stipulated that the RSC should consist of delegates from the Arabs, Europeans, Bohoras, Goans, Hindus, Ithnasheris, Ismailis, Memons, and Parsees.[3] Second, officials also amended the draft lease controlling use of the proposed site to make sure that the pavilion would be open to "*all* Indian and Arab residents."[4] Despite the narrow basis of these inclusions, the added conditions imposed by government were resented by the committee, and protracted negotiations delayed the project well into 1920. Finally, on 1 September of that year, the chief secretary wrote to what he now called the Indian Representative Sports Committee. The government's offer of land had now lapsed, he said, and could only be renewed on condition that the committee "endeavor to definitely ascertain the opinion of the general public on this project & also whether they are ready to raise the money necessary for a suitable building."[5] A member of the RSC tartly replied that "it was rather late in the day now to reascertain the opinion of the general public on this project as the authorities know perfectly well that the only thing left to be done is the signing of the lease by the parties."[6] Nevertheless, the committee went ahead and surveyed the "public," albeit in a typically colonial form: by corresponding with and asking for support from the Indian National Association, the head of the Ithnasheria community, the Goan Sports Club, the Parsee Cricket Club, Hindoo Gymkhana, and the Hindu Cricket Club. While all concerned echoed their support and willingness to subscribe funds, this "public" survey did little to ease doubts. As the supervisor of sport later complained, "from a purely Indian Scheme it was gradually modified until it became a 'Public' one controlled by Asiatics. . . . It would be most unwise and unjust—in my opinion—for Government to allow any one or various sections of the inhabitants to build and control a Sports or Social Club in which all who are permitted to utilize Recreation Park, would not, in certain circumstances, have an equal right."[7] While the idea for the pavilion was repeatedly postponed and revived between 1919 and 1926, these objections were never surmounted and the structure was never begun.

This minor dispute reflects the degree to which "in a town so cosmopolitan as Zanzibar the task of providing games facilities for so large a number of Sectional clubs is by no means a light one."[8] While the author of this statement, the chief secretary, may have recognized the difficulty of this task, he offered no explanation for how such a cosmopolitan milieu as urban Zanzibar had managed to produce so many narrowly based sports clubs. Official recognition of the problem was highly ironic at several levels, not least because the division of the urban public into sectional, bounded interests was largely a colonial creation in the first place. Standing above a fray of their own making, pretending to defend the general interests of a public that they worked to deny, colonial officials refused to acknowledge the consequences of their own practices, projecting blame instead on various groups held to be insular, self-seeking, and narrow. The Indians indeed may well have been seeking to follow European precedent, creating a sports club on the lines of the European-controlled Mnazi Moja club. Yet the lesson drawn from this was not that Europeans were setting a bad example but rather that the Indians should be denigrated both as self-seeking and second-class mimics. The pretension of the colonial government to represent the public was further revealed to be hollow insofar as it sought only to ensure that the pavilion would be open to "all *Indian* and *Arab* residents," excluding thereby the majority African population from any place in the public.

Colonial policy created and dealt with a public carved into communities: throughout the period prior to World War II, official efforts to gauge local opinion, or to include token representation on governing boards and committees, were always channeled through racial or religious associations and clubs. The earliest of these were the Indian National Association and the Arab Association, dominated by prominent merchants and landowners. The "communities" were not created out of whole cloth by the British, products of false consciousness foisted upon a gullible population. From at least the nineteenth century onwards, communal identifications certainly existed on Zanzibar based on localities of origin and religious orientation. These identifications could and did serve as the basis of social solidarities during the precolonial period, but they were not exclusive boundaries of social action and coexisted with other, more diverse, practices. What colonial policy worked to do was to seize on these identifications and fix them into rigid domains of political and social organization. In particular, colonial officials went to great lengths to ensure that access to the state by subjects would only be recognized in terms of racially or religiously based "communities," headed by elites.

The same was true when the colonial state sought to contact the "public," which it routinely did only through the "heads of communities."[9] Although there are many examples, the construction of the Beit el Amani (Peace Museum) in the early 1920s serves as an apt illustration. Designed by John H. Sinclair (a long-serving official who later became resident) in the "Saracenic" style, a British vision of what Muslim monumental architecture should be, the building was intended to commemorate the end of World War I. More than a museum, it was primarily intended to serve as an "Institute of Native Development"—which its colonial founders, led by Dr. A. H. Spurrier, saw as involving the paternalistic role of "fostering native crafts and industries" and spreading "an active propaganda . . . against disease of every kind in humans, animals, and the vegetable kingdom."[10] The colonial construction of the public purpose of this building was essentially to co-opt it as the propaganda wing of the Public Health Department (popularly known as the "Rat Office," or Ofisi ya Panya, due to the dissections carried out there as antiplague measures).

The public nature of the Peace Museum was further belied by the manner of its construction and dedication. The building was erected by a quasi-official committee and was completed by the colonial government when private funds ran out. The General Committee of Peace Celebrations included a "subcommittee to collect subscriptions," consisting of well-connected representatives of the Hindus, Ismailis, Ithnasheria, Bohoras, and two Arabs; clearly, the role of the "public" was to channel donations to colonial purposes by means of "community appeals." Again, the exclusion of any African participation was simply taken for granted. At the ritual dedication of the structure on Armistice Day in 1925, only the august heads of these "communities" were allowed on the ceremonial platform to greet the sultan along with high colonial officials.[11] The "general public" was cordoned off below and prohibited from entering the museum until after the dignitaries had toured it and departed.[12]

The opening of the Peace Museum echoes in many respects the function of the imperial durbars and assemblages in India so richly analyzed by Bernard Cohn (1983), revealing the conjuncture between ritual displays of power, representations of authority, and the politics of colonial space. As one example drawn from many, the dedication of the structure succinctly illustrates the way in which officials on Zanzibar routinely sought to keep the general public well off the colonial stage, treating it as an inchoate mass. At moments of collective spectacle, the public would be summoned to serve as audience to imperial displays, bearing mute witness to the ceremonial posturings of power. Otherwise, it had no role or place. As "generalized subjects," Zanzibaris were excluded by the colonial state, never being recognized or granted official standing. But if they mobilized against their disempowerment and began to organize along accepted communal lines to gain representation and voice, therein lay the trap. For the British would then simply disparage such groups as parochial and self-seeking, invoking a fictive "public interest" to disable the claims of any single community.

The contours of this colonial double bind can be seen in numerous domains. However, one arena in particular deserves to be explored in greater detail: the struggle over Mnazi Mmoja ("one coconut tree"), a large tract of urban ground held by the Ismaili religious council and used by members of the sect for ceremonial and burial purposes. Gaining control of unbuilt land was an early and enduring preoccupation of the colonial regime, especially through the manipulation of religious trusts *(wakfs),* as both Laura Fair (1994) and Garth Myers (1993) have recently argued. Holding this particular piece of property came to be seen as crucial by authorities largely due to late-nineteenth-century sanitary preoccupations common to colonial cities elsewhere. As Mnazi Mmoja was the largest open space adjoining densely populated urban areas, it was held to be the "lungs" of the city, essential for ventilation and public recreation (a social rather than merely physical kind of "venting"). The fight over the disposition of this space offers a particularly rich perspective on the constitution of a colonial public, providing insight into disputes over community rights and governmental powers, the ownership of land and law.

"Necessity Knew No Law": Clubs, Communities, and the Colonial Double Bind in Mnazi Mmoja

The contestation over Mnazi Mmoja, a large and valuable neck of land between the sea and the creek on the edge of Stone Town, was exceedingly complex and protracted. Eventually, the struggle became more than merely local in scope, widening to include the Aga Khan (the Ismaili spiritual leader), the Government of India, and the Foreign Office. From the 1890s well into the 1920s, the colonial government repeatedly attempted to wrest the property out of Ismaili control, abrogating previous agreements and provoking vigorous protests. The first attempt came in 1894, soon after the formal imposition of protectorate rule. As the new regime was casting about for a pretext to seize Mnazi Mmoja, the recently installed consul general, Arthur H.

Hardinge, had little grasp of the facts of the case. He was compelled to write to the distinguished former consul, Sir John Kirk, who had retired to the English countryside after twenty years of service on Zanzibar. In the letter, Hardinge inquired whether any evidence existed concerning the history of ownership, proposing two ways by which the British might advance a claim on the site. First, he propounded the theory that the land had originally belonged to a British Indian subject who died intestate, and hence should be administered by the British consul; second, he suggested that the sultan could be compelled to assert his rights to Mnazi Mmoja, which then would be taken over by the protectorate government. In his reply, Kirk held out little hope that either of these ploys might suffice. He stated that the sultan had no legal claim whatsoever, as the real estate had long ago passed from his jurisdiction. Nor did he believe that the British could acquire it for themselves: "If a British Indian dies intestate and without heirs generally speaking his estate would fall to the British Crown but if he were a member of the Khojas [Ismailis] I suspect the Aga Khan might sustain a good claim anyhow it would be a delicate question. But this question does not arise as the property passed to the Jamaat [Ismaili religious council] before we asserted ourselves in Zanzibar and when the bulk of the Khojas were not under British law."[13]

The ambiguity surrounding ownership here was typical of Zanzibar, especially in the domain of religious trusts. From the imposition of Omani rule in the 1830s, the sultan asserted his authority over unoccupied land in accordance with Islamic law. Most of this property, especially in the peri-urban areas, was allocated to his followers and family, who settled their clients—ex-slaves and dependents—on it under usufruct tenure, allowing them to build or plant and enjoy the fruits thereof. Wealthy patrons did not need to incur personal expense to develop the sites granted them; they could simply deploy their title as a source of social capital, enhancing their status and cultivating loyalty by (re)distributing rights of occupation and use (Fair 1994). Formal documents detailing these arrangements were often nonexistent, and the passage of time only complicated matters further. Well into the twentieth century, no central registry existed, deeds were a rarity, and plots were typically demarcated by features of the landscape (usually trees) that were difficult to trace over time. Colonial officials found it possible to exploit these ambiguities as they themselves sought to seize open land and convert religious trusts—on which the poor customarily lived rent free—into private property. Note how Hardinge used the lack of legal proof of ownership as a wedge to advance a counterclaim: the consul general had no evidence that it was any *particular* British Indian subject who had deeded the land to the Ismailis, but he took the absence of a will on the part of the Ismailis as an excuse to make such a claim.

In the same letter, Kirk further asserted that, when he arrived in Zanzibar in 1866, he "found Khoja [Ismaili] rights more or less acknowledged." Although no record existed as to how the Ismailis came to possess the property "as owners or trustees," they held it "more or less" and enjoyed "full rights." In spite of this, Kirk took it upon himself to make incursions upon these "full rights" in ways that later regimes would repeatedly copy. As he told it, the Ismailis were in "undisputed possession" of a block of land used as a cemetery, a mosque site, and a mortuary chapel with fenced-in vegetable and flower gardens; a profusion of tombs and sacred structures testified to long-term, widely recognized communal use. But there was a much larger contiguous piece of land, consisting of almost the entire neck between the foreshore and the creek, to which the "Khojas" also laid claim. "These claims however were less evident seeing that the sect did not use this portion for burial of their creed people."

Kirk here enunciates the principle that would later be used to erode Ismaili rights: because they had not built upon all the land in their possession, their ownership could be disputed. The fact that the real estate was to be held in trust for a future expansion of the graveyard or for other religious purposes made no difference. If the property was "open," then to him it was open for the taking. When serving as British consul during the cholera epidemic of 1870, Kirk had already given expression to this view, intervening in the question of the larger neck of land. Two American sailors who had succumbed to the epidemic were summarily buried there by their own consul. The Ismailis, feeling that their long acknowledged right to be consulted over the use of their graveyard had been violated, reacted with outrage, threatening to disinter the bodies. Kirk insisted that they be allowed to remain. He cited the earlier instance of a French consul, who had received permission from the Ismailis to bury his concubine there and erect a tomb. Kirk noted that the Ismailis were always accommodating and "never refused if application was made. No application was made in the case of the American seamen, but as we were then burying at the rate of 400 a day I held that necessity knew no law. . . . Before the cholera epidemic had ended the whole of the ridge down to the water's edge from end to end was covered with graves of natives chiefly slaves etc. There was not a yard of ground that had not been turned up so that the whole looked a sweet-potatoe garden."

Kirk's interventions had not rested with his summary seizure of the ridge as a burial ground. In fact, the Ismailis' willingness to accommodate the needs of others, just as long as their authority was recognized, worked further to their disadvantage. As the former British consul observed to Hardinge, because "part of the cemetery was left so long open to native burial and to burial of Europeans under special permission . . . I held myself justified in regarding the Khoja title as limited after so long usage." Kirk informed the Ismailis that he held their right to the land as limited, a threat later realized. Having rationalized his interference, he soon became suspicious that others were hatching plots to grab the property away from him. In the letter, he alleged that the sultan at the time, Seyyid Barghash,

> formed a plan to seize the whole of the ridge in order to erect on it a row of shops and houses. The plan he took was this, he got some poor people, lepers, to erect a hut, then to enclose a garden. These lepers became a nuisance sitting by the roadside by which all the vegetables and shamba [farm] produce passed. This I regarded as dangerous and tried to have the lepers kept within their compound. The Sultan one day soon after that had a large part of the ridge marked out for building plots. I most strongly objected on public grounds to the ridge being built on as I thought it would add to the filth of the creek and make it a cess pool and because I regarded the low neck of land as the lung of the town which if built over would affect the quarters to the north. My difficulty was that I was never quite satisfied whether the Khojas were not acting in collusion with the Sultan and under an agreement to share the estate which would then be made a valuable and marketable property instead of a barren trust.

Kirk suspected, with no foundation or proof, that the Ismailis had cut a deal with the sultan to share in the "plunder." He did not deign to consider the equally plausible possibility that something much less nefarious was going on: the granting to the sultan by the Ismailis of a plot of community land to be used for the kind of charitable purpose for which it was intended—namely, the settlement of lepers. And so he "threatened to intervene both against the Sultan and the Khojas by advancing claims on behalf of the Crown if I did not get my own way." This threat amounted to little more than a bluff, but it worked. Kirk admitted to Hardinge that "had the matter gone into a Court of Justice I believe the Khojas could have established a good case to possession free of all obligation of trust." Moreover, given the substance of the case, he judged that the Aga Khan had the power to dispose of the property at will. Nonetheless, faced with a threat backed by military force, and with uncertain recourse to law, the Ismailis reportedly agreed to recognize their "limited right" to the land while the sultan disavowed any rights whatsoever.

What "limited right" in this case might have involved is not clear, which laid the grounds for divergent interpretations and disputes. As Kirk saw the question in 1894, the Ismailis had unlimited right to their cemetery and connected buildings and a "limited right" to the rest of the land. If they wanted to extend their graveyard, it would be a "very delicate matter to prevent them" and "as long as burials go on, the Ismailis are the trustees and their assent must be obtained." On the other hand, Kirk assured Hardinge that he had the power as consul to prevent building or obstructions of any kind on the whole neck and could regulate or prevent further burials if this should prove threatening to public health. Kirk summed up his understanding of this vexed issue by suggesting a resolution: "I think the ridge should be planted and used for open recreation and kept in trust by the Khojas."

Kirk's correspondence with Hardinge did not lay the issue to rest. In 1899 the colonial government was still disputing the extent of the Ismaili claim and their right to burial. As a result, a legal agreement was reached in September of that year between the Ismaili Jamat, the British consul, and the sultan's government (in the person of the British first minister). This agreement served to codify Kirk's earlier views. The government undertook to recognize the Ismailis' exclusive possession and right to burial in the smaller plot of land, as well as its use for religious rites and ceremonies. Furthermore, once the graveyard was filled, the government promised to provide the community with another close to town. For their part, the Ismailis agreed to "hereby renounce and for ever give up and relinquish all claim to or right title or interest in the residue of said land which is outside of and not included in the boundaries of the said piece of land." Most crucially, the government committed itself to keeping the territory which the Ismailis had renounced "open as a recreation or pleasure ground and no buildings except those suitable for recreation, pleasure ground, or ornamental purpose . . . shall be erected thereon."[14]

Colonial officials regarded this as a contract that confined Ismaili control to a limited plot of land, while allowing the government to administer the rest as a public recreation ground. What the Ismailis thought they were consenting to was another question, but it seems that they regarded the accord as an extension of earlier practice, much like the burial of the French consul's concubine. While agreeing to grant use of a part of the property, they still believed that they retained their rights of ownership and expected to be consulted and deferred to in its use. In this view, the government could only be considered a temporary trustee.

Colonial authorities precipitated a full-blown conflict over these issues beginning in 1909. In that year, at a meeting of the town council—a nonrepresentative body consisting of the consul, first minister, town collector, director of public works, director of agriculture, commandant of police, and medical officer of health—objections were raised by Dr. Spurrier to the practices of the Mnazi Moja Sports Club, a private golf club run by Europeans on Mnazi Mmoja. The club had been cutting turf to repair greens, leaving bald patches where standing water collected and malarial mosquitoes could breed. The council proposed to prevent this in future, recommending that a notice be published in the *Official Gazette* to the effect that the Mnazi Mmoja was under the control of the first minister. Solicitous of their golfing brethren, however, the council members first wrote to the sports club to ask its advice before taking action. The club sought to safeguard its putative "rights," as town collector Andrade reported back to the council: "The land between the Khoja cemetery wall and the Canteen was formerly claimed by the Khojas but they relinquished their claim some years ago on condition that the ground be kept by the Government for the use and enjoyment of the public. The Club are afraid that if the present proposals are unopposed they may serve as the thin edge of a wedge and that the Government might in a few years time appropriate the land to its own use. They propose therefore that a decree should be published stating that the land is dedicated to the public use and enjoyment and that it is under the control of the government."[15]

This framing of the issue involves multiple ironies. The Mnazi Moja Sports Club was essentially identical in form to the Indian RSC that tried to construct Pearce Pavilion, and yet the treatment accorded them was vastly different. The club was a private association, recognized as representing a privileged segment of the "public": European sportsmen. As such, it had been granted access to a considerable portion of Mnazi Mmoja for the purpose of establishing and maintaining a golf course. Over time, this turf became the club's exclusive domain, as the members controlled access, made rules of use, and paid for upkeep out of the dues collected. In contrast to the rejection of the RSC, however, authorities never accused club members of usurping a public right and turning it to private gain, though that was exactly what they were doing. As individuals, many colonial officials enjoyed the privileges of membership; a handful of clubs allowed the tiny white minority to circulate socially in elite milieus drawn up to maintain the color bar.[16] As public servants, colonial officers never questioned the racial ideology that created these fora, bending over backwards to protect the interests of the so-called European community. For instance, despite the fact that the sports club had no right to Mnazi Mmoja (and had been established there only a comparatively short time), the town council deferred to it when deciding the legal disposition of the property. After the draft decree was ultimately drawn up, it was circulated among club members for comment. By contrast, the party most concerned with the land—the Ismailis—was neither notified nor consulted. In an ironic twist, though, the Europeans and Ismailis had at least one thing in common: despite their favored position, the club members evidently shared Ismaili suspicions that the government might eventually move to seize Mnazi Mmoja for its own purposes, which prompted them to request an ironclad legal guarantee of the park's public purpose.

When the decree had been reviewed and polished into final form, Edward Clarke, the consul general, transmitted it to the Foreign Office for approval. In a letter, he explained the rationale behind the measure:

> In 1899 an agreement was drawn up between His Highness the Aga Khan . . . and the Zanzibar Government, by which, in return for certain privileges, the former withdrew all claims, on the understanding that the Zanzibar Government would undertake to dedicate the ground to the public in perpetuity. The rights of control by the Zanzibar Govern-

> ment, however, have never been legally defined and it has recently been questioned by the Mnazi Moja Sports Club. Mr. Grain and Judge Murison, whom I consulted in this matter, are of opinion that the difficulty could best be met by the issue of a decree defining the rights of the Government. . . . This draft has been shown to and approved by the members of the Mnazi Moja Sports Club and as it does not appear likely that the issue of the decree will raise any opposition, I trust you will authorize me to proceed.[17]

The decree was passed in 1910, but little did Clarke imagine the opposition it would arouse. Partly this is due to the fact that the measure, which Clarke saw merely as the legal codification of an already established agreement, involved yet another step in the erosion of Ismaili prerogatives—tantamount almost to the complete erasure of their rights over Mnazi Mmoja. The 1910 decree directly violated the 1899 agreement in numerous aspects. First, the park was intended to be dedicated to the public, but a sizable section of it was now occupied by a private European golf club. Second, the regime had taken over a further portion of the land for the erection of a government wireless station. Even so, the Ismailis tolerated these incursions, until a further violation in 1911–12 finally provoked them to react.

The earlier agreement had given the Ismailis the right to conduct religious festivals and ceremonies adjacent to their burial ground. During these celebrations, typically around the close of Ramadan and the Hajj, tents for food stalls, bioscopes, and cinematographs would be erected and a public fair held. Until 1911, vendors were charged rents, although no entrance fees were ever taken from the public. In the wake of the decree, colonial officials abruptly declared that the Ismailis had no authority to collect these rents. The manner by which they came to this decision testifies not only to the long-standing British practice of eroding Ismaili rights whenever possible but also to bureaucratic incoherence and the weakness of institutional memory. The long history of prior negotiations never came into play, and various authorities even seemed uncertain of the basic facts of the case. The change came about when the legal member of council (LMC) suddenly noticed the stalls one day and became curious. He then happened to ask the town collector what rents he was levying on Mnazi Mmoja. Nothing whatsoever, replied the town collector, as the stalls were on land claimed by the Ismailis. The LMC then wrote to the first minister with the following query: "Is not this ground vested in you under the terms of the Mnazi Moja Decree?"[18] Accordingly, the first minister raised the question with Clarke, who decided to seize the rental income. In doing so, he cited clause 3 of the 1899 agreement in which he believed the "Khojas renounced all right and interest outside the boundary" and directed that "such rents should be paid to the credit of the Mnazi Moja account as provided in section 3 of the Decree No. 8 of 1910."[19]

Clarke clearly believed he was simply upholding the law as defined by the 1910 decree. But he did not recognize how the measure itself was in violation of previous agreements, constituting yet another show of bad faith on the part of the regime. As a later attorney general admitted, while the 1910 decree was created to codify the 1899 agreement, it plainly contravened the earlier accord by sanctioning the existence of the illegal wireless station. Furthermore, he continued, "in the following year [1911] the Government unintentionally infringed the terms of the agreement by renting certain sites for circuses and merry-go-rounds. This was done in all good faith, and by virtue of a clause (Section 3 paragraph [g]) in the Decree, the existence of which, in latter day opinion is considered to be an additional infringement of the spirit of the 1899 agreement."[20]

However "unintentional" Clarke's decision may have been, by this time the Ismailis had plentiful cause to doubt the "good faith" of the colonial regime. Accordingly, they sent off a protest over the seizure of the rents to the Aga Khan, who was at that time in India. He forwarded their complaints to the Government of India, who passed them on to the Foreign Office in London. The Foreign Office then wired Zanzibar that the Aga Khan had complained about a violation of the 1899 accord and asked for full details from Clarke. The Foreign Office emphasized that the Ismailis had objected to their general treatment at the hands of Clarke and underlined that it was crucial to maintain good relations with the Aga Khan.

Clarke replied by protesting his innocence and taking umbrage at the fact that the Ismailis had not respected the formal chain of command: "I have received absolutely no complaint as to 'general treatment' of Aga's followers and am quite at a loss to understand what they mean. Would urge that their first duty as British Subjects is to lay any grievances they may have before me and would earnestly deprecate any encouragement being given to them to go straight to Home or India Governments without first coming to Agency: a course which can only result in shaking my position and causing great delays."[21] Clarke's insecurity about being undercut or even mildly questioned was matched in a subsequent telegram by his insistence that the forms of the law be adhered to: "Without making any complaint to me these people [the Ismailis] endeavor to collect the rents in disregard of their own renunciation and in direct defiance of decree to which they have never objected."[22] On the basis of this highly selective reading of the facts of the case, Clarke dogmatically asserted that a law is a law, and that if the Zanzibar government were to show any flexibility whatsoever, it might be vulnerable to ceaseless challenge. His representations were received unsympathetically in London. Given the insignificant nature of the rents involved, the Foreign Office seemed willing to find a compromise in order to protect its relations with the Aga Khan (who was deemed crucial to the success of policy in India). Metropolitan officials emphasized the need to make concessions and urged again that Clarke do nothing to insult the Ismailis on Zanzibar. Until the dispute could be resolved, London ordered that the status quo be reinstated pending the Aga Khan's arrival in East Africa—in other words, that the Ismailis be allowed to continue to collect rents. Clarke took offense at this move, feeling that it conceded too much legal ground to the Ismailis; he insisted that neither party to the dispute should be allowed to collect rents. In doing so, he inflated the dispute into a war threatening the very foundations of colonial authority:

> It has been represented to me by L.M. of C. [Legal Member of Council] (1) that prestige of Government would suffer severely if after having told Zanzibar natives that Indians had no right to collect rents which should be paid to us, we were now suddenly to inform them we had been wrong and that it was to the Indians they must apply. (2) Also that if, as I believe is the case, Indians intend to endeavor to upset agreement of 1899 in the Courts it might severely prejudice our position if, after negligently allowing them for years to exercise rights which under that agreement are nonexistent, and after having at length put an end to this state of things, we were now to retreat. Both these arguments have considerable weight: and the consequences especially of the greater part of the Mnazi Moja falling to the Indians as, if the agreement were upset, it would, are unthinkable.[23]

Clarke sought here to bolster his position by subtly insinuating the terms of battle into his discourse, raising the prospect of "retreat" and conquered ground "falling" into the hands of the enemy, predicting a loss of "prestige" and "unthinkable" consequences. His increasing hyperbole left the Foreign Office largely unmoved. London replied that the Ismailis had indeed been contemplating a suit but that the Aga Khan would ask them to drop the litigation on condition that Clarke agree to restore the status quo pending the Ismaili leader's arrival in 1913. Clarke was ordered to summon the Ismaili council and inform its members that he would suspend the 1910 decree.

Despite Clarke's instructions to settle the matter amicably, his meetings with the Ismaili leaders on 3 and 10 April 1912 did not go well, prompting them to send off another cable of protest to the Aga Khan. The Foreign Office then called upon Clarke to explain what had gone wrong. His eventual reply highlights the nature of the dispute:

> These people [the Ismailis] have no doubt led his Highness [the Aga Khan] to believe that the Zanzibar Government had been interfering with their actual "burial ground" whereas, as you are already aware, that is enclosed on all sides by a high wall and gates which are always kept shut. With this, no interference of any kind has ever been attempted or even contemplated. I pointed out to the deputation that to speak of the ground outside the cemetery wall as a "burial ground" was very

> misleading. They replied that they considered that practically all the ground known as Mnazi Moja covering 27 acres *was* a "burial ground." I said I could not accept this view for a moment and declined altogether to look upon the piece of land in question in such a light.[24]

Clearly the Ismailis did not view the 1899 agreement as involving a formal renouncement of their right to control the larger plot of land: in their view all of the property involved should be regarded as a burial ground to which they alone could give outside parties conditional access. With good cause they felt that the Zanzibar government had repeatedly violated the understanding by which it had been granted limited use of the land. The Foreign Office echoed this view in a telegram to Clarke, reporting the results of an interview with the Aga Khan: "The Aga Khan stated that the real difficulty as regards the rent, the wireless telegraph station, and all the other points in dispute, was that the Khojas saw in each of these things the thin edge of a wedge. They feared that the Government having once got a footing on the Mnazi Moja might eventually give some rights over the land to some sect on unfriendly terms with the Khojas."[25]

It seems crucial here that the Ismailis were not seeking to deny the government access to the land. As Kirk long ago observed, they always sympathetically entertained and approved requests to use the property. However, they firmly rejected that they ever transferred or alienated to colonial authorities the right to decide what use was to be made of the property, and they sought to prevent the British from arrogating that right to themselves or bestowing it upon any other group. The Foreign Office assured Clarke that the Aga Khan promised to work with the Zanzibar authorities to convince his followers that no such thing would ever occur—if Clarke would provide His Highness with a commitment reflecting that fact. The telegram concluded: "[The Aga Khan] was aware that the Agreement [of 1899] would not allow of such a concession being granted, but the Agreement was, according to his view, not legally binding, as the signatories had no real power to act on behalf of the Khoja Community."

This last assertion infuriated Clarke, insofar as he saw it as an attempt to disavow a legal agreement, duly signed and registered by the Aga Khan's representatives. So consumed was he by visions of "Indian" perfidy—the alleged inability of "Asiatics" to live up to their covenants—that he completely ignored the numerous violations of the accord on the part of the colonial government. The conventions of diplomacy undercut by his vitriol, Clarke began by stating that the Aga Khan's position had no "validity in law":

> No court in the world would, I am assured, admit that a document drawn up under such conditions . . . , legally registered at the time and acted upon by both the parties to it for the space of nearly thirteen years without ever having been questioned, could now be set aside because

one of the parties had suddenly chosen to declare that it was null and void.

The Zanzibar Government can certainly never on its part admit that it is so seeing that it holds the rights this agreement gives it, not for itself, but in trust for the inhabitants of the town, Europeans, Arabs, Indians and Swahilis. I feel convinced that you would never ask it to surrender rights which from every point of view are of such vital consequence to the population of Zanzibar, and to surrender them in favour of one small community notorious for its narrowmindedness, its passion for quarrelling to the death about trifles and of its entire absence of anything approaching public spirit or gratitude to the country where it has so long thriven.

Moreover, it is to be observed that were the whole question of the validity of this famous agreement to be "thrown," so to speak, "into the melting pot," it is quite possible that the Khojas might find that they would not come off so well as in 1899 and that, instead of gaining the Mnazi Moja, they would lose a large part of the rights which they at present enjoy in regard to the existing cemetery.

I observe further that the Agha Khan [*sic*] says that he feels sure that he will be able to make his followers here happy if the Zanzibar Government will give him an assurance that it will never convey any rights over the Mnazi Moja to some sect on unfriendly terms with the Khojas.

These people are everything that is stupid and ignorant but I altogether decline to believe that they are stupid and ignorant to such a point as to think that anything in the nature of the danger thus indicated can possibly exist. The Mnazi Moja grows every year more necessary to the town: it is covered every afternoon with English people playing golf and Indians playing cricket. Can anyone pretend that in these circumstances the Zanzibar Government is likely to give rights over the ground so employed "to some sect unfriendly to the Khojas"? . . . I am very much afraid that if the Agha Khan comes out here next year with such ideas in his head as those indicated in your despatch under reply, it will be impossible for us, whatever good will I may show—and I desire nothing better than that this tiresome dispute should be once and forever laid to rest—it will be impossible for us to come to an understanding.[26]

This is the voice of colonial power when challenged—petty, vindictive, and threatening in turn. First, Clarke pretends that the Zanzibar government has no interest of its own to press in this affair but instead is committed to protecting a vital public interest, held in trust for all the residents of the town. The hypocrisy of this claim should by now be amply apparent. His protestations of innocence, high-mindedness, and beneficent public spirit serve to cloak a record of colonial arrogance, usurpation, and contempt for the law.[27] The regime's sordid record of dealing with the Ismailis is eclipsed by an attempt to blame the victim. In a stunning instance of colonial projection, Clarke seeks to defend himself not by arguing the facts of the case but by launching a vicious attack upon his adversaries, casting them as narrow-minded, quarrelsome, and devoid of public spirit—charges unsupported anywhere else in the voluminous archival record. He crowns his attack by threatening that the Ismailis stand to lose everything should the case come to court. And finally, of course, there is the appeal to necessity: that the town could not live without Mnazi Mmoja. But his assertions that he was defending the land for all residents and that it was vital to the town at large are contradicted by his own illustration: "The Mnazi Moja grows every year more necessary to the town: it is covered every afternoon with English people playing golf . . ." How can English golfers and Indians playing cricket be conflated with the "town"? What kind of public is this, and whose rights was he actually seeking to defend?

Clarke's dispatch was, once again, received unsympathetically at the Foreign Office. Sir Edward Grey sent off a frosty reply, informing the consul general that his "tone" indicated a lack of sufficient appreciation for "the importance which His Majesty's Government and the Government of India attach to their relations with the Aga Khan and how unreasonable it would be to allow those relations to be disturbed by a comparatively small question of this kind." Clarke's superior told him that the validity of the 1899 agreement was moot, as the Aga Khan did not seek to overturn its "material effects." The only question to be resolved related to "the purposes for which you are to use the Mnazi Moja and the collection of some trifling rents which you, rather unwisely I think, took away from the Khojas." He insisted that every courtesy and consideration must be shown to the Aga Khan, concluding, "He evidently is perfectly willing to help you and has no idea of depriving Zanzibar of that part of the Mnazi Moja which you want for recreation grounds and that is all that matters. He wants to do what is reasonable for us without losing prestige with his own community and we should make it as easy as we can on points of form for him to do that."[28] The diplomatic reason of the Foreign Office held sway over Clarke's extreme rigidity, and the status quo prevailed pending the arrival of the Aga Khan. He finally managed to pass through Zanzibar in 1914, but his visit was cut short by the outbreak of World War I. The question of Mnazi Mmoja, while discussed, remained unresolved at his departure, and in the face of war the dispute retreated into insignificance. It would remain unsettled until 1925–26, when the Ismaili leader managed once again to reach East Africa.

On the face of it, the qualified intervention of the Foreign Office might make the depredations of local colonial functionaries seem less powerful than they actually were. Note that, in many respects, the Ismailis were better positioned than others. First, unlike other Zanzibari groups, they possessed the international heft to obtain a hearing at the highest levels of the imperial administration via the diplomatic influence of the Aga Khan. Second, again through the Aga Khan, they had an independent channel to press their case and provide testimony on their own behalf, which was highly unusual. In most other instances, British bureaucrats on Zanzibar had great administrative latitude and used their control over the information selectively transmitted to London to their advantage; most often, local complaints never reached the ears of higher authority or were forwarded on in such a way as to bolster the position of the regime. Third, the Ismailis were the "community" best prepared to face concerted attacks from colonial authorities. They possessed considerable collective resources and internal organization and were educated in the intricacies of the colonial legal system. Other Zanzibaris, particularly Africans, whether of indigenous or mainland origin, lacked these comparative advantages; the colonial administration hardly even deigned to recognize them. Even if they had managed to organize themselves into civic associations, the colonial double bind was still in force: as a generalized mass they lacked standing, but as a group they were branded as parochial and self-seeking. Despite wielding advantages that other Zanzibaris lacked, the Ismailis still found their rights progressively eroded as they were shut out from control of the land they formerly possessed, vilified as selfish and insular, and restricted to the tiny portion of the neck walled off as a burial ground.[29]

Of Politics and Parks: Colonial Hegemony in Play

It might be argued that the intermittent character of confrontations over Mnazi Mmoja—the fact that the British bureaucracy by turns tried to exercise command over the land and then let the matter rest—signals the inefficient nature of the colonial regime. In certain respects this is true. But ineptness should not be mistaken for incapacity. The administration's efforts to seize Mnazi Mmoja over the long haul testifies to the diffuse nature of its rule, providing evidence of rotating personnel, gaps in institutional continuity and memory, even abrupt shifts in focus. At key junctures, if officials seemed woefully ignorant of even the basic history of the case, the government's control of the legal system and documentary record left them free to revisit questions thought settled, framing or revising past agreements in such a way as to curtail the established rights of groups. What is significant here is the temporality of struggle and the strategic advantage of lags and lacuna; these underlay the disproportionate power possessed by the administration to fight a battle over the long term and, hence, to wear down opposition. Note how, at each round of dispute, the "full rights" of the Ismailis were progressively winnowed away, even as, at times, the regime retreated or conceded minor points. Few communities, no matter how determined or well-organized, could hold their own in the face of such diffuse, irregular, and yet prolonged assaults.

The outcome in Mnazi Mmoja was not produced by an omniscient or monolithic state. The structured quality of debates about land control over an extended period didn't arise from regularity in state apparatus or power, but rather from a widespread and generally accepted ideology that shaped notions of colonial governance at a very general level. This ideology was so tied into a ruling common sense that it can fairly be described as hegemonic, accepted widely by successive residents and officials—accounting for how different historical agents could approach the Mnazi Mmoja question in similar ways at different points in time. Colonial hegemony was constituted out of broad understandings that were inextricably part of modern political rationality in its liberal guise—to begin with, the conception of government as a guardian of a "public" order, a fulcrum for balancing competing private social interests. Such an idea, capable of broad application at home and abroad, could only be reinforced in the colonial context by the ideology of indirect rule and the paternalism on which the whole vision of a "protectorate" was based. Similarly, few colonial officials on Zanzibar or elsewhere in the empire ever questioned the assumption that the administration had a right and duty to control unoccupied land, or that disputes should be adjudicated within a legal order based on private property, title, and the sanctity of formal contracts. And from the nineteenth century onward, European observers and officials operated out of a general consensus that Zanzibar's diverse population could be broken down into distinct groups, usually classified in broad terms as Arabs, Indians, and Africans, each of which was "naturally" suited to certain social positions, places, and roles.[30] The fact that this racial ideology masked a more complicated reality and created many contradictions did not stop the authorities from continuing to act as if the "public" was a mosaic of competing communities. Taken together, these ideological elements and others made hegemony possible. But if this framework of belief was fairly consistent, that does not mean that the state was unified or that it possessed "power" and exercised it as the instrument of a harmonious will.

Holding the ground in Mnazi Mmoja was not a strategic plan hatched and carried out over the long term by a Machiavellian regime, confident in the uncanny and wily reach of its power. Colonial rule on Zanzibar, as elsewhere, was anything but all-encompassing or capable of dominating the totality of the everyday. The government possessed neither the means nor the capacity to control social life in all its myriad detail. But colonialism was not dependent upon achieving this objective in the first place. Rather than total domination, what we see in the conflict over Mnazi Mmoja is the hegemony of certain kinds of political forms and practices. As limited and incomplete as the regime was, in certain areas it possessed greater leverage for influencing and shaping social action. The public-private double bind only worked because the colonial government deployed these tactics in limited domains over which it could exercise a great deal of control—the disposition of open lands; the doling out of bureaucratic positions; and access to education, rations, and other state resources. In these areas officials had considerable means to shape the political rules of engagement by which subjects could access the state or place demands upon it—in other words, to frame the modalities of "public" interaction, shaping a fragmented civil sphere. While the authorities could not and did not dictate the content, agenda, or process of associational life (much less the internal workings of "communities"), they could structure a political field in crucial ways that placed its opponents at a distinct disadvantage. As well, the changes the British presided over were not incompatible with Zanzibari precedent and practice. Communal solidarities and identifications of various sorts existed long before the protectorate was established, and the new colonial associations accorded well with the aspirations of elite Zanzibaris, especially the Arab aristocracy and rising Indian merchants. Moreover, the colonial construction of the civil sphere was difficult to struggle against insofar as it relied upon ostensibly liberal, neutral, and abstract modalities. The imposition of new juridical-political forms was not a program or plan that allowed for totalizing domination; instead, it was a subtle, top-down process that allowed the regime in certain respects to shape the terms by which subsequent struggles would be waged. Thinking about hegemony in these terms takes us very close to David Scott's understanding of colonial governmentality:

> In the colonial world the problem of *modern* power turned on the politico-ethical project of producing subjects and governing their conduct. What this required was the concerted attempt to alter the political and social worlds of the colonized, an attempt to transform and redefine the very conditions of the desiring subject. The political problem of modern colonial power was therefore not merely to contain resistance and encourage accommodation but to seek that *both* could *only* be defined in relation to the categories and structures of modern political rationalities. (1995, 214)

By the early 1920s, Clarke was long vanished from the scene, and a new set of officials were free to reinterpret or ignore the past to suit their own ends. In 1923, in direct violation of the 1912 status quo and the 1899 agreement, the colonial government rented part of the Mnazi Mmoja to the Wallet Circus Company to erect stalls and tents for a cinematograph and a circus play. The company began to build a fence on the site, close by and directly blocking access to the Ismaili cemetery and sacred sites—a further violation of the accords. Dismayed by the incursion, the Ismailis removed the fence. This prompted an angry summons by the British resident, John Sinclair, who called on them to explain their actions. Sinclair opened the meeting by informing the Ismailis that "their action was very high handed and illegal." If they believed they had "any rights" in the matter, he stated, they should apply for a court injunction rather than take direct action. The Ismailis responded that they had only demolished the fence because the man installing it had claimed to be doing so with Ismaili permission, which had never been granted. They added that the late Consul Clarke, through the Foreign Office, had granted them the right to collect rents from the erection of booths on the Mnazi Mmoja.

Sinclair allowed that Clarke had given the Ismailis this "concession." But he judged it null and void because it was given only pending an imminent visit from the Aga Khan. Since His Highness had come and gone, it was no longer in effect. Besides, the resident alleged that the concession was offered "without prejudice to the rights of the Govt under the Agreement of 1899 and the Mnazi Moja Decree. . . . So as far as I can ascertain from the P.P. there is no question of the Khojas having any legal rights over the ground at all and the concession was only made purely out of consideration to the personal request of the Aga Khan." He closed the meeting by stating that, even if the Ismailis now desired to give the circus owner use of the ground, he "could not recognize that their permission was necessary." Consequently, he directed the commandant of police to see "that no further interference with workmen employed on the ground takes place."[31]

Sinclair conceded no ground in staking out the government's legal position. But he did not want to inflame the dispute unnecessarily and provoke a rebuke from the Colonial Office. He proposed that any final decision be postponed pending the arrival of the Aga Khan, who was expected shortly in Zanzibar. If the Ismailis would consent to place the Mnazi Mmoja rents in an escrow account managed by a local law firm until then, he would press the matter no further. The Ismaili council endorsed this interim compromise, while firmly reiterating its position: "We further request the Government to make arrangements that the control of the said Mnazimoja ground should remain in our hands as it is since the time of the Ex-Consul the late Mr. Edward Clarke, til his Highness the Agakhan's visit to this place and the ground should not be given by the Government to any one as given to the Circus Company in the present instance without our previous consent."[32] In return, Sinclair added a further condition, stipulating that if the Aga Khan didn't arrive within a year the concession would cease and the government resume full control.[33] This arrangement might seem a mere repetition of the past, echoing the status quo established after 1913. But notice how the authorities managed at each successive cycle of dispute to subtly shift the terms of debate. Sinclair may have acted less intemperately than Clarke in offering a truce, but he combined this with a hard-edged insistence that these concessions were "without prejudice to the Govt legal rights of control over the land in question and are made purely as an act of grace and courtesy to H.H. the Aga Khan."[34] Suddenly, by 1923, "there is no question of the Khojas having any legal rights over the ground." Any consideration shown them by the government was granted as a favor or an act of grace, rather than a recognition of their rights. The realities of the case had been neatly reversed.

Once again the Aga Khan was delayed in traveling to Zanzibar. His Highness satisfied the Colonial Office that he was unavoidably detained by his responsibilities in India; the secretary of state for the colonies therefore sent a cable to Sinclair instructing him to remove the one-year limit on the concession, leaving the question of Mnazi Mmoja in abeyance for an indefinite term. The Aga Khan finally managed to arrive in Zanzibar in 1925, and by that time Sinclair had been replaced by Alfred Claud Hollis. The new resident approached the issue of Mnazi Mmoja in ways substantially different from his predecessors. First, he was fresh to Zanzibar and had no stake in the dispute or familiarity with the parties involved. Since the Colonial Office had assumed control in 1914, two "old hands" on Zanzibar had been appointed as residents (Pearce, Sinclair); Hollis was the first external bureaucrat to be named to the post, and he accorded much more neatly with the new orthodoxy. By contrast, Sinclair, who had come to Zanzibar in the earliest years of the protectorate, was "the last official link with the old order of things," part of a world that stretched back to Hardinge, Portal, and Kirk.[35] Second, Hollis had no illusion that Zanzibar was his personal fiefdom. Trained by and promoted within the Colonial Office, he was much more likely to explicitly follow directions from the metropole. He showed the Aga Khan every consideration, meeting at length with him to go over the case. He even went so far as to allow the Ismaili leader to read his draft dispatch to London, seeking his approval before sending it. Third, because Hollis was unfamiliar with the facts, he ordered an extensive review of the case history, personally reading the "voluminous correspondence on the subject."[36]

As the resident's subsequent memorandum to the secretary of state for the colonies indicates, his findings wholly vindicated Ismaili claims. In his judgment, the Ismaili council was correct: the 1910 decree "violates in one or two small, but to them important, details the Mnazi Moja agreement of 1899." He also admitted that the government broke the agreement with the erection of the wireless station and had further violated it "on a few occasions"—most notably in 1912 and 1923, when efforts were made to rent out the ground to carnivals. The Ismailis, said Hollis, had no intention of preventing the land being used for recreation, and he found their concerns altogether justified: "All they wish to prevent is that the land in question should be let, even for short periods, to persons who wish to erect merry-go-rounds, booths, Punch and Judy shows, tents for circuses, etc., just outside their cemetery. On such occasions large crowds assemble, bands play, and the solemnity of a funeral which may be taking place is interfered with."

The settlement was possible because Hollis recognized that the aims of the government had already been achieved; he could act magnanimously and concede diplomatic ground while still retaining substantive control of Mnazi Mmoja. The result of all this was a 1926 decree that canceled the 1910 measure and dedicated all the land outside the Ismaili cemetery as a public recreation ground held in trust by the government. Yet even here a final, revealing tussle broke out. Much like the European sports club before them, the Ismailis sought a written guarantee from the colonial administration that it would never let any part of the land for any purpose whatsoever. The council, in response to the draft decree provided to them, asked for the following amendment: "The Ismailia Council also desires that a provision be introduced to the proposed decree which would effectively prevent the use of the Mnazi Moja ground by any one section of the public or by the members of any one community to the exclusion of the other sections of the public or the members of the other communities inhabiting Zanzibar."[37]

Rather than view this request as an attempt to protect the sanctity of their religious sites and guarantee the public character of the land, the chief secretary responded to the Ismaili petition with suspicion and distrust. In so doing, he showed just whose public interests the colonial regime was anxious to defend. As he wrote to the resident, "The ground is already dedicated to the public. What they [the Ismailis] evidently want is to be able to demand that golf should not be played there. *Although only Europeans play,* there is nothing to prevent anyone joining in who may wish to, but if it was used by others the M.M. Club would probably cease spending money on upkeep of grounds" (emphasis added).[38] Hollis concurred with the chief secretary's rejection of the Ismaili amendment, stating: "I do not wish to insert any clause in the decree that might make it possible to turn people off the golf course."[39] The degree was passed without the amendment, and the Ismaili council and the Aga Khan later reluctantly acquiesced in the decision.

Here, then, we have the colonial "public." While the chief secretary was correct in stating that the golf course was technically public, this amounted to nothing more than an empty form. If nothing in law *prevented* others from joining in the game, the practical fact was that only whites were ever likely to play. Very few Zanzibaris possessed the inclination or desire to engage in such a quixotic sport, which in any case required expensive imported equipment. Nor were "natives" ever likely to avail themselves of their "public" right to invade this exclusive European preserve, paid for and maintained by a private European golf club; indeed, any attempt to do so would have provoked a hostile response. Throughout the colonial period, the only Zanzibaris who were allowed on the links were there in capacities more congenial to European expectations of subordination: in the tropical heat, as caddies, carrying the white man's burden—his golf clubs.

Maintaining the fiction of the "public" was only possible in the absence of scrutiny. The existence of the Mnazi Moja Sports Club was so long accepted, its use of the land so well protected by European hegemony, that it went virtually unprotested; this in spite of its violation of both the letter and spirit of the law. Over time, the administration could rely upon its powers to erode public rights and to appropriate them bit by bit. The way public affairs were managed to suit private interests was frankly acknowledged by government officials. In late 1938, for instance, the director of agriculture, R. W. R. Miller, raised objections to the ad hoc management of the sports club grounds. As members, he and four other Europeans had been overseeing the groundskeeping crew, but the results were less than satisfactory. Their efforts were not coordinated, and if they were away on business or holiday, the course and croquet lawn would run to seed. As he saw it, the overriding problem was the "constant lack of supervision of the labour force." In his unofficial capacity, Miller wrote to the sports club committee, suggesting that it formally request the government to allow Mr. Machado, the superintendent of gardens, to take over the job of directing the upkeep of the course. The club should also ask for the right to pay this government servant an "honorarium" for his work. On the same day, in his official capacity, the director forwarded this proposal to the chief secretary, emphasizing the merit of the appointment on the following grounds: "The upkeep of the Golf Course will become a matter of considerable importance," he stated, "in view of the Government's interest in establishing a hotel in Zanzibar."

The chief secretary referred the issue to the acting financial secretary, who then raised a crucial question: what was the exact legal status of the property, and to whom did it belong? After some research, the land officer reported back in early 1939 that the ground occupied by the sports club was "common land" held by the government; under the terms of the 1926 decree, it was dedicated to the recreational "use and enjoyment of the public forever." The acting financial secretary expressed no concern about this clear usurpation of the public interest. Indeed, in a letter to the chief secretary supporting Miller's proposal, he openly accepted the contradiction: "The golf course appears to include the whole of the area described in Cap. 108 [the 1926 decree] as the 'Mnazi Moja.' The control and management of the golf course is in the hands of the Mnazi Moja Club, though no rule to that effect appears to have been made under Cap. 108. . . . If the proposal is agreed to, Mr. Machado would supervise these areas as a servant of the Mnazi Moja Club, which in fact does actually supervise these areas at the present time. . . . There would seem therefore to be no legal objection to the Mnazi Moja Club employing a supervisor to these grounds."[40] Shortly thereafter, the proposal was accepted and implemented.

It is not as if these colonial functionaries simply forgot to make a rule to authorize what they were doing. Instead, their practice flagrantly violated regulations to which they, or their predecessors, had solemnly agreed. That at least some high officials knew and tolerated this is more than clear. Moreover, British administrators understood that they could continue to break the law so long as Zanzibaris remained indifferent to their formal rights or unwilling to seek redress through the courts. Given the expense of legal action, the hostile reaction it would provoke, and the social costs that would follow, no "native" was likely to bring suit over the usurpation of the ground—even if he or she possessed the awareness that such action was theoretically possible.

A later discussion fully reveals the way in which the ostensibly liberal forms of civil society could function as a convenient mask for more subtle (and extralegal) practices of exclusion. In 1944, the honorable secretary of the Mnazi Moja Sports Club wrote to the chief secretary, expressing anxiety about wartime shortages that he feared would threaten the very existence of golf in the islands:

> 1). I have been asked by the Committee of the above club to bring to the notice of the Government the following facts relative to the continued use of that land known as the Mnazi Moja for the purposes of a Golf Course. 2). As you are doubtless aware, under Sec. 2 of the Mnazi Moja Decree Cap. 108, this has been "dedicated as a recreation ground to the use and enjoyment of the public for ever." Full advantage of this gift has not hitherto been taken by the public for two probable reasons, the first one being ignorance of their rights, and the second a knowledge that personal danger of being struck by a golf ball is involved. . . . 3). The maintenance of the above "statu quo ante bellum" [*sic*] is therefore dependent upon daily use by golfers of the greens and fairways into which thousands of pounds of the Club's money has been sunk, a condition which due to the inability of the players to obtain golf balls, is liable to lead to the total loss of concessions enjoyed until now without protest or hindrance from any section of the community. 4). I take the liberty of suggesting therefore, that these are fit and proper grounds for making representations to the Home Governmant [*sic*] for help in obtaining a minimum supply of golf balls, say 60 doz., in order to enable the European Community to continue to enjoy a privilege which is in danger of becoming irretrievably lost.[41]

The "honorable" golf club secretary seems to evince no shame in pleading for special consideration that would allow the continuance of a leisure pastime while other members of the "European Community" were fighting and dying on the battlefields of Europe. His real concern is with a different sort of privation: the wartime restrictions on rubber, which had depleted the supply of tennis and golf balls on Zanzibar. Given this shortage, the secretary worries that the exclusive European possession of the course might lapse. He frankly admits that the club has usurped a public right, made possible solely by continuous occupation and use. He denies the force of the law, however, by describing the public dedication of the park as a "gift"—an act of benevolence that confers benefits but bestows no rights.[42] The club's appropriation of

Mnazi Mmoja was made possible, he smugly asserts, because the public remained "ignorant" of its full rights and felt threatened by a sense of risk. This state of affairs, the secretary fears, might soon be subject to change, as the shortage of balls threatens to curtail play. And if the links fell into disuse, club members could not hold their ground. Others—the Zanzibaris to whom the land was dedicated—might begin to take over the open space for cricket practices or football matches. Once there, they could not be evicted: having no basis in law or right, the golf club would be unable to reassert its exclusive privilege and retake the turf. The game would be up.

Conclusion

This sorry tale reveals much about the construction, over time, of the public sphere and civil society on Zanzibar. The fight for the Mnazi Mmoja golf course was hardly a defining event in colonial history; nor was the Ismaili land claim. But this conflict speaks to much broader processes, to a much more embracing field of colonial power and representation. It was, after all, a protracted battle, one that lasted for more than a half century, over the possession and control of territory. As Myers (1993) and Fair (1994) have argued, bureaucratic attempts to regulate urban space—manipulating Islamic law to invalidate religious trusts and turn inalienable ground into private property—were at the heart of the imperial project. Furthermore, the contestation over Mnazi Mmoja replayed itself in numerous other domains. Most pertinently, the administration relied upon similar divide-and-rule tactics and discursive strategies to frustrate the efforts of urban Zanzibaris to gain municipal power and public representation over an extended period.

It is implausible to dismiss the Ismailis as either isolated or unrepresentative. While they were exceptional in terms of the relative advantages they possessed, their fate was all too typical of other Zanzibari "communities" caught in the colonial double bind. By making access to the state, to its institutions, and its official policies dependent upon membership in racial or religious communities, the regime structured a public that was vulnerable to divisive tactics. As Fair has written, "Beginning in the earliest days of the colony, the Administration encouraged the men of the island to organize themselves into ethnic associations which more clearly reflected European conceptions of bounded racial groupings. All policy discussions between the state and island residents were directed through these ethnic associations and it was only through these recognized bodies that people could officially communicate with the state" (1994, 252).

Any attempt to petition the administration other than in the name of a recognized community was summarily rejected. Similarly, the colonial government routinely distributed educational opportunities, bureaucratic positions, health services, and other public resources along racial lines—which always worked to the disadvantage of the majority African population. Perhaps its most bitterly resented practice was the doling out of rations on racial lines during World War II, a policy that reserved staple goods for Arabs and Indians, leaving Africans largely to fend for themselves or do without. This arrangement infuriated many Africans as a patent injustice, and the unevenness by which it was applied (other African groups, such as the Comorians, successfully lobbied to obtain "Arab" rations) led a good number to redefine their identities, claiming Shirazi descent to obtain better rations—a move perfectly understood by those left behind, but resented nonetheless (Fair 1994, 243–49).

The colonization by the state of civil society and the public sphere—their racialization and rationalization—was by no means total. Many urban neighborhoods were mixed to a greater or lesser degree, and certain fora (mosques, *barazas*, even some sports teams) continued on a multiracial basis. Yet these rarely, if ever, provided opportunities for challenging the colonial government. Widespread resistance to the divide-and-rule policies of the British by mixed groups of Zanzibaris only occurred in a few notable instances—for example, the Ng'ambo rent strike of 1928 and the islandwide General Strike of 1948, both led by the poor and working classes of Zanzibar's "other side." As Fair (1994, 88–139, 361–77) has shown, however, such movements arose in the context of egregious and concerted assaults by local elites and the state on widely held, deeply cherished understandings of customary rights and moral economy. These popular expressions of outrage and organized resistance eventually dissipated once they were successful in forcing the colonial state to back down and alleviate the oppressive conditions that caused the struggle in the first place. While their achievements were profound, they did not translate into ongoing political organizations.

Indeed, the colonial regime worked assiduously to separate politics from culture, disabling the former by linking it to racist divide-and-rule policies, bounded communities, and the state. By the time the struggle for independence began to take off after World War II, these negative associations were firmly in place and structured much of what was to follow. As nationalist aspirations and interparty competition increasingly pitted "African" against "Arab," and as political strife began to poison everyday existence, colonial authorities continued to divide and rule; this while conducting public relations campaigns against racialism (Fair 1994; Myers 1993; Clayton 1981; Lofchie 1965). Token efforts to engage in humanist pieties fostered by the new metropolitan Labour government did little to erase decades of colonial experience. To this day, many Zanzibaris continue to view "politics" as decidedly negative, something never to be equated with "public debate and choice":

> The kiswahili word for "politics," *siasa,* has an extremely negative connotation on Zanzibar, associated with the formation of largely ethnically-

> based political parties, colonial manipulation of the pre-independence elections, the unfortunate and unnecessary slaughter of many thousands of persons at the time of the "revolution," and the rise to power of an autocratic and tyrannical regime in the years immediately following independence. . . . In Zanzibar, "politics" is by definition associated with the state, formal parties, and authoritarian men. (Fair 1994, 5)

By the time of the revolution on Zanzibar in 1964, "politics" was indissolubly linked to racial division, antagonism, and unspeakable violence. The revolutionary regime, attributing this as part of the colonial legacy, moved early on to ban all ethnic associations and to nationalize their schools, dispensaries, and other communal assets. As it sought to reverse historic injustices and overthrow colonial social forms, however, the new administration exceeded its predecessor in its efforts to control civil society. (In fact, it was only under the revolution that the Ismailis were finally excised altogether from Mnazi Mmoja, as the material signs of their historical ownership were wholly eradicated from the land. Their considerable burial ground is no longer marked by headstones or walls; the land is open and empty, and few Zanzibaris today realize its former use or long-term connection to the Ismailis.) More than ever, the state constituted the public: basic rights of speech and assembly were strictly curtailed, as the government tried to monopolize both the civil sphere and the economy. This centralization of power, backed by an extensive East German-trained security apparatus, enabled the regime to act as the sole source of mass mobilization, controlling all associational and public life. For many Zanzibaris, the revolutionary era was a time of considerable insecurity, as the smallest miscues—wearing bell-bottoms or having an overly long Afro were regarded as signs of being in thrall to the West—could result in a public whipping or six months' compulsory labor. In such a climate, very few were foolhardy enough to attempt outright opposition, and those who were even suspected of doing so were placed in a highly precarious position.

Given the long history of the manipulation of civil society on Zanzibar, current discourse about the city and the lack of public participation seems strikingly misplaced. By treating civic engagement as a cultural trait rather than a political problem, conservationists fundamentally distort the realities of power in the present. Restoration efforts inevitably raise the question: For whom is the city being conserved? Expatriates and Zanzibari officials involved in rehabilitation projects claimed to be working for the benefit of all Zanzibaris; yet popular involvement was minimal at best, as the planning process allowed little scope for even the mere consultation of local residents. At the end of several years of effort, conservationists were dismayed by the lack of public engagement with their work; they voiced complaints about the absence of civic culture in the islands, suggesting that Zanzibaris had no commitment to community involvement. Often I was told sotto voce that residents of Stone

Town needed to be "educated" to understand the importance of preserving the city and to appreciate its role as the central site of "Zanzibari" cultural heritage and identity. Failing this, conservation plans would be ignored and citizens would continue to build on graveyards, to seize public space, to convert houses into hotels, to dump trash in alleys, and, in various other ways, to raid the public domain for private gain. Phrased in an ahistorical, essentializing vein, such statements hinted at an intrinsic lack of public spirit and morality. Ignoring the fact that there *is* a community of residents living in the town, they allege its absence in order to explain why people do not respond to top-down, hierarchical planning initiatives that excluded them in the first place. The double standard involved in such comments is reminiscent of the colonial claim that Zanzibaris have (note the tense) no civic sense. There is, of course, a disturbing irony here: while willfully ignoring the legacy of the past, conservationists reproduced its terms on another level, echoing colonial paternalism in its most perverse form.

Under colonial rule, this putative lack of "civic consciousness" was often blamed for "violations" of petty etiquette such as littering, urinating in public, defecating in little used alleys, and reckless bicycling, all of which were taken to indicate low moral worth. Rather than, say, providing funds for building an adequate number of public toilets, the government adopted various measures to educate the masses on the value of "making Zanzibar a tidy town" and the like. In 1943, for instance, an "Anti-Litter Campaign" was initiated "in an attempt to inculcate, in the young in particular, a pride in the appearance of Zanzibar Town, through which a civic sense of collective responsibility can also be encouraged."[43] This was just the first in a series of similar propaganda efforts, culminating in the extensive program to motivate residents to clean and decorate the town in anticipation of Princess Margaret's royal visit in 1952. Such efforts were disingenuous, for, while the British may have wanted an idealized public committed to "keeping our city clean," they took pains to avoid handing over power to anything resembling a municipal body and assiduously worked to prevent the rise of a more genuinely political and representative civic sphere.

Given this history, we can now fully comprehend the political consequences—the selective erasures and enforced silences—involved in regarding civil society as the normative condition of possibility for any democratic order. John Harbeson has recently claimed that "the idea of civil society" testifies to a gap in our analysis of "African problems of political and socioeconomic development on the ground." Are these then purely "African" problems? Is it possible to foreclose the question in so neat a fashion? Harbeson goes on to argue that the social scientific neglect of civil society "has been reflected in less-than-successful policy formation by African governments and donor development assistance agencies." He spatially restricts the issue to the internal workings of bounded nation-states and compounds this flaw by adopting a resolutely presentist temporal focus. Does then "postcolonial" mean we have truly gotten past the past? Can we close off and preclude any historical consideration of the legacy of colonial regimes, soundly laying blame for the current state of affairs on recent governments? This very active form of historical amnesia underlies Harbeson's normative conception of the premises of civil society: "1) The existence of civil society is inevitable and necessary; 2) consensus exists on how civil society is to function and on its substantive principles; 3) civil society is synonymous with society's conception of optimal normative bases of governance and societal organization; and 4) civil society is the blueprint and design for the structure of the state" (1994, 3).

The Zanzibari case throws each of these assumptions into profound doubt. How can a renewed focus on civil society lay the basis for "political reform in Africa" when it is conceived in abstract and idealist terms that bear little connection to past or present conditions? The extent of Harbeson's naivete can be seen most fully in the way he sums up his thesis: "The missing dimension supplied by the idea of civil society is that, in process terms, working understandings concerning the basic rules of the political game or structure of the state emerge from within society and the economy at large. In substantive terms, civil society typically refers to the points of agreement on what those working rules *should* be" (1994, 3). As the example of Mnazi Mmoja shows, exactly the opposite was true. The "basic rules of the political game" were established by the colonial state, which worked to disable and control the public sphere. In this instance, the "working understanding" that emerged was precisely that the game was loaded from the start: while there may have been "points of agreement" between indigenes and expatriates on what the rules should be, the colonial state repeatedly felt free to ignore or manipulate them. This legacy has direct connections to contemporary state practices on Zanzibar—as well as on forms and levels of public participation. As Zanzibar has moved through its various "postcolonial" political forms, becoming successively an independent nation, a revolutionary encampment, and a liberalized playground for tourists, the contours of civil society have remained all too consistent with those established long before. Without recognizing such connections we can hardly even begin to consider "less-than-successful policy formation by African governments." The so-called problem of civil society is a historical one, with its origins in the colonial epoch, not a function or figment of postcoloniality.

An interrogation of the colonial public sphere also sheds light on debates started by Jürgen Habermas (1992, 1989; see also Calhoun 1992). Many have questioned whether Habermas saw the bourgeois public sphere as a normative ideal or a historical reality in Europe. Such critics note that his focus on the "quality of discourse," and on the existence of critical-rational debate, led him to underplay its exclusionary character. They highlight the issue of the "quantity of participation," noting how a propertied, educated, male public sphere was only made possible by silencing a host of others (Eley 1992; Fraser 1992; Ryan 1992); some go so far as to argue that Habermas's work serves to compound this erasure, and advocate that focus be placed on multiple "publics," on issues of identity and difference, and on questions of power. But the debate has remained sturdily Eurocentric, privileging the metropolitan nation-state as analytical focus—as if it developed apart from a much broader colonial context. If Habermas considered eighteenth-century Britain to be home to the very model of the public sphere, clearly he was concerned solely with the English metropole, not with its expansive empire, at many of whose "capitals" local public spheres were deformed, disrupted, and silenced. Indeed, the expansion and transformation of the public sphere "at home" had much to do with the flow of commodities, ideas, and people from those very places. To consider the imperial center in isolation from its colonies is to indulge a highly selective historical vision. It is also to foreclose what Gary Wilder identifies (see chapter 2) as the crucial question: "In what ways must we rethink a category like civil society when we recognize both state and colony, reason and race to be intrinsic elements of an irreducibly imperial nation-state, the political form of a colonial modernity?" Insofar as the public sphere directly invokes issues of inclusion, we must begin to grapple with the ways it operated across boundaries in an interconnected and dynamic colonial space. As this Zanzibari story shows, the history of civil society in a remote outpost may tell us a great deal about the practical politics of colonialism, about the failures and exclusions involved in the construction (and destruction) of political community in the cartography of empire.

Notes

1. For a fuller discussion of the tangled history of colonial urban planning on Zanzibar, see Bissell 1999, Sheriff 1995, and Myers 1993.

2. Jenks to chief secretary, 9 July 1926, Zanzibar National Archives (ZNA): AB 39/271. As will become clear in what follows, "Mnazi Moja" designated both a plot of land and the European sports club that came to occupy a portion of the ground. Various forms of this name appear in colonial documents, but more recently, in line with correct Kiswahili, "Mnazi Mmoja" has replaced the older variants. I will use the more recent form unless it occurs in direct quotation.

3. "Draft Regulations for the Pearce Pavilion Committee" [1919], ZNA: AB 39/271.

4. Jenks to chief secretary, 9 July 1926, ZNA: AB 39/271.

5. Chief secretary to honorable secretary of the Indian Representative Sports Committee, 1 September 1920, ZNA: AB 39/271.

6. Tayab Ali to honorable secretary of the Indian Representative Sports Committee, 25 September 1920, ZNA: AB 39/271.

7. Jenks to chief secretary, 9 July 1926, ZNA: AB 39/271.

8. Chief secretary to the honorable secretaries of the various Indian sports clubs, 8 September 1926, ZNA: AB 39/271.

9. This practice cannot be limited just to the colonial period. The most recent conservation plan, sponsored by the Aga Khan Trust for Culture, was completed only after several years of effort. During this time, popular input was kept to the bare minimum. The "public" entered into the process at the end, and only then in its usual guise. To explain the plan to citizens, the lead planner convened a meeting in late April 1994 of the heads of various religious communities. They were given a detailed presentation of the scheme in hopes that they would subsequently go back to their flocks, clarifying the methods and aims of conservation to "the people." Other public initiatives during this time included some handbills posted throughout Stone Town and an exhibition of the plan that lasted a few weeks.

10. A. H. Spurrier, "Memorandum on the Peace Memorial Research and Educational Museum," 31 January 1923, ZNA: AB 41/1. Dr. Spurrier was the former medical officer of health; after his retirement he continued to live for a time on Zanzibar and was asked by the government to organize the new museum.

11. These occasions did not only serve to validate the established leaders of communities, but also sometimes to create new ones. A figure who later became quite prominent in the Comorian community, Juma Aley, said that he was asked to give a speech at the Peace Museum dedication while he was still quite young. He stated in an interview that this performance was "the event that propelled him into the view and graces of the colonial authorities" (Laura Fair, 24 January 1997, E-mail).

12. Resident to chief secretary, 21 October 1925, ZNA: AB 41/1. The ceremonial arrangements were made at the direction of the resident, Alfred Claud Hollis. As he explained in detail to the chief secretary: "Opening to take place at 4 P.M. on 11 November 1925 at which hour His Highness will arrive at the outside entrance where he will be met by the Chairman of the Committee and the Curator, who will accompany him to the steps. At the foot of the steps he will be received by myself, a few of the principal officials, heads of communities, and members of the committee. His Highness and I will mount the steps, followed by the Chairman and Curator. The general public will be in front of the steps." As he further elaborated, at the conclusion of the ceremony the sultan would be the first to tour the Beit el Amani: "While he is in the Museum only heads of communities and a few principal officials should be allowed to enter, the general public being admitted after his departure." See also *Supplement to the Official Gazette*, 14 November 1925, ZNA: BA 104/43.

13. Kirk to Hardinge, 12 August 1894, ZNA: AB 40/42. In order to make clear the relations between the British consul, the sultan, and the protectorate government (government of Zanzibar), it is necessary to delineate the questions of legal standing and forms of governmentality that colonialism created. Due to the complicated way colonial rule was imposed, the British maintained the fiction of having a consul general on Zanzibar who was charged with representing the Crown's interests in the court of the sultan, who headed a nominally "separate" government. The consul general posed as a mere diplomatic representative, but in actuality he controlled everything the pro-

tectorate government did, making all appointments and budgetary decisions. Furthermore, all government departments were led by British-imposed officers, mostly Europeans, including the first minister, who ran matters on a day-to-day basis. This form of indirect rule, which lasted until 1913, meant that the British were compelled to recognize foreign treaty rights granted by the sultan prior to their assumption of control—rights that granted trading privileges and extraterritorial legal status to foreign nationals. Various groups, such as Comorians, could claim to be French subjects, gaining "community" privileges and special treatment under the treaties negotiated by the French consul. Most Arabs, of course, along with indigenous African groups and long-resident ex-slaves, were considered subjects of the sultan and were governed by a hybrid mix of British and Islamic law. Some Indians, on the other hand, were considered "British Indian subjects" following the conquest of India. If, however, certain groups—the Ismailis, for example—had gained rights on Zanzibar prior to the time the British took over their "homelands" in India, then British law could not be applied to them.

14. "Mnazi Moja Agreement, Registered No. 53 of 1899," 15 September 1899, ZNA: AB 40/42.

15. "Town Council Minutes," 14 January 1910, ZNA: AC 16/13.

16. Among others, Norma Lorimer recognized the significance these social fora possessed in the colonial world, speaking of the importance of the golf club to English identity and "satisfactory colonization" overseas. A seasoned traveler who had lived in Uganda, she managed to reach Zanzibar during the reign of Sultan Seyyid Ali (1902–11). In her subsequent account, she reflected upon Mnazi Mmoja, writing that "for the English community, the two most important institutions in Zanzibar are the golf course and the [English] Club. . . . Along the road [to the course] you pass as many nationalities as you do when you cross the bridge at Constantinople which divides Pera from Galata. . . .You journey on with this amusing river of Eastern humanity, until you pass the Marconi station on the cliff, then you suddenly come to the greenest of green golf courses, which runs along by the sea. It is indeed a charming spot, for it is bordered with luxuriant vegetation, and there is a beautiful walk just beyond it, where the soul that delights in tropical flowers and wild birds can wander, while the sons of Britain overseas follow the little white ball which makes their happiness and their home" (1917, 337–38). I am very grateful to Laura Fair for bringing this text to my attention. For similar views from the same period, see Younghusband 1910.

17. Clarke to Sir Edward Grey, 10 February 1910, ZNA: AB 40/43.

18. Legal member of council to first minister, 26 August 1911, ZNA: AB 40/42.

19. Clarke to Foreign Office, 14 February 1912, ZNA: AB 40/42.

20. Cyril Brooke Francis, "Memorandum: The Mnazi Moja Decree, 1926," 14 January 1926, ZNA: AB 40/43.

21. Clarke to Foreign Office, 14 February 1912, ZNA: AB 40/42.

22. Clarke to Foreign Office, 16 February 1912, ZNA: AB 40/42.

23. Clarke to Foreign Office, 28 February 1912, ZNA: AB 40/42.

24. Clarke to Foreign Office, 27 April 1912, ZNA: AB 40/42.

25. Foreign Office to Clarke, 22 June 1912, ZNA: AB 40/42.

26. Clarke to Foreign Office, 27 July 1912, ZNA: AB 40/42.

27. Nor was this an isolated instance. Prior to World War II, colonial officials often paternalistically invoked the need for the regime to protect the rights of "vulnerable" subjects, usually Africans, as a means of delaying or disabling demands for more representative governing bodies. They claimed that creating such public fora would work to the advantage of more "advanced" Indians or Arabs, arguing that the status quo—in which colonial officials controlled the rules of the game—should be indefinitely maintained.

28. Sir Edward Grey to Clarke, 11 September 1912, ZNA: AB 40/43.

29. The burial ground was filled with graves, materially marked as sacrosanct. Colonial officials feared making outright assaults on established religious domains, believing that such actions would only serve to inflame indigenous "passions." Hence they considered this smaller portion of the land as beyond their reach, simply out of bounds. But if the site lacked this sacred character and had not been used for purposes of interment, the British certainly would have moved to seize it, ejecting the Ismailis from the entire area. For example, the principal medical officer, Dr. Henry Curwen, cast a jealous eye upon the space in 1916, lamenting its "loss" to the Ismailis. He regretted the fact that it could not be used for the purposes of urban planning, writing that it would have made a perfect (and highly salubrious) setting for a segregated European quarter, laid out on English garden city lines: "A time has come in the history of nearly all old Eastern towns, built and continually added to with any regard to the tenets of hygiene, that Europeans, realizing the unhealthiness of obstructed houses thronged round by native dwellings, have emigrated to open districts beyond the town's confines and there built themselves suitable well ventilated houses in country surroundings. In the case of Zanzibar the ridge alongside the golf links, an ideal site for detachable houses of bungalow type with surrounding gardens, was irrevocably lost many years ago to an Indian community as a burial ground." With Mnazi Mmoja out of the question, it was many decades before another "suitable" site for European housing was developed—in Mazizini, well outside the city on the road to the airport. See Curwen, "Annual Report of the Public Health Department," 1916, pp. 18–19, ZNA: BA 7/40.

30. For more detail on the development of racialized categories in colonial Zanzibar, see Bissell 1992 and Fair 1994.

31. Sinclair to chief secretary, 7 March 1923, ZNA: AB 40/42.

32. Honorable secretary, Shia Imami Ismailia Council to chief secretary, 6 July 1923, ZNA: AB 40/42.

33. Sinclair to honorable secretary, Shia Imami Ismailia Council, 27 July 1923, ZNA: AB 40/42.

34. Ibid.

35. "Farewell Entertainments to the British Resident and Mrs. Sinclair," *Supplement to the Official Gazette* 32, no. 1652, 24 September 1923, 605. The quote is from Dr. A. H. Spurrier. Sir Gerald H. Portal was the figure most responsible for giving shape to protectorate rule, serving as consul general in 1891–92.

36. Resident to secretary of state for the colonies, 17 February 1925, ZNA: AB 40/42.

37. Honorable secretary, Shia Imami Ismailia Council, to chief secretary, 21 January 1926, ZNA: AB 40/43.

38. Chief secretary to resident, 21 January 1926, ZNA: AB 40/43.

39. Resident to chief secretary, 21 January 1926, ZNA: AB 40/43.

40. See ZNA: AB 40/43: director of agriculture to the honorable secretary of the Mnazi Moja Sports Club, 14 December 1938; director of agriculture to the chief secretary, 14 December 1938; acting financial secretary to the land officer, 18 December 1938; land officer to the acting financial secretary, 6 January 1939; acting financial secretary to chief secretary, 11 January 1939.

41. Honorable secretary of the Mnazi Moja Sports Club to chief secretary, 21 July 1944, ZNA: AB 40/43.

42. This construction of law as "gift" or "concession" echoes Sinclair's earlier description, when he held that Clarke's sworn agreement with the Ismailis could only be understood as a "favor," "act of grace," or "courtesy." What this suggests is a certain equivocation in British understandings of law in the colonial context. In the case of native subjects, legal terms would be insistently emphasized as neutral rules and procedures to which all must conform. Obedience to the law—the supposed essence of any "civilized" society—was not required, however, when the tables were turned: if "natives" tried to enforce agreements, seeking to ensure the compliance of colonial rulers to established legal terms, the force of the law would no longer be recognized as binding. If they could not evade its terms, Europeans would symbolically recast the law so as to deny its compulsory power. When applied by natives to whites, the law was no longer the law, so to speak: instead, it would be construed in the language of the gift, and adherence coded as an act of benevolent charity or indulgent patronage.

43. Address from the colonial secretary of the Town Board, written for publication and broadcast, 4 October 1943, ZNA: AB 39/317.

References

Bissell, William Cunningham. 1992. "Race to the Head of the Class: Richard Burton in the Interstices of Colonial Power and Knowledge." Master's thesis, University of Chicago.

———. 1999. "City of Stone, Space of Contestation: Urban Conservation and the Colonial Past in Zanzibar." Ph.D. diss., University of Chicago.

Calhoun, Craig. 1992. "Habermas and the Public Sphere." In *Habermas and the Public Sphere,* ed. Craig Calhoun. Cambridge: MIT Press.

Callaghy, Thomas M. 1994. "Civil Society, Democracy, and Economic Change in Africa: A Dissenting Opinion about Resurgent Societies." In *Civil Society and the State in Africa,* ed. John W. Harbeson, Donald Rothchild, and Naomi Chazan. Boulder: Lynne Rienner.

Clayton, Anthony. 1981. *The Zanzibari Revolution and Its Aftermath.* London: Archon.

Cohen, Jean, and Andrew Arato. 1992. *Civil Society and Political Theory.* Cambridge: MIT Press.

Cohn, Bernard. 1983. "Representing Authority in Victorian India." In *The Invention of Tradition.* New York: Cambridge University Press.

Eley, Geoff. 1992. "Nations, Publics, and Political Cultures: Placing Habermas in the Nineteenth Century." In *Habermas and the Public Sphere,* ed. Craig Calhoun. Cambridge: MIT Press.

Fair, Laura J. 1994. "Pastimes and Politics: A Social History of Zanzibar's Ng'ambo Community, 1890–1950." Ph.D. diss., University of Minnesota.

Fraser, Nancy. 1992. "Rethinking the Public Sphere: A Contribution to the Critique of Actually Existing Democracy." In *Habermas and the Public Sphere,* ed. Craig Calhoun. Cambridge: MIT Press.

Gramsci, Antonio. 1971. *Selections from the Prison Notebooks.* Translated by Quintin Hoare and Geoffrey Nowell Smith. New York: International Publishers.

Habermas, Jürgen. 1989. *The Structural Transformation of the Public Sphere.* Cambridge: MIT Press.

———. 1992. "Further Reflections on the Public Sphere." In *Habermas and the Public Sphere,* ed. Craig Calhoun. Cambridge: MIT Press.

Harbeson, John W. 1994. "Civil Society and Political Renaissance in Africa." In *Civil Society and the State in Africa,* ed. John W. Harbeson, Donald Rothchild, and Naomi Chazan. Boulder: Lynne Rienner.

Hardt, Michael. 1995. "The Withering of Civil Society." *Social Text* 45:27–44.

Lofchie, Michael. 1965. *Background to Revolution.* Princeton: Princeton University Press.

Lorimer, Norma. 1917. *By the Waters of Africa.* New York: Frederick Stokes.

Myers, Garth Andrew. 1993. "Reconstructing Ng'ambo: Town Planning and Development on the Other Side of Zanzibar." Ph.D. diss., University of California, Los Angeles.

Pearce, Major Francis Barrow. 1920. *Zanzibar: The Island Metropolis of Eastern Africa.* London: T. Fisher Unwin.

Ryan, Mary P. 1992. "Gender and Public Access: Women's Politics in Nineteenth-Century America." In *Habermas and the Public Sphere,* ed. Craig Calhoun. Cambridge: MIT Press.

Scott, David. 1995. "Colonial Governmentality." *Social Text* 43:191–220.

Sheriff, Abdul, ed. 1995. *The History and Conservation of Zanzibar Stone Town.* London: James Currey.

Young, Crawford. 1994. "In Search of Civil Society." In *Civil Society and the State in Africa,* ed. John W. Harbeson, Donald Rothchild, and Naomi Chazan. Boulder: Lynne Rienner.

Younghusband, Ethel. 1910. *Glimpses of East Africa and Zanzibar.* London: John Long.

Yúdice, George. 1995. "Civil Society, Consumption, and Governmentality in an Age of Global Restructuring." *Social Text* 45:1–26.

6

Staging *Pɔlitisi:* The Dialogics of Publicity and Secrecy in Sierra Leone

Mariane Ferme

In this chapter, I explore the vicissitudes of postcolonial politics in Sierra Leone and their articulation within a public sphere, through an examination of elections that appeared to contradict their democratic potential. Sierra Leonean participants in the 1986 ballot considered the management of ambiguity and the coexistence of covert and public strategies to be central elements in electoral politics, and their ultimate goal was to build consensus through processes of consultation designed to eliminate public opposition. This, in the view of many participants, was the only viable avenue to a peaceful project of democratization. By contrast, the distinction between winners and losers at the ballot generated resentment, and hence the potential for violence. This feature of electoral politics in turn was linked in the local social imaginary to the historical development of the colonial and postcolonial nation-state.

An alternative logic of power to that of public debate and competition was at work, one of dissimulation. Individual success and political effectiveness were seen as being predicated on the ambiguous and sometimes illicit cohabitation with different powerful agencies. The ever-present possibility of politicians resorting to covert politics and the occult to attain power by unconventional means shaped how people decoded events in public, and made these

---

My fieldwork in Sierra Leone was carried out in 1984–86, 1990, and 1993. A Hellman Family Faculty Grant (through the University of California, Berkeley) supported a leave in 1997 during which this essay was written. I am grateful to John Comaroff and Luca D'Isanto for their editorial input, though I am responsible for selectively following their advice. Helpful comments on earlier versions were also given by two anonymous readers, by colleagues in the Berkeley Anthropology Department, and by Janet Roitman, Rijk van Dijk, Patsy Spyer, Rafael Sanchez, and Françoise Vergès. I am especially grateful to Paul Richards and Murray Last, and to Peter Geschiere and Wim van Binsbergen, for inviting me to present some of this material at seminars held in 1997 at University College, London, and Leiden University. Their comments and those of other seminar participants greatly enriched my thinking about the topics addressed in this chapter.

very events unpredictable and potentially violent. The point here is not to romanticize an authentically "African" political idiom of consensus building and ambiguous outcomes, or to minimize the violent elements embedded in these processes. On the contrary, autocratic Sierra Leonean regimes have appropriated this indigenous idiom of consensus in pursuit of their own ends, through the skillful manipulation of symbols rooted in local and regional history. In modern Sierra Leonean politics, the idiom of consensual "hanging heads" (*ngu hitɛ* in Mende) articulated with that of competitive elections to create tension and ambiguity, and these together—not as dialectical stages alternating with peace and clarity—produced outcomes that were remarkably democratic in spirit, even under single-party rule.[1] The case I examine here underscores the different ways a society's membership can "be counted," and count, at the ballot, and make a difference in a collective act of self-construction.

I also raise questions about the relationship between covert strategies and principles of publicity, transparency, and open rational debate, which are central to normative definitions of democratic processes and of the public sphere. For if a defining feature of the public sphere is its accessibility to the broadest possible spectrum of citizens, then its existence in the Sierra Leone case is beyond doubt—except that the conditions under which so many can participate in creating "a public opinion" are that debates be as much secret as they are public, and that outcomes remain ambiguous. A central tenet to the continued existence of a public sphere in Sierra Leone is that its deliberations remain partly secret, especially when these deliberations concern the ballot, given the modern history of electoral abuses in the country. Only through the careful and sometimes unpredictable management of rumors of secret gatherings and strategies can the abuses of the electoral system be kept in check. At the same time, these covert strategies open the way to those very abuses. Both state agents and social actors opposed to them share a view of these shifting idioms and strategies of political culture, a complicity that has been identified as one of the defining features of postcolonial subjectivity under autocratic regimes in Africa (see Mbembe 1992). These shared terms of engagement further complicate the distinction between state and civil society—and the public sphere's mediating role between them—challenged by other contributors to this volume and by previous critical assessments of civil society in an African context (e.g., Harbeson, Rothchild, and Chazan 1994). An understanding of this complicity is at the heart of the African project of political modernity.

Public events in Sierra Leone must be seen in the context of polysemic symbols from the past, symbols whose open character makes them fundamentally appropriable for a variety of purposes. These events unfold on the terrain of a long history of earlier sedimentations. They are "built on the ruins of earlier symbolic edifices and use their materials—even if it is only to fill the foundations of new temples, as the Athenians did after the Persian wars" (Castoriadis 1987, 121). In this patently pre-postmodern world, political actors inherit cultural forms that shape their practices and visions of a moral community, even when these are aimed specifically at subverting a particular legacy (in which case the past is often consciously addressed), or when this legacy is relatively unconscious and emergent.

It is indeed the practices that most explicitly link societies to their past, such as rituals, that also bear within them the "experimental technology" necessary to make sense of, and respond to, novel and contradictory circumstances of modernity (Comaroff and Comaroff 1993, xxx). Thus, for example, Peter Geschiere (1995) has shown that "traditional" Cameroonian witchcraft beliefs and practices—because they potentiate *both* individualistic accumulation *and* social leveling—have become a potent idiom in national politics. The intrinsic ambiguity of witchcraft mimics the opacity of the affairs of the Cameroonian state. However, the unprecedented speed and scale of modern forms of enrichment in Cameroon have tested the fluid limits of existing witchcraft idioms, and have warranted the introduction of new ways of operating in the domain of the occult, a domain in which the Cameroonian state itself has become an actor (Geschiere 1995, 157–62, chap. 5). Hence the need to analyze the ways in which existing cultural idioms may also be mobilized, and transformed, to articulate unbridgeable gaps between past and present, albeit in the guise of a mediation between them.

Public Consensus, Secret Competition

In the rural Wunde chiefdom, the 1986 parliamentary elections were fraught with ambiguity and violence. These were widely perceived by participants to be common features of the political process in Sierra Leone at large. By contrast, the same elections were characterized by Western observers as among the least violent and the most "democratic" of the postindependence period (Hayward and Kandeh 1987, 27); for social scientists, of course, the *absence* of physical coercion, the presence of rational debate, and the peaceful exercise of free individual choice are the hallmarks of liberal democratic forms of participation.

Habermas ([1962] 1989), for example, links democracy in Europe, and the displacement of the absolutist state, to the rise of a bourgeois public sphere and its cultural institutions (the theater, the literary salon, the café, and especially the press), in which communities of interest can negotiate their differences. For Habermas, the substitution of physical force—which he sees as a symptom of the irrational—with the force of discursive argument is central to the emergence of modern political forms. So, too, is the presence of public spaces and procedures for transacting different interests—such as eighteenth-century English parliamentary and press debates—after the secrecy that had characterized court politics (52). Indeed, Habermas perceives the potential demise of the bourgeois public sphere in the return to greater political secrecy in nineteenth- and twentieth-century European states, exemplified by the shift of deliberations and negotiations back to the restricted domains of ministerial cabinets and committees—while political institutions of the public sphere, such as parliament, were only left with a "rubber-stamping" role. This shift coincided with the transformation of public debate in the nineteenth century from an earlier focus on the *principle* of publicity, to the problem of the *enlargement* of the public sphere through electoral reform and the extension of the franchise beyond the property-owning, literate bourgeoisie (133).

From an anthropological perspective (e.g., Hann 1996; Rabo 1996; Spülbeck 1996), and especially from an Africanist one (e.g., Ekeh 1975; Woods 1992) Habermas's theory of political modernity appears partial and Eurocentric. The experience of colonialism, where European political and social institutions were applied in situations of racialized hierarchies of difference, often made "the bourgeois legal fiction of citizenship . . . a farce" (Chakrabarty 1992, 9). At best, it was a fiction applied to an emerging African urban bourgeoisie and not to the majority of rural "native" subjects: "civil society, in this sense, was presumed to be civilized society, from whose ranks the uncivilized were excluded."[2] In Africa and elsewhere in the postcolonial world, the colonial state has left a "bifurcated" legacy, where a hybrid juxtaposition of direct and indirect rule separates urban citizens from rural subjects governed by "native authorities" (Mamdani 1996, 16). More generally, indirect rule facilitated the practice by European and indigenous agents of the colonial state of "straddling" between administration and business, between "official duties and lucrative activities" (Bayart 1993, 70–71). The fusion of public and private spheres upon which these straddling practices were predicated has led to the privatization of many state functions in postcolonial Africa (Bayart 1993, 97–98). Indeed, an outright "criminalization" of the state has occurred: police prey on the civilian population they are supposed to protect, financial institutions falsify the extent of their insolvency, and so on (Bayart, Ellis, and Hibou 1997).

While these developments in postcolonial Africa seem to contradict Habermas's normative definition of the public sphere, they have also produced critical spaces where "public opinion" has taken shape, albeit in hybrid, covert forms.[3] Habermas himself saw in modern politics a return to covert, secretive practices, linked to the dramatic rise of the public sphere since the nineteenth century—a process marked by the growth of competing interests within the public sphere in such a way as to limit its critical role vis-à-vis the state; and, in the twentieth century, by a breakdown of the separation between the state and the institutions of civil society. Note that, for Habermas, it is the expansion of voting privileges, above all else, that enlarged and multiplied the institutions of the public sphere in the nineteenth century, and that dramatically limited their "publicity." At the same time, the separation between state, civil society, and the public sphere began to be redefined; the state took on "private" roles (e.g., the oversight of social welfare), while societal institutions assumed statelike functions in the domain of economic activity ([1962] 1989, 142–60). These transformations, though, were not necessarily reflected in the public's continued self-image as a critical body—an image or fiction that, according to Habermas, was (and continues to be) an equally important element in the historical constitution of a public sphere. This is especially evident in the context of elections, which are at the core of participatory democracy and underpin the very idea of a free, transparent political society; party platforms, public debates, and critical press scrutiny are, after all, conventions that perpetuate "the liberal fiction of a public sphere in civil society" (211).

In the Sierra Leonean instance examined here, this fiction was called into question, even when it was invoked. The rituals and events of the electoral process were *not* articulated through the contestation and debate that constitute the main "periodic staging of a political public sphere" (Habermas [1962] 1989, 211). Rather, what was staged during the 1986 national ballot in Sierra Leone, and in others before it, was a performance of consensus and unity, which on the surface seemed inimical to democratic competition. Struggles for power and political argument did occur. But they took place elsewhere: in domains whose restricted access made them antithetical to those normally associated with institutions of the public sphere. Political debates straddled public and secret settings, but the general awareness that this was the case makes possible an argument that a public opinion of sorts was nonetheless being formed, one whose straddling techniques—in the interest of avoiding violence—owed its origins to the violent, alien logic of "outvoting." Like other intergroup negotiations,

> voting, too, is a projection of real forces and of their proportions upon the plane of intellectuality; it anticipates, in an abstract symbol, the result of concrete battle and coercion. This symbol, at least, does represent the real power relations and the enforced subordination which they impose on the minority. (Simmel 1950, 242)

The electoral process might be an ill-adapted, alien political institution in Sierra Leone. And its introduction here may have been deformed by the single-party state. Yet, as its outcome suggests, the 1986 ballot produced unexpected results that seemed, indeed, to coincide with the will of the majority.[4] Where they occurred, public displays of consensus were usually framed *both* in the idiom of "traditional" political culture *and* as shared values of modern national politics. Some rural people questioned the part played by competition in elections and decried the relationship between public and secret politics. But they saw them as an inevitable aspect of *pɔlitisi,* of national electoral politics, and of the violence engendered by this process.

The General Election of 1986: Kpuawala

The 1986 general elections were held a few months after the installation of a new president, Maj. Gen. J. S. Momoh, to succeed Siaka Stevens. At the time, the peaceful transition from the aging Stevens—who had led the country for most of its postindependence years—to his handpicked successor was hailed by the international media and by political observers as a rare event in Africa. All the more so because political and economic life in Sierra Leone were at a particularly low point. Hopes for real change were reflected in the high percentage of contested seats in this ballot—90 percent compared to about 71 percent in 1982—the first held after the declaration of a single-party state under the All Peoples' Congress (APC) in 1978 (Hayward and Kandeh 1987, 36). The electoral campaign and vote canvassing, the process of finalizing candidate lists, the elections, and their outcome were fraught with anxiety and ambivalence in the rural village of Kpuawala (see Ferme 1992, 66–82).

In addition to the public appearances and speeches made by politicians and their supporters at regular intervals, another kind of politicking was at work: in secretive, nocturnal conclaves. Initially these two domains existed in parallel to each other, the one shadowing the other. Open gatherings in the central communal spaces during daytime hours were followed by nighttime meetings known to only a few. These were held inside darkened houses or in the secluded forest enclosures of the men's Poro society; open, verbal allegiance to a candidate was often followed by private avowals of support to his opponent. Occasionally, however, the articulation of these different arenas became apparent through unexpected circumstances, highlighting the implicit connections between them.

The ambivalence about the elections among village people in Kpuawala was brought on, in part, by the configuration of a particular struggle. The incumbent member of Parliament (M.P.) for the area, who was the paramount chief's (P.C.'s) brother and a Freetown physician, was challenged by the brother of the local section chief. In Sierra Leone, rural villages and hamlets are grouped into sections, several of which make up a chiefdom, and each of these nesting administrative units are represented by a chief and his or her speaker, in addition to select elders. In sparsely populated rural areas, a political constituency may encompass multiple chiefdoms. Here, in Bo South I, it included two: Wunde and Jaiama-Bongor. The candidates, however, came from the same chiefdom, Wunde, and, in fact, from neighboring sections and communities. Kpuawala was roughly equidistant from the chiefdom and section headquarters that were, respectively, to be identified with the opposing contestants. As a result, it would be caught in the middle.

Both candidates had close, overlapping kinship and social ties to all communities in Wunde. The challenger was a civil servant in the chiefdom administration known as "V.J." (for Vandi Jimmy, his surname). He had been begged *not* to run against Dr. Dabo, the P.C.'s brother, who was his elder. This happened at a public meeting in early February 1986, when leaders and representatives of the chiefdom were called ostensibly to discuss the implementation of a national price regulation program. The introductory speech was given by the central chiefdom administration clerk, who stressed "our" need to "make sacrifices" in accepting price reductions and in resisting the temptation to hoard goods. "We," he told the audience, "are the government." This speech was delivered in English and translated simultaneously into Mende for the benefit of a member of the national press who had accompanied Dr. Dabo from Freetown to follow his campaign. The imprecise rendering of expressions such as "making sacrifices" with *saa gbua* (the vernacular term for ritual sacrifices of food and animals) must have given a somewhat surreal quality to the discussion of price controls and international loans. In any event, the assembled audience seemed not to pay much attention to the official speeches. It only perked up when the list of commodities and prices was introduced. After having reached an agreement on a uniform price list for locally produced goods, the gathering turned to other political matters.

Visiting dignitaries were introduced. These included B. A. Foday Kai, the elderly but energetic paramount chief from Jaiama-Bongor, the other chiefdom in the constituency. Foday Kai was also a figure of national renown and a member of the APC's central committee, and was thus asked to chair the proceedings.[5] On this occasion, he wore his usual attire: blue jeans with a "Pierre Cardin" belt, a "Wisconsin" T-shirt emblazoned with his own initials, a "Miller Beer" baseball cap, and thick prescription spectacles. The chain-smoking Foday Kai cut a very different figure from the Wunde P.C., whose long, white robe, round skullcap, and abstention from smoke and drink identified him as a "praying," or practicing, Muslim. However, Foday Kai also had a leather whip casually draped around his neck, a traditional marker of Mende chiefship that complicated his cosmopolitan appearance. This blend of imported and locally manufactured commodities, of new and old, and of cosmopolitan fashion and the historic symbols of indigenous rule underscored Foday Kai's carefully crafted identity as a cultural broker. Widely respected for his knowledge of Mende "tradition" and his interest in and patronage of vernacular arts and crafts, he was consulted in matters relating to local culture and history by rural people as well as by foreigners and urban Sierra Leoneans.[6] His roles as paramount chief and a member of the APC's central committee, as native ruler, and as one of a handful of chiefly representatives on the national scene extended his brokerage skills into the political domain as well. Foday Kai was a powerful reminder of the integral role played by "traditional" rulers in modern African politics, especially in bridging the gap between state and civil societal institutions, between democratic and lineage politics (whose idiom he always employed).

The political meeting had begun with a cheering drill, orchestrated from the dais by men wearing matching white trousers and red caps. These men incited the crowd to shout each letter of the ruling APC party logo, followed by slogans about unity. The attire of these cheerleaders, later referred to by Dr. Dabo as his "Unity Force," corresponded to the party's flag, or "symbol," a red rising sun against a white background. Their opening ritual set the stage for the official proceedings, situating them within the purview of the ruling national party. Then there was an announcement that the educated descendants of the chiefdom—those who had migrated to urban areas or abroad and who held white-collar jobs—had formed the "Sewa Descendants Association," which recently had met in Bo, the provincial headquarters.

At that gathering, they had discussed the upcoming parliamentary elections. Their secretary had told those present that two men had expressed a desire to run: the incumbent, Dr. Dabo, and V.J., the section chief's brother, who was a government clerk in the neighboring Sherbro district. The meeting was not able to reach a consensus on a single candidate to support, nor could it manage to convince either one to drop out of the race; so it decided to put the matter to the constituency itself. Members of the association in the audience, which included professionals, civil servants, and businessmen, were identified by their T-shirts silk-screened with the organization's acronym—which had been sent by a chapter in the United States. The composition of such associations in Sierra Leone further confuses the division between the state and civil society, and emphasizes the increasing importance in political processes at home of the wealthier and better educated expatriates in Europe and the United States. In the wake of the hardships brought about by previous economic policies, the financial support given by these foreign groups to the grass roots, and the networks they have established, has made them an important factor in constituting a transnational civil society.[7]

Following the announcement about the association, and its earlier meeting, V.J., the challenger, made a theatrical, late entry, conspicuously taking up a position with his followers at the back of the audience. By contrast, Dr. Dabo, the incumbent, was seated on the dais in front of the assembly, with the other dignitaries—many of whom were his relatives. P.C. Foday Kai stood up and spoke forcefully, saying that he disliked the gossip and the vicious rumors (*sɔlɛ*, literally "noise") that might be generated by a contested election. He expressed fears about the infighting to which it would lead. It would have been bad enough if the candidates had been from two different chiefdoms in the constituency. But with both coming from nearby areas of Wunde, there was sure to be trouble. Foday Kai asked the interested parties and their supporters to "hang heads" *(ngu hitɛi):* to engage in consultations until they reached "one voice," or unity *(ngo yila),* and agreed on a candidate.

In making this request, Foday Kai was not merely rejecting competitive electoral politics out of a regressive attachment to tradition. He was affirming a principle central to single-party rule in Sierra Leone since 1978; the principle that also underlay the ritual display of unity at the start of the meeting. The move away from a multiparty constitution had been justified on the ground that it was inconsistent with the consensus building implied in the customary practice of "hanging heads." This, President Siaka Stevens had argued at the time, was a more "African" approach to the democratic process and would prevent the widespread violence and corruption that had characterized earlier elections (see Kpundeh 1995; Reno 1995, 66; Scott 1960, 187; Zack-Williams 1989, 125). Significantly, he had called a referendum to pass the constitutional change, to show that the process of transition had itself been consensual; that "hanging heads" had occurred on a national scale (see Hayward and Dumbuya 1983, 663–64). With this creative reading of "tradition," Stevens and his supporters implied—as other Africans have done—that democratization might be better served by being grounded in vernacular political styles, rather than in liberal theories without local resonances (see Haugerud 1995; Karlström 1996). But this modern appropriation of "hanging heads" could also be seen as antidemocratic: its fundamental premise, to enable participation in decision-making processes in a relatively egalitarian setting, was easily subverted by exclusionary strategies aimed at eliminating threatening political opponents. Simply put, Stevens had appealed to consensus politics as a preliminary step toward instituting a single-party state, because his APC party had barely won the 1977 elections. During that ballot, the APC's strong-arm tactics against candidates of the largely Mende-based Sierra Leone People's Party (SLPP) had gained the latter considerable popular sympathy. As a result, many believed that the SLPP would have won in future contests (see Hayward and Dumbuya 1983, 663). More immediately, in Kpuawala in 1986, the paramount chief sought to achieve an uncontested election by building on a modern use of *his own role* in politics; from the very first elections at the eve of independence, in 1957, local rulers used the strategy of "hanging heads" to run unopposed in their own local ballots and to support their favorite candidates on the national stage (Scott 1960, 185–87).

Unlike those early, uncompetitive elections, the move now to "hang heads" in search of consensus, and the fears expressed by Foday Kai of the consequences of a contested race, belied the very high percentage of contested seats fought in all Sierra Leonean elections since independence. Indeed, Foday Kai's concern may have been prompted by a recent ballot closer to home: in 1982, in the neighboring Pujehun district, the division of the constituency between two candidates from the same area resulted in unprecedented violence, deaths, destroyed property, and the burning of entire villages (see Kandeh 1992, 96; Hayward and Dumbuya 1985, 80–81). Many refugees from those events were now living in Wunde and were among Foday Kai's audience.

Thus the search for consensus in this setting might be read both as a response, by the APC leadership, to recent experiences of similar electoral contests *and* as an evocation of an older, more encompassing political culture. Local political practices always carry a multiplicity of meanings and symbolic articulations.

After Foday Kai, virtually every one of the dignitaries from his chiefdom gave speeches openly supporting Dr. Dabo, even though some used ambiguous language suggesting that they did not oppose the challenger either. In following their P.C., these speakers exemplified exactly the consensus they were trying to elicit from the two candidates. They intimated that having an open contest would be embarrassing, and that it would be a disgrace if the matter could not be settled "in the chiefdom family." The reference to family immediately triggered a response from V.J.'s close relatives. They protested against the assumption that they had encouraged him to stand. The audience around Alhaji Vandy Jimmy, V.J.'s brother and the local section chief, murmured in agreement; it was well-known to them that the latter had tried to "sweet talk" his brother out of running *(i ngi ma nɛnɛa).* The very fact that Alhaji Vandy Jimmy—to whom no direct reference was made—presumed that he was being called into question is itself instructive. It suggests that political speech is always thought to comprise multiple, often concealed messages. The exchange offered a glimpse into that other, less visible domain of politics, as Chief Vandy Jimmy articulated what would normally have remained unsaid in public. At that point, various friends of the challenger scrambled to chronicle their efforts to dissuade him from his candidacy—acknowledging, in effect, that the hanging heads process had not succeeded at that level.

All through this discussion, V.J. stood in stone-faced silence on the margins of the gathering, conspicuously unaffected by efforts to provoke his participation. Then he was asked again, in front of everyone, if he still intended to run. He replied in the affirmative. This gesture indicated his unwillingness to go along with what was in effect a performance. Recall that the meeting had begun with a theatrical cheering session, a ritual expression of unity; also, the protestation of the section chief, which suggested that real political negotiations ought to be concealed, never more than partially enacted in public. English, a language well understood by only a handful of the audience's members, was used earlier in the meeting, which added to the notion that substantive deliberations were a secondary aspect in this kind of open political gathering. Indeed, the proper domain for hanging heads and reaching consensus here is never the public arena, whose oppositional, competitive dynamics underscores the authoritarian logic of "open," rational debate. With his statuelike posture and his refusal to be drawn into the discussion, V.J. underscored the staged character of these proceedings, whose sparrings were a mere *overture* to both the electoral campaign and the negotiations characteristic of any political process (see Murphy 1990). The tension was palpable, until the P.C. changed the subject with a formal speech that made no reference to what had just transpired.

This last intervention signaled a shift. Negotiations over the issue of political elections would now move to another register, away from the public domain to the parlors and backrooms of village compounds. Accordingly, the gathering adjourned. Later, young men discussing the day's events in Kpuawala seemed quite skeptical of the public expression of support for the incumbent: "That's what they said, but who knows what is in their hearts?" They speculated that the backing for V.J. was much greater than was apparent—even if he was a newcomer with relatively few patronage networks in the area. Some criticized the M.P. for never having set foot in the villages of his constituency since his election; his rare visits had been confined to the chiefdom headquarters. They pointed out that his challenger had built a beautiful, modern cement house in his hometown (the most attractive house in the community), and took this to indicate that he would spend more time locally than his opponent did. Eventually, however, it was announced that the two candidates had come to an agreement. V.J. had withdrawn from the race.

The (Body) Politics of Ambiguity

V.J.'s change of mind turned out not to have been, in Mende terms, a change of heart. Nor had most people thought so. In the days following the February meeting, casual conversations in the village turned to the dangers of *pɔlitisi,* and to the "bad medicine" (*hale nyamui,* also "unattractive, ugly") often deployed to acquire power and wealth. One man remembered a court case in the neighboring chiefdom some years before; he described the metal claws found on an alleged member of the leopard medicine society indicted for murder. Members of this society and a handful of other banned secret cults were thought to mimic the attack techniques of wild animals to procure human bodies, whose parts were used to make amulets or substances that endowed their wearers or consumers with special capacities (Kalous 1974; Richards 1996a, 143–45). Women and children were said to be the most common victims of bad medicine, as they were easier prey. The covert manner in which these substances were thought to work under ordinary clothes and appearances was analogous to the way in which political speech was assumed to evoke hidden meanings and to project its significance to the outside world. When politicians or performers displayed unusual oratorical skills, when they seemed particularly charming and persuasive, Kpuawala bystanders often wondered what made them so attractive. Jokes about things hidden under clothes or inside bellies revealed the preoccupation with potency medicines, and brought the issue of bodily substance to the forefront of their evaluation of people.

Beyond the practices they address, such public discussions of bad medicine have political effects as well. Rumors, suspicions, accusations, and denials of witchcraft activities in the national media as well as village gossip circuits are the discursive extensions of power medicine's strategic, concealed deployment. Politicians enhance their reputations by circulating rumors of their own occult powers, while attempting to undermine their rivals with suspicions of consorting with much worse concealed agencies (see MacCormack 1983); public accusations of involvement in bad medicine may trigger reactions of horror and fear toward the accused, but they also add to their power, especially when there is no evidence with which to prosecute in a court of law.

Not a week had passed after the February political meeting when it was rumored that V.J. was again a candidate. According to local gossip, as soon as the gathering had ended, the Jaiama-Bongor people who had publicly opposed V.J.'s candidacy had written to his brother, the section chief, declaring their secret support. Those who reported this rumor found nothing strange in this shift from a vocal public stance against somebody to surreptitious support for him—or vice versa. The backing for Dabo at a meeting of all the constituency notables, where even the national press had been present, was thus countered by a personal letter to V.J.'s brother; what is more, the latter was seen to reflect real loyalties more than the former. This domain of concealed actions and relations carried greater weight than did the open debate of political meetings.

The months leading up to the May ballot saw visits from both candidates and their supporters, who extolled the virtues of their man and the shortcomings of his opponent. At one point, V.J. reported the P.C. to the national electoral commission in Freetown for publicly backing his own brother and intimidating his subjects, instead of keeping out of the campaign. V.J. also mentioned being harassed by his opponent's allies when he went to Freetown to collect the party "symbol" that was necessary to stand in the election, and which would grace official candidate posters (see figures 6.1 and 6.2). Supporters of each side gave speeches saying that people should follow their hearts in "dropping the paper," in voting *(a wu kɔlɔ gula wu li woma),* but then tried to turn those hearts in a particular direction through gifts of cash, food, and even drugs. On one occasion, a group of young men said that V.J. had brought a big bag of *jamba* (marijuana) for his followers. This substance was consumed mostly by young men, who made up the bands of escorts/thugs that protected the candidates and threatened their adversaries. V.J. courted this constituency most openly, thus reinforcing his image as the candidate for change and youth and against the status quo. In this aspect, this political struggle conformed to a generational conflict evident throughout Africa (e.g., Hutchinson 1996; Marchal 1993; Richards 1995, 1996b).

In addition to its formal public appearances, each camp held unan-

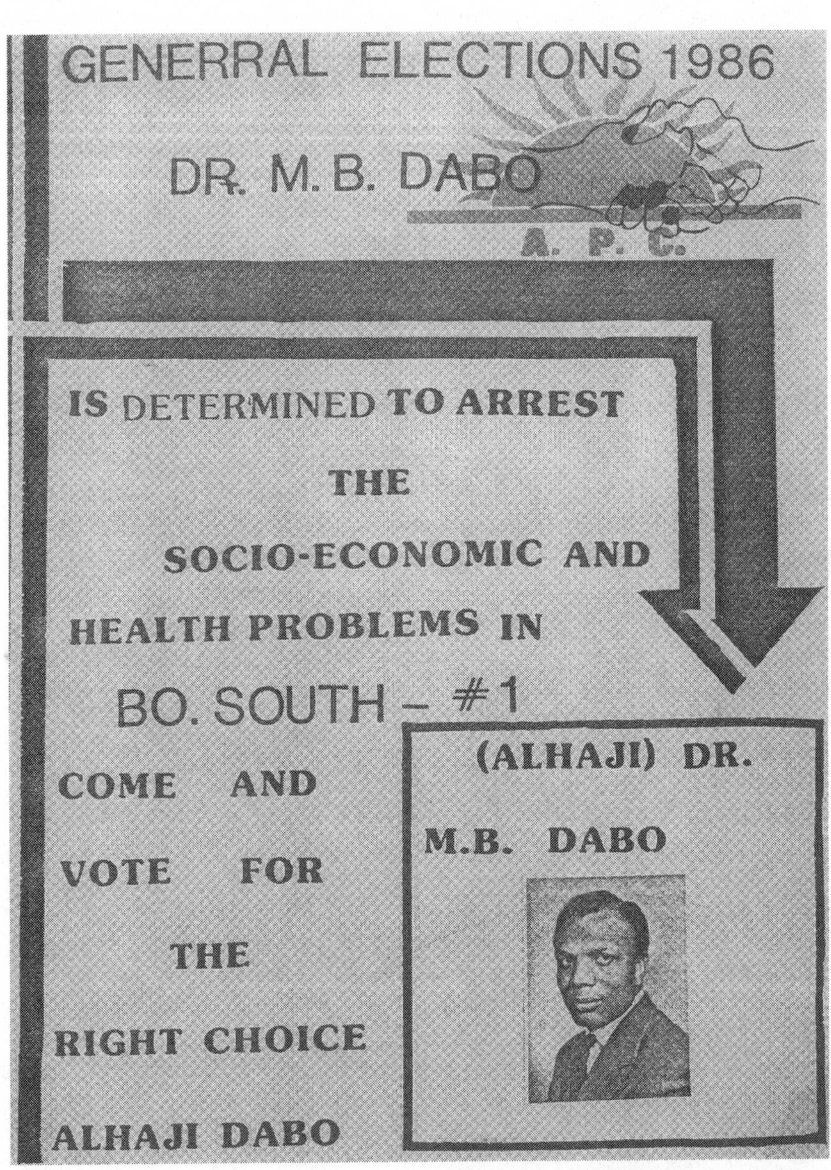

Fig. 6.1. Incumbent M.P. (Alhaji) Dr. Dabo candidate poster, Bo South I constituency general elections, 1986.

Fig. 6.2. Challenger Vandi Jimmy (V.J.) candidate poster, Bo South I constituency general elections, 1986.

nounced, "secret" meetings. One April day, I dropped by without advance warning at the section chief's house and found him surrounded by local notables and Kpuawala men, who were obviously embarrassed to be seen with him. Among those eating at his table were some of the most eloquent supporters of his brother's political opponent. Like the Jaiama-Bongor elders, these people seemed to be backing one candidate in public and another in private. Turning surprise to advantage, the section chief approached the man accompanying me—a known follower of his brother's opponent and a brother-in-law of the P.C.—and began "sweet-talking" him into changing his mind. In a context in which it was assumed that loyalties were often multiple and dissimulated, and where special attributes were thought to endow political figures with irresistible powers of persuasion, it was always worthwhile to sow the seeds of alliance. And, concomitantly, to court *all* potential voters.

Courting the voter is characteristic of democratic elections, where the undecided, who lack a strong commitment to any side, may determine the outcome. In Kpuawala voters are courted for a different reason: because an eloquent campaigner, aided by concealed powers, can always entice followers with *multiple* loyalties to turn—if only long enough to effect the desired result. The notion that unusual personal attributes, or persuasive ways, can alter political balances at any time also suggests that political contests remain undecided until the last.

When sweet talking was not enough, more or less open threats of action followed. A group of elders from the chiefdom headquarters visited Kpuawala in May to beg the gathered community to vote for the incumbent. Insisting that they had come at their own initiative, without the P.C.'s knowledge, they at first repeated the familiar litany that they were not there to campaign and that everyone should vote according to their hearts. But, on two separate occasions during the meeting, speakers reminded the audience that votes would be counted by village. It would be obvious, therefore, whether they had "followed" Dr. Dabo or V.J. This thinly veiled threat was also one of the few open acknowledgements that despite public declarations, the M.P.'s backers were aware that secret machinations might be afoot to put an end to his long political career.

The candidates' platforms shared common elements: both Dr. Dabo and V.J. focused on "development," on the benefits that would accrue to their constituencies from their election, and on their kinship ties to the chiefdom. But significant contrasts were apparent as well. The two men could not have been more different, nor could the symbolism invoked by them. While they both ran under the same party icon, a red rising sun, each had a distinctive set of allegiances to its colors. The incumbent belonged to the country's educated elite: a European-trained physician who had spent many years abroad, he had a private practice in Freetown and traveled upcountry in a Mercedes. His electoral poster portrayed him in suit and necktie (figure 6.1). His pilgrimage to Mecca had also earned him the title of *Alhaji,* but this was bracketed in his poster, which privileged the "Dr." Nonetheless, Dr. Dabo's Muslim identity helped bridge the distance between his European education and his political reliance on the religious rural leadership in the constituency.

Despite the kinship rhetoric in Dr. Dabo's speech and his appeal to a common Muslim faith, he remained for many constituents a distant, foreign relative. Much was made by his opponents of the fact that he did not own a house in the chiefdom or spend much time there; also that his family was of Mandingo origin, from neighboring Guinée. Dr. Dabo's speeches emphasized the public works projects he had steered toward the chiefdom, but whispered comments from the audience suggested that, by living in the capital, he distanced himself from his constituency. A story circulated about how, when the local men had helped clear a large farm for the M.P. after his previous election, they were fed "white people's food"—sweets and finger food instead of the customary rice meal—and had left hungry.

By contrast, his opponent was said always to feed people generous meals when they assisted him in major farming tasks. "At least with V.J. we will eat rice and fill our stomachs," declaimed his supporters. In his campaign, the challenger exploited the rich political symbolism of his populist appeal to earthiness and full stomachs. V.J. also capitalized on the fact that he had not received a sophisticated education, or traveled abroad. He labeled himself a "son of the soil," whose closeness to his homeland and its problems was demonstrated by his having built a house there (figure 6.2). Another strand of V.J.'s strategy to claim the higher moral ground was in the very domain of religious symbolism in which the opposing camp appeared to have its most solid credentials. In contrast with the urban, professional attire of Dr. Dabo in his campaign poster, V.J. chose to be portrayed in the white gown worn by the P.C. and all other local Muslim clerics.[8] His followers presented him as a candidate for change, one who would spend more time locally than his opponent ever did. As evidence, they stressed the difference between V.J.'s section chief brother, who worked on his farm every day, and the paramount chief, who "stayed in town." While Dr. Dabo's identification with the APC regime was brought home by the constant presence of an escort wearing the party logo and chanting its "unity" routines, V.J.'s campaign bore no such markers; to wit, his distance from the ruling party took on even more radical overtones as events unfolded.

The campaign came to a fever pitch with the approach of the elections in May, and the fear of slander and violence in local communities increased apace. People from the neighboring chiefdoms—where the 1982 elections had been marked by assault and destruction—had begun to arrive over the preceding weeks. Carrying their possessions and settling in with local friends and relatives, they hoped to avoid the worst political turmoil. It was said that at times like these, such places as Kpuawala, being in the "bush," were far safer than the big towns.

The isolation of these bush communities was not accidental. The work to maintain roads and bridges within the chiefdom was scheduled by the P.C. and local authorities, and depended on voluntary cooperation. Thus one of the ways in which political sympathies in the various areas could be gauged at election time was through the willingness of people to participate in such communal labor. For a long time now, the palm log bridges and paths leading to Kpuawala had been left to deteriorate, and things were getting worse with the onset of the rains. Residents complained about the state of the road every time a vehicle tried to get through. But no effort was made to clear the vegetation engulfing it, I was told, in order to limit the risk of thugs coming in from outside to cause trouble. Kpuawala, in short, had deliberately pushed itself farther into the bush through the strategic neglect of road maintenance. This tactic also bespoke the political factionalism that divided the chiefdom, cutting off the village, now increasingly opposed to Dr. Dabo, from the P.C. and his headquarters, which had come to be identified with the incumbent.

Three days before the elections, two rotting bridges were finally repaired so that a vehicle carrying the electoral commission and ballot boxes could get through. The voters' roll was wildly inaccurate. It included over twice the number of people recorded by the national census five months earlier. No attempt was made to update the lists by dropping duplicate entries and by deleting the names of the deceased and departed—or by registering immigrants and those too young to vote at previous elections. As before (see Scott 1960, 197–200, 245–51), the lists were treated as inviolable documents. As a result, several young men and women were not mentioned in the roll call preceding election day. After some objection, the commissioner said that people on the list who were still in Kpuawala would vote first; those not on it could do so later.

Election day saw people converge on Kpuawala from the four other communities that were to vote at this polling station. Crowding around the meeting place where their names were read, voters received a blue marble and had their fingers marked in green to prevent them from casting more than one ballot. They went alone to a nearby house, where two boxes were placed. Each was marked by a photographic portrait of a candidate, and voters were instructed to drop the marble into the box of their choice. Nobody left the village for the whole day. Despite these arrangements, which were intended to guarantee the secrecy considered crucial to "free and fair elections"—and the fact that nobody openly discussed their ballots—everyone seemed to assume that voting preferences would be known to the opposing camp. When asked how this could happen, people said that there were ways in which what went on inside the closed room could be ascertained. Some seemed particularly uneasy about having the candidates' portraits looking on. These pictures were alluded to as indexical symbols of the human beings they represented, rather than being neutral icons to differentiate ballot boxes.

At the end of the day, when the polls closed, the electoral commissioners were besieged by complaints about irregularities; some people even refused to let them leave with the ballot boxes. After arguments and physical struggles, they were allowed to depart in a vehicle sent to fetch them—but with an escort of young male leaders who went along to register their objections and to prevent further irregularities. The following two days were spent in almost unbearable anticipation of the results, and hardly anyone went off to their fields. Slanderous speculation began even as we were waiting, when one local man said loudly—to nobody in particular—that, if V.J. won, the Kpuawala chief was sure to be replaced; that nobody would ever listen to him or respect him again. This chief had never wavered in his support of the M.P., whose brother, the paramount chief, was his son-in-law.

Finally, at daybreak on 2 June, the third day after the elections, the arrival of a crowd of shouting people from the path to the section headquarters made plain that V.J. had won. Most of the community broke into song and dance. The losing M.P.'s most prominent supporters were slandered—including the village chief. Piles of palm branches were left in front of his house—the first public display of a different party symbol in a supposedly single-party election. The palm tree had been the symbol of the Sierra Leone People's Party (SLPP), which had led the government in the pre- and postindependence years, and had then been the APC's main opposition until its suppression (discussed in the following section). The crowd intoned a song addressing the local chief by his first name rather than the respectful *maada* ("grandfather") and the Dabo surname, and he was told that he was now an "ordinary person" and would soon be replaced. The song went on to say the same of the paramount chief; also that a new chief would "sit in Wunde." This was a play both on the word for chief (*mahɛi*, "he who sits upon") and on the fact that Wunde is, at once, the name of the chiefdom and the name of the particular village where V.J. was from and where his brother lived. The implication was that the section chief was being put forth as a likely successor to the P.C. Other local people were accused of having acted as spies for Dr. Dabo's campaign during the preceding months, and they were beaten or driven out of town over the following days. The same happened in neighboring communities.

Later, a large crowd gathered in the section chief's village to celebrate his brother's victory. His compound was surrounded by palm tree branches planted in the ground, and palm fruits were hung on strings from the eaves of his house. The section chief proclaimed, publicly, that palm trees had been the source of his wealth, adding: "This is where I found money for my brother's campaign. The Dabos are rich [from diamonds and trade and politics], but [palm] oil is what made *me* rich."[9] People ate and collected the palm fruits throughout the day. One Kpuawala man came back from the celebration proudly displaying what by his own reckoning were 150 palm fruits: he said that he would plant them and begin his own palm tree nursery. Thus it was that palm fruits, the symbol and instrument of V.J.'s election, became a tangible expression of political and economic patronage, helping others to reproduce wealth elsewhere.

Palm Trees against the Sunset: Political Symbols and Their Transformations

Alhaji Vandy Jimmy's victorious display of palm leaves and fruits was more than a celebration of hard work and honestly gained wealth. It also tapped into political symbolism with deep historical roots in Mendeland. The palm tree, as I mentioned, was the symbol of the illegal, mostly Mende-based Sierra Leone People's Party (SLPP), which dominated the national scene from before independence to 1969, when it became the opposition. During the 1973 general elections, the SLPP was marginalized by the APC; it was formally outlawed with the establishment of single-party rule five years later. Thus Alhaji's celebratory display could also be interpreted as an assertive resuscitation of the SLPP, as a challenge to the process of "hanging heads" associated with decades of oppressive APC rule, and as a rejection of the leadership of the likes of Dr. Dabo. Indeed, V.J.'s campaign, beginning with his defiant stance at the margins of the APC-dominated meeting in February, might be read as the symbolic reenactment of a suppressed oppositional politics, appealing specifically to Mende ethnicity.

The periodic evocation of ethnic sentiment has been an increasingly common feature of modern party politics in Sierra Leone (Kandeh 1992) and elsewhere in Africa. In particular, it has been linked to political dynamics in single-party states, where ethnicity "became the home of the opposition" in the absence of other unifying factors such as a developed class consciousness (Vail 1989, 2). Ironically, oppositional ethnic politics have been exacerbated by calls in the early 1990s for multiparty elections across Africa on the part of international donors (e.g., Moore 1996, 589–92).[10]

In sum, the "son of the soil" rhetoric accompanying that display of palm leaves went beyond a generic opposition against the foreign values and cosmopolitan lifestyle of Dr. Dabo, whose wealth was based both on professional and political activities and on family mercantile enterprises. It also had a more specific link to modern party politics in Sierra Leone, pointing toward the emergence of an opposition. In addition, the image of V.J.'s generously nurturing roots in Mendeland invoked a specific local history. Among the claims made by some of his relatives was that they were "warriors" descended from the legendary Ndawa of Wunde, founder of their village. A century earlier, Ndawa had led a blockade against the coastward transport of commodities on demand by European merchants—a move that resulted in the intervention of British colonial authorities (Abraham 1978, 37, 85; Fyfe 1962, 483).[11] Their connections to a lineage of landowners and warriors was contrasted with the alien origin of Dr. Dabo and his brother, the P.C. It was pointed out that being tall and fair, the Dabo family even *looked* different from "real" Mende, and still spoke among themselves the Manding language of their Guinée homeland, which none of the local villagers could understand.

The palm leaf also carried another yet deeper historical significance in this Mende setting. It was said to have been the signal sent among communities by leaders of Poro, the men's secret society, to organize a rebellion against the imposition of taxes, in 1898, in the Sierra Leone Protectorate (Abraham 1978, 159; Chalmers 1899). Thus its association with unity and consensus went back a long way, much longer than the red-and-white "Unity Force" of the APC. By appropriating this symbol to express discontent with the government, V.J.'s supporters recast their victory as continuous with those century-old events. The secret role of Poro and other esoteric societies in orchestrating political outcomes has long been a preoccupation in modern Sierra Leone (e.g., Cohen 1981; Kilson 1966; Little 1965, 1966; Scott 1960, 174); this was underscored in a comment made by a still-furious Dr. Dabo several months later. After referring to the palm leaves, he said that the election turnout had been secretly arranged by the Poro initiation chapters in the villages of the chiefdom. "*They* kept on meeting in the bush," he said, and promised that this was not the end of the story. His meaning was clear: he, too, had recourse to covert ways of getting even.

Of Bees, Warriors, and Politics by Other Means

The official vote count in the Bo South I constituency was reported in Kpuawala a few days after the ballot. A representative from the electoral commission toured the chiefdom villages accompanied by the P.C.'s messenger, and posted a typed copy of the vote breakdown by polling station near the main meeting places (see the appendix to this chapter). V.J. had won a majority of votes in all polling stations of both Wunde and Jaiama-Bongor chiefdoms, with the exception of the headquarter towns, Gboyama and Telu, and of P.C. Foday Kai's hometown of Bendu. In other words, despite the ambiguity surrounding Chief Foday Kai's political loyalties, and his followers' covert support for V.J., both P.C.s and their closest allies ended up backing the incumbent candidate. This outcome underscores the strategic linkages between "traditional" authorities and politicians at the national level in modern Sierra Leone. The profile of the two candidates in this election suggests why this is the case: there is no fundamental discontinuity between these two kinds of political elites, their formation, and the sites they inhabit. Within the same family, close brothers may hold "traditional" or national political office, or, as in the case of P.C.

Foday Kai, both at the same time. Though the continuity between "traditional" and modern educated elites has been seen to be especially strong in postcolonial Sierra Leone (see Bayart 1993, 148; Kilson 1966, 71–79), and their political alliances a feature of single-party states elsewhere in Africa, this linkage also owes much to the institutional legacy of the colonial state and its role in shaping "native authorities" (see Geschiere 1995; Mamdani 1996, 16–23). In particular, Mamdani has seen a major obstacle to the development of a modern African civil society in the racist exclusion of rural peoples from full citizenship in the colonial state, and their subjection to "traditional" authorities and "customary" laws that differed from the citizenship rights of urban dwellers. However, this chapter points to a more optimistic future for civil society, given that in practice the same social actors can straddle the two domains of traditional and national politics, and of rural and urban locations.

During the weeks between the elections and the inaugural celebrations for the new M.P. on 15 July, supporters of Dr. Dabo, relatives of the paramount chief, and local authorities were harassed, insulted, and threatened. Some relocated to the chiefdom headquarters, which had become isolated from all other communities despite its prominent location on the main road. Bush paths and back roads connecting villages suddenly came alive with travelers, thus opening up an alternative geography—one previously concealed—to that associated with the out-of-favor regime. On inauguration day itself, the "unity" conveyed by the uniform attire of the crowd—*ashɔbi*s, clothes made especially for the occasion from a single fabric pattern—belied the uneasiness of the new M.P.'s followers. They were less than delighted to hold the festivities, according to protocol, at the political center of the chiefdom, right "at the feet" of the losing M.P.'s constituency; many of them stayed away. But a large gathering, with masked dancers and a variety of other entertainments, took place anyway. As was customary, these were accompanied by licentious language and political and social satire.[12] Chiefdom officials and visiting dignitaries spoke about mending old enmities and "forgiving" each other, to general applause and vigorous nodding in the audience. But, at the high point of the festivities, a war dance was performed by P.C. Foday Kai and some of the elders. On this, his first visit to the chiefdom since the February meeting, Foday Kai put aside his jeans and baseball cap. Along with his cohort, he wore "traditional" warrior garb: a rust-colored, kola-nut-dyed tunic, breeches, and a cap made from strip-woven local cotton, on which were sewn amulets and animal horns filled with protective medicines. In this attire, the handful of elders performed one of the carefully choreographed dances for which Foday Kai was known, waving swords over their heads and staging mock duels.

Although intended as a form of celebratory entertainment, this dance seemed to speak of political battles of another time and kind, and to relate them to the contest just concluded. In the event, the dancing warriors' protective garb was put to the test not by bullets or blades, but by a swarm of dangerous killer bees, which suddenly descended on the crowd in the midst of this performance. In a few minutes, the village's open spaces were deserted as people ran shouting in all directions, shutting doors and windows behind themselves. Amid the eerie silence, the only sound was the drone of insects and the running engine of a single abandoned car: its doors were open and its white interior was alive with bees.

One of the paramount chief's brothers said that the bees must have been nesting in the roof of a an abandoned kiosk nearby, a building whose fading sign read "Post Office." Perhaps it was fitting that the bees had chosen this site. It stood as a reminder of the collapse of state services and of the severed communication links between outlying rural areas, the country's urban centers, and the world beyond. The man argued, quite reasonably, that the commotion from the unusually large crowd must have disturbed the nest. His sister, however, seemed skeptical of this explanation. Eventually the swarm began to lift and people emerged from hiding, many with multiple stings on their bodies. Visitors were anxious to get away as fast as possible. Few doubted that this attack had been the work of witches *(hɔnabla)*, unleashed by vengeful, disappointed Dabo supporters.

"*Hɔnabla mia a tie, kpɛlɛ!*" "They are all witches!" one woman said excitedly, adding that she just *knew* she should have stayed away. An alternative gathering was held in the new M.P.'s hometown, where the main topic of songs, speeches, jokes, and other performances was the bee attack, whose meaning was interpreted with variable degrees of explicitness. All along, most people seemed to think, there had been intentions other than reconciliation in the minds of the P.C., the losing candidate, and their supporters. They had tricked people into coming to their territory, only to unleash their evil medicines on them, even to try and kill them. Thus the unpredictable, terrifying bee attack that put an end to the "celebration" hosted by the losing candidate's brother spawned an open discussion about the relationship between public and secret political practices. Among its recurring themes was the impossibility that the losing party would accept the results. This followed the assumption that it was driven by witchcraft. But the violence was also seen as an inevitable consequence of electoral politics in general, a process that produced winners and losers rather than consensus through negotiation.

Because it played into a long history of oppositions, and called upon powerful symbols, the conflict continued for a long time after the elections. Seven months later, when I left Sierra Leone, followers and relatives of the P.C. and Dr. Dabo were still being harassed and ostracized; in extreme cases they had abandoned their home villages. Procedures were under way to depose chiefs who had been too openly supportive of the losing candidate, and others were made to apologize profusely with gifts, money, and public humiliation. Then my farewell party in Kpuawala turned into a political confrontation, in which

Foday Kai had yet again to intervene as peacemaker in order to avoid open violence. This was the fate of most major gatherings in the chiefdom thereafter. The bee attack came to be accepted as conclusive proof that the losers were not going to resign themselves gracefully and were planning to use witchcraft to even scores. It should be said, however, that some people in the P.C.'s compound at the time of the attack interpreted the event in very different terms: as a covert punitive action by V.J.'s supporters. Secret strategies and connections were seen to have been a major factor in his victory; hence Dr. Dabo's comment about V.J.'s "meetings in the Poro bush."

In March 1987, only a few months after his inauguration, the new M.P. was implicated with five others in an alleged coup attempt against President Momoh, supposedly mounted by a Mende antismuggling agent with the support, among others, of Vice President Minah. A prominent Mende politician from the neighboring Pujehun district, Minah was also considered responsible for the violent *ndɔgbɔsui* attacks there following the 1982 elections. The accused men were imprisoned and most of them were executed. V.J. managed to get his sentence converted to house arrest in Freetown, where he died in 1990, apparently from complications from diabetes (Paul Richards, personal communication, London, March 1997). In Wunde, however, his death was imputed to more mysterious agencies.

These events turned politics inside the chiefdom upside down, as the persecuted supporters of Dr. Dabo regained control of the local scene and began to exact their own revenge. Some of those who had been chased from their villages as spies were installed as village chiefs, albeit very unpopular ones. The section chief was deposed and heavily fined by the P.C., with the backing of police sent in by the national government. The police also helped track down, imprison, and mistreat many elders who had followed V.J. Had Dr. Dabo been prophetic when he had said, in 1986, that the political fallout of the election was far from over? Or had he been at work behind the scenes, marshaling his own resources and networks to bring all this about? Many Kpuawala people felt they knew the answer as soon as the bees attacked.

In light of the conflict, the president of Sierra Leone, Momoh, decided to pay a visit to the chiefdom to "settle the land" *(a ndɔlɔ hugbatɛ)*, arriving by helicopter with the inspector general of police, Bambay Kamara. But resentment continued to brew over the crackdown by the P.C. after V.J.'s death. Rumors began again to circulate about gatherings in the Poro bush. As it happened, the civil war overtook the affairs in the chiefdom. The military regime that seized power in 1992 weakened the authority of all P.C.s installed under the APC government, accusing them of having been corrupt. When elections were held again in February 1996 to establish a civilian government, they were open to more than one party for the first time in twenty years. Among those fielding candidates were several with names harking back to "pre-APC times," including the SLPP, which won the ballot.

Conclusion

I began this analysis of the 1986 elections outlining some of the challenges posed by the straddling strategies and bifurcated historical legacies that make the application of normative models of the public sphere and civil society problematic in the context of the postcolonial Sierra Leonean state. The permeability in Africa between spheres that might arguably have limited autonomy elsewhere, if only under specific circumstances, is also an aspect of the "illicit cohabitation" between authority and its subjects in postcolonial regimes (Mbembe 1992, 4). In the Sierra Leonean case, this cohabitation was exemplified by the shared idiom of covert power at different levels of state and civil society. Regardless of the implications for struggles in local, national, or even transnational political arenas of any electoral reforms in Sierra Leone, the continued link between these domains is also ensured by a shared political culture among their actors. One of the defining features of postcolonial subjectivity in Sierra Leone is the fundamental ambiguity of political intentions, practices, and agencies. Modern politics and life also presume the coexistence of multiple public and covert dimensions of reality. That "numerous contents of life cannot even emerge in the presence of full publicity" (Simmel 1950, 330) is taken for granted; but this, as Habermas himself has noted, has come increasingly to characterize the "democratic" formations of late capitalist societies as well.

The potent social imaginary of ambiguity, rumors, and occult forces deployed in the more "ordinary" political setting of the 1986 ballot and its aftermath also provides a context for understanding the extraordinary forms of violence that took place at the outbreak of civil war some five years later.[13] Both events drew on symbols linked to the historical genealogy of the modern state, its violent genesis in colonialism and its more recent history under the corrupt, sometimes brutal APC regime. This genealogy includes previous instances of belligerent resistance, such as the 1898 "tax war"; and of bitterly oppositional party politics, such as those evoked by the silent deployment of SLPP icons during the 1986 elections, itself a protest against single-party rule.

The SLPP's rapid transition from banned party to majority government in the 1996 elections was foreshadowed by the continued invocation of its key symbols in major political events during the years of its suppression. Its existence in peoples' memories and desires, as they lived through the excesses of what came to be known as the "APC time," conforms to Mende notions of how power operates. Power is seen to work in secret, covert spheres, whose existence is tantalizingly evoked by the use of polysemic symbols in the public domain, such as the palm branches displayed by the section chief or the rhetoric of hanging heads. These symbols are sufficiently rich in their resonances to conjure up many other meanings as well. Palm branches speak of ancestral links to the land, of a commitment to feed one's followers, of Mende political history in both postcolonial and colonial times. Hanging heads may be understood, generically, as a means to achieve unified, concerted political action through consultation and compromise; but it is also associated with the introduction of a single-party constitution, and with the APC era. Furthermore, the polysemy of political symbols like the palm leaf—as icons of authority in some contexts and as oblique calls to resistance in others—challenges any simple antinomy between hegemonic and counterhegemonic signs.

After V.J.'s involvement in the 1987 coup attempt, his brother was not reinstated as section chief, although he commanded a loyal personal following. By contrast, the paramount chief displayed remarkable staying power. He continued to hold office, despite periodic threats to his authority posed by changes in government and by the civil war that has displaced him and many of his subjects. However, the 1996 (multiparty) elections did not resolve the issue of the M.P. for the constituency, and the post did not return to its previous holder.

On the face of it, the discourse of democratization and reform that has engulfed Sierra Leone and other African states seems to favor the concentration of electoral politics in urban centers. In Sierra Leone, the civilian government elected in the 1996 multiparty elections, and restored to power in 1998, ran on a platform that included electoral reform proposals. Future elections might restrict voters to a choice of parties, not individuals, and this might shift competition for political patronage and office from the local constituency to the party headquarters in Freetown. At the same time, multiparty elections may also facilitate the politicization of ethnic identities; witness, for example, the formation of new, ethnic-based parties in the 1995 Tanzanian elections (see Moore 1996).

What is most striking, finally, about the 1986 elections in Wunde is the remarkably democratic spirit at their core. And this in spite of real anxieties and fears of violence; in spite, too, of the "foreignness" of the idiom of government and of the electoral process embodied in *pɔlitisi.* The counterpressures to conform and compete, to renounce political ambitions in favor of consensus and yet to struggle to the very end, is embedded in the logic of covert politics. While electoral politics enact the fiction of free and fair competition, many Sierra Leoneans are uncomfortable with the way in which this creates winners and losers; for them, it is a process, more akin to court cases, that inevitably causes resentment and potential violence. Throughout the relatively short history of elections in Sierra Leone, therefore, efforts have been made to transform political institutions and practices inherited from the colonial state through their integration with local political idioms, like that of hanging heads. While the autocratic potential of these idioms was demonstrated both by their appropriation on the part of the APC and by the role of paramount chiefs in national politics during the early postindependence years, they remain a powerful symbolic resource. In any event, recourse to covert strategies, to the occult, and to the rumors that amplify their potency in public domains provide a powerful check to political excesses.

Together, these features of modern Sierra Leonean political culture give voice to another kind of civility. It is one—and here is the crucial point—that resituates civil society and moral discourse at the very center of national politics; that treats these things as inseparable in the first place. This, to be sure, is the corollary of a public sphere based, in the local imagination, on a dialogics of compromise, of consensus forged through both overt and covert consultation, of communal and sectarian interest, of civility.

Appendix

1986 Sierra Leone General Election Results for Bo South I Constituency

Polling Station Number	Polling Station Name	Votes for Dr. Dabo	Votes for V.J. (Vandi Jimmy)
1	Mendekelema	162	245
2	Mano	31	234
3	Pelewahun	75	179
4	Ngelehun	45	232
5	Largor	62	205
6	Koribundu I	64	131
7	Koribundu II	53	137
8	Koribundu III	50	220
9	Jombohun	13	249
10	Kpetema	48	214
11	Bendu	219	129
12	Kandor Old	128	162
13	Mamboma I	153	282
14	Mamboma II	42	152
15	Mamboma III	130	277
16	Telu	268	75
17	Bawomahun	114	372
18	Gbaama I	222	309
19	Gbaama II	230	274
20	Hegbebu	77	172
21	Ngogbebu	39	130
22	Kponima	94	219
23	Gboyama I	1,050	19
24	Gboyama II	746	31
25	Gboyama III	504	14
26	New Dia	180	445
27	Kpuawala	112	199
28	Fanima	137	189

Polling Station Number	Polling Station Name	Votes for Dr. Dabo	Votes for V.J. (Vandi Jimmy)
29	Wunde I	22	537
30	Wunde II	8	259
31	Yengema	81	358
32	Yanihun	68	151
33	Niagorehun	99	180
34	Pelewahun	70	161
	Total	5,396	7,132

Note: Roman numerals following a location's name indicate that these are larger towns encompassing several polling stations.

The first half of the polling stations on this list are located in Jaiama-Bongor chiefdom, the remaining ones in Wunde. Note that the only places where Dr. Dabo won a majority of votes were the chiefdom headquarter towns of the constituency, namely Telu (16) and Gboyama (23–25). Also notable is the disparity of votes cast in each chiefdom, especially compared to figures from the national census carried out only a few months earlier. The December 1985 census of Wunde chiefdom reported a total population figure of 6,973 inhabitants, while the Jaiama-Bongor population was roughly three times as large. However, the table shows that Wunde voters outnumbered those from Jaiama-Bongor.

Several factors may account for this discrepancy. Seasonal population movement is one: the census was conducted in early December, a dry-season month during which many people visit relatives and attend social occasions. This is also the season in which younger men travel to alluvial diamond-mining areas to supplement their income during a gap in the farming cycle. By the time elections were held at the end of May, the dry season was at its end, and most people returned home. Furthermore, the fact that Jaiama-Bongor chiefdom was itself the site of significant diamond-mining operations, which accounted for its larger population, also meant that it contained a greater number of strangers, including non-Sierra Leoneans. The latter, although not entitled to vote in elections, would have been counted in a census.

Despite these factors, the discrepancies remain significant. It suggests that, at the very least, a large number of people not normally resident in Gboyama (Dr. Dabo's hometown)—where by far the largest number of votes were cast—were encouraged to return home to vote. The results may give substance to accusations of vote tampering, but if improprieties did occur in Gboyama, it is remarkable that they did not succeed in obtaining a victory for the home candidate.

Notes

1. The February 1996 ballot, held ten years after the events analyzed in this chapter, was the first attempt to reestablish multiparty politics and state accountability in

Sierra Leone in some twenty years—a result of both internal popular demands and international pressure. Fifteen months later, the government elected in 1996 was ousted by a coup. However, in March 1998, it was reinstated to power, thanks to the military efforts of Nigerian-led West African troops.

2. For the relationship between notions of civility, civilization, and civil society, see chapter 4 and Elias 1978.

3. Habermas's analysis of the rise of the bourgeois public sphere as a set of institutions that enabled the political participation of increasing numbers of citizens has also been criticized from the perspective of European and American history. The exclusion from the public discursive exchanges of the voices of women, the illiterate, the propertyless, slaves, and other significant portions of the population has always raised questions about "the limits of actually existing democracy" (Fraser 1992, 110; see also Eley 1992; Ryan 1992). Even when these groups have gained access to this conversation, the shift away from an engagement with formal politics—signaled, for example, by the failure to exercise the right to vote—underscores the need to move beyond identifying who is "legally eligible to participate" to reach an understanding of the changing forms and sites of the political (Schudson 1992, 147–48).

4. A high degree of control over results at the local level is possible in single-party states precisely because power tends to become more personalized, and patronage negotiations take place locally rather than on the national scene (see Hayward and Dumbuya 1985, 79). Throup (1993, 377–80) argues that in Kenya, too, single-party rule has not excluded electoral competition and real political change. In addition, Fauré (1993, 324–26) explores the diffidence of Ivoirian voters toward openly competitive electoral contests as a feature of African forms of political culture that directly challenges prevailing Western notions of democratization.

5. Chief Foday Kai was related to the village chief in Kpuawala. He was also a graduate of the prestigious Bo School, a former civil servant, and a recipient of the Order of the British Empire.

6. Foday Kai supported in his chiefdom the few weavers who could still make the older, complicated cloth patterns using only natural dyes, and he ensured that a younger generation was trained by them. He also supervised in his compound the training of dance groups in largely abandoned forms of performance. Foday Kai had represented Sierra Leone at a number of international cultural events in Nigeria (e.g., FESTAC 1977), the United Kingdom, and the United States, as well as being a regular lecturer for the Peace Corps and the international diplomatic community in Freetown. For his role as cultural broker and interpreter-inventor of his peoples' traditions for outsiders, he was once referred to as "Mr. [Mende] culture" (Lamp 1987, 72). See James and Tamu 1992 for Foday Kai's biography.

7. The notion of a transnational civil society deserves a more sustained discussion, which space limitations prevent me from undertaking here. Guyer (1994) explores its implications for Nigeria, and Basch, Glick Schiller, and Szanton Blanc (1994) discuss the role of U.S.-based transnational Asian and Caribbean communities in political and other developments in their home countries.

8. V.J.'s brother, the section chief, had gone on pilgrimage to Mecca several years ahead of Paramount Chief Dabo, and was thus himself an *Alhaji.*

9. *Mbeindo ngi navo majɔa nya ndee va. Daboisia, ti gbatɛngo, kɛ nya ta, ngulɔ mia a nya gbatɛa.*

10. The link between multipartyism and an oppositional ethnic politics was explicitly made by factions in the Sierra Leone civil war. In 1991, the Revolutionary United Front (RUF)—the main (non-Mende) rebel group in the civil war—launched its first incursions into Sierra Leone through Mende territory on the Liberian border and tried to stir up ethnic rivalries in the region through, among other things, the display of SLPP symbols. Though the rebels were unsuccessful in this effort (Richards 1995, 139), their move points to the likelihood that in the 1986 elections, the display by V.J.'s supporters of palm fronds could also be read as a sign that the APC faced a growing threat from a Mende opposition.

11. V.J.'s supporters drew parallels between their candidate's opposition to a corrupt government and Ndawa's (literally, "big mouth," "big name") activities against the colonial administration. They made much of the fact that Dr. Dabo had been sacked in 1984 from his ministerial post in social welfare and rural development because of financial irregularities. They also claimed that V. J. had stronger roots in the area because of his putative links to a famous indigenous lineage. However, the paramount chief could trace his own family's presence in this region for at least as long as V.J.'s. The P.C.'s father and grandfather had preceded him in the chiefdom's leadership, even though their family came during the nineteenth century from the Guinée-Sierra Leone border region.

12. For a discussion of the politics of masking and the masking of politics in Sierra Leone, especially under the APC regime, see Nunley (1987, 203–15).

13. During the civil war, for example, the resistance to clearcut oppositions, and the effort to blur boundaries, gave form to the figure described by the Krio neologism, *sobel,* the soldier-rebel. Unable to distinguish between the attire or behavior of the government's military forces and their rebel enemies, the civilian population recognized the shifting boundaries between these purported opponents well in advance of the events that in 1997 brought just such a paradoxical alliance to power. The saying "Soldiers by day, rebels by night" (Richards 1996b, 7) located the articulation of these identities in the relationship between day and night, open and covert action, in a dynamic of shape-shifting that has its antecedent in the Mende political imaginary in the figure of *ndɔgbɔsui* alluded to in connection with the 1982 elections in the Wunde region. More generally, *ndɔgbɔsui* is an anthropomorphic trickster, a shape-shifting figure common in Mende lore (see Harris and Sawyerr 1968).

References

Abraham, Arthur. 1978. *Mende Government and Politics under Colonial Rule: A Historical Study of Political Change in Sierra Leone, 1890–1937.* Freetown: Sierra Leone University Press.

Basch, Linda, Nina Glick Schiller, and Cristina Szanton Blanc. 1994. *Nations Unbound: Transnational Projects, Postcolonial Predicaments, and Deterritorialized Nation-States.* Langhorne, Pa.: Gordon and Breach.

Bayart, Jean-François. 1993. *The State in Africa: The Politics of the Belly.* Translated by M. Harper and C. and E. Harrison. London: Longman.

Bayart, Jean-François, S. Ellis, and B. Hibou. 1997. *La Criminalization de l'état en Afrique.* Espace International. Paris: Éditions Complexe.

Castoriadis, Cornelius. 1987. *The Imaginary Institution of Society.* Translated by K. Blamey. Cambridge: MIT Press.

Chakrabarty, Dipesh. 1992. "Postcoloniality and the Artifice of History: Who Speaks for 'Indian' Pasts?" *Representations* 37:1–26.

Chalmers, Sir David. 1899. *Report by Her Majesty's Commissioner and Correspondence on the Subject of the Insurrection in the Sierra Leone Protectorate, 1898.* London: Her Majesty's Stationery Office.

Cohen, Abner. 1981. *The Politics of Elite Culture: Explorations in the Dramaturgy of Power in a Modern African Society.* Berkeley: University of California Press.

Comaroff, Jean, and John Comaroff. 1993. Introduction to *Modernity and Its Malcontents: Ritual and Power in Postcolonial Africa,* ed. J. and J. Comaroff. Chicago: University of Chicago Press.

Ekeh, Peter. 1975. "Colonialism and the Two Publics in Africa: A Theoretical Statement." *Comparative Studies in Society and History* 17:91–112.

Eley, Geoff. 1992. "Nations, Politics, and Political Cultures: Placing Habermas in the Nineteenth Century." In *Habermas and the Public Sphere,* ed. C. Calhoun. Cambridge: MIT Press.

Elias, Norbert. [1938] 1978. *The History of Manners.* Translated by E. Jephcott. Reprint, New York: Pantheon.

Fauré, Yves. 1993. "Democracy and Realism: Reflections on the Case of Côte d'Ivoire." *Africa* 63 (3): 313–29.

Ferme, Mariane. 1992. "'Hammocks Belong to Men, Stools to Women': Constructing and Contesting Gender Domains in a Mende Village." Ph.D. diss., University of Chicago.

Fraser, Nancy. 1992. "Rethinking the Public Sphere: A Contribution to the Critique of Actually Existing Democracy." In *Habermas and the Public Sphere,* ed. C. Calhoun. Cambridge: MIT Press.

Fyfe, Christopher. 1962. *A History of Sierra Leone.* Oxford: Oxford University Press.

Geschiere, Peter. 1995. *Sorcellerie et politique en Afrique: La viande des autres.* Paris: Karthala.

Guyer, Jane. 1994. "The Spatial Dimensions of Civil Society in Africa: An Anthropologist Looks at Nigeria." In *Civil Society and the State in Africa,* ed. John W. Harbeson, Donald Rothchild, and Naomi Chazan. Boulder: Lynne Rienner.

Habermas, Jürgen. [1962] 1989. *The Structural Transformation of the Public Sphere: An Inquiry into a Category of Bourgeois Society.* Translated by Thomas Burger with Frederick Lawrence. Reprint, Cambridge: MIT Press.

Hann, Chris. 1996. "Introduction: Political Society and Civil Anthropology." In *Civil Society: Challenging Western Models*, ed. C. Hann and E. Dunn. London: Routledge.

Harbeson, John W., Donald Rothchild, and Naomi Chazan. 1994. *Civil Society and the State in Africa.* Boulder: Lynne Rienner.

Harris, W. T., and Harry Sawyerr. 1968. *The Springs of Mende Belief and Conduct.* Freetown: Sierra Leone University Press.

Haugerud, Angelique. 1995. *The Culture of Politics of Modern Kenya.* New York: Cambridge University Press.

Hayward, Fred, and Ahmed Dumbuya. 1983. "Political Legitimacy, Political Symbols, and National Leadership in West Africa." *Journal of Modern African Studies* 21 (4): 645–71.

———. 1985. "Changing Electoral Patterns in Sierra Leone: The 1982 Single-Party Elections." *African Studies Review* 28 (4): 62–86.

Hayward, Fred M., and Jimmy Kandeh. 1987. "Perspectives on Twenty-Five Years of Elections in Sierra Leone." In *Elections in Independent Africa*, ed. Fred M. Hayward. Boulder: Westview Press.

Hutchinson, Sharon. 1996. *Nuer Dilemmas: Coping with Money, War and the State.* Berkeley: University of California Press.

James, F. B., and S. A. J. Tamu. 1992. *B. A. Foday-Kai: A Biography.* Freetown: People's Educational Association of Sierra Leone.

Kalous, Milan. 1974. *Cannibals and Tongo Players of Sierra Leone.* Auckland: Wright and Carman.

Kandeh, Jimmy. 1992. "Politicization of Ethnic Identities in Sierra Leone." *African Studies Review* 35 (1): 81–100.

Karlström, Mikael. 1996. "Imagining Democracy: Political Culture and Democratisation in Buganda." *Africa* 66 (4): 485–505.

Kilson, Martin. 1966. *Political Change in a West African State: A Study of the Modernization Process in Sierra Leone.* Cambridge: Harvard University Press.

Kpundeh, Sahr John. 1995. *Politics and Corruption in Africa: A Case Study of Sierra Leone.* Lanham, Md.: University Press of America.

Lamp, Frederick. 1987. Review of *Radiance from the Waters: Ideals of Feminine Beauty in Mende Art*, by S. A. Boone (1986). *African Arts* 20 (2): 17–26; 72–74.

Little, Kenneth. 1965. "The Political Function of the Poro," part 1. *Africa* 35 (4): 349–65.

———. 1966. "The Political Function of the Poro," part 2. *Africa* 36 (1): 62–71.

MacCormack, Carol P. 1983. "Human Leopards and Crocodiles: Political Meanings of Categorical Ambiguities." In *Ethnography of Cannibalism*, ed. P. Brown and D. Tuzin. Washington: Society for Psychological Anthropology.

Mamdani, Mahmood. 1996. *Citizen and Subject: Contemporary Africa and the Legacy of Late Colonialism.* Princeton: Princeton University Press.

Marchal, Roland. 1993. "Un Espace urbain en guerre: Les Mooryann de Mogadiscio." *Cahiers d'Études Africaines* 33–2 (130): 295–320.

Mbembe, Achille. 1992. "Provisional Notes on the Postcolony." *Africa* 62 (1): 3–37.

Moore, Sally Falk. 1996. "Post-Socialist Micro-Politics: Kilimanjaro, 1993." *Africa* 66 (4): 587–606.

Murphy, William. 1990. "Creating the Appearance of Consensus in Mende Political Discourse." *American Anthropologist* 92 (1): 24–41.

Nunley, John W. 1987. *Moving with the Face of the Devil: Art and Politics in Urban West Africa.* Urbana: University of Illinois Press.

Rabo, Annika. 1996. "Gender, State and Civil Society in Jordan and Syria." In *Civil Society: Challenging Western Models,* ed. C. Hann and E. Dunn. London: Routledge.

Reno, William. 1995. *Corruption and State Politics in Sierra Leone.* Cambridge: Cambridge University Press.

Richards, Paul. 1995. "Rebellion in Liberia and Sierra Leone: A Crisis of Youth?" In *Conflict in Africa,* ed. Oliver Furley. London: I.B. Tauris.

———. 1996a. "Chimpanzees, Diamonds and War: The Discourses of Global Environmental Change and Local Violence on the Liberia-Sierra Leone Border." In *The Future of Anthropological Knowledge,* ed. H. Moore. London: Routledge.

———. 1996b. *Fighting for the Rain Forest: War, Youth and Resources in Sierra Leone.* London: International African Institute, in association with James Currey and Heinemann.

Ryan, Mary. 1992. "Gender and Public Access: Women's Politics in Nineteenth-Century America." In *Habermas and the Public Sphere,* ed. C. Calhoun. Cambridge: MIT Press.

Schudson, Michael. 1992. "Was There Ever a Public Sphere? If So, When? Reflections on an American Case." In *Habermas and the Public Sphere,* ed. C. Calhoun. Cambridge: MIT Press.

Scott, D. J. R. 1960. "The Sierra Leone Election, May 1957." In *Five Elections in Africa,* ed. W. J. M. Mackenzie and K. Robinson. Oxford: Clarendon Press.

Simmel, Georg. 1950. *The Sociology of Georg Simmel.* Edited and translated by K. Wolff. Glencoe, Ill.: Free Press.

Spülbeck, Susanne. 1996. "Anti-Semitism and Fear of the Public Sphere in a Post-Totalitarian Society: East Germany." In *Civil Society: Challenging Western Models,* ed. C. Hann and E. Dunn. London: Routledge.

Throup, David. 1993. "Elections and Political Legitimacy in Kenya." *Africa* 63 (3): 371–96.

Vail, Leroy. 1989. "Introduction: Ethnicity in Southern African History." In *The Creation of Tribalism in Southern Africa,* ed. Leroy Vail. Berkeley: University of California Press.

Woods, Duayne. 1992. "Civil Society in Europe and Africa: Limiting State Power through a Public Sphere." *African Studies Review* 35 (2): 77–100.

Zack-Williams, A. B. 1989. "Sierra Leone 1968–85: The Decline of Politics and the Politics of Decline." *International Journal of Sierra Leone Studies* 1:122–30.

7

Civil Lives: Leadership and Accomplishment in Botswana

Deborah Durham

During a visit to Botswana in July 1995, I heard numerous critiques of President Ketumile Masire, often coupled with paeans of praise to South Africa's Nelson Mandela. At the time, the Batawana, one of the "eight major Tswana tribes" in the country, were installing Tawana II, just twenty-six years old, as chief. Press coverage of the installation and people with whom I spoke conveyed an ambivalence about Tawana's leadership that paralleled that over President Masire. Also in the press that winter were reports of strife and factionalism within the various political parties (which held their conventions in July), typically revolving around leadership and leaders. In spite of characterizations of the Botswana populace as politically overwhelmed, complacent, or weak by some academics (Good 1992; Holm and Molutsi 1992; Molutsi 1998; Picard 1985), none of this vigorous debate surprised me. I was familiar with complaints about presidents, chiefs, and chairmen in Botswana. When I first arrived in the urban village of Mahalapye in 1989, questions of leadership were continually argued—over the person of the local Herero chief, over the heads of local associations, over the role of the increasingly active Herero Youth Association in the community.[1]

What are we to make of these complaints? Were they evidence of a break-

---

I conducted over thirty-two months of fieldwork in Botswana between 1989 and 1996. This research was supported by Fulbright-Hays (Department of Education), the National Science Foundation, Wenner-Gren, the National Endowment for the Humanities, the American Philosophical Society, and Sweet Briar College Faculty Grants. I have participated in various manifestations of a Botswana Internet discussion list server from 1993 to 1998. Most of the participants are Batswana studying abroad; a few live in Botswana. When I first joined a group in 1993, it was run from McGill University as <botswana@cs.mcgill.ca>. When the list manager graduated and returned to Botswana, the list server was relocated to Duquesne University at <botswana@mathcs.duq.edu>. The list manager at Duquesne then graduated and at the end of 1996 two lists were formed, <botsnet@newton.ccs.tuns.ca> and <botswanacf@sheffield.ac.uk>.

down in Botswana's much-lauded democracy, an increasing distance between the personnel and institutions of government and the people of the country? Did they reflect a failure to resolve the legacy of a parallel or dual political system (with both hereditary chiefs and elected officials)? Or did they reflect, as others might claim, the nascent stirrings of a civil society, an emergence of a politicized, active citizenry able both to legitimate and to restrain state powers, against which it stands in vigilant opposition? These latter questions, however, presuppose that states and civil societies are natural, distinct, and historico-evolutionary features of the political landscape; "power, coercion, and resistance" would then serve as intervening variables.[2] I argue that to understand the nature of political life in Botswana and the criticisms of its leaders, it is necessary to examine more fundamental concerns with "civility" itself—local, cultural concerns with the moral nature of political action and the political aspects of a person's agency. I suggest that these discourses derive from a perduring concern with the possibilities of egalitarianism and hierarchical privilege, a concern that pervades social life here, from casual street encounters and household economies to government inquiries and political careers.

Critiques of leadership of all sorts, and concern with egalitarianism and privilege, are not new to the political landscape in Botswana. Nor do "Radio Mall" complaints offered in street-side gossip, media critiques, and public accusations index a unique moment of political crisis in this fairly quiet country. To the contrary, criticism of chiefs has long been a feature of public debate here (Comaroff 1975) and has been embedded in the vivid imagery of courtly praise poetry since time immemorial (Schapera 1965). Present-day discourses of dissatisfaction, then, are best seen as contemporary historical transformations of tensions that have marked political culture and everyday lives in this part of the world for more than a century. The enduring concern with rank and equality, with ascribed privilege and achievement, and the legacy of critique and indeed accountability have given a distinctive quality to Botswana's so-called model democracy. These are the cultural foundations on which we must understand contemporary political forms and processes.[3]

In this chapter, I examine debates about leaders and about leadership in the national media, within the Herero ward of Mahalapye, and among subscribers to a Botswana Internet discussion list. The circulation of critiques through the various public spheres is part of the process whereby Botswana's democracy is remade on a daily basis.[4] Examining that process will *not* answer the question put by Gloria Somolokae: "Do Batswana think and act as democrats?" (1989; the question also in Crowder 1988; Good 1996; Holm 1988, 1993; Holm and Molutsi 1992; and van Binsbergen 1995). Indeed, the question is itself unanswerable, given the ideological distractions that surround attempts to define "democratic" behavior (see Mamdani 1995; Comaroff and Comaroff 1997). But the arguments over leadership do reach to the heart of political culture and civil society—in Africa as in North America, these arguments delineate the possibilities for agentive performance and frame questions about the bases of action, legitimate and illegitimate, by members of society.

Leadership may be considered an "institution," studied for its rights and responsibilities, for its modes of legitimation, and for the way in which it partakes in the accumulation and exercise of power. But it may also be considered part of the social context within which institutions take form, are effective or ineffective, and undergo transformation. Putnam (1993), in his influential study of the workings of democracy in modern Italy, argues that the ways in which all such institutions actually work depend on their social contexts, which are richly varied and historical. Many anthropologists, including myself, are reluctant to distinguish quite so sharply between an institution and its context. Mbembe (1992), for example, has shown how the discourses of state may be refracted and recaptured in the discourses of "the people." His provocative essay reminds us that both institutions and individuals are perpetually embroiled in struggles over meaning. For Mbembe's argument, political struggles produce cultural discourses. Here, I shall consider how cultural struggles over the presence and place of equality and distinction, achievement and privilege, produce political discourses—discourses replete with tensions that are centrally implicated in the reproduction of Botswana's democracy. My objective, then, is to illustrate the ways in which a cultural context can creatively reimagine institutions of leadership—be it chiefship, the presidency, or whatever—and in so doing reconstitute the very framework of a "civil" society.

Botswana and the Struggle for Civil Society

Elections held every five years with a significant impact on policy (Charlton 1993), a free press whose reporting restraints are largely self-imposed (Zaffiro 1993), and an economy whose growth led the world (prior to a recent recession) in underwriting a countrywide increase in incomes and infrastructural growth confound the idea of "struggle" between people and government (see Crowder 1988; Durham 1994; Solway 1995; Tsie 1996). Violent clashes between the government and citizens have been few, although student riots in sympathy for a murdered girl disrupted the capital city and a neighboring village in 1995 and again in 1997 (see Durham 1998). But confrontations of this kind are unusual: more typical are the lengthy discussions in village courts, a public sphere in which opinions tend to be voiced with direct reference to the ideals of a *civil* society (Comaroff 1975; see also Alverson 1978, Kuper 1970). In 1989, when two Herero men began fighting in a ward *kgotla* (chief's court) in Mahalapye, it was the subject of general ridicule for days; years later, in 1996, the incident was still laughingly recalled. When men in the Mahalapye *kgotla* became openly hostile to persons or to the general debate, they would be compelled to leave and their comments dismissed as "*dipolitiki*"—

politics. Thus Gulbrandsen (1995, 426, 439; see also Lekorwe 1989) argues that the disinterest in political parties among most Batswana, at least until the 1990s, owed in part to the stridency of harangues in "Freedom Squares," local public meeting places created across the land at the behest of the state.[5] Almost weekly a politician announces in one forum or another—as reported in the government paper—that Botswana is a nation of "peace-loving people."

The "peace-loving" nature of Botswana's citizenry, however, has raised serious questions among political scientists and other observers. Good (1996), Holm (1988), and Molutsi (1998) are perhaps the most vigorous spokespersons of the view that Botswana's democratic present rests on authoritarian silencing of dissent, popular ignorance of "modern" political process, and a hierarchical and authoritarian past in the shape of the chiefships.

Analysts are often drawn to the articulation of institutions based upon a Weberian "traditional" legitimacy with those of a "legal-rational" legitimacy—the copresence, in Botswana, of both inherited chiefships and a state authorized by electoral politics and constituted in people's lives in the form of professionalized bureaucratic offices, a copresence with its roots in the colonial period (Charlton 1993, 331; cf. Wylie 1990). The success of the Botswana Democratic Party (BDP)[6] regime, runs a common argument, has rested on its ability to weaken "customary" authority without going so far as to provoke outright rebellion (Parson 1990). This is accomplished by sustaining a dual legal system, one "traditional" and the other Roman-Dutch, with the latter taking precedence in cases of appeal; also by having an advisory House of Chiefs sit in government.[7] This view has it that Batswana remain persistent traditionalists, deferential to the authority of inherited statuses and only superficially loyal to a liberal democratic system (see especially Holm 1988; also Gulbrandsen 1995, van Binsbergen 1995). Traditionalists or not, the contradictions of *bogosi* ("chiefship") were fiercely debated by Batswana in September 1996 on an Internet list server: chiefs were alternately seen as "voicing the concerns of the people" against government ministers and as antiquated relics of a system of hereditary privilege and rights out of step with the principles of representative democracy. More than one contributor suggested "develop[ing] our chieftainship in a democratic way," either by having each ethnic group represented in the House of Chiefs or by arranging to elect chiefs in a manner consistent with the prevailing democratic system (<botswana@mathcs.duq.edu> 18–30 September 1996).[8] This discussion was thick with ideas on leadership, privilege, access to position, and status; I shall refer to it again later in this chapter.

Countering the idea that chiefship represented an authoritarian past, and that the copresence of chiefships and a Parliament weakens civil society in Botswana, is a debate as to whether the system under which chiefs gained and exercised authority in the past was not itself democratic, at least in some sense of the word. The chief's councils and court, after all, were the forums in which legislation was formulated; a chief invited open argument about policy and criticism of officeholder by adult male citizens in his *kgotla*. And succession to the chiefship, while limited to those with some genealogical claim, ultimately rested upon the consent of the people (see Kuper 1970; Comaroff 1978; Wylie 1990; see Parson 1990 for the view that, once chiefs became monogamous and were supported by the ideas of British colonialists, primogeniture has been the sole source of authority). The most extreme version of this perspective sees Batswana as fiercely competitive, deploying a language of ascriptive rights in order to negotiate power relations and effectively achieve access to offices. However, the term most frequently applied to Botswana's "political culture" of the past and sometimes of the present is "consensual democracy," a term that in Western democratic theory suggests weakness in civil society in that it does not acknowledge debate, difference, and opposition.[9]

Critics of Botswana's contemporary democracy often note that outside of chiefs' courts and rather weak national interest groups—trade unions, women's rights groups, church councils; those that conventionally gauge the strength of civil society—political life is fairly attenuated. This view is entirely wrong in my opinion. It derives from two sources. One is a lack of familiarity with everyday life in villages and towns on the part of those Western social scientists who have been most vocal in dissecting the public sphere in this African context; this is underscored by their insistence on measuring "civil" society in purely Eurocentric terms.[10]

A second source is the conventional view that, historically, Tswana society was uniform in structure, that all of its component units—households, wards, villages, and tribes—were founded on homologous patterns of authority, status, membership, and political participation. This representation may not be untrue in strictly formal terms, but it conceals a great deal; the picture itself shores up the claims of male seniority and ruling cadres to sustain a monopoly on power and political legitimacy. Ever since the mid–nineteenth century, Tswana chiefdoms have witnessed the growth of other public spheres alongside the royal court—voluntary associations, commercial projects, and especially the church—which have existed sometimes in opposition to and sometimes in support of the chiefship (Brown 1982; Comaroff and Comaroff 1991; Durham 1993, 1995; Gulbrandsen 1995; Landau 1995).

Women, in studies of "traditional" Tswana political society, are too often analytically confined to the household, until they begin to join churches. This notwithstanding the fact that women's activities—in arranging labor for funerals, for example, or in forming short-lived purchasing associations for bulk cloth—have long transcended households: such activities are highly significant in the political life of a chiefdom, but have never been neatly encapsulated within formal structures. During the late colonial period, for example, women in Mahalapye demonstrated on behalf of Seretse Khama during his succession crisis. Whether to protect their market activities at the busy train station (protesting a prohibition on alcohol) or, as "the Mahalapye women's leader" later reported, just to support Seretse (Parsons 1990, 90–92; see also Wylie 1990, 201), the women were organized, had a leader, and were politically engaged. It is simply false to assume, as is so often done, that prior to the rise of such Western-modeled women's rights groups as *Emang Basadi* local politics had been restricted to contests for male authority. Beyond this arena, we find a full and vigorous public life in rural Botswana, in which the struggle between claims to privilege and hierarchical status and to individual action and egalitarianism is also waged.

Hierarchical Privilege and Egalitarian Achievement

At the core of that life—whether taking place in the streets, in homesteads, in the *kgotla,* in newspaper reports, or in the new forum of the World Wide Web—is an ongoing tension between the possibilities of, on the one hand, hierarchy, status, and privilege, and on the other of equality and opportunity for achievement. The tension is most fundamentally between potential agentive positions, between the capacities of persons that allow certain kinds of action and activity, whether commanding others or oneself.[11] This tension takes many forms and occurs in different domains. Claims to hierarchical status difference, and to equality and openness of opportunity, may both be argued in discourses of liberal individualism and of kinship and patronage (see Solway 1994b, 1998). It has, as a tension between modes of interaction, considerable historical depth, although it has undergone significant transformations—with the extension of private property, for example, and the commercialization of the cattle economy; with colonial forms of coercion, constraint, and accumulation; with education and the bureaucratization of political institutions (cf. Kuper 1970; Peters 1994; Wylie 1990).

Comaroff and Roberts (1981) have suggested that endogamous marriage within the Tswana world created an ambiguous field of multiple ties among people who were linked to one another as agnates, matrilateral kin, and affines. Because these forms of linkage were inimical—agnation implied rank and rivalry over property and position; matrilateral bonds were unranked and supportive—social relations had constantly to be managed and negotiated. This process entailed a delicate, unstable balance within households and family groups between (1) hierarchy, asymmetry, and inequality, and (2) egalitarian complementarity. Similar contrasts prevailed with the chiefship and the public *kgotla.* Most precolonial rulers were regarded, above all, as the "first among equals" (Wylie 1990, 27)—but they were also beneficiaries of a system "of hereditary rank [reflecting] the material dependence of clients on their patrons . . . expressed in the deference and subordination of juniors" (25). They were, simultaneously, "chiefs by birth" and "chiefs by the people";[12]

access to office was determined, equally, by "rules" of ascription and by practices of achievement (Comaroff and Roberts 1981; Kuper 1970). In the nineteenth and early twentieth centuries, moreover, the tension between hierarchical order and individuated achievement manifested itself in the periodic rise and fall of highly centralized political communities, in which status was marked by *kgotla* rituals—and in dispersed, egalitarian settlements, both possibilities within the political culture (Comaroff and Comaroff 1992b).

Today, the same set of tensions are reproduced in everyday street-side encounters, as small requests for gifts are made playfully between casual acquaintances in order to establish relations of equality between them—in contrast with requests insistently made in terms of kinship, which involve claims of dependency, responsibility, and hierarchy (Durham 1995). Enactments of command, both of self and others and of subjection shape comportment and dress, especially of women (Durham 1999). On the national stage, transformations of this tension are reproduced, in altered form. On the one hand is the insistence on equal citizenship for all; "we are all Batswana" is the oft-repeated claim made by functionaries of the state and by villagers across the country. On the other hand is the widespread and persistent suspicion of discrimination based on Tswana "tribal" difference, ethnicity, or race (cf. Durham 1993; Motzafi-Haller 1998). For example, rumors still circulate in Mahalapye, relayed with surprise and condemnation, that in the 1970s Kalanga who knew to put a "small mark" on their applications to university were automatically accepted (the minister of education then was Kalanga). Such unfounded gossip attests to contradictory perceptions and expectations of both preferential treatment and open and equal opportunity for achievement, expectations that pervade public discourse in Botswana today.

Unemployment rates of 20 percent or higher in the mid-1990s (Hope 1996, 58) make access to work particularly contentious. In the workplace, ethnicity is both denied as significant (by many employed minorities with whom I spoke) and is also widely suspected as grounds for either employment or dismissal. The *Guardian* (Botswana) reported in "Fired for Ikalanga?" that two workers at BotswanaCraft, a crafts marketing enterprise, had been fired for speaking Ikalanga, the Kalanga language, on the job (17 March 1989, 1). The story was hotly debated in the press. Can workers be distinguished on the grounds of ethnicity? Should "private," inaccessible languages be spoken in a space of public employment? One contributor to an Internet discussion linked the hereditary status of chiefs to ethnic (actually racial) discrimination. Hereditary *bogosi,* he said, "has no moral basis any more than apartheid on the basis of skin pigmentation" (<botswana@mathcs.duq.edu> 19 September 1996). Leaving aside issues of race and ethnicity, some employers in Mahalapye strive to avoid all ties of ascribed dependency and rights: they purposefully hire nonrelatives to work as housemaids, shop assistants, and herd boys. Relatives, I was told, make demands; they rely upon kinship, not performance, to keep their jobs. Nonrelatives also have their problems as employees, however, in a society in which equal status is something to be defined in the course of ongoing social interaction. Employers, local as well as expatriates, frequently complain about the slowness and laziness of their staff. But laziness is not the issue; these same workers toil hard and long on other projects. Rather, they tend to resist the imposition of a relationship of hierarchy and dependency in the work environment.[13] This, after all, is a society in which equality is valued and must be accomplished within the course of ongoing social interaction; those relatives who make demands may also more readily acknowledge commands.

If anything, talk of prejudice and preferential treatment suggests that expectations of egalitarianism and equal opportunity have increased in the twentieth century. This has come about through a number of social and economic transformations. It is now commonplace to note that employment opportunities, first in South Africa and now within Botswana itself, have provided young men and women with access to resources outside of family property under control of senior male relatives. Able to earn cash and acquire cattle, those willing to leave home to search for work could become independent. Work, and hard work at that, are valued means of achievement: many younger men told me that their fathers had given them nothing, and that they had accomplished what they had (cattle, jobs, households, status) on their own. In a 1 March 1991 article titled "SPIL Meet on Logistics," the *Guardian* printed a delightful aphorism: a guest speaker to the Society for the Promotion of Ikalanga Language (SPIL) in the capital city of Gaborone described his own success as "someone who dances while clapping hands for himself"(9). Often, however, this kind of achievement is linked to education. "No one is born with skills, we all acquire them, don't we?" asked a member of the Botswana Internet discussion list (<botswana@mathcs.duq.edu> 1 November 1996), who went on to ask whether everyone had the same opportunities to learn, acknowledging that opportunity and privilege were encountering new twists and turns.

When, after independence, the Botswana government embarked upon a massive program to make primary education available to all (it is now trying to make secondary education universally accessible) the possibility of equal access to "symbolic capital" was recognized. Nonetheless, numerous complaints about the unequal opportunity to achieve have arisen from discrepancies in competence in the dominant language of instruction (Setswana). At the same time, attitudes toward private schools, available to those with money for tuition, reveal a deep ambivalence over status. Many younger, working adults in Mahalapye, although by no means from wealthy families, aspire to send their children to such schools. They expect that this, along with their own incomes, can give their children an advantage in seeking positions at university and in employment. And yet private schools are also the subject of newspaper cartoons and critical letters to editors: graduates of these schools, which are often taught in English, are shown to be ignorant in Setswana language and culture, unable to pass the standardized exams in the vernacular, and unable to perform in a Setswana-speaking society.

The tensions surrounding access to public schools and the status conferred by private schooling underscore the concern in Botswana with the contrast between privilege and open opportunity. Schooling is still seen as the most reliable route to jobs and income, and also to receiving a kind of respect formerly accorded to the wisdom of the elders. The well-grounded suspicion that its availability may be restricted by hidden forms of discrimination puts it at the epicenter of debates about the nature of contemporary Botswana—and also, as we shall see, at the center of public arguments over leaders and their capacity to lead.

Debated Leadership: Citizenship and Selfishness

Let us return, then, to the complaints heard in 1995, about President Masire and Tawana II, the newly instated Tawana chief. In critiques of President Masire, politicians, the press, and street-side gossip questioned the limits of liberal citizenship, of egalitarian membership in a state whose premise was "civic nationalism" (see Greenfeld 1994). Just before I arrived in the country in July of that year, members of the major opposition party in Parliament—newly confident after 1994 elections in which they increased representation from three to thirteen—tabled a no-confidence motion in the government. While the motion itself referred to a number of problems perceived to be plaguing Botswana (unemployment, income disparities, rural-urban relationships), the newspapers focused on "swipes at" President Masire.[14] The *Guardian*, 7 July 1995, reported M.P. Michael Dingake of the Botswana National Front as saying, "A President or government official with doubtful trust, honour and integrity has no right to exhort the public at large towards social responsibility." Dingake, the article added, had called for "dynamic, farsighted, sensitive and examplary [*sic*] political leadership"(2). The same newspaper also reported a challenge to Knight Maripe, leader of the Botswana People's Party, by the "youth" of that party for largely the same set of reasons (including a more direct reference to financial integrity).

While M.P. Dingake and the Botswana National Front (BNF) went on to criticize specific BDP policies, the press focused instead upon the president's qualities as a leader. Three issues were raised, each relating to larger social concerns: finances, steadfastness and competence, and forward-looking leadership. I shall examine these issues in terms of local expectations of fiscal accountability and ideas about equal citizenship, and connect them to concerns about age-based and educational status. Public discussions of financial accountability consistently expressed a strong commitment to equality of access and opportunity, and a thoroughgoing opposition to hierarchy, preference, and discrimination. With respect to age and education, however, the ambivalence that I have described becomes more evident.

The *Guardian* came down especially hard on President Masire's financial trustworthiness. It mentioned that his name was among those government officials recently listed as bad debtors to the Botswana Agricultural Marketing Board (BAMB). This concern with the integrity of the national leader followed the creation of the Directorate on Corruption and Economic Crime in 1994—itself a response to a rising "moral panic" over corruption in government circles after the discovery of mismanagement and irregular allocations by the Botswana Housing Commission (BHC). The official report on the BHC scandal was followed, in 1992, by the resignation of the vice president and some cabinet ministers; the scandal is held partially responsible for BDP losses in the 1994 elections. Housing figured prominently in discussions of corruption and privilege: along with the financial aspects of the BHC affair, there were widely voiced complaints that relatives of the vice president had been moved to the top of the long waiting lists for government-sponsored accommodation in the capital. Phakalane Estates—a new, expensive residential development just outside Gaborone—was frequently referred to as "Magangsburg." This South African–sounding name links the financial involvement of former M.P. David Magang to the discriminating practices of apartheid South Africa. While outside observers of Botswana often mention the high level of probity in government, many citizens are troubled by such scandals and by evidence of official corruption.

It has long been recognized that several BDP policies, while helpful to the poor rural voters who form the party's electoral base, also enable some politicians to prosper. "Government Ministers Only Enrich Themselves" proclaimed a headline in the government newspaper in 1989 (Zaffiro 1993, 10). Masire himself, in fact, is the one most noted for having benefited from state agricultural initiatives; he is now one of the largest cattle owners in the country. But people in Mahalapye, even when they acknowledged this, did not denounce the president for it (unlike students overseas, who expressed their disapproval on the Internet). In Mahalapye, it was normal, and even admirable, that leading figures become well-to-do partly as a consequence of their positions. Chiefs, elected officials, administrators, and those in business knew many people; they wheeled and dealed, and cars and houses were a consequence of their politicking. Indeed, prosperity could be read as a sign of qualities of achievement, and not part of unequal ascriptive privilege. But—and this is a big but—it was expected that any industrious person with the energy and some know-how could also achieve wealth in the same manner. The Herero chief, Johannes Maharero, scorned by many in the 1980s, has won considerable respect over the years by advancing from an impoverished, uneducated mineworker living in a small mudbrick rondavel to a fairly prosperous cattle trader (and general wheeler-dealer), tractor owner, and resident of a large house wired for electricity. Everyone recognizes that some of his prosperity comes from the business contacts made through his political position, combined with determination and work. ("I don't sleep, I am always thinking" he often told me in English, a language he was trying to learn.) But, as long as he adheres to the business codes by which everyone is bound, no one begrudges him his success. This same attitude was invoked again in an Internet discussion in November 1996: when one contributor intimated that the wealthy were "thieves," numerous responses affirmed that "most of these people worked hard for what they have today," and urged people to report actual corruption (<botswana@mathcs.duq.edu> 6–12 November 1996).

Where President Masire strayed, implied the *Guardian,* was not in profiting but in claiming privileges not available to others and creating his own differentiated relationship to the nation-state. The same may be said of the corrupt officials even now being sought by the anticorruption unit. Many people in Mahalapye, and throughout the country, take advantage of the government-backed credit programs that seek to underwrite development, and every month they are burdened with loan repayments for tractors, cars, sewing equipment, small buildings, businesses, and agricultural improvements. Others scramble around—selling goats or cattle, calling in personal debts or taking out others—to pay the interest on private bank loans or store hire-purchase agreements. Within just three weeks in 1995, two of my Herero acquaintances in Gaborone had furnishings repossessed when they failed to meet credit payments. When President Masire removes himself from the obligations weighing so heavily upon his fellow citizens, he is censured. Commenting on his "failure to service his NDB loan," one discussant on the Internet added sarcastically, "Like any farmer??" (<botswana@cs.mcgill.ca> 5 February 1995). Nor are privileged facilities for other politicians much approved. During the summer of 1995, for instance, a block of "luxury flats" was being prepared for occupation by members of Parliament—drawing outraged comments from the press and people on the streets. While "ordinary citizens" were waiting up to fifteen years for houses built by the Botswana Housing Commission, and while the cost of those houses went up and up, M.P.s were given preferential housing. Echoes, again, of segregated South African cities, of a dual system of laws and rights. And unlike the subjected citizens of Mbembe's "vulgar" postcolony (1992), people in Botswana were neither amused nor zombified.

The idea that President Masire was no longer an equal citizen was expressed by one Herero critic in terms of clothing. Speaking of South Africa's President Mandela, she commented approvingly on his clothing, especially his informal shirts and jerseys, adding, "*ma suvera ovandu, ma tjiwa ovandu*" ("he loves people, he knows people"). President Masire, on the other hand, wears very finely tailored suits, and my critic noted "*u ri kombanda*" ("he is above [the people]"). It is true, he does not dress like them. Although fine attire is much admired even in everyday affairs, clothing can also signify unity within groups, both symbolically and through the pragmatics of mutual endeavor in design and construction (see Durham 1999). Although people certainly would not expect to see their president in a uniform or in clothes matching anyone else's, clothes did offer a ready metaphor: a way of saying that the national leader had abstracted himself from what one Internet contributor called "the level field of play" (<botswana@mathcs.duq.edu> 27 September 1996).

The idea of the community being formed through material goods and interests is central to understanding the BAMB loan scandal. To a large extent, people in Botswana envision their citizenship in terms of rights to the resources of the country (see Durham 1993). *Omang* cards, national identity cards issued in 1989, were often explained as a means of preventing foreigners from taking jobs, school places, land, and development resources belonging to the country. In using public assets, President Masire acted as any citizen, as an equal member of the national community; that these were development funds made the point even stronger.

Public funds in the village are open matters. In both of the voluntary associations that I joined, and others I witnessed, financial accounts were meticulously kept, down to the *thebe* (in 1996, about a third of a cent). Dues, contributions, fines, and income from concerts were carefully recorded; after each funeral or celebration or trip, all expenses were dutifully reported—with remarkable exactitude. One form of fund-raising for village and association projects stands out for the way in which it reflects popular attitudes toward collective responsibility. Sometimes groups would raise money by asking for contributions from all and sundry. Members of a choir, school, ward, or whatever community are then chosen to conduct the collections. (I was even drafted on one occasion by the Herero Ward Crime Prevention Committee.) The collectors are usually women, although men are not barred from the job. Collectors carefully record each donation—from the usual 25 *thebe* (10 cents) to 10 *pula* ($3.50)—and the inscription of each and every donor's name, along with the amount, is the central ritual of the collection. These sheets and scraps of paper are collected with the monies to great applause; they later languish in a notebook or paper bag in some dusty corner. No donor is allowed to escape uninscribed (as I often tried to do), even though it might enable unrecorded donations to be pocketed. And as the collectors circulate, or in collections in larger gatherings, chiefs, officials, and wealthy men are expected to contribute generously, as is everyone according to his or her means.[15]

When the president and other officials abused the development programs, then, it is no wonder that they were condemned for "failing to lead by example" (<botswana@cs.mcgill.edu> 7 February 1995). Batswana expressed concern that the president and his ministers had abstracted themselves from the nation and were operating outside of it; that they had ceased to be citizens of the state, invested in and investing in its public resources. In violating standards of repayment, the president elicited some devastating negative imagery indeed: he was condemned as "selfish." Selfishness is the inverse of loving and caring for others, and as such is indirectly linked to "jealousy," harmful in itself and the motive behind witchcraft. Both these ideas, of jealousy and stepping outside the moral and national community were voiced by a young Herero woman living in Gaborone in 1995. This young woman, a BNF supporter (as are many youth in Botswana), expressed her dissatisfactions with the BDP president at great length. Much of her commentary focused on funerals—upon, in fact, the rites for three Batswana killed in a 1995 mine disaster in South Africa. President Mandela, she noted, attended the services for the South Africans killed; President Masire did not attend those in Botswana.

Funerals in Botswana are *the* central forum for reestablishing moral communities, in which dispersed peoples and interests enter into the process of self-construction (see Durham 1993, chap. 7). For those willing to read it that way, the national leader had withdrawn from the collective process of fabricating identity. His absence further undermined the possibility of building presidential authority along "traditional" lines of gerontocratic patriarchy. In village households, senior men may be poor and uneducated, but they still exert considerable power through their ability to intermediate with the dead. The Herero chief in Mahalapye, who was scorned in the 1980s but gained credibility in the 1990s, partly effected that transformation through attendance at funerals and annual graveside commemorations.

Attendance at burials is highly valued, for it signifies both membership in the community of grief and in a community of caring. Funerals doubly evoke the caring associated with "love" (*oku suvera* in Otjiherero). *Oku suvera ovandu* (to love people, as the casually shirted Mandela was said to do), a quality attributed appreciatively to people, involves most centrally caring for their physical well-being. Gifts of clothes, money, food, and even furniture are concrete manifestations of love. A well-attended funeral attests to the love the deceased had for the mourners, which is reproduced in the food and drinks provided by the family. But it also attests to the love the mourners had for the deceased, and many of their actions as mourners are addressed to the body, the physical remains. Yet this second form of "caring" is double-edged: it can be benevolent, but it has a negative, malevolent form as well. Jealousy, which is thought to pervade everyday life, has its effect on the physical well-being of others; a jealous heart harms its object. It can even kill. Hence, while people ought to go to funerals out of love, they may also go to conceal or even satiate their own jealousy.

No one in Botswana would suspect President Masire of jealousy (or its potent ally, witchcraft) in not attending the mine-disaster funerals. But his indifference could suggest the "selfishness" of which he was elsewhere accused; political discourse does not here center on witchcraft itself, as Geschiere (1997) describes for elsewhere in Africa, but it does invoke moral behavior that is in other contexts associated with witchcraft. Selfishness is akin to jealousy and—the point being invoked by the young woman—is directly opposed to loving and caring for people. But more subtly, some of the complaints about the president's financial activities invoke some of the imagery associated with directed malevolence. Just as witchcraft figures in a "zero-sum" moral economy of material success (see Austen 1993), contemporary interpretations of profit and accumulation in Botswana suggest that profit for some is achieved through others' loss. This arose, for example, in an Internet discussion of a statement by the president of BOCCIM (Botswana Chamber of Commerce, Industry, and Manpower) that Botswana had produced no millionaires (<botswana@mathcs.duq.edu> 6–11 November 1996). While many noted that wealth could be achieved through hard work, they also observed that it could be acquired by means of selfishness and theft. "Batswana do not like to see fellow Batswana succeed," the BOCCIM president was reported as saying, adding that "some even use their official position to destroy other Batswana."[16] Batswana responses on the Internet included such comments as "Being a millionaire means you are either hardworking or exploiting other people," and the repeated assertion that the wealth of "plenty of millionaires" is based on theft—indeed, upon "pathological greed." In all of these, the imagery of riches based on selfishness and malevolence mirrors directly the imagery of more esoteric actions of jealousy and its companion witchcraft. When President Masire's wealth is mentioned, when he is noted for not attending funerals, when he is called "selfish," there is always a flirtation with very serious notions, notions of inhumanity, notions of the profoundest of uncivil acts.

Age, Knowledge, and the Ambivalence of Status

The other terms on which the national newspapers indicted President Masire in July 1995 were steadfastness, leadership, and competence. The issue of steadfastness was raised because the BDP had recently waffled on a number of issues: initially resisting a court case that declared existing citizenship laws unconstitutional, it suddenly retreated and acknowledged citizenship for the children of Batswana women married to foreigners (see Dow 1995); again after long resistance, it lowered the voting age from twenty-one to eighteen (possibly to the advantage of the opposition); having dismissed the Ngwaketse chief, Seepapitso, for insubordination, the government acceded to extensive protests and reinstated him; and after many years of defending the constitutional clause designating the "eight principal tribes" of Botswana, the BDP now seemed willing to abandon it.

These are all "reactive" motions. One of the most frequent criticisms of Masire's leadership has been his lack of initiative, his failure to introduce new policy. This critique resonates with what members of the Herero Youth

Association (HYA) seek in *their* president: someone with ideas, someone to suggest new goals and initiatives. A leader does, in fact, need to stand apart from the general population. In the social imagination of many in Botswana, the source of novelty, of surpassing, lies in the paired set of youth and (Western) education. But these sources of energy and achievement carry their own perils, which again recapitulate the tensions between status hierarchies and achievement-oriented egalitarianism.

Masire, goes this line of critique, had been following the same program that has guided Botswana since independence in 1966. Now outdated, that program no longer addressed the problems faced by a rapidly urbanizing population, by women, youth, and other groups; nor could it resolve the economic issues that now confront the entire country. Ironically, it was the BDP's own campaign strategy of emphasizing specific accomplishments (providing schools, jobs, literacy, infrastructure) (Charlton 1993, 364) that suggested this line of critique. The time had come, according to this argument, to surrender the leadership to younger members of the party, to those with new ideas, new energies. This reasoning was paired, in some circles, with the observation that the president had only a junior certificate education. In short, he was taken to task for being too old, and for lacking education now needed to do a job that he was sometimes depicted as having simply "inherited" when Botswana's first president died in office. By mid-1996, predictions of a midterm retirement in favor of a younger leader were common on the streets, on the Internet, and even in the press, and Masire did indeed retire in 1998.[17]

At first glance, the age factor would seem a curious basis for criticism. Age, after all, is usually taken to be a criterion for status and leadership within "traditional" domains—as noted in the reference to funerals. And indeed, the most widely voiced doubt leveled in 1995 against the new chief of the Tawana tribe, Tawana II, was that he was too young at twenty-six. Similarly, in 1989 I was frequently told that the Herero chief, then in his early thirties, was too young, "just a child." The fact that Masire was too old for the presidency and the party leadership while Tawana II and Maharero were too young for chiefship may point to the distinction between "modern" and "traditional" spheres of leadership. But, as I noted earlier, the two spheres are not distinct: they have formed and reformed each other; they overlap considerably in that chiefs are salaried parts of the government bureaucracy; and both are subject to the ongoing cultural discourse about privilege and achievement. Age has become a highly ambiguous criterion for status in Botswana today in all domains.

People are today ambivalent about the respect they ought to accord age; yet age itself is less a biological state than a social achievement. Deference to age is widely understood to have underpinned "customary" behavior in the past, although older people have been complaining about disrespectfulness for at least seventy years (cf. Tlou 1994). Age ostensibly yielded an accumulation of experience and wisdom, as well as other resources to which younger people sought access, most notably cattle and command of human resources (through kinship and other networks). It is no accident that deference to the elderly today is most strongly marked at funerals, within the homestead, and at the village *kgotla.* Or that it is seen by some people to override even such status distinction as that between chief and commoner. For age, after all, can be seen as an equal-opportunity accomplishment. One contributor to the Internet discussion wrote: "Should my 70-year-old grandfather stand up when a 31+ young man who is chief simply because he is born of a certain couple appears?" (<botswana@mathcs.duq.edu> 24 September 1996).

With the advent of new avenues to success, avenues not dependent upon family cattle or local labor or political support, the position of the elderly has weakened (cf. Comaroff and Comaroff 1992a; Bruun et al. 1994). Outside of the *kgotla,* older people are often derided as superstitious, as failing in personal hygiene, as making political choices based on loyalty rather than informed judgment, as ignorant of the workings of the machinery of modern life—in particular the government bureaucracy and the hospital system. And, while aged parents are generally treated with respect within household compounds, their authority in decision making and in initiating projects is often usurped by sons and daughters—who may have little interest in owning cattle or goats, who provide the monetary resources for the education and upkeep of their siblings or cousins, and who solve many of the problems of contemporary life. As I have noted, almost all the life stories told me by men in their thirties and forties utterly discounted contributions by male parents or guardians. These men typically ascribed their achievements to hard work and self-determination.

The other ambiguity surrounding age flows from the fact that it is not a simple by-product of passing time—it is not necessarily, in fact, an equal-opportunity accomplishment in Botswana. Maturity and seniority are as much an achieved status as one ascribed through biological processes. Innumerable males in their sixties in Mahalapye remain effectively social juveniles or fall directly into dependent "old age" without ever having been "elders" (cf. Bruun et al. 1994). Treated with patronizing good humor by people of all ages, they never become heads of households or attain the financial autonomy (whether based on cattle or salaries) that would enable them to command others' labor and attention. Such biological children as they have had remain in other households. Conversely, some men in their late thirties—still within the general age-range of "youth" in Botswana—achieve the kind of social respect that encourages them to join the seniors' circles at weddings and "admonish" the young couple, to command the services of others at public events, and to sit with the elders at public *kgotla* meetings.

The ambiguities surrounding age as a basis for leadership and status are well illustrated by the shifting evaluations of Johannes Maharero, the Herero chief in Mahalapye. When I first met him in 1989, Maharero had been Herero chief about five years and working in the main Mahalapye *kgotla* for three years. Before then, he was a mineworker in Rustenburg, South Africa; he was raised out at cattlepost, as he said, "in the bush."[18] In the early years, many expressed considerable doubt about his ability as a leader. He was often dismissed as a "child" and as lacking the skills for the job. Maharero had a terrible reputation for "chasing girls," and in December 1988 broke off his wedding just days before the event. Both the chasing of girls and the broken marriage were used to point out his childishness: "It is time for him to grow up," said one of my frequent companions in the village. By this she meant that it was time for him to marry, for in the absence of other initiation rituals in contemporary Botswana, only marriage confirms the passage into full adulthood (see Durham 1998). In 1995, it was rumored that the senior tribal authority for the region—the regent Sediegeng Kgamane—had spoken to Maharero, saying that his reluctance to marry was holding back his advancement in office. Not only grade promotions (and accompanying salaries) were at stake—in 1995, people believed that Maharero's bachelorhood could disqualify him from succeeding to the chiefship of the village as a whole.[19] It is no accident that Tawana II, upon his accession the same year, was asked by the press when he would wed and was urged to do so in editorial exhortations. A ruler who claims authority to regulate others' relationships should certainly be master of his own.

At issue with Maharero was not only his marital status but also his education. Raised in the bush, schooled in mine compounds, he seemed at first ill-fitted to the position. Rulers, after all, should be steeped in the lore and practices of their people; it is they who are responsible for applying, protecting, and augmenting *mekgwa le melao*, the laws and customs of the *morafe* (nation). As is clear from the doubts voiced over Tawana II, who had an LLB (honors) degree in business law but little exposure to customary proceedings, chiefly competence comes from experience and not "school" learning. And yet the doubts voiced about Maharero's qualifications for office very often referred not to his ignorance of Tswana or Herero custom but to his lack of a Western education. People believed he could not speak any English, or read or write in any language—although he was, in fact, haltingly literate in Setswana and Otjiherero, and was learning to speak English. The talk of Maharero's illiteracy was a figurative expression of both doubts about his suitability for the position and an insistence that even chiefship has requisite qualifications. As Maharero sat in the village *kgotla*, hearing disputes and other court cases and assisting people with administrative procedures such as cattle registrations, he inevitably held a pen in his hand. The pen served, it seemed, as a badge of office—not only an instrument for signing various documents put before him, but as a scepter of the basic educational skills mastered, a mark of his qualification.[20] He often also clasped a copy of the *Botswana Daily News;* although I never saw him actually reading it, it was covered with scribbled names, phone numbers, and business figures. By 1994, Maharero's status had risen considerably. Much of that increase can be attributed to the success of his cattle-dealing, brick-making, and tractor-hire businesses, reflected in a multiroomed, neatly painted house. But it was also often mentioned that he could read and write now—he wrote notes prodigiously—and could speak some English. His public speeches and his conversations at home were peppered with English phrases, in the manner common among younger people in Botswana and urban residents.

The fact that Tawana, with his university degree, and Maharero, with only rudimentary schooling, could *both* be criticized for their educational qualifications points to a double uncertainty over their positions. On one side are the ambiguities surrounding the chiefship today as a "traditional" status embedded in a "modern" bureaucratic civil service. On the other is the ill-defined relationship of education to social and political position. As noted previously, President Masire's formal qualifications in this respect are occasionally questioned. A former schoolteacher, his credentials were notable thirty years ago; today, after impressive government initiatives in education, they seem less so. Many newer members of Parliament, including some of those involved in the corruption scandals of the past years, hold university degrees, often in law or business. Government in Botswana seems to be becoming increasingly "technocratic," focused around the specialized training and competencies of functionaries.[21] A similar ethos of offices and specialization has come to pervade life in the village as well (see Durham 1993). Social and other associations are replete with offices and task-oriented committees—the Herero Youth Association has a president, chair, secretary, treasurer, publicity secretary, choir officer, and stores officer. Elections to these positions have, over the past nine years, consistently taken into consideration the skills and training of the candidates; Chief Maharero, although nominated regularly, has not been elected to one of these offices.

The increasingly technocratic nature of these offices, and of the Botswana government as a whole, implies two things. One, it focuses attention upon achieved skills, skills increasingly accredited by degrees. Two, achievement itself is becoming more and more compartmentalized; even education and (social) age, qualifications that might legitimize leadership across a broad range of situations, are valid only within the scope of specific activities. To what does schooling entitle one? Broad claims to status? Or merely specialized roles, outside of which one is again "equal" to others? Sentiments on this issue are ambivalent, reflecting the general ambiguity surrounding privilege and equality. Education, believed in Mahalapye to be openly accessible through work, epitomizes the achievement-oriented aspects of egalitarianism. But at the same time, it establishes new forms of inequality—and claims for privilege and deference. And the contradictions allow for profound disquiet concerning the nature and legitimacy of leadership, contradictions picked out in a

Botswana Internet discussion in October and November 1996 (<botswana@ mathcs.duq.edu>). Is "a semi-illiterate miner" with "political lineage" but "unable to read a balance sheet" out of place on a bank board? Is a professor in a "higher league," as another member claimed? Or, as yet another suggested, might a carpenter do as well on a board of directors? While the discussants, all engaged in tertiary training for highly specialized careers, were all destined for positions of prestige, their contributions showed the extent of the discomfort felt over hierarchical implications, and in particular those situated outside kinship, where status difference is more readily accepted.

Conclusion

One Botswana "netter" wrote of chiefship in Botswana, "we have mixed feelings about it" (<botswana@mathcs.duq.edu> 26 September 1996). Batswana have deeply mixed feelings across a variety of domains about the possibilities for status and privilege, about distinction and inequality that recur in their society. At the heart of this ambivalence is the ever-present tension between possibilities of hierarchical privilege and egalitarianism, a tension that has taken different forms in different historical periods and social spaces. It is this tension that provides the specific framework for the complaints, debates, and arguments about current leaders and also about the nature of leadership positions in the country.

Putnam (1993) found that differences in the effectiveness and practices of regional governments and politics in Italy could not be attributed to the constitutional form of the regions. Instead, "civic culture" and the sociohistorical context shaped political and administrative practices. The turn to "culture" must not result in a series of characterological assessments: even a short stay in a village shows that the Batswana are not entirely a "peace-loving people"; they do not everywhere avoid argument, contestation, and violence; they are neither consistently egalitarian nor patriarchal-authoritarian, even within one domain. Nor do hierarchy and egalitarianism refer to a homogeneous, coherent, or unambiguous ensemble of ideas. Hierarchy may involve inherited status; it may also involve claims to differential privileges and responsibilities. Egalitarianism, as I have illustrated, sometimes is used to imply equal status for all persons regardless of achievement, and it sometimes refers to equal opportunity; sometimes it is used in quite different ways. This is not merely a matter of definition: each usage comes with a moral and political vision of citizenship and the nation. The ambiguities engendered and the arguments engaged over these terms—over status, privilege, and opportunity; and over leadership, citizenship, and the nation—resist hegemonic resolution by any political faction, social class, or other collectivity.

And this is where the struggle for civil society takes place. Embracing the arguments that make up political culture, Batswana construct—in homes, on the streets, in chiefs' courts and the national media, on the World Wide Web—the visible forms of their political society. In the course of debating the performance and propriety of leaders, Batswana address fundamental issues of morality and personhood, legitimate action, and accomplishment. It is the ongoing argument itself—rather than any particular conclusion—that guarantees the civility, the regard given to the morality of personhood and status, in Botswana.

Notes

1. My time in Botswana has been spent largely in the Herero ward of Mahalapye, although I have paid lengthy visits to other parts of the village and country. Mahalapye is a large settlement (more than 28,000 inhabitants by the 1991 census) situated along the main north-south highway and rail line through eastern Botswana. It is technically an "urban village" for, in spite of its size, a large proportion of its residents are involved primarily in agriculture. Most households are, however, heavily dependent upon wage income earned locally, by dispersed members, or remitted by relocated former members. Mahalapye also remains a village in that it has a very active chief's court and is organized into wards, each with at least a nominal headman. It has something of a schizophrenic character: along the main highway is a busy, rather dirty town with supermarkets, banks, clothing and furniture stores, and, by the mid-1990s, a number of fast-food chains. But off the main roadways, houses cluster in dusty compounds around which paths wind unpredictably.

Mahalapye is home to some 3,000 or so Herero, concentrated around Herero ward, one of the oldest settled parts of the village, where many Tswana also live. Since their flight from Namibia in 1904, and in particular since their settlement as a distinct unit under Khama III in 1923, these Herero have lived within a Tswana-Botswana political system, and for the purposes of this chapter I treat them as "citizens of Botswana." They should not be thought untypical as Botswana citizens because of being Herero: in spite of the popular ideas that the success of Botswana's postcolonial democracy is based upon ethnic homogeneity, the modern nation-state is ethnically diverse; so too were the old Tswana polities (see Schapera 1952).

Although Mahalapye Herero are concerned with their ethnic distinctiveness (Durham 1993), they have not made it the basis of political claims, as have other, more oppressed, non-Tswana groups (cf. Solway 1994a) or as have Herero in northwestern Botswana who maintained extensive ties with Namibia (cf. Almagor 1982). Mahalapye Herero participate fully in Botswana's political system and, more to the point, in its political culture. They run for political office and campaign for the BNF and for the BDP, and sometimes win. The Mahalapye Herero chief sits in the central *kgotla* of Mahalapye as a junior chief, and some think that he will be designated the senior subordinate tribal authority of Mahalapye when the current one retires. Tensions between openness and voting, and secrecy and privilege were voiced by Herero in July and August 1996, in complaints that the sitting senior village chief had attempted to nominate his own preferred candidate by bypassing a popular election, which when held was won by the Herero chief. Herero of Mahalapye, in discussing this incident, focused almost entirely on the attempts by the sitting senior chief personally to nominate a preferred candidate and on the rights of popular election, and not on the more obvious issue of ethnic discrimination. It is quite possible, however, that the succession conflict will later be construed as evidence of discrimination against Herero—for the central tension here is not between Herero and Tswana, but between discrimination and privilege versus equality and opportunity. As this chapter argues, this tension may be recapitulated in many registers.

2. See, for example, the papers in Harbeson, Rothchild, and Chazan 1994. Fatton (1995) provides a more subtle portrait of a conflict-ridden, heterogeneous civil society, but retains the basic civil society-state relationship with which I take issue. Mamdani (1995) critiques Africanist discourse on civil society as rooted in an evolutionist paradigm, repeating such bipolarities as tradition-modernity, underdeveloped-developed, community-society. See Mitchell (1991) for a Foucauldian critique of universalist, reified notions of "the state" and his call to analyze the conditions under which "states" take shape and objective form. See Clastres (1987) for a critique of the notion of "power" as rooted in violence and coercion in Western political analysis; Clastres limits his analysis, however, to the study of nonstate societies.

3. I argue here for taking "culture," as problematic as the term may be, seriously in political studies; this in spite of the fact that Mitchell (1991), a political scientist, takes earlier political culture approaches to task for failing to delimit the subject of their studies.

4. Political culture ought not be seen as a set of agreed-upon standards, precepts, and orientations or dispositions. It is instead shaped in disagreements and struggles for expression; also by different "technologies" media of argument (e.g., letters to the editors of a popular press, songs, political rhetoric or market gossip, the Internet, and so on). Hence, while Crowder (1988, 466) may be correct to claim that the multiethnic population of Botswana had historically "shared a common political culture" under the various Tswana polities, we do not want to think of that common political culture as comprising intransigent, homogeneous, and consistent political beliefs or even practices.

5. Detracting from this rosy picture are several factors. One is an extraordinarily high population growth rate in the 1970s and 1980s. Estimates ran as high as 4 percent; there has been a significant downturn since then (VanderPost 1992). This means that well over half the population is below the age of seventeen, which exacerbates problems of high unemployment, rapid urbanization, and a slowing economy. Furthermore, increases in incomes have been poorly distributed, and disparities of wealth have been described as among the highest in the world (Good 1992; Hope 1996). A pronounced "moral panic" looks at increases in crime, especially theft and assault, and high HIV infection rates. Decreasing government revenues from diamond and copper-nickel mines may also constrain government salaries and development initiatives, introducing

further strains. And, in 1997, the government formulated a highly restrictive media policy, which drew immediate international criticism and which may not be introduced.

6. The Botswana Democratic Party has been in power since independence in 1966. The main opposition party was the Botswana National Front (BNF), until it split in 1998. The Botswana People's Party (BPP) has a regional base around Francistown. As of September 1997, Botswana had twelve registered political parties.

7. Kuper (1970), writing soon after independence, discusses how the national (bureaucratic) and local (traditional) political structures and processes transformed each other; see also Maundeni 1998; Molutsi 1998.

8. The idea of having chiefs from all ethnic groups (sometimes called "tribes") in the House of Chiefs, frequently suggested, is unworkable. Not all ethnic groups have rulers, and few have any political unity. The proposal for more democratic means of selecting chiefs was directed in particular at the hereditary sovereigns of the major Tswana polities. Subordinate authorities ("headmen") are already subject to elective or consultative appointment.

9. See Ngcongco (1989) on Botswana's democratic tradition. But cf. Holm (1988; also van Binsbergen 1995) for the view that the traditional political processes were more authoritarian, with chiefs and ruling families ultimately controlling political discourse; he calls the current system a "paternalistic democracy." Good (1992, 95; 1996) uses the terms "open elite democracy" and the harsher "authoritarian liberalism."

10. See note 1 above.

11. The tension between hierarchy and equality is significantly different than the analogous tension in the United States. Stuart Ewen (1988, 32, 68), in his study of "the politics of style in contemporary culture," speaks of a "consumer democracy" in which the antinomy between "democracy and privilege" is struggled over in the domain of style, in which "judgment . . . is not based on what one *does* within society, but rather upon what one *has*." Ewen also notes that the iconography of status in the United States has "tended to mask the relations of power that prevailed within society," as surface and substance become more and more disarticulated.

12. These are Tswana proverbs. *Bogosi boa tsaleloa, ga bo loeloe* (Wylie 1990, 18) translates as "one is born to the chiefship, it is not fought for." *Kgosi ke kgosi ka batho*, "the chief is the chief by the people," is still uttered often in Botswana.

13. Note Evans-Pritchard's observations on the "fiercely egalitarian" Nuer: "Among themselves even the suspicion of an order riles a man and he either does not carry it out or he carries it out in a casual and dilatory manner that is more insulting than a refusal. When a Nuer wants his fellows to do something he asks it as a favour to a kinsman, saying, 'Son of my mother, do so-and-so', or he includes himself in the command and says: 'Let us depart'" (1940, 182).

14. The term "swipe" was used by both the *Guardian* and the *Mmegi*.

15. For more on solicitations and subscriptions in Botswana and the making of a national community, see Durham 1995.

16. This was quoted in the Botswana Internet discussion list (<botswana@mathcs.duq.edu>) on 8 November 1996, and was ostensibly from the *Business Observer*, 16–20 October 1996.

17. Masire turned seventy in 1995, the year in which most of these complaints were registered. He is younger than Nelson Mandela, an irony not lost on some of the critics. Complaints about age were also linked to the emergence of two major factions within the BDP. One, known as the "Kwelagobe faction," after its leader, was considered to represent the "old generation"; the other, as of yet unsuccessful in its challenges, was lead by Momphati Merafhe, former head of the army and newly minted M.P. from Mahalapye. Masire's inability to contain the intraparty rivalries must be considered an index of his waning power.

18. Although the chiefship is inherited patrilineally among Herero (who belong to both matrilineal clans and patrilineages), Johannes Maharero inherited the chiefship through his mother's father. As is common in Botswana, the children of unmarried women are treated legally as the children of their mothers' families. No one in Mahalapye ever disputed the unusual line of succession, although some Herero in Namibia did. Maharero's claim to have been raised "in the bush" was part of his assertion of personal achievement, discounting any parental contributions (here including being sent to school). Others pointed to his cattlepost childhood, however, to express their doubts about his qualifications for his position.

19. By the summer of 1996 the issues had shifted. As mentioned in note 1, people were talking about the unfair nominating practices used by the retiring village chief. In 1998, Maharero married a university student.

20. Although I referred to the pen as a metaphor, it may be better termed a metonym. Metonymic imagery is particularly apt in establishing hierarchical relationships (Durham and Fernandez 1991).

21. The trend toward professional competence and specialization in the bureaucracy began in colonial times as the British administration built up a system of offices that effectively served to transfer power from the chiefs (left "intact" through a system of indirect rule) to the state (see Parson 1990); and also as the chiefs themselves reorganized their own governments (Wylie 1990). Principles of bureaucratic specialization guided the staffing of many offices with expatriates after independence, and dominates strategies for "localization." As Charlton (1993, 364) notes, while the framework of "typically African patterns of bureaucratic domination" seems present, the bureaucracy does not dominate the political life of the country.

References

Almagor, Uri. 1982. "Pastoral Identity and Reluctance to Change: The Mbanderu of Ngamiland." In *Land Reform in the Making*, ed. R. Werbner. London: Rex Collings.

Alverson, Hoyt. 1978. *Mind in the Heart of Darkness: Value and Self-Identity among the Tswana of Southern Africa*. New Haven: Yale University Press.

Austen, Ralph. 1993. "The Moral Economy of Witchcraft: An Essay in Comparative History." In *Modernity and Its Malcontents: Ritual and Power in Postcolonial Africa*, ed. J. Comaroff and J. L. Comaroff. Chicago: University of Chicago Press.

Brown, Chris. 1982. "Kgatleng Burial Societies." *Botswana Notes and Records* 14:80–83.

Bruun, Frank Jarle, Mbulawa Mugabe, and Yolande Coombes, eds. 1994. *The Situation of the Elderly in Botswana*. NIR-SUM programme on Health, Population and Development, report no. 1. Gaborone, Botswana: National Institute of Development Research and Documentation.

Charlton, Roger. 1993. "The Politics of Elections in Botswana." *Africa* 63 (3): 330–70.

Clastres, Pierre. 1987. *Society Against the State*. New York: Zone Books.

Comaroff, Jean, and John Comaroff. 1991. *Of Revelation and Revolution: Christianity, Colonialism, and Consciousness in South Africa*, vol. 1. Chicago: University of Chicago Press.

Comaroff, John. 1975. "Talking Politics: Oratory and Authority in a Tswana Chiefdom." In *Political Language and Oratory in Traditional Society*, ed. M. Bloch. New York: Academic Press.

———. 1978. "Rules and Rulers: Political Processes in a Tswana Chiefdom." *Man* 13 (1): 1–20.

Comaroff, John, and Jean Comaroff. 1992a. "Goodly Beasts, Beastly Goods." In *Ethnography and the Historical Imagination*. Chicago: University of Chicago Press.

———. 1992b. "The Long and the Short of It." In *Ethnography and the Historical Imagination*. Chicago: University of Chicago Press.

———. 1997. "Postcolonial Politics and Discourses of Democracy in Southern Africa: An Anthropological Reflection on African Political Modernities." *Journal of Anthropological Research* 53 (2): 123–46.

Comaroff, John, and Simon Roberts. 1981. *Rules and Processes: The Cultural Logic of Dispute in an African Context*. Chicago: University of Chicago Press.

Crowder, Michael. 1988. "Botswana and the Survival of Liberal Democracy in Africa." In *Decolonization and African Independence*, ed. P. Gifford and W. R. Louis. New Haven: Yale University Press.

Dow, Unity. 1995. *The Citizenship Case: The Attorney General of the Republic of Botswana v. Unity Dow*. Gaborone, Botswana: Lentswe la Lesedi, for Metlhaetsile Women's Information Centre.

Durham, Deborah. 1993. "Images of Culture: Being Herero in a Liberal Democracy." Ph.D. diss., University of Chicago.

———. 1994. "Cultured Citizens, Culture of Citizens: Being Herero in Botswana." Paper presented at session, New States, Old Regimes: The Resurgence of Tribalism and Ethnic Rivalries in Africa. American Anthropological Association annual meeting, Atlanta.

———. 1995. "Soliciting Gifts and Negotiating Agency: The Spirit of Asking in Botswana." *Journal of the Royal Anthropological Institute* 1 (1): 111–28.

———. 1998. "Re: Mankgodi Burns. Missing Children, Youth, and the State in Botswana." Paper presented to the African Studies Workshop, University of Chicago, 3 March 1998.

———. 1999. "The Predicament of Dress: Dress, Ambiguous Meanings, and the Ironies of a Cultural Identity." *American Ethnologist* 26 (2). Forthcoming.

Durham, Deborah, and James Fernandez. 1991. "Tropical Dominions: The Figurative Struggle over Domains of Belonging and Apartness in Africa." In *Beyond Metaphor,* ed. J. W. Fernandez. Stanford: Stanford University Press.

Evans-Pritchard, E. E. 1940. *The Nuer.* Oxford: Oxford University Press.

Ewen, Stuart. 1988. *All Consuming Images: The Politics of Style in Contemporary Culture.* Basic Books.

Fatton, Robert, Jr. 1995. "Africa in the Age of Democratization: The Civil Limitations of Civil Society." *African Studies Review* 38 (2): 67–99.

Fox, Richard. 1990. Introduction to *Nationalist Ideologies and the Production of National Cultures,* ed. R. Fox. Washington: American Ethnological Society Monograph Series, no. 2.

Geschiere, Peter. 1997. *The Modernity of Witchcraft: Politics and the Occult in Postcolonial Africa.* Charlottesville: University Press of Virginia.

Good, Kenneth. 1992. "Interpreting the Exceptionality of Botswana." *Journal of Modern African Studies* 30 (1): 69–95.

———. 1996. "Authoritarian Liberalism: A Defining Characteristic of Botswana." *Journal of Contemporary African Studies* 14 (1): 29–51.

Greenfeld, Liah. 1994. *Nationalism: Five Roads to Modernity.* Cambridge: Harvard University Press.

Gulbrandsen, Ornulf. 1995. "The King Is King by the Grace of the People: The Exercise and Control of Power in Subject-Ruler Relations." *Comparative Studies in Society and History* 37 (3): 415–44.

Harbeson, John W., Donald Rothchild, and Naomi Chazan. 1994. *Civil Society and the State in Africa.* Boulder: Lynne Rienner.

Holm, John. 1988. "Botswana: A Paternalistic Democracy." In *Democracy in Developing Countries,* vol. 2, *Africa,* ed. L. Diamond, J. Linz, and S. Lipset. Boulder: Lynne Rienner.

———. 1993. "Political Culture and Democracy: A Study of Mass Participation in Botswana." In *Botswana: The Political Economy of Democratic Development,* ed. S. J. Stedman. Boulder: Lynne Rienner.

Holm, J., and P. Molutsi. 1992. "State-Society Relations in Botswana: Beginning Liberalization." In *Governance and Politics in Africa,* ed. G. Hyden and M. Bratton. Boulder: Lynne Rienner.

Hope, Kempe Ronald. 1996. "Growth, Unemployment and Poverty in Botswana." *Journal of Contemporary African Studies* 14:53–67.

Kuper, Adam. 1970. *Kalahari Village Politics: An African Democracy.* Cambridge: Cambridge University Press.

Landau, Paul. 1995. *The Realm of the Word: Language, Gender, and Christianity in a Southern African Kingdom.* Portsmouth, N.H.: Heinemann.

Lekorwe, Mogopodi. 1989. "The Kgotla and the Freedom Square: One-way or Two-way Communication?" In *Democracy in Botswana,* ed. John Holm and Patrick Molutsi. Athens: Ohio University Press.

Mamdani, Mahmood. 1995. "A Critique of the State and Civil Society Paradigm in Africanist Studies." In *African Studies in Social Movements and Democracy,* ed. M. Mamdani and E. Wamba-dia-Wamba. Dakar, Senegal: CODESRIA.

Maundeni, Zibani. 1998. "The Struggle for Political Freedom and Independence." In *Botswana: Politics and Society,* ed. W. A. Edge and M. H. Lekorwe. Pretoria: J.L. van Schaik.

Mbembe, Achille. 1992. "The Banality of Power and the Aesthetics of Vulgarity in the Postcolony." *Public Culture* 4 (2): 1–30.

Mitchell, Timothy. 1991. "The Limits of the State: Beyond Statist Approaches and Their Critics." *American Political Science Review* 85 (1): 77–96.

Molutsi, Patrick. 1998. "Elections and Electoral Experience in Botswana." In *Botswana: Politics and Society,* ed. W. A. Edge and M. H. Lekorwe. Pretoria: J.L. van Schaik.

Motzafi-Haller, Pnina. 1998. "Beyond Textual Analysis: Practice, Interacting Discourses, and the Experience of Distinction in Botswana." *Cultural Anthropology* 13 (4): 522–47.

Ngcongco, L. D. 1989. "Tswana Political Tradition: How Democratic?" In *Democracy in Botswana,* ed. J. Holm and P. Molutsi. Athens: Ohio University Press.

Parson, Jack, ed. 1990. *Succession to High Office in Botswana.* Ohio University Monographs in International Studies, Africa Series no. 54.

Parsons, Q. Neil. 1990. "Seretse Khama and the Bangwato Succession Crisis, 1948–1953." In *Succession to High Office in Botswana,* ed. J. Parson. Ohio University Monographs in International Studies, Africa Series no. 54.

Peters, Pauline. 1994. *Dividing the Commons: Politics, Policy, and Culture in Botswana.* Charlottesville: University Press of Virginia.

Picard, Louis, ed. 1985. *The Evolution of Modern Botswana.* Lincoln: University of Nebraska.

Putnam, Robert. 1993. *Making Democracy Work: Civic Traditions in Modern Italy.* Princeton: Princeton University Press.

Schapera, Isaac. 1952. *The Ethnic Composition of Tswana Tribes.* Monographs in Social Anthropology, no. 11. London School of Economics and Political Science.

———. 1965. *Praise-Poems of Tswana Chiefs.* Oxford: Oxford University Press.

Solway, Jacqueline. 1994a. "From Shame to Pride: Politicized Ethnicity in the Kalahari, Botswana." *Canadian Journal of African Studies* 28 (2): 254–74.

———. 1994b. "Drought as 'Revelatory Crisis': An Exploration of Shifting Entitlements and Hierarchies in the Kalahari, Botswana." *Development and Change* 25 (3): 471–95.

———. 1995. "Political Participation: Ethnicity and Multiparty Democracy in Botswana." *Canadian Research Consortium on Southern Africa, Collected Research Papers*, vol. 1.

———. 1998. "Taking Stock in the Kalahari: Accumulation and Resistance on the Southern African Periphery." *Journal of Southern African Studies* 24 (2): 425–41.

Somolokae, Gloria. 1989. "Do Batswana Think and Act as Democrats?" In *Democracy in Botswana*, ed. J. Holm and P. Molutsi. Athens: Ohio University Press.

Strathern, Marilyn. 1988. *The Gender of the Gift*. Berkeley: University of California Press.

Tlou, Sheila. 1994. "The Elderly and the Youth's Perception of Each Other." In *The Situation of the Elderly in Botswana*, ed. Frank Jarle Bruun, Mbulawa Mugabe, and Yolande Coombes. NIR-SUM programme on Health, Population and Development, report no. 1. Gaborone, Botswana: National Institute of Development Research and Documentation.

Tsie, Balefi. 1996. "The Political Context of Botswana's Development Performance." *Journal of Southern African Studies* 22 (4): 599–616.

Van Binsbergen, Wim. 1995. "Aspects of Democracy and Democratisation in Zambia and Botswana: Exploring African Political Culture at the Grassroots." *Journal of Contemporary African Studies* 13 (1): 3–33.

VanderPost, Cornelis. 1992. "Regional Patterns of Fertility Transition in Botswana." *Geography* 77 (2): 109–22.

Wylie, Diana. 1990. *A Little God: The Twilight of Patriarchy in a Southern African Chiefdom*. Hanover: Wesleyan University Press.

Zaffiro, James. 1993. "Mass Media, Politics, and Society in Botswana: The 1990s and Beyond." *Africa Today* 40 (1): 7–26.

8

Debating Muslims, Disputed Practices: Struggles for the Realization of an Alternative Moral Order in Niger

Adeline Masquelier

Fighting in the Mosque: An Introduction to the Divided Muslim Community of Dogondoutchi

IN HIS ANALYSIS of the Maitatsine movement in northern Nigeria, Watts notes that wherever Islam provides the moral framework for the elaboration of an oppositional culture aimed at challenging dominant hegemonies, it acts "as both an alternative political and economic platform to the state and a critical oppositional discourse" (1996, 284). Like other Islamic reformist movements in West Africa and elsewhere that spring from the constant negotiation and reinvention of Muslim tradition, Maitatsine compels us to rethink critically the relation between state and society. It is the role of Islam in its mediation and critical understanding of state-society relations that I briefly explore in this chapter through a focus on Izala, an anti-Sufi movement whose recent spread in southern Niger sparked intense struggles over the meaning of Islam and Islamic identity. In 1992, a violent dispute erupted between *'yan* Izala,[1] a group of Muslim anti-Sufi reformists and *'yan* Tijaniyya (members of the Tijaniyya brotherhood, a Sufi order[2]) in the main mosque of Dogondoutchi, a

---

Funding for my 1994 research was provided by a Summer Fellowship from Tulane University's Committee on Research. I want to thank all the participants of the Struggle for Civil Society conference for their comments and assistance on an earlier version of this essay. I am especially grateful to Andy Apter, Misty Bastian, Jean Comaroff, John Comaroff, and Debbie Durham for their critical discussions of the material. Special thanks to Jean Comaroff for her careful editing of the essay. Ralph Austen gave me many insightful comments and words of encouragement. I also received valuable suggestions from the participants of a 1997 colloquium at the University of Helsinki, Finland. Kerriann Marden provided helpful editorial advice. More special thanks to Elisha Renne for providing me with valuable information on the history of Izala in Nigeria and for raising critical issues with which I am still struggling. I am also grateful to Luise White for her helpful suggestions and to Michael Fischer and Medhi Abedi for writing their book, *Debating Muslims*, which inspired the title of this chapter.

bustling Mawri community located in the Hausa-speaking region of Arewa. Foreign proselytizers who had come to stimulate the religious fervor of Izala followers, but inadvertently offended their religious opponents, spurred a furious commotion one afternoon, as Muslims assembled on the prayer grounds. What started as a heated argument between Mawri members of the two Muslim factions soon escalated into physical confrontation, and, before the police could intervene, villagers were fighting with knives, clubs, and machetes on the prayer grounds. When the police finally managed to disarm some of the assailants, many had been wounded, though no one was critically injured. Several individuals were escorted to police headquarters and detained there but, as far as I was able to determine, no one was actually charged with anything. Mamane, a thirty-year-old Mawri butcher and member of Izala, recounted the incident for me two years later:

> I was with some visitors [and members of Izala] who had just arrived [from Nigeria], having been authorized by the state to preach.[3] Sarkin Arewa [the customary chief] was absent, [having gone to] the fields. We went to see Kona [the town chief] to let him know that we had some guests. It was a Saturday. The Tijaniyya clerics were informed that *'yan* Izala would preach. It was time for the four o'clock prayer. They [*'yan* Izala] decided to go to the main mosque and pray. They parked their car inside the mosque grounds to protect it from any damage [at the hands of opponents of Izala]. But Tijaniyya *malamai*[4] told the neighborhood hoodlums [about the Izala's presence] and they started to throw stones at the car, warning the *'yan* Izala to get out of the mosque because it wasn't *their* parents' mosque. The *'yan* Izala realized that the hoodlums had been acting on the orders of the local *malamai.* The police arrived to settle things. They [the *'yan* Izala] got in touch with the mayor and the town chief and they visited one of the Tijaniyya leaders to ask for reparations. Things were settled, and they [the *'yan* Izala] were authorized by the mayor's office, the village chief and the police to preach wherever they wanted. (20 June 1994)

In his version of what happened in the mosque, Mamane makes no mention of the scuffle that ensued between members of the two Muslim sects. He depicts Izala followers as the innocent victims of parochialism and prejudice.

According to Zeinabou, a young woman who allegedly witnessed the incident, the fight erupted after the *'yan* Izala argued that half of the *grande mosquée* (main mosque) was rightfully theirs, because they too were Muslims, and, as such, were just as legitimately entitled to the prayer grounds as their Sufi opponents. It was a Friday, market day in Dogondoutchi. The *'yan* Izala, who had just arrived in town from Nigeria, had parked their car in the mosque grounds. The Sufi Muslims assembled there for the Friday prayer were outraged by what they perceived to be total disrespect on the part of the foreign visitors. They told them to leave. "Why do you enter the mosque in your car? Who are you to do such a thing?" they allegedly asked. The *'yan* Izala answered that they wanted half the mosque to pray, that it was theirs as much as it was the *'yan* Tijaniyya's. And this is when they started fighting, Zeinabou told me. Soon feeling outnumbered, the *'yan* Izala had tried to leave the premises, but their car would not start. A powerful cleric, Malam Boubakar, had used his medicines to pin their car to the ground. The *'yan* Izala tried in vain to get the car started. Eventually, the *mai gari* (chief of town) Kona, who was himself a *'dan* Izala, offered excuses to Malam Boubakar just as his Nigerian guests were able to start their automobile and leave the scene precipitously.

Contradicting Mamane's and Zeinabou's reports, other versions of the incident portray Izala followers as mean, aggressive, and intolerant individuals whose sarcastic—and often merciless—critiques of mainstream Islam only foster friction, and whose thoughtless acts lead to violence. According to opponents of the Izala movement with whom I spoke, the *'yan* Izala only entered the mosque to cause trouble: they parked their car within the walls of the mosque in order to provoke the *'yan* Tariqa and they got what they deserved for trespassing on sacred grounds with an automobile. In these versions of the affair, a *malam* spoke very harshly of Izala during his preaching, allegedly claiming that if the corpse of a *'dan* Izala was disinterred the day following the burial, one would find the carcass of a donkey in place of human remains. The *malam* also challenged *'yan* Izala to swear on the Qur'an—presumably to test their faith in the doctrine they were preaching and defending. In response, one *'dan* Izala, an old and respectable man, allegedly agreed to put his faith to the test despite warnings that he would die if he dared. But before he was able to approach the Qur'an, his daughter begged him to desist. The old man came closer but did not actually touch the Holy Book. Other *'yan* Izala intervened. They were jostled by *'yan* Tariqa eager to witness the old man's humiliation and unnerved by his supporters' attempts to protect him. This is what led to the violent fight that jolted Dogondoutchi, a community where previous religious debates pitted Muslims as a group against *bori* spirit mediums.[5]

Even if ultimately no one was charged with destroying property or endangering life, and even if, on the ground, nothing was visibly changed, the fight at the mosque was a significant episode in the local history of religious politics because it ushered in a new era of debate and division over Muslim identity, knowledge, and power. Many of those who had not previously taken sides now felt forced publicly to acknowledge their views on doctrinal differences and ritual discrepancies. That none of the versions of the incident seem to agree on what prompted the violence, what concluded it, and what it implied for the two religious factions is in itself indicative of the multiplicity of perspectives and the wide-reaching tensions that divide the local community.[6]

According to Rabi—mother of nine, who had joined Izala three years before to follow her husband—the old man was actually assaulted by his opponents, who had never intended to let him prove his faith. When he returned home after things had quieted down, concerned kin reprimanded him for having risked his life. As Rabi put it, "Why did he go there at all? He had no friends, no neighbors [to watch out for him]. They [the *'yan* Tariqa] could have killed him." Rabi's anguished statement highlights the violent hatred that now existed between *'yan* Izala and *'yan* Tariqa, a hatred that, some said, could lead a man to watch his own brother helplessly die without lifting a finger if the two belonged to opposite Muslim factions. *'Yan* Izala were believed always to carry knives with them, adding to the anxiety of many villagers who were pessimistic about the implications of growing rivalries between the two religious groups. Stories of fathers mercilessly beating their newly converted sons with clubs or riding crops were legion in Muslim circles that adhered to the locally established Islamic tradition that had, until recently, ruled unchallenged.

As could be expected, the incident at the mosque was followed by other disputes that pitted reformists against traditionalists, brother against brother, fathers against sons, contesting the nature of Islamic knowledge and the legitimation of Islamic authority. Despite their often divisive outcome, what is significant about these confrontations is that they would not have occurred had there not been an "opening up" of Islamic consciousness that allowed for the emergence of multiple perspectives.

These religious debates offer points of departure for a discussion of civil society that is "neither homogenous nor unitary [but rather] fragmented by the contradictory historical alternatives of competing social actors, institutions and beliefs" (Fatton 1995, 73). The conservative *'yan* Izala have struggled to articulate their vision of an alternative Islamic civil society that promotes a philosophy of "each man for himself," stresses education for all, and redefines women's roles. Like other increasingly prominent religious reforms elsewhere that compel us to rethink the state's articulation with local moralities,[7] the successful spread of Izala in southern Niger forces us to address the concept of civil society broadly, as a social space where issues of power, freedom, and responsibility can be entertained in the context of utopian visions designed to challenge what *'yan* Izala perceive as oppressive or "un-Islamic" institutions and relations.

Izala members have been referred to as fundamentalists by scholars and commentators who see "family resemblances" between the Izala project and Islamic movements elsewhere. Fundamentalism can be broadly defined as a militant desire to defend religion against the onslaught of modern, secular culture, based on the assumption of a fixed truth that has its source in the Scriptures. Besides referring to a belief in the inviolability of sacred texts, however, the term "fundamentalism" connotes fanaticism and bigotry. Rather than clarifying the Izala conception of Islam, the word reflects our hostility toward movements of this sort (Munson 1993, 152). It also breeds misconceptions. Fundamentalism is inevitably associated with conservative ideologies of gender, family, and society that, in the Izala case, only inadequately recapitulate key values and attitudes. Mindful of the cautionary notes sounded by Harris (1994) and others on the use of the term "fundamentalism," I refer to *'yan* Izala as reformist Muslims, in an attempt to extend the well-worn dichotomy between "modernist" and "conservative" Islam, and to stress the ambiguities inherent in the Izala vision of Islamic society. Elsewhere, the term "Islamism" has been invoked as a generic concept to refer to individuals or organizations aiming at a renewal and reform of existing social conditions (Westerlund 1997). While it might appear more neutral than "fundamentalism," "Islamism" is not a designation Nigerien Izala members employ to refer to themselves, whereas the term "reformist" reflects an Izala self-designating concept that refers to the suppression of certain undesirable innovations and the return to the golden age of Islam. As we shall see, this reformist impetus also implies a significant revision of what we might term civil society.

Civil Society and Islam in Contemporary Niger

For Nigeriens—who in January 1996 witnessed the return of military rule in their virtually bankrupt country and were later effectively disenfranchised by the fraudulent presidential election that installed the coup leader as commander of the nation—the path to democracy has been bumpy and filled with disappointment. The government's human rights record worsened considerably in 1996 as a result of the numerous abuses committed. In addition, persistent drought, soil degradation, high import prices, a flat uranium market, and burdensome debts have further weakened the already troubled economy. Even if the political situation of Niger were to improve in the near future, a return to democracy would most likely not bring an immediate solution to the country's most burning fiscal problems. Major domains of economic and civic enterprise have come to a standstill since the recent slump in uranium prices—the country's major export product in the seventies and early eighties—that reduced tax revenues to 9 percent of the GNP. Intent upon maintaining public expenditures at their boom level despite an inexorably shrinking tax base, the Nigerien government has been unable to pay bills submitted by local suppliers or to finance an adequate level of public service. The government's external debt more than doubled during 1984–88, and since 1990 the payment of state employees' salaries have been substantially delayed. Thus far, attempts to generate revenues by raising tax rates and strengthening enforcement have met with failure. While some civil servants accepted philosophically the fact that they received their April salaries in May or June, the armed forces occasionally reacted with mutiny. In 1993, 1994, and 1995, growing discontent, fostered by further withholding of salaries to government workers (some of whom had not been paid for six months), led to a series of strikes, further crippling public services and causing major disruptions throughout the country—particularly on the national education system, most students having spent more days outside than inside the schools in the last few years.

Urged by international donors in the wake of growing fiscal deficit to undertake thorough reforms, the Nigerien government has resorted to a series of desperate stopgap measures that have only resulted in a transfer of civic operations out of the formal sector—commonly referred to as *la fuite vers l'informel* (Barlow and Snyder 1993). Moreover, while Niger's participation in the artificially maintained franc zone protected the country from currency fluctuation, the fixity of the CFA franc to French currency for over forty years has also abetted the slow but consistent impoverishment of a population encouraged to buy French imported goods. The 1994 devaluation of the CFA that was designed to increase domestic production and investment by boosting exports only worsened the situation for many Nigeriens, who have seen their living standards decline steadily and who must now pay twice what they used to for many of the imports they have come to depend upon.

It is too early to offer a prognosis on the impact of recent events on Niger's path to democracy and pluralism. What is more certain is that the *décrispation* (liberalization) introduced in the late 1980s to facilitate Niger's transition to a civilian, democratically elected regime has promoted an upsurge of popular ambitions and fostered the emergence of new forms of social protest. For instance, the democratization promoted by former Nigerien president Ali Saibou ushered an era of public debate on politics and policy through the opening of two new independent newspapers, *Le Républicain* and *Haske* ("light" in Hausa) that challenged the formerly government-controlled *Le Sahel* by offering their readers previously suppressed information on various topics. Since then, other newspapers—such as *Le Soleil, Le Paon Africain* ("The African Peacock"), and *Alternative*—have been created by political parties. Since the January 1996 coup, however, the government has taken action to limit press freedom and stifle political discussion through intimidation, harassment, and detention. Even radio stations, which are widely popular among the largely illiterate population, are not immune to censorship. Despite such efforts to control media content, the local independent press, composed of about fifteen privately owned newspapers, has remained relatively assertive in protesting government actions.[8]

Although civic and political organizations were banned from holding gatherings for much of 1996, people throughout the country nonetheless have become increasingly aware that they belong to specific groups and that they need to organize in order to address and defend their own interests.[9] These mechanisms of self-determination reflect the multiple forms that postcolonial "public opinion" may take when it emerges in broad daylight. From the five-year Tuareg struggle for secession to the students' major demonstrations in 1993 and 1994, or the recent rejection of the government's family code by Islamic women's groups,[10] we witness a "complete transformation of the conditions in which politics emerge." For Nigeriens who lost—or perhaps never had—rights to full participation in the civil and political life of their nation, and who suffered an austere, authoritarian regime until the late 1980s, these movements of social protest are "a way of reclaiming the right of self-expression, all too long confiscated by the official institution of power" (Monga 1995, 360).

Against this background, I will highlight some of the defining characteristics of the Izala doctrine and its success in canalizing communal discontent to show how the reformist group has contributed in its own way to the affirmation of social identity and the definition of individual rights. The Islamic organization has a very short history in Arewa. Because its members faced the threat of being imprisoned for subversive activity, the Izala movement remained in its embryonic stage until a few years ago, when its leaders felt it was safe to emerge from the shadows. It now operates in a climate conducive to identity-based politics. Though they speak of transforming Niger into an Islamic republic on the Iranian model,[11] *'yan* Izala do not, at least for the moment, play a determining role in the course of political events. Yet, as is attested in neighboring Nigeria, where the Maitatsine uprisings resulted in hundreds of deaths (Isichei 1987; Lubeck 1987; Barkindo 1993) and where *'yan* Izala's aggressive preaching has often led to violent physical confrontations (Umar 1993), the mobilizing potential of the movement cannot be ignored. A cursory examination of the "mosque incident" described earlier makes clear that Izala has this potential in the Nigerien context as well.

'Yan Izala profess to liberate Muslims and "animists" alike from the shackles of superstition and idolatry through education and enlightenment. But their virulent denunciation of Sufism and its founders (Umar 1993, 168) have virtually ostracized them from the rest of the Muslim community (Masquelier 1996). In addition to incurring the wrath of their elders for challenging their authority, Izala followers have angered the *marabouts* (Muslim clerics) by relentlessly accusing them of quackery and calling them parasites who live off a credulous and ignorant population. They themselves have been castigated by traditionalists who object to their novel conceptions of society and social hierarchy (Masquelier 1996; Loimeier 1997; Grégoire 1993). They also have made enemies of former friends and neighbors by contesting the scheduling and length of daily prayers,[12] and by promoting an ethic of work and frugal commensalism that contradicts fundamental Mawri values based on generosity and ostentation. In forging the boundaries of their new moral order, they have exacerbated local competition for power among the Muslim elite. Their widely disseminated, cleverly advertised doctrines have also raised passionate resentment among devout traditionalist Muslims, who see themselves as

having followed the precepts of the Qur'an long before *'yan* Izala undertook their reformist mission.

In the past, the official promotion of an admittedly liberal Islam had helped to minimize sectarian competition and promote national unity. Today, the confrontation between Sufi and anti-Sufi factions suggests that Islam has become a medium for expressing ideological, political, and even socioeconomic cleavages (see Al-Karsani 1993). It is no surprise that Izala is seen by many of its opponents as a subversive force backed by foreign Muslim powers who wish to transform the country into one of their satellites. One need only attend any of the preaching sessions organized by Izala on a semiweekly basis to assess the divisive effects of the movement in Dogondoutchi. Rather than giving voice to shared values, the words of Izala preachers widen oppositions and sharpen rivalries. In challenging the authority of the state and redefining their place in society, *'yan* Izala are thus contributing to the emergence of a civil society that is "neither homogenous, nor wholly emancipatory [but rather] contradictory, exhibiting both democratic and despotic tendencies" (Fatton 1995, 93).

Such efforts to redefine the terms and boundaries of moral community raise central questions as to the applicability and usefulness of the concept of civil society to analyses of postcolonial African states. As Karlström shows in chapter 4, there are inherent difficulties in assuming the uniform and uncritical generalizability of an analytical category that emerged in specific historical circumstances. While a general discussion of the relevance of "civil society" to African realities is beyond the purview of this essay, using the concept at all nonetheless necessitates shifting the focus away from the narrow institutional context of voluntary associations that has traditionally been the concern of political scientists. A more useful definition of civil society should refer to the more extensive and diffuse domain of social discourse and practice in which ordinary Nigeriens have the possibility of imagining an alternative modernity. Broadening the concept in such a way allows us to focus on the issues of power and gender, identity and morality, citizenship and egalitarianism that are emerging and contemplated in the context of Izala discourse. And if the concept of civil society is to be of any value to an analysis of the politics of Islamic identity in Niger, it must define and describe a plural—rather than a uniform and unitary—political space. Rather than democratically imparting enlightenment and opportunities, it is often "the domain of profoundly inegalitarian and obscurantist institutions and lifestyles" (Fatton 1995, 77) that fuels widespread tension and bitter conflicts.

The Expansion of Islam in Arewa

Islam is a fairly new arrival in this part of Niger. The first occupants of Arewa delegated the propitiation of land deities to priest elders. Then, in the seventeenth century, government became the responsibility of the descendants of conquering Bornuan warriors, while religious authority remained entrusted to the *'yan kasa* (literally, "sons of the land": indigenous priest elders). War was the backbone of Mawri society, a source of wealth and prestige for the ruling class and an avenue to fame and fortune for commoners (de Latour 1982). By the turn of the nineteenth century, the Sokoto caliphate had gained control over many of the neighboring Hausa states; but Dogondoutchi, a region of subsistence agriculture, was relatively insulated from the influence of Islam until after World War II. In Arewa up until the 1930s, the spots where itinerant Qur'anic preachers prayed were systematically burned by villagers, eager to preserve their communities from what they perceived as the polluting influence of Islam (see de Latour 1982). Once the territories that now make up the Republic of Niger were "pacified" and Muslims came to be perceived as useful servants of the administration, colonial policies, which had long expressed the French suspicion of itinerant *marabouts,* started encouraging conversion to Islam (Fuglestad 1983). Yet, these policies did not come to full fruition until after independence, when Islam became an important catalyst in the establishment of a shared national identity for the citizens of the newly formed republic (Bernus 1969, 208). While the number of Muslims did slowly grow, it was not until the 1970s that villagers started converting massively to the religion of the Prophet.

To postcolonial urban elites, as well as struggling rural villagers, Islam has now come to signify status, power, and *arziki* (a concept that evokes notions of wealth, prosperity, and well-being). Though many Nigeriens—particularly women—often secretly continue to rely on spirits as more powerful mediators with a distant God than prayers in Arabic, they are nonetheless forced by circumstance to acknowledge the economic benefits of becoming Muslim (Masquelier 1993). Since prosperity is viewed as an undeniable sign of God's goodwill, the wealth and success of respected *Alhazai* (those who have gone on a pilgrimage to Mecca) provide powerful incentives to turn to prayer. Yet, wherever it has taken hold in Arewa, Islam has adapted to Mawri norms and values even as it drew on indigenous practices. In Niger, as elsewhere, Islam thus is not an invariant, homogenous, and cohesive force; rather it is composed of many realities and expressed through many localized visions, all of which contribute to the highly pluralistic nature of the community (see Al-Azmeh 1993, 4).

Although earlier regimes made substantial efforts to promote Islam as the unified religion of the Nigerien people through the patronage of the Hajj to Mecca, the construction of mosques, and the establishment of a Muslim university in Say, it is generally true that a localized sense of ethnic identity prevails over one's sense of being Muslim. Thus while Islam may operate as a social cement within ethnically homogenous communities, it rarely has the power to draw connections across ethnic boundaries. Many Nigeriens are recognizable by their ethnic facial scars; these scars as well as people's language and region of origin divide them more effectively than Islam can ever unite them. Perhaps in part because becoming Muslim in Dogondoutchi does not necessarily mean belonging to a national brotherhood that transcends local ethnic rivalries, most villagers have now embraced the religion of the Prophet and ostentatiously display the visible signs of their adherence. Claiming a Muslim identity is for many primarily a way of fitting in and conforming to practices that are now the norm in Arewa communities, where *bori* mediums have become marginalized minorities. Yet, being a Muslim means different things to different people. Thus, some rigorously follow Qur'anic principles while others live with significant compromises, even though all claim Islamic status and wear the *babban riga* (male Islamic robe). It is through a recognition of these numerous, if subtle, distinctions that we can appreciate how postcolonial identities have been multiplied, transformed, and circulated (Mbembe 1992) amid the impact of reformist debates within the Muslim diaspora in Niger. Thus civil society in Niger is not simply about the power of the Muslim collectivity against the state; it also means the coexistence of multiple and competing Muslim voices that struggle to be heard in the cacophony.

Truth, Authority, and Authenticity

Comparing customs of syncretic Muslims with those of other more "authentic" Muslims, many in Dogondoutchi wonder whether there exists more than one Qur'an. Confronted with the multiplicity of arguments against or in favor of a particular religious practice allegedly based on the Scriptures, they feel confused. The current debate about the nature of Islamic knowledge and the way one practices Islam has forced them to question previously axiomatic truths and traditions (Masquelier 1996). While they remain confident of the superiority of Islam over other religions, they are no longer certain that their own conception of Islam is correct and that the challenging perspective is erroneous. The Qur'an is the ultimate reference for those who seek legitimation for practices that were once justified by a simple appeal to tradition. Thus *'yan* Izala reformers constantly invoke the Holy Book in their criticism of a faith corrupted by syncretism and innovation.[13] As custodians of truth and piety, they condemn the wearing of amulets because the Qur'an makes no mention of protective charms. Yet, traditionalist Muslims, many of whom wear amulets or buy them for their children, also insist, along with an appeal to timeless "traditions," that their faith too is based on a thorough knowledge of the Qur'an.[14]

For those inclined to give credence to the claims of both parties, their widely divergent views could only mean that there must exist more than one Holy Book. Those committed to the uniqueness of the Qur'an invoke practical sources of difference—like the man who told me that doctrinal discrepancies between *'yan* Tariqa and *'yan* Izala originated in the fact that Abubakar Gumi, one of the founders of Izala in Nigeria, had translated the Qur'an from Arabic to French, his different rendering of key terms leading to diverging understandings of what constitutes proper Islamic precept and practice. For others, doctrinal differences stem from the fact that some have *really* read and memorized the word of God, while others simply pretend to have done so. From the *'yan* Izala perspective, Islam is one, and to suggest otherwise is blasphemy: Muslims may disagree about what is or is not "Islamic," but such disagreement assumes the existence of a single true Islam (Launay 1992, 5). Yet others, less textual in their view of truth, insist that their "book" resides not on paper but in their chests, having been thoroughly memorized; the written book, after all, is but an imperfect transcript. For them, engaging in Qur'anic discussions is an intimate part of how one lives one's life as a Muslim; Islamic truth lies less in doctrinal debate than in lived practice.

That the Qur'an should generate such confusion about its ontological status is hardly surprising. It is, as Fischer and Abedi have noted, "a profoundly enigmatic text. For Muslims, it is the word of God, divine in both its meanings and its language, infinite, beyond human capacity for definitive exegesis" (1990, 97). At the same time, the very structure of Qur'an and hadith—"a fun house of mirrors playing upon appearances and resemblances *(mutashabih)* that may or may not be grounded" (100)—lays in being open to debate, dialogue, and reinterpretation. In addition, the manner in which the text itself is held to relate to actual everyday practice also changes over time and space. Understanding the powerful reformist movement that is currently sweeping through Islamic communities in Arewa and elsewhere requires that we pay close attention to the interpretive and dialogic tradition that is at the very heart of Islam. Only by acknowledging the current struggles for the definition of truth and the control of knowledge can we begin to approach the multiplicity and richness of expression that have emerged out of universalist Islamic principles. At the same time, Islam's long history of revival and reform is rooted not simply in its own traditions, but also in its response to Westernization and secularization (see Watts 1996). Anti-Sufism, in its most recent incarnation as Izala, promotes an alternative moral order that contests the legacies of Western colonialism. This is what makes Islamic reform movements in Africa and elsewhere so relevant to a discussion of postcolonial identity and civil society. For in such cases, Islam becomes the vehicle for the invention and sustenance of new traditions as well as the idiom in which a culturally convincing critique of the postcolonial state can be shaped.

Origins of the Izala Movement

While Izala and Tariqa leaders compete for the power to define Muslim reality, their fellow villagers have been prompted to review their own Islamic identities within an ostensibly unified tradition. Regardless of how they felt toward the reformist doctrine, few of them were even dimly aware of the origins of Izala. Often beliefs in Izala's origins were comments on the movement's legitimacy. One *'dan* Tariqa, a wealthy trader, knew of Abubakar Gumi, the charismatic leader of Izala who died in 1992. "Abubakar started Izala," he declared, "but before he died, he reconverted to Islam. He told everyone, it [Izala] wasn't a true religion" (28 June 1994). According to a local butcher who had been a member of the organization for three years, the founder of Izala was "a man like everyone else, a Moroccan. Tijani is his name." Other villagers believed the movement had no specific origin. To them, Izala was nothing but a moral and spiritual philosophy based on the rigorous application of Qur'anic precepts. As one of them—a wealthy entrepreneur in his fifties—put it, "those who know how to properly abide by the principles of the Qur'an are *'yan* Izala."

One man, who described himself as a "*true* Muslim,[15] not a *'dan* Izala," offered the following opinion:

> Izala comes from Sokoto [Nigeria]. Over there, they fight. They [*'yan* Izala] have killed more than one hundred people. But here [in Dogondoutchi], we prevent the people from fighting among themselves—especially after the fight at the mosque where people came with axes, bows, and clubs. (23 June 1994)

What is striking in this particular testimony is the emphasis on the aggressive nature of the organization whose members allegedly "killed more than one hundred people" in the name of Islamic authenticity and piety. It is true that no less than thirty-four clashes involving Izala and the Tijaniyya and Qadiriyya brotherhoods occurred between June 1978 and December 1980 in Plateau State—and that most of them "called for the intervention of the Police and often resulted in loss of life and damage to vehicles or properties" (Umar 1993, 169). But such violence is by no means specific to anti-Sufism.[16] It characterizes previous disputes between the now reconciled Islamic brotherhoods. For instance, the intense rivalry between the followers of the Qadiriyya (called *sadalu*, a reference to the fact that they pray with their arms at their sides) and Tijaniyya (referred to as *kabalu* because they pray with their arms crossed over their chests) occasionally led to violent clashes in the 1950s and 1960s in Nigeria (Umar 1993; see also Launay 1992 for a similar case in the Ivory Coast). In Dogondoutchi, this disagreement over what constituted "proper" and therefore morally acceptable prayer also tore the rural community apart. Today, however, such bitter arguments are the stuff of memory in the wake of new divisions. *'Yan kabalu* and *'yan sadalu* everywhere have put their differences aside, and they are now working together to oppose Izala reformists (Grégoire 1993).

Conventional social history suggests that the Izala movement was founded by Malam Ismaila Idris, a Fulani, with the support of Sheikh Abubakar Gumi, who had close ties with Saudi Arabia and the Muslim Students Society (Ibrahim 1991). Gumi had long denounced Sufism as un-Islamic because, he argued, no Sufi orders existed during the lifetime of the Prophet and his immediate successors (Umar 1993, 164). Feeling the need to create an organized forum for the continuation of Gumi's anti-Sufism, the followers of Gumi founded the *Jama'atu Izalat al-Bid'a wa Iqamat al-Sunna* (Movement for Suppressing Innovations and Restoring the Sunna) in 1978 in Jos, Nigeria. Thus was born Izala. The Izala vision of a better society was the product of, and response to, particular forces and events in Nigerian society, but it also emerged from global concerns about the nature and future of Muslim practice, as is attested by the multiplicity of Islamic movements.

The movement spread quickly via the distribution of taped cassettes of Gumi's sermons and the preaching of his doctrine throughout the country. Sheikh Gumi also made strategic use of Radio Kaduna,[17] the Nigerian Television Authority, and the Hausa language newspaper *Gaskiya ta fi Kwabo* to promote his message (Watts 1996, 275).[18] While the history of Izala in Nigeria is well documented, less is known about the early beginnings of the movement in Niger,[19] and particularly in Arewa. This is one *'dan* Izala account of how the organization took root in Dogondoutchi:

> Izala has existed for a long time but, in Doutchi, no one knew about it. No one knew the leaders of the association. Those who belonged to Izala would leave for Matankari [a nearby village] for the Friday prayer and the police would arrest them. They were forbidden to practice [their brand of Islam]. This is because everyone was afraid of this new religion. Later, the state and everybody else understood what it was about. The state then issued an authorization that allowed them [Izala members] to practice their religion. We have even been granted a plot of land to build our mosque. (12 June 1994)

The project of building a new place of worship on land granted by the local administration developed after the fight in the *grande mosquée,* when the *'yan* Izala realized that to ensure the strength and growth of the movement, they would need a mosque of their own to concretize their opposition to the "traditional" religious establishment. Knowing very well that they would not be granted subsidies to pay for the construction of the building, Izala members decided that they would all "pitch in": the mosque would be not only a place to attend prayers and sermons; it would also stand as a tangible reminder of the unity of the Izala community for the generations to come.

Today Izala leaders enjoy a growing popularity, most notably among younger Muslims—a segment of the population that is particularly receptive to the reformist ban on conspicuous consumption. But the movement also counts several wealthy entrepreneurs among its constituency. In contrast to both the Nigerian situation (where many of the followers of Malam Idris are poor) (Isichei 1987) and the context described by Grégoire (1993, 114) in Maradi, Niger (where Izala seems to attract "young rich kids") adherence in Dogondoutchi cuts across all social strata. Izala might be construed as a form of protest against Sufi corruption, or against the redistributive ethos around which much of everyday life is ordered in Mawri communities—gifts are crucial in forging or cementing social relationships. Yet, although it has clearly provided a forum for pursuing political objectives and airing grievances in the absence of other outlets, the movement is more adequately understood in relation to profound existential changes in the lives of its devotees. It must be analyzed in the context of what has been described as a "reorientation from a communal to an individualistic mode of religiosity [that] seems to be more in tune with the rugged individualism of capitalist social relations" (Umar 1993, 178).

Individuality, Equality and Frugality in Izala Discourse

In adapting itself to the local cultural context over the past several decades, Islam has successfully synthesized Muslim values with indigenous ways, something that, in the eyes of outsiders and purists, has greatly contributed to the religion's "syncretic" character. It is precisely these syncretized practices that *'yan* Izala want to eradicate through their militant preaching. Believing that the Muslim world is "in a state of decline" (Esposito 1992, 19), and that the ills of the present are a consequence of the failure to follow proper Qur'anic principles, *'yan* Izala urge all followers of the Prophet to return to an authentic Islam, devoid of heathenism and innovations. Indigenous elements that have become an integral part of local Islamic life such as wearing amulets, practicing divination, or drinking the ink used to write Qur'anic verses are declared *haram* (forbidden) because no mention is made of them in the Qur'an.

A return to the pristine Islam of the Prophet and caliphs is also a call to frugality, *'yan* Izala insist, repeating tirelessly the Prophet's admonition against spending more than one can afford. Thus, whereas Sufi elders and neighbors engage in ostentatious gift giving among kin and friends, and redistribute their resources widely among dependent clients, Muslim clerics, and the indigent, members of Izala preach individualism, conservation, and the rational utilization of resources. This means that 10,000 CFA francs ($20) is regarded as sufficient a sum to pay bridewealth, instead of the customary 100,000 or 200,000 CFA francs ($200 or $400). It also means that, as one charismatic Izala leader put it, "For the naming ceremony [of your infant], all you need to slaughter the ram is a sharp knife." This ironic referent is the conspicuous—and in his opinion, needless—distribution of money, kola nuts, and other gifts when a child is given a name on the seventh day of its life. The simpler, the better: if you cannot afford a ram, a chicken will do; it is more in accord with the teachings of the Prophet to economize than to go heavily into debt.

Because they claim that one's chief responsibility is to care for immediate dependents, not to entertain neighbors, *'yan* Izala have earned a reputation for being tightfisted, selfish individuals who turn their backs on social obligations. In a society that has traditionally condemned private accumulation of wealth, the Izala ban on conspicuous consumption has angered many for whom generosity is inseparable from friendliness, moral engagement, and sociality. In contrast, those who have embraced the tenets of Izala philosophy are for the most part young men who, in an era when most villagers struggle to make ends meet, welcome the movement's injunction against needless expenditure.

Generational divisions have grown in recent years. As the extended family has splintered under the impact of increasingly individualistic modes of farming, individuals are no longer able to depend on shared family resources and must fend for themselves (Sutter 1979; de Latour Dejean 1980). Thus, young men have become largely responsible for raising the money they need for the payment of bridewealth and taxes. While this growing individuation has freed the younger generation from the control of a gerontocracy often perceived as abusive, increasing economic privatization has not in fact relieved villagers of social and economic obligations. On the contrary, the social and financial pressures placed on salaried workers, seasonal laborers, and heads of households have become *more* acute—especially since the 1994 devaluation of the national currency. The demands for money placed on those who have the good fortune to enjoy a regular income often far exceed the meager supply. Endless requests for cash—to celebrate the birth of a child, to buy new outfits for the family, to help a friend in need, or to entertain important guests—flow in from the social networks that pull against an increasingly bureaucratic, urban-centered economy. Amid falling standards of living, growing unemployment, and disintegrating family support, the Izala endorsement of frugality provides a publicly sanctioned avenue of "escape" for young men who are reluctant to burden themselves with costly traditions yet also unwilling to appear disrespectful of them.

In addition to advocating a different way of managing one's wealth, Izala followers also promulgate conceptions of society and social relations that contrast sharply with those of their Sufi "elders," exacerbating latent intergenerational conflicts. Until quite recently, or so traditionalist Muslims would have us believe, Mawri sons hardly ever questioned the authority of their fathers who, by definition, "knew better" about issues ranging from marriage to Muslim practice to wealth management. Today, many sons have left their fathers' households never to return because, they say, following the dictates of their non-Izala elders would mean violating Muslim principles and leading a sinful life.[20] Further arguing that hereditary distinctions in terms of ethnic origin or social status have no place in Islam, *'yan* Izala oppose all practices—from saint worship to Sufi ritual—that presume a differential basis of power and authority among believers. In their opinion, Mawri society—and by extension, Nigerien society at large—is too hierarchical. No one, they insist, should be at the mercy of elders, especially if, through their ignorance and lack of piety, the latter perpetuate[21] a system of values that flaunts Qur'anic principles. As we shall see, this position is consistent with the Izala view of education, which is characterized by a fairly egalitarian ethos. *'Yan* Izala thus repeatedly challenge the authority of their "elders" in terms of their failure to obey the teachings of Muhammad. They generally refuse to eat with kin who have not embraced the reformist message: it is sinful to sit down with a pagan, even if it happens to be one's father. And they do not kneel in the presence of father, mother, father-in-law, mother-in-law, or anyone else whose age or social status would customarily dictate that they be shown deference (Grégoire 1993, 112). For most traditionalist Muslims, showing respect to one's parents, whatever the circumstances, is one of the most important personal obligations: for them, Izala followers are just power-hungry, selfish individuals whose total disregard for social tradition erodes their humanity (Masquelier 1996).

Even more offensive to their Muslim opponents is the Izala claim that Muhammad was a man like everybody else and ought to be remembered as such. "They do not believe in prophets and they say that Muhammad is just a man. If there are no prophets, then, who brought the Muslim religion?" a young trader angrily demanded during a conversation about the reformist doctrine. For many traditionalists, lack of respect for prophets both predisposes one to join Izala, and typifies "Izalaness." To Hajjiya Bibata, a loquacious and successful trader whose views coincide with many of her neighbors, such radical egalitarianism is treason:

> They [the *'yan* Izala] have betrayed the Muslim religion by saying that the Prophet is a man like other men. Everyone knows he is God's messenger. God sent him so he would teach people how to serve him. And since the *'yan* Izala serve him wrong, he [God] punishes them and they become donkeys. I will never give my daughter to a *'dan* Izala. The people of *bori* follow God better than do *'yan* Izala. (29 June 1994)

To maintain, as Ajiya Bibata does, that those who engage in spirit possession—an activity deemed sinful and anti-Muslim by followers of the Prophet—are actually more pious than Muslim reformists[22] is a serious insult. It is also a good measure of the ire that the reformist message has provoked among traditionalist Muslims for whom the assertive individualism and egalitarianism of Izala are a threat to society and family. Yet, it is precisely the lack of filial piety and altruism that has attracted many young Mawri to the reformist movement. In Maradi, it is school-leavers who find the Izala doctrine to be the brand of Islam best adapted to the exigencies of modern life (Grégoire 1993, 112–13).

The unparalleled appeal to youth of the *'yan* Izala campaign for an "order of rectitude" (Al-Azmeh 1993, 25) harking back to the time of Muhammad has also given rise to local speculation concerning the legitimacy of the movement. One of the most commonly held opinions is that *'yan* Izala tempt would-be converts with offers of money, using funds funneled in from Saudi Arabia, Egypt, or Nigeria. Clearly the power of the movement is closely associated, by those outside of it, with the management of wealth. *'Yan* Izala retort bitterly that local leaders receive nothing but Qur'ans from Saudi Arabia, though they invest their energies tirelessly in teaching the Sunna and recruiting new members.

Literacy and Enlightenment for All

The Izala movement is also an intervention in the definition of knowledge and its control. Traditionally, very few Muslims in this region of Niger completed Islamic studies or even learned how to read Arabic. While they demonstrated their adherence to Islam through multiple acts of piety—attending daily prayers, fasting, giving alms—their lack of literacy forced them to rely on *malamai* whose own lack of education further diversified local Muslim practice. While the number of children attending Qur'anic school has been increasing in recent years, it is still lower than the numbers attending schools based on the French system of education, and few progress beyond oral recitation of the Qur'an in Arabic. The relative absence of *ulema* (educated clerics who have been thoroughly initiated into the Scriptures) has long ensured that the authority of *malamai* goes unchallenged in the region, save an occasional confrontation with members of the *bori*. *'Yan* Izala deplore this situation. Intent upon eradicating quackery and ignorance, they strive to give the faithful a chance to learn about Islam on their own, and they insist on the need to make education accessible to all, regardless of age, sex, or social status. Rather than send their children to Qur'anic school, they have set up their own educational centers to provide an intensive education in Arabic. Izala children attend school from 8 A.M. to 12 P.M. and return from 4 P.M. to 6 P.M.

But education is not simply for children. In an attempt to promote their vision of an enlightened *umma* (Muslim community), *'yan* Izala have singled out *jahiliyya* (ignorance about Islam) as one of the targets of their reformist mission. *Jahiliyya* has become imbued with moral overtones that suggest that ignorance of Islam is a sin that can be overcome by exposure to the salvatory effects of Qur'anic education. In their efforts to raise the level of knowledge of the average Muslim in Nigeria, Izala attempt to teach certain modern skills in addition to religious instruction. Whereas traditional Qur'anic schools run by Sufi clerics taught children to memorize the Qur'an and also some basic ritual obligations, Izala schools strongly emphasize learning Arabic as a means to pursue independent Islamic studies (Westerlund 1997). Precisely because they perceive knowledge to be potentially accessible to all, *'yan* Izala are especially critical of religious leaders who define *ilimi* as esoteric or mystical knowledge and who use their control of it to justify their status as possessors of "blessing" *(baraka).* Arguing that knowledge is for all, Izala leaders regularly engage in rhetorical battles with Sufi *malamai* whom they accuse of quackery and deceit. Sufi clerics, they say, use secrecy as a front to cover up their lack of education and to exploit gullible clients in need of reassuring advice.

People's alleged gullibility and their willingness to trust the powers of *malamai* is rooted in the fetishization of the written word, literacy remaining a fairly mysterious capacity for many villagers. The patent effectiveness of writing as a means of human communication that defies temporal and spatial boundaries makes it a privileged candidate for use in intercourse between people and distant deities. Goody (1968; 1987) suggests that writing, as embodied speech, has often been valued more by illiterate peoples for its role in superhuman than in human communication, and that the initial appeal of Islam to outsiders is tied to the power of inscription. Whether or not this applies to the Mawri case, local people tap into the reservoir of power vested in sacred texts.[23] As is demonstrated by the debate concerning the existence of one versus several versions of the Qur'an, very few villagers have access to the Holy Book, much less decipher it. As happens in cases when literacy is primarily religious, "the Book becomes less a means to further enquiry, a step in the accumulation of knowledge, than an end itself, the timeless depository of all knowledge" (Goody 1968, 237). By democratizing literacy,[24] *'yan* Izala are thus not only demoting *malamai* from their position as guardians of sacred and restricted knowledge; they are also reconceptualizing the whole relationship of Muslims to the Holy Book and to the written word. Qur'anic verses, the *'yan* Izala vehemently argue, are not meant to be written so their power can be manipulated and absorbed through charms or *rubutu* ("drinking the word"), mistakenly attributing to the Scriptures godlike powers they never had. Qur'anic verses should not be fetishized in this way because ultimately only God has the power to heal. The aim of Islamic leaders should be to demystify religious texts by empowering believers with Qur'anic knowledge, not capitalizing on ignorance and belief in magical powers. The Scriptures, the *'yan* Izala insist, only have one set of correct interpretations; people must be taught them so that they can ignore all else (see Bowen 1993).

That the *'yan* Izala maintain not only men's but also women's rights to education—actively encouraging even married women to participate in their free evening classes—allows them to counter their opponents' claims that they aim to deprive women of their freedom. Women should be schooled, Izala followers assert, because they are invested with the sacred task of educating their children and taking care of their household. Because this activity should have priority over any other, women should be given the tools (i.e., an

Islamic education) they need to carry out their important task successfully. The future of the Islamic community is in their hands.

Izala thus glorifies the role played by women in Muslim society. "Women are queens, it says so in the Qur'an" volunteered one local Izala leader, who added that

> They should not work in the fields. It is also men who must provide water and wood supplies for the household. It is *haram* [forbidden] to take one's wife to the fields and put her to work. But [women] can become teachers, nurses, midwives, office clerks [as long as] they cover their bodies before stepping out of the house. (5 July 1994)

Education and seclusion should encourage the creation of a society in which women are honored, favored, and free of the struggle for survival. It is the Prophet himself, *'yan* Izala insist, who, when asked about the distinct tasks of women, replied that "to manage a house well, to keep a husband happy, and behave appropriately was equal to anything men might do" (Metcalf 1987, 148). Staying at home and attending to her domestic chores was the best way for a woman to earn respect, but keeping one's wife at home—even secluded—did not entail keeping her in ignorance of religious laws and principles. In fact, it was a husband's responsibility to ensure that his wife be properly taught, because knowing the precepts of Islam was the best way to serve God.

Seclusion, Movement, and the Veil

In fact, in Dogondoutchi and elsewhere in Niger, the Izala concern to restore a pure and authentic Islam increasingly focuses on women as the repositories of Islamic morality. In Islam, in general, morality translates into a set of rules that prescribe male and female action and the presentation of the body. But in the reformist discourses of Izala, it is women's bodies in particular that have become the object of meticulous attention. As is the case elsewhere in the Islamic diaspora (Ong 1987, 1995; Bauer 1985; Abu-Lughod 1986; Delaney 1991; Rugh 1986; Gaspard and Khosrokhavar 1995; Mernissi 1987; Hawley and Proudfoot 1994) much of the debate over what constitutes respectability, piety, and modesty centers on women's dress and deportment. For wives and daughters of *'yan* Izala, acknowledging membership into the reformist movement has meant wearing the *hijabi,* a veil whose color and fabric match the rest of their outfit, encompassing the body down to the ankles. Though the luminous yellow, deep pink, bright green, or vivid turquoise shades of the *hijabi* cloth paradoxically ensures that women wearing such an outfit will be noticed wherever they go (more so than their "heathen" counterparts wearing mostly earth-tone wrappers and matching blouses), the professed intent is to hide women from the public eye and protect their virtue. According to a *'dan* Izala,

> In the Muslim religion, the woman must hide her body and be dressed modestly. She cannot just walk wherever she wants. My wife remains at home; we have another woman who comes to bring us water from the pump, and I pay someone to bring us firewood. My wife is free to leave [the house] and visit her mother or go to the dispensary during the day as long as she asks my permission. All Muslims should keep their wives at home. (19 June 1994)

The *hijabi* covers a woman's hair and hides the contours of her upper body. It is held around the face with an elastic band, enabling her to retain the use of her hands. The veil signifies respectability and propriety. Girls as young as five years old may be seen donning a *hijabi* in Dogondoutchi even though, in the opinion of the *'yan* Izala I talked to, it is only when they reach puberty that wearing the veil in public becomes an absolute necessity.[25]

Moussa Boubakar, a tailor and member of Izala who started making veils for his wives after returning from the Hajj eight years ago, insisted that "It is God who said that women should hide their bodies." After he saw what Muslim women were wearing in Mecca, he copied their models of *hijabi:*

> Any color can be used [for a woman's garment] as long as the fabric doesn't shine: red, green, black. But shiny material [*mai walkiya*] is no good because it attracts men's attention. Some veils are very long [shrouding the ankles], others are shorter. But for grown women as well as little girls, the veil should normally fall to the ground. Women can wear beautiful outfits made of *bazin* [brocade] but only to wear at home.[26] They can't wear them in the street, in town. (12 June 1994)

Besides exemplifying allegiance to God, Moussa Boubakar concluded, wearing the *hijabi* is an expression of positive virtue: like other pious act such as praying or giving alms, it increases a believer's chances of being justly rewarded on judgment day. Moussa Boubakar's statement of sartorial modesty was quickly imitated by other Izala men who requested that the tailor copy his design for their own wives. Foreign practices are thus reinterpreted by individuals eager to answer local concerns. Soon, every Izala woman in Dogondoutchi was wearing an outfit tailored by Moussa Boubakar or his assistants, declaring her family's purifying intentions.

Women outside the movement have also recently started wrapping themselves in gauzy veils or cloth when they leave their homes instead of wearing a simple head scarf. While their head coverings connote respectability—failure to cover one's head in public widely implies *karuwanci* ("prostitution"), and even young girls are enjoined to wear a head scarf when leaving the home—they are also a matter of fashion: in 1994, sheer veils imported from

South Asia, adorned with subtle impressions in pale blue, yellow, or green shades were the latest rage. Though their appearance on local markets is probably no coincidence in this era of intense debate over what constitutes appropriate female dress, their appeal to women outside of Izala partially resides in the fact that they generally reveal more than they conceal while nonetheless allowing for a semblance of propriety.

Unlike sheer veils that hug shoulders suggestively and espouse their wearer's movements gracefully, the stiff brocade of the *hijabi* hides a woman's upper torso so completely as to render impossible the definition of her body contours. Although seclusion is often more systematically enforced in Izala households, the *hijabi* nonetheless allows Izala women to enter places that would otherwise be prohibited to them in this highly gender-segregated society. Other Muslim women, who perceive their Izala counterparts to be victims of overzealous husbands, would probably laugh at the suggestion that the *hijabi* is an emancipatory device: Izala women remain mostly indoors while their husbands spend a great deal of their time preaching or attending meetings—so much so, in fact, that they are rarely home to grant their wives permission to go out. Whether or not Izala wives or daughters actually enjoy more freedom, it is clear that the *hijabi* "enables women to move in and out of [enclosed living] spaces in a kind of portable seclusion" (Papanek 1973, 295). From this perspective, while the marketplace is too public for Izala women—and for many non-Izala women as well, who are by and large constrained by their domestic duties—access to the mosque is not denied them: women belonging to the movement may pray in the back because they are covered with the *hijabi* that physically and symbolically secludes them from the outside world, while paradoxically enabling them to carve out a moral space for themselves.[27] In so allowing women to move within previously inaccessible spheres, the *hijabi* compels us "to turn our attention away from fixed and reified spaces . . . and to begin attending more closely to how individuals move through spaces over time, simultaneously defining and transforming them" (Cooper 1997, 198), but such consideration is beyond the purview of my present discussion.

Veiling of any type, however, reflects local understandings of female respectability in the context of wider redefinitions of Muslim identity and morality. As elsewhere in the Islamic world, Mawri reformists are actively involved in the construction of the virtuous woman in direct contradistinction to Western models of womanhood, which they believe to be the source of moral degeneracy in Europe and America. Though the custom of veiling predates the advent of Islam, *'yan* Izala insist that the order to veil comes directly from the Scriptures. It is the Prophet who told his wives to cover their bodies; therefore, pious women should emulate these archetypical figures of Islamic virtue and wear a veil, especially if, despite the admonition to stay home and serve their God through marriage and reproduction,[28] they have to leave their compound.

My discussion of Izala raises the question of the movement's vision of femininity and domesticity within the larger debate about women's civil rights in Islamic societies. Studies of conservative Islamic movements have often revealed how control over women's sexuality, and over their social and economic roles, has been one of the cornerstones of the Islamist agenda. The rhetoric of many of these movements joins a condemnation of women's aspirations for greater freedom to a broader critique of the pernicious effects of European and American social and political institutions on the Muslim world (Awn 1994). In Iran, one of the first measures taken by Khomeini's Shi'i government was to pressure women into wearing the veil in an attempt to Islamicize the society as a whole. The "morality police" that wandered the streets of Tehran would coerce women into conforming to proper Islamic values. In the Sudan, reforms instituted by the powerful National Islamic Front since it gained power in 1990 have similarly forced women to veil, and have attempted to replace the traditional Sudanese dress with a heavy, floor-length "Islamic costume" (Wheelwright 1992). In Pakistan, a woman who steps outside her home without a veil is considered morally corrupt (Banghash 1985). In these contexts and elsewhere, reformist Islamic movements have clearly defined themselves as "antimodernist" organizations, extending religiously sanctioned control over women's bodies as metonyms for control over society at large.

While the Izala case bears undeniable similarities to the Iranian, Algerian, or Sudanese contexts in these respects, it is important not to erase some fundamental differences between these various Islamic societies or organizations. When it comes to the education of women, for instance, Izala is anything but a conservative movement. Rather it is an attempt to forge an alternative modernity for Muslims in this region of West Africa, one that is not rooted in Western notions of power, morality, and accountability. Recall, for instance, that a woman's primary obligation is to learn to read the Qur'an so that she can be a better and more responsible member of Muslim society. It is worth pointing out that in Nigeria, many women have been attracted to the movement because they see its doctrines and practices as a move forward in comparison to the situation within the Sufi orders (Westerlund 1997).[29] The *'yan* Izala's commitment to further the education of women has already resulted in the expansion of the Islamic school system in Dogondoutchi, though it is not clear whether such strategies will lead to an increasing integration of Muslim women in "public" affairs—as has been the case in Nigeria where women, through their roles as political actors, have affected particular outcomes in the public realm. After all, many *'yan* Izala say that though women are theoretically allowed to go out as long as they are appropriately dressed, it is best to keep them partially or entirely secluded. Izala thus shares with other Muslim reformist movements a concern with defining itself in opposition to the secular modernity of the West, yet its stance toward women and education gives it a certain modernist dimension that should not be overlooked if one is to understand the intricacies of the Izala vision of Islam and role as defender of family integrity.

Izala efforts to forge a community of believers united in the common struggle against illiteracy, immorality, and profligacy exemplifies how civil society can become the source of a counterhegemonic social movement that is directed not simply—or so much—against the state but also against local-level, village, and family structures: through their insistence that a son's primary allegiance is to his God, rather than to his father, *'yan* Izala actively question the moral legitimacy of parental authority, especially when it is, as they often claim, based on decidedly un-Islamic principles. Their rejection of the patrilineage, occurring in tandem with the subversion of local religious authorities, suggests that we cannot simply analyze Nigerien politics of emerging identities, power, and self-representation in terms of conventional state-society oppositions. The Izala message inserted itself within the spaces of doubt and ambiguity introduced by the *décrispation* of the late 1980s, and it is on these spaces—in which the meanings of truth, legitimacy, and tradition are constantly being negotiated—that we must focus to understand how, for instance, local competition for control of the main mosque in a Nigerien town may contribute to an emerging critical consciousness about Islamic identity.

Conclusion

The recent emergence of an overarching civic and political culture in Niger has been promoted partly by the liberalization of Muslim discourse and the proliferation of distinct, and often fiercely opposed, Islamic invented "traditions" whose competing visions of order, morality, and social control have resulted in violent disputes over mosque ownership. Bowen notes that the control of a mosque has great political significance in any Muslim society, adding that while a struggle over mosque control may have as its explicit object a relatively minor liturgical issue, it often brings to the surface a much broader set of sociopolitical divisions (1993, 309). In the case recounted here, such divisions are themselves part of wider transformations in Islamic lifestyles and thinking. As modes of reflection over, and criticism of, Islamic practice, they contribute to a public sphere of discourse that differs markedly from European formulations of civil society—in which religion is markedly absent.

In Dogondoutchi, the recent critical debates over the nature of Islamic knowledge and worship has put increasing pressure on religious practitioners to articulate their beliefs. Such debates share similarities with religious disputes elsewhere in that Mawri protagonists eschew culturally specific rationalizations for current practices to advocate religious action based on its degree of fit with the universal set of norms provided by the Qur'an and hadith (Bowen 1993, 321). Concerned that the onslaught of Westernization and secularization threatens the Islamic order, members of Izala have implemented sweeping reforms, which they insist will establish religious, moral, and social practices more in keeping with Qur'anic injunctions. In so doing, they have also redirected the course of the ongoing debate on spirituality, knowledge, and piety that had long shaped *'yan* bori and Muslim relations. Having successfully managed to rally certain discontents and declare war on a society that had long tolerated polytheistic and syncretistic practices, the goal of these zealots is now to reform Mawri society—and the rest of Niger—so that no aspect of social, familial, political, or economic life is left outside of Islam's purview.

In the *'yan* Izala's vision of a Muslim civil society, religious truths are conceived as fixed and unchanging, which is precisely why one can aim to live one's life guided by the very words and deeds of the Prophet (as they are transcribed in the Qur'an and hadith). Eickelman and Piscatori note that "eternal religious truths . . . are perceived, understood and transmitted by persons historically situated in 'imagined' communities, who knowingly or inadvertently contribute to the reconfiguration or reinterpretation of those verities, even as their fixed and unchanging natures are affirmed" (1990, 2). While this captures the essence of the reformist movement, it does not mean that Izala rejects "modernity" to return to a mythical past: that much is clear from their egalitarian vision of society, their stress on self-centered achievement, and their insistence that women be educated. As a particular form of invented tradition based on a new scripturalist interpretation of Islam, Izala provides a framework for the growing individualism that has come to characterize postcolonial identities and increasingly monetized relations. In Dogondoutchi, this form of anti-Sufism actively engages with capitalist processes and a certain form of consumerism. As we have seen, its oppositional culture, while countering aspects of Euromodernism, also counters long-standing local traditions of economic redistribution.

It is through its contestation of a previously unquestioned orthodoxy and its cultivation of an alternative socio-moral order, one of entitled individuals and loyal followers, that Izala can be said to contribute to the emergence of a Nigerien civil society. Granted, Izala's sustained efforts to reaffirm the centrality of Islam in both public and private life has often promoted dissent rather than unity in the Muslim community. The reformist movement's struggle to establish a moral order accessible and useful to all through Qur'anic teaching has only highlighted the clash of incompatible interests in Dogondoutchi. Moreover, despite its seemingly egalitarian ethos and its valorization of women's roles, Izala is not all enlightenment and emancipation: it is contradictory, simultaneously practical and hopelessly utopian, democratic yet also despotic. Nevertheless, Izala in Niger clearly "sounds a warning to the widespread belief that African societies have tended to be ineffective counterweights to African states" (Watts 1996, 184). By contributing an Islamic alternative to more secular models of nationhood, citizenship, family, and identity, the Izala discourse is actively shaping the emerging Nigerien public sphere, providing a religious framework for scrutinizing contemporary social arrangements and speculating on the forms that public and private life should take. That such critical discussions about society are primarily religious in nature should not surprise us given Mawri society's persistent history of confrontation between Muslims and spirit mediums (Masquelier 1993, 1994). These debates that divide communities and families under different religious banners broaden our understanding of civil society's potential when it is exported to social contexts in which people are urged—through the media of televised sermons, printed words, taped admonitions, or unmediated confrontations—to reorder their lives, from matters of dress and commensalism to how they should earn and spend money.

Notes

1. *'Yan* literally means "sons of" (*'dan* is the singular form), but usually refers to membership in a group or organization. Hence, *'yan bori* is translated as "members of the *bori*," while *'yan Izala* means "followers, or members, of Izala."

2. There are two major Sufi brotherhoods in Niger: the Tijaniyya and the Qadiriyya. Uthman dan Fodio, who in the 1800s led a *jihad* against the Islamicized Hausa states and founded the Sokoto caliphate, was a member of the Qadiriyya. Many of the wealthiest merchants of Niger belong to this brotherhood, whose members are locally referred to as *'yan sadalu.* The Tijaniyya brotherhood was founded in Algeria by Sheikh Ahmad Tijani in the eighteenth century and later was introduced in Niger in the 1950s by the members of the brotherhood from Kano, Nigeria. Members of the Tijaniyya are referred to as *'yan kabalu.* Together the two religious organizations constitute the Tariqa brotherhoods.

3. Itinerant *malamai* intending to preach must first obtain official clearance.

4. *Malamai* are muslim clerics/scholars.

5. Communities throughout Arewa were traditionally split between those who followed the Prophet and those who followed the spirits—a situation that sometimes led to bitter confrontations between the two parties (Masquelier 1993, 1994), even though Muslim and non-Muslim identities have remained rather fluid, multidimensional, and overlapping.

6. I first heard about the "mosque incident" from a top town official with whom I had an informal chat after I came to offer greetings and introduce myself. While he deplored the violent outcome of the dispute and was very critical of Izala activities, he did not hesitate to discuss such matters with me. However, when I visited the local police station in the hope of gaining access to police records of the whole affair, I was told by several persons that no such records existed and that, to their knowledge, no such fight had ever taken place.

7. With its focus on thriftiness and individual realization, the Izala movement bears interesting parallels with the spread of Calvinism and the associated emergence of

particular ethical and economic aspirations in modern Europe (Weber 1958). Just as Protestantism's stress on ascetic labor, moral accountability, and individual agency provided the social context for the growth of modern capitalism, Izala contributes a model of utilitarian moral economy that seems best adapted to the contemporary logic of market relations. Moreover, the Protestant ethic's concept of a world that "has been provided by God as the context in which man was to labor in His name" (Comaroff 1985, 130) is not unlike the Izala notion that a Muslim's primary duty is to create an environment in which all can learn how to serve Allah properly by leading self-determined and morally accountable lives. Despite these intriguing similarities, the moral community envisioned by *'yan* Izala is resolutely anti-Western in its formulation of citizenship, family, and gendered identity.

8. Ironically, economic factors might prove more decisive than any political decision as the costs of paper and printing, both imported from neighboring Nigeria, continue to rise.

9. According to Voice of America Hausa broadcaster Aliyu Mustaphawas, the new openness that characterized talk about politics and the state in Niger in the early 1990s was largely due to the "National Conference" that was deliberating the political future of the country in 1991. His description of the new climate in the capital is revealing of the current changes the whole country has been experiencing:

> If you have been away from the city of Niamey for say two or more years, you would feel the change immediately, as soon as you come into the town. You will observe right away the change in people's facial expressions, and they talk a little louder than before. . . . It looks like virtually everyone is involved in one activity or the other, from politicians, academicians, members of the business community to workers, students and women. Everyone, that is, except the military. One gets the feeling that the entire country has suddenly become politically alive in sharp contrast with the past when Niamey used to be politically boring. (1991, 1, 4)

10. In June 1994, Islamic women's groups rejected the government family code saying that 603 of its 906 articles were a breach of Qur'anic principles. The code, which Islamic activists oppose unanimously, forbids repudiation of a wife by her husband and allows couples to opt formally for a monogamous relationship. In a formal statement, women from six different Muslim organizations said that all the issues the code intended to oversee were already regulated by the Muslim religion and should not suffer human interference (Mayer 1995, 1).

11. Iran provides the model for the *'yan* Izala's utopian dream of an "Islamic civil society," but, paradoxically, Shi'ite doctrines are thought to be just as un-Islamic as the views advocated by Sufi orders.

12. *'Yan* Izala insist that the "traditional" prayer schedule adopted by local Muslims is incorrect. They have created a prayer schedule of their own, in which three of the five daily prayers take place half an hour after the *'yan* Tariqa prayers. Arguing that the Prophet allegedly remarked that "praying on time" was the most important obliga-

tion of a pious Muslim, they warn their followers and foes alike that exactitude in prayer is a good way of ensuring one's place in heaven (see Masquelier 1996).

13. Of course, what constitutes "innovation" is also a matter of debate. *'Yan* Izala may condemn the wearing of amulets on the basis that there is no mention of such healing practices in the Holy Book, but like their Sufi counterparts, they see no problem in using the technological innovation of a public address system to broadcast the call to prayer.

14. One *malam,* a *'dan* Tijaniyya with whom I discussed doctrinal and practical differences between Izala members and followers of Tijaniyya and Qadiriyya, noted philosophically that "prayers are more efficacious than amulets but for those who know nothing, who cannot read the Qur'an, amulets work. One cannot tell them 'Go read this *sourate* [verse of the Qur'an], it will protect you.'" Though this informant did not encourage people to wear amulets, he disagreed with the *'yan* Izala position that the practice of wearing *layya* (charms) was sinful in all contexts, regardless of one's educational and social standing.

15. Mainstream Muslims often refer to one another as "true Muslims" *(mutanen kwarai)* to emphasize the fact that, in their views, *'yan* Izala are impostors.

16. It seems only fair to point out that according to Sheikh Gumi himself, violence was perpetrated by members of the Muslim brotherhoods on Izala followers rather than the other way around. This is how Gumi describes in his memoirs what happened:

> At first the Tariqa leaders and their followers did not take any particular notice of the preachers, but soon it became apparent that Izala was spreading fast and the people were questioning their past mistakes. That was when organized violence began against the association.
>
> The first victim, I think, was Malam Ali, a Nupe man living in Kawo, a Kaduna suburb. . . . One day, he went to . . . preach as usual. He had hardly begun when many Tariqa followers surrounded him and demanded that he should stop. He stopped immediately, but as he was getting ready to go away a few of them shouted that he should be killed. A scuffle ensued and in the process someone brought out a knife and stabbed him to death.
>
> Also, not long afterwards, an Izala public meeting was attacked by irate Tariqa followers in Lafia, Plateau State. Many were wounded and their vehicles were shattered or burnt. . . .
>
> Then also the Tariqa leaders resorted to other tactics, like threats and intimidation against the law enforcement agencies in order to force them to ban Izala meetings. (1992, 158)

17. Radio Kaduna is the most listened-to radio station in West Africa. It broadcasts over much of Nigeria, Niger, and many surrounding countries (Larkin 1996).

18. For an insightful discussion of the role of the media in shaping the knowledge and practice of Islam in northern Nigeria, see Larkin 1996.

19. As far as I know, there are no studies of the Izala movement in Niger, except for Grégoire's (1993) essay on Islam and identity among the merchant class of Maradi.

20. While family obligations and loyalty to one's parents are morally sanctioned, loyalty to the Umma, united in submission to the one God, must take clear precedence. Muslims who want to remind their brothers of such principles like to invoke the story of Abraham's willingness to sacrifice his son Isma'il, and of Isma'il's willingness to be sacrificed: The father-son relationship, "while undeniably strong, was subordinated to God's wishes" (Eickelman and Piscatori 1996, 82).

21. *'Yan* Izala are very bothered by the *'yan* Tariqa's claim that "those who belong to Izala do not like their fathers, mothers, brothers, or sisters." In their defense, they insist that following the Prophet's teaching to the letter—which may mean alienating oneself from one's family—is more important to Allah than upholding traditions that simply strengthen the power of the local gerontocracy.

22. The enmity that now characterizes mainstream Muslims and Izala followers has had a salutary effect on the relations between Muslims and "animists." *Bori* practitioners are no longer so systematically targeted in zealous diatribes on the part of those eager to distance themselves from the "backwardness" and "immorality" of their animist neighbors.

23. As Doutté explains,

> since the graphic signs which represented the words are much easier to handle than the sounds and are capable of enduring, as they have a material form, it is inevitable that magical force is seen as encapsulated in them; in other words, writing itself is reputed to have magical powers. (Goody 1968, 227)

24. The Izala dissemination of religious education through radio sermons and the circulation of cassettes was also instrumental in reconceptualizing the role of the *ulema,* who made the religious meanings contained in the Qur'an available to those who could not read (Larkin 1996, 5).

25. According to Malam Idris Ali'o, "A girl must start wearing a veil when she starts menstruating. But there are four-year-olds who already wear a veil and it is fine."

26. The same logic dictates that women should not wear heavy bracelets that make noise and attract unwanted attention. Moussa Boubakar further elaborated:

> All the things that women wear to attract men are *haram* [forbidden by religion]. Perfume, for instance. A woman can make herself beautiful but only within [the confines of] her compound and for the benefit of her husband. Not to attract another man; that's sinful.

27. Muslim women are allowed in the mosque only once they have reached menopause and no longer constitute a sexual threat to men. "Young women cannot go [to the mosque] because they would attract attention and distract men from their prayers," Malam Boubakar Hamidou once explained to me. *'Yan* Izala respond to such blatant disregard for women's own religious aspirations by asking: "Why should women be prevented from praying at the mosque?" For them, the obvious solution to women's curtailed freedom lies in the veil, which, together with the pants and long-sleeved robe

that constitute the rest of the Izala outfit for females, creates a protective limited enclosure.

28. Islamic reformists are especially pronatalist. They oppose family planning and birth control because they believe God decides how many children a couple begets. This is why women are such assets to their communities: by producing children who grow to become pious followers of Izala, women will increase the size and strength of the *Umma* (Islamic community). The ultimate goal in producing large families is to ensure that Muhammad will be the prophet with the largest following.

29. With respect to women's right to vote, Izala leader Abubakar Gumi repeatedly urged Muslim men to allow their women to register for the elections and to let them go to the polls. Asserting that "politics is more important than prayer," Gumi stressed the "necessity that every man take . . . his women and children above the age of eighteen to register so that [they could] predominate over the Non-Muslims" (Christelow 1984, 7).

References

Abu-Lughod, Lila. 1986. *Veiled Sentiments: Honor and Poetry in a Bedouin Society.* Berkeley: University of California Press.

Al-Azmeh, Aziz. 1993. *Islams and Modernities.* London: Verso.

Al-Karsani, Awad Al-Sid. 1993. "Beyond Sufism: The Case of Millennial Islam in Sudan." In *Muslim Identity and Social Change in Sub-Saharan Africa,* ed. Louis Brenner. Bloomington: Indiana University Press.

Awn, Peter J. 1994. "Indian Islam: The Shah Bano Affair." In *Fundamentalism and Gender,* ed. John Stratton Hawley. New York: Oxford University Press.

Bangash, Mohsin A. 1985. "Women Rally to Tear Down Veil and Four Walls." *New Statesman and Society,* 2 August, 19–20.

Barkindo, Bawuro M. 1993. "Growing Islamism in Kano since 1970: Causes, Form and Implications." In *Muslim Identity and Social Change in Sub-Saharan Africa,* ed. Louis Brenner. Bloomington: Indiana University Press.

Barlow, Robin, and Wayne Snyder. 1993. "Taxation in Niger: Problems and Proposals." *World Development* 21 (7): 1, 179–89.

Bauer, Janet. 1985. "Sexuality and the Moral 'Construction' of Women in an Islamic Society." *Anthropological Quarterly* 58:120–29.

Bernus, Suzanne. 1969. *Particularisme ethnique en milieu urbain: L'Exemple de Niamey.* Paris: Institute d'Ethnologie.

Bowen, John R. 1993. *Muslims through Discourse: Religion and Ritual in Gayo Society.* Princeton, N.J.: Princeton University Press.

Christelow, Allan. 1984. "Religious Protest and Dissent in Northern Nigeria: From Madhism to Quranic Integrism." Manuscript. Quoted in Roman Loimeier, "Islamic Reform and Political Change: The Example of Abubakar Gumi and the *'Yan* Izala Movement in Nigeria," in *African Islam and Islam in Africa,* ed. Eva Evers Rosander and David Westerlund (Athens: Ohio University Press, 1997), 7.

Comaroff, Jean. 1985. *Body of Power, Spirit of Resistance: The Culture and History of a South African People.* Chicago: University of Chicago Press.

Cooper, Barbara. 1997. "Gender, Movement, and History: Social and Spatial Transformations in 20th Century Maradi, Niger. Environment and Planning D." *Society and Space* 15:195–221.

Delaney, Carol. 1991 *The Seed and the Soil: Gender and Cosmology in Turkish Village Society.* Berkeley: University of California Press.

de Latour, Eliane. 1982. "La Paix destructrice." In *Guerres de lignages et guerres d'états en Afrique,* eds. Jean Bazin and Emmanuel Terray. Paris: Editions des Archives Contemporaines.

de Latour Dejean, Eliane. 1980. "Shadows Nourished by the Sun: Rural Social Differentiation among the Mawri of Niger." In *Peasants in Africa: Historical and Contemporary Perspectives,* ed. Martin Klein. Beverly Hills: Sage Publications.

Eickelman, Dale, and James Piscatori. 1990. "Social Theory in the Study of Muslim Societies." In *Muslim Travelers: Pilgrimage, Migration and the Religious Imagination,* ed. Dale Eickelman and James Piscatori. Berkeley: University of California Press.

———. 1996. *Muslim Politics.* Princeton, N.J.: Princeton University Press.

Esposito, John L. 1992. *The Islamic Threat: Myth or Reality?* New York: Oxford University Press.

Fatton, Robert, Jr. 1995. "Africa in the Age of Democratization: The Civic Limitations of Civil Society." *African Studies Review* 38:67–100.

Fischer, Michael M. J., and Mehdi Abedi. 1990. *Debating Muslims: Cultural Dialogues in Postmodernity and Tradition.* Madison: University of Wisconsin Press.

Fuglestad, Finn. 1983. *A History of Niger: 1850–1960.* New York: Cambridge University Press.

Gaspard, Françoise, and Farhad Khosrokhavar. 1995. *Le Foulard et la république.* Paris: Editions La Découverte.

Goody, Jack. 1968. "Restricted Literacy in Northern Ghana." In *Literacy in Traditional Societies,* ed. Jack Goody. Cambridge: Cambridge University Press.

———. 1987. *The Interface between the Written and the Oral.* Cambridge: Cambridge University Press.

Grégoire, Emmanuel. 1993. "Islam and the Identity of Merchants in Maradi (Niger)." In *Muslim Identity and Social Change in Sub-Saharan Africa,* ed. Louis Brenner. Bloomington: Indiana University Press.

Gumi, Sheikh Abubakar, with Ismaila Abubakar Tsiga. 1992. *Where I Stand.* Ibadan: Spectrum Books.

Harris, Jay M. 1994. "'Fundamentalism': Objections from a Modern Jewish Historian." In *Fundamentalism and Gender,* ed. John Stratton Hawley. New York: Oxford University Press.

Hawley, John Stratton, and Wayne Proudfoot. 1994. Introduction to *Fundamentalism and Gender,* ed. John Stratton Hawley. New York: Oxford University Press

Ibrahim, Jibrin. 1991. "Religion and Political Turbulence in Nigeria." *Journal of Modern African Studies* 29:115–36.

Isichei, Elizabeth. 1987. "The Maitatsine Risings in Nigeria 1980–85: A Revolt of the Disinherited." *Journal of Religion in Africa* 17:194–208.

Karlström, Mikael. 1999. "Civil Society and Its Presuppositions: Lessons from Uganda." In *Civil Society and the Political Imagination in Africa,* ed. John and Jean Comaroff. Chicago: University of Chicago Press.

Larkin, Brian. 1996. "The Holy Qur'an, Tafsir, and the Uncertain Development of Religious Media in Northern Nigeria." Paper presented at the African Studies Association annual meeting, San Francisco.

Launay, Robert. 1992. *Beyond the Stream: Islam and Society in a West African Town.* Berkeley: University of California Press.

Loimeier, Roman. 1997. "Islamic Reform and Political Change: The Example of Abubakar Gumi and the *'Yan* Izala Movement in Nigeria." In *African Islam and Islam in Africa,* ed. Eva Evers Rosander and David Westerlund. Athens: Ohio University Press.

Lubeck, Paul. 1987. "Islamic Protest and Oil-Based Capitalism." In *State, Oil, and Agriculture in Nigeria,* ed. Michael Watts. Berkeley: Institute of International Studies, University of California.

Masquelier, Adeline. 1993. "Narratives of Power, Images of Wealth: The Ritual Economy of *Bori* in the Market." In *Modernity and Its Malcontents: Ritual and Power in Postcolonial Africa,* ed. Jean Comaroff and John Comaroff. Chicago: University of Chicago Press.

———. 1994. "Lightning, Death and the Avenging Spirits: *Bori* Values in a Muslim World." *Journal of Religion in Africa* 24:2–51.

———. 1996. "Identity, Alterity and Ambiguity in a Nigerien Community: Competing Definitions of True Islam." In *Postcolonial Identities in Africa,* ed. Richard Werbner. London: Zed Press.

Mayer, Joel. 1995. "Nouvelles du Niger." *Camel Express: Newsletter of the Friends of Niger* 12.

Mbembe, Achille. 1992. "Provisional Notes on the Postcolony." *Africa* 62:3–37.

Mernissi, Fatima. 1987. *Beyond the Veil: Male-Female Dynamics in Modern Muslim Society,* rev. ed. Bloomington: Indiana University Press.

Metcalf, Barbara D. 1987. "Islamic Arguments in Contemporary Pakistan." In *Islam and the Political Economy of Meaning: Comparative Studies of Muslim Discourse,* ed. William R. Roff. London: Croom Helm.

Monga, Celestin. 1995. "Civil Society and Democratization in Francophone Africa." *The Journal of Modern African Studies* 33:359–379.

Munson, Henry, Jr. 1993. *Religion and Power in Morocco.* New Haven, Conn.: Yale University Press.

Mustaphawas, Aliyu. 1991. "The New Niger: A Reporter's Notebook by a VOA Hausa Broadcaster." *Camel Express* 7.

Ong, Aihwa. 1987. *Spirit of Resistance and Capitalist Discipline: Factory Women in Malaysia.* Albany: SUNY Press.

———. 1995. "Postcolonial Nationalism: Women and Retraditionalization in the Islamic Imaginary, Malaysia." In *Feminism, Nationalism and Militarism*, ed. Constance R. Sutton. Arlington, Va.: Association for Feminist Anthropology, American Anthropological Association.

Papanek, Hanna. 1973. "Purdah: Separate Worlds and Symbolic Shelter." *Comparative Studies in Society and History* 15:289–325.

Rugh, Andrea B. 1986. *Reveal and Conceal: Dress in Contemporary Egypt*. Syracuse: Syracuse University Press.

Sutter, John. 1979. "Social Analysis of the Nigerien Rural Producer." *Niger Agricultural Sector Assessment* 2 (part D). Niamey: USAID.

Umar, Muhammad Sani. 1993. "Changing Islamic Identity in Nigeria from the 1960s to the 1980s: From Sufism to Anti-Sufism." In *Muslim Identity and Social Change in Sub-Saharan Africa*, ed. Louis Brenner. Bloomington: Indiana University Press.

Watts, Michael. 1996. "Islamic Modernities? Citizenship, Civil Society and Islamism in a Nigerian City." *Public Culture* 8:251–89.

Weber, Max. 1958. *The Protestant Ethic and the Spirit of Capitalism*. Translated by Talcott Parsons. New York: Charles Scribner's Sons.

Westerlund, David. 1997. "Reaction and Action: Accounting for the Rise of Islamism." In *African Islam and Islam in Africa*, ed. Eva Evers Rosander and David Westerlund. Athens: Ohio University Press.

Wheelwright, Gael. 1992. "Holes in the Veil: The Strong Tide of Anti-Feminist Islam in Arabic-Speaking Africa Is Facing Resistance." *New Statesman and Society*, 27 March, 24–25.

9

Curl Up and Dye: Civil Society and the Fashion-Minded Citizen

Amy Stambach

Hair Talk

ON 9 OCTOBER 1988 an editorial appeared in the *Tanzanian Sunday News* titled "Beware! Hair Curling Is Dangerous!" More than a dozen letters followed, most of them urging Tanzanian women not to purchase hair-care products imported from the United States and Europe.[1] Some warned that chemicals used in "curl kits" could cause convulsions, blindness, and possibly madness, and could harm the fetuses of pregnant women. Others argued that buying these products was a waste of money and contributed to the impoverishment of Africa at the hands of the West, or that straightening and curling one's hair was an imitation of "white aesthetics," a form of "cultural degradation and subjugation."[2]

Issues discussed in the editorials—and the very editorials themselves—render concrete many of the competing ideas Tanzanians hold about civil society. To some Tanzanians, particular hairstyles signify cultural vulnerability in an unexpected, political way; they raise concern about capitalist investment and the erosion of cultural identity. To others, these same styles are signs of vitality; they attest to personal freedom and sexual liberation that characterizes a truly *civil* society. The double character of women's hair fashion—as an icon of corruption and as a testament to personal and national growth—has implications for our understandings of the changing moral and political relationship between the citizen and the state. It points to a complex of values and beliefs people use to comment on and modify their worlds, and it illustrates that, regardless of the presence or absence of formal organizations for people to negotiate access to power, the media provides a vital political arena in which citizens can debate questions of governance. "Civil society" in this chapter is thus useful for reflecting on the visible manifestations of citizens' ideas about good citizenship and governance, and for examining the ways editorials offer evidence of a civil society in operation—an emergence of a civil domain of public debate via the media.

Tanzania has been one of the most openly politicized countries in Africa;

everything has been debated—from miniskirts to university admissions—and hair curling is but one extension of this political mode. Tanzanians' propensity to read the political into the everyday gives an interesting twist to civil society. Editorials reflect a legacy of early independence African socialism in which citizens were politicized to scrutinize themselves and others for ideological conformity (see Abrahams 1987; Rubin 1996). Writing about the moral and economic implications of hair curling in the newspaper redirects an older socialist ideology onto the capitalist workings of markets and states. Editorialists' passionate discussion about good governance and moral community indicates that civil society is not necessarily—or only—a buffer zone created "by donors as the connective tissue of democratic political culture" (see Wedel 1995, 323) but is more generally a politicized arena in which citizens minutely inspect themselves and others. Significant here is that this domain of political action occurs in contest with foreign organizations, and that the citizen-policing of daily life and personal conduct occurs in the government-run media. The media provide a critical institution for a more productive engagement between state and society (Hann 1996, 12), and editorials themselves enable citizens to express their views in a collective space—a precondition, as others have argued (cf. Habermas 1989; Loizos 1996; Spulbeck 1996, 76), for the political workings of civil society.

My time frame here, October 1988 through March 1993, spans nearly five years of dramatic social, political, and economic change. During this interval, the Tanzanian government endorsed a multiparty political system, reprivatized farms and industries, permitted private presses to open, and legalized privately owned exchange bureaus. In the context of these political and economic changes, women's retextured hair took on new meaning. Popular images portrayed consumers as morally obligated citizens, unleashed as it were in this free-market economy. "Hair"—and especially women's hair—became a marker of ideological loyalties. If one did not curl, one affirmed an ideal of economic self-reliance, but if one *did,* one indicated a personal and political commitment to reinterpreting older policies.

By the early 1990s, when cash was free-flowing, hairstyles were seen increasingly as evidence of religious orientation and capitalist economic activity. Hair both signaled the changing moral and political relationship between citizen and political community and evoked historically shifting sets of conventions and norms by which civil society ought to be defined and organized. As we shall see, hair was not only, or necessarily, a symbol of psychosocial development and sexual transformation.[3] It also objectified—like fashion in general (cf. Barthes [1967] 1986; Fox-Genovese 1987; Heath 1992; Russell 1996; Turner 1980)—sociopolitical differences and competing views about economic liberalization. Hair in the Tanzanian debate became an expression of contemporary nation-building, one that had different meanings for different people at different times.

Civil Society in 1988: Corruption in a Privatizing State

The plurality of views revealed through the editorials indicates that visions of civil society are neither homogeneous nor indisputable, not even when they are managed in a government-run newspaper.[4] Discussion in the *Sunday News* began with a letter from Sr. Arna Xevier[5] of Dar es Salaam, titled "Beware—Hair Curling Is Dangerous":

> This is to inform my dear ladies and gentlemen in Tanzania that hair curling is a dangerous practice, the effects of which will take place after 10 years.
>
> These include night blindness, total body weakness, *mydriasis, pebroptosis, palomotor,* head tremour and persistent frontal headaches. This is due to chemical reaction between the nuclei particle of the hair with embryo of the external tissue of the skin during curling, which may lead to madness and confusion.
>
> Experiment done on rabbit hair curling showed that after a period of 5 years all of the above were positive. Institute of Bio-Chemistry at the University of Burma in Asia has isolated the tissues of invivo test, the results will be published soon. (9 October 1988, 4)

Mathew H. K. of Dar es Salaam responded in another letter titled "Beware of Dangerous Chemicals":

> Sr. Arna Xevier's article . . . wouldn't pass without comments.
>
> I personally agree with her recommendable views regarding future consequences of hair curling. Frankly, hair curling to women and few men is dangerous. If not dangerous why don't Europeans curl?
>
> And why are they interested in changing African natural hair? This is purely trading and testing of chemicals on poor African women's bodies.
>
> Expectant women who are members of the hair curling club have experienced some problems during delivery.
>
> For the past decade, western countries have tried to use Africa as a dumping ground of toxic wastes, chemical tests. As if not enough they now dump chemicals on our African women through hair curling, contraceptive pills, etc.
>
> Lastly, I call upon women and the few poor men to beware of any dangers posed by imported drugs and chemicals. (*Sunday News*, 16 October 1988, 4)

Two weeks later, the *Sunday News* published another letter, titled "Curl Your Hair and Die Soon." Dionister Enicety Temba of Morogoro also supported Sr. Arna's point:

> I would like to support, and indeed, praise Sr. Arna Xevier for her views. . . .
>
> As Sr. Arna pointed out, it is extremely dangerous to indulge in hair curling as the bill for this abuse of nature is issued ten years later—long after the practice has been discarded and, possibly, forgotten.
>
> Those who curl their hair now should be prepared to pay their bill in the form of unpleasant medical complications that could be far-reaching. Some people turn a blind eye to these early warnings but, surely, they have a price to pay.
>
> . . . Our shops are stocked to the ceiling with chemicals and cosmetics which have been banned in Europe and America. Even South Africa of all countries prevents its black community from using the chemicals and cosmetics—not because of apartheid—but due to the dangers the chemicals and cosmetics pose to the regular user.
>
> Why should women undermine their health or cut short on their life expectancy for the sake of beauty?
>
> Our women always copy foreign culture without studying possible consequences to themselves and the community at large. Do our women really need to have red or pink faces like those of white women? . . .
>
> . . . the Government should stand up and take notice. Our meagre foreign exchange should be spent judiciously. Our women do not need all the trash we see in our shops. (30 October 1988, 4)

The substance of these editorials suggests that "civil society" is quixotically defined. It emerges here through debates about a privatizing, market-oriented economy. Curled hair is not the issue per se. Rather, editorialists debate the implications of a privatizing economy, including the anxieties "curl kits" evoke about the impact of transnational flows on local worlds. What begins as a cautionary word to women regarding the physical effects of hair curling becomes an extended discussion about a modernity of fluids and medical testing. Zainab Mwatawala of Morogoro notes that "We are the losers, make no mistake about it! We are the ready market for their trash!" (*Sunday News*, 13 November 1988, 4). And Dionister Temba, also from Morogoro, asks, "Who authorises the importation of such chemicals? Who issues the foreign exchange to the businessmen who import such junk? Someone should stand up and tell us why our foreign exchange is being misused like this" (*Sunday News*, 30 October 1988, 4).

Writers' references to global issues of environmentalism, neocolonial exploitation, and foreign exchange reveal that citizens are keenly aware of the ways commerce shapes the interrelationship of citizen and state. In some letters, writers associate broad issues with the dangerous "heat" of curl kits. Several suggest a connection between personal beautification and the responsibilities of good citizenship. In one of the more alarming letters, titled "Want to

Lose Your Head?" Leah Medard of Dar es Salaam makes a crucial, if partial, connection among curl kits, medical testing, and electricity:

> I would like to support all those who are against hair curling. One does not need to be told of the imminent dangers of careless exposure of man's greatest asset—the head—to electricity.
>
> It is high time the supporters of hair-curling realized that there is no replacement for the brain once destroyed or impaired by electric shock. However the choice is theirs—to live or not to live. . . . (*Sunday News*, 29 January 1989, 4)

The suggestion that hair curling can cause electric shock to the brain resonates with Sr. Arna's comment about head tremors, madness, and persistent frontal headaches, and with the title of another letter, "This Hair Curling Fever!" (*Sunday News*, 25 December 1988, 4). Concern about electrical shock signifies to some people in this context disquiet about the import of foreign products. Mention of the physical dangers of hair curling conflates the boundaries of the individual subject with the health of civil society. An earlier letter to the editor raised this subject through the topic of illegal dumping. In June and July 1988, the Tanzanian media had carried stories about toxic wastes: an Italian vessel, the *MV Piave,* was unloading radioactive material in Bendei State, Nigeria. One incident (*Daily News,* 15 June 1988, 2) sparked investigation into other cases, and the editors of the *Daily News* reported that "illegal dumping" was politically revealing. It was a prime example of the way Western countries treated former African colonies. Winston Msowoya, a Tanzanian living in Alberta, Canada, wrote an editorial titled "Africa Not a Nuclear Waste Bin." His words burn with condemnation and, like the debate on hair curling, reflected heightened concern about the dangers of importing and exporting dangerous chemicals around the globe, an anxiety conceived in terms of a violation of Africa as Woman:

> My profound indignation on the recent reports of unwarranted and treacherous endeavours by foreign industrialised nations to dump hazardous nuclear and industrial waste on African soil.
>
> The naked willingness and lust for money by some African states to allow foreign companies to turn our Mother Africa into a nuclear waste dumping ground has not only portrayed Africa's unprecedented betrayal of her continental integrity, but also an outright degradation of African dignity.
>
> Our Continent has been a playing ground for foreign soldiers of fortune and of recent, the western nations have been carrying malicious news coverage on AIDS being exported from Africa. . . . (*Daily News*, 16 June 1988, 4)

The parallels Temba and others draw between hair products and European waste, and between women's bodies and the African continent, attract attention to the highly metaphoric ways in which people conceive of governance. Msowoya's "foreign soldiers of fortune" figuratively attacked "Mother Africa." And rapacious entrepreneurs competed to find markets in "poor," feminized Africa.[6] The question writers are grappling with is, who bears responsibility for the abuse of the African continent? And who, in the end, is responsible for cleaning up the debris? Civic-minded citizens? Government officials? The answer in most of the letters is clear. This is a matter that calls for civic responsibility: government action is capricious and ill founded, and only "the people" can repel neocolonial interests.

Conventional notions of civil society, developed most recently in conjunction with transformations in Eastern Europe and Latin America (cf. Cohen and Arato 1992; Harbeson, Rothchild, and Chazan 1994; Wedel 1995), focus largely on voluntary associations as key institutions for mediating the state and society. Yet here we have a vital forum in which people are grappling with the distinctions between private and public. Their political engagement within the government press challenges many established notions of civil society. Indeed, the critical tenor of writers toward government, and, especially, toward themselves as responsible citizens, warrants a call for broadening our understanding of the scope, content, and institutional packaging of civil society. Civil society may very well be "defined as the domain of political action outside the party-state's control" (Kaminski 1995, 18). Loizos emphasizes that the "nurturing of free media is important for civil society" (1996, 63). However, the Tanzanian case suggests the issue may not be not whether citizens contest power within or outside the realm of the state, or whether civic-minded citizens speak for or against capitalist economic activity, but that civil society engages competing groups in discussions about good government, responsibility, and virtue. When we examine this dynamic, we find tremendous variability in institutional forms and political loci. As David Anderson (1996) puts it, there is an amazing variety of "citizenship regimes," many of which are represented in competition with one another—and, in Tanzania, in the government-sponsored media.

As the media then reported, the political climate in Tanzania in the late 1980s was exciting and hopeful. In contrast to the empty shelves of 1984 and 1985, shops were full of soaps, oils, sugar, and cigarettes. The Structural Adjustment Program (1983–85) and the Economic Recovery Program (initiated July 1986) revised economic policies of the late 1960s and early 1970s and facilitated the import of luxury items like hair curling kits, dyes, and relaxers. As a result of the Own Funds Imports (OFI) Scheme, a program implemented in 1985 under the Structural Adjustment Program, Tanzanians no longer had to hide illegally owned foreign exchange; they could use their reserves to purchase licenses for import and thus convert foreign wealth into Tanzanian shillings (Rösch 1992, 35). Although they could not hold foreign currency for any other reason at the time, many did apply to this program, and the result was a steady increase in the number of Tanzanian-owned import companies and what appeared, from some angles, to be a positive stimulation of the domestic economy.

From other perspectives, however, OFI was less successful. It resulted in dramatic currency adjustment and subsequent inflation. In 1985 alone, the Tanzanian shillings (/=) bought by the U.S. dollar went from 10/= to 40/=; and by January 1990 it was at 200/= (Rösch 1992, 37; Stein 1992, 70–75). Most Tanzanians did not have any hidden capital to invest, much less money to purchase luxury items. The discrepancy between those who could buy curl kits and those who could not became only more pronounced as a result of these changes. One person described the costly items that flooded Tanzanian stores as "all the trash we see in our shops." In 1988, when one U.S. dollar bought 125/= on the official market (Rösch 1992, 37) and as much as 200/= on the "parallel" black market, an imported curl kit cost about 2,000/= (U.S.$10–16).[7] Many people believed that those who bought curl kits and other luxuries relied on funds from sources other than official jobs.

During this period of structural adjustment and privatization, the media—particularly the *Sunday News*—was key in articulating and maintaining the government's positions on the direction taken by the new developments.[8] Official steps toward privatizing the press accompanied the move to a multiparty system of government. In June 1988, the *Family Mirror* published its first issue. By early 1993, several other publications were available: the *Business Times, Michapo, Cheka,* and a host of local, privately produced newspapers. In the face of privatization, the government-run media was challenged to change its own political and public image. In addition to running a series of articles about the need to balance investigative reporting with state interests (and subtly arguing in the course of it that free media journalists should work to defend their government), the *Daily News* and its Sunday component presented increasingly controversial issues in editorial sections. Among the controversial topics were South African apartheid and Mandela's imminent release, the fall of the Berlin Wall and the future of communism, and the International Monetary Fund's proposal for economic restructuring and its impact on rural citizens. Like the hair curling debate, these subjects provided readers and writers with a way of talking about, and shaping, civil society. They brought to the fore the overriding conception that civil society was rife with political tensions.

In the hair curling debate, for instance, writers varied in their views about the social and political outcomes of the import of "dangerous chemicals." Among the most vocal proponents of hair curling were an educated elite for whom curled hair attested to upward mobility and economic privilege. Two Morogoro secondary school students, Lucy Herman and Jaqueline Yunge, represented this contingent in a letter titled "... No, Hair Curling Is Fine and Okay."

> We would like to differ with Sr. Arna Xevier's views regarding the practice of curling hair. In her article on October 9, she claimed that side effects emanating from hair curling surface after ten years. We would like her to furnish us with proof and statistics in relation to her claims. . . .
>
> We are surprised to see that the issue of hair curling effects is confined only to Tanzania and not the entire world. If hair curling is really harmful then the Americans who introduced the practice would have experienced the problems Sr. Arna is citing.
>
> Could Sr. Arna tell us how many people have so far suffered from side effects resulting from hair curling? If hair curling is dangerous, the World Health Organization (WHO) would have already stood up to halt it.
>
> We understand that lengthy experiments are carried out before anything is applied on the human body. And indeed, nothing is one-hundred percent harmless to the body. Even medical drugs can be as detrimental to health as such stuff as poison and alcohol.
>
> We therefore believe hair curling has more merits than demerits. That is why it has not yet been banned. (*Sunday News*, 30 October 1988, 4)

In a letter titled "Hair Curling Is Safe," A. Dominic Swai of Moshi echoed their argument by noting that

> . . . The dangers cited in Sr. Arna's, Mathew H. K.'s and N. Mwaibasa's letters do not befall all users but only those who are allergic to the chemicals.
>
> Hair treatment has advantages such as enabling one to easily comb his/her hair into any style one wants, thus enhancing beauty. Is there anything shameful in making one's self attractive?
>
> Hair treatment has been going on for more than 20 years. It is indisputable that there are women who have been curling their hair for a long time, but they have never experienced any of the said "dangers."
>
> For the allergic ones, they may opt for other means such as hair relaxing, etc., just like patients allergic to *Penicillin, Quinine, Chloroquine* etc. look for other medicines that do not ill-affect them. (*Sunday News*, 27 November 1988, 4)

In contrast to claims made by opponents of curl kits, proponents contended that consumers were *not* in league with foreign profiteers who sought to extract value and wealth from Africa, but rather were among an international group of consumers who used, and potentially profited from, an increasingly globalized economy. From Lucy and Jaqueline's point of view, consumers are themselves in a position to turn around the power equation. By joining an international community that shares universal standards, women who curl have greater political capital to appeal to international organizations for representation and protection. The confidence of their arguments and their appeal to greater cosmopolitanism suggest impatience with "old wives' tales." International alliances reinforce, rather than undermine, African rights to fair treatment. From Swai's point of view, curled hair offers a practical solution to hair management; more than this, it is a response to accepted aesthetic canons. Both letters suggest that curled hair and cultural identity are positively related, and they reinterpret transnational contacts as beneficial relations.

In a sense, the students and A. Dominic Swai are appealing to a higher order of governance, arguing that people are citizens of the world and, as such, should turn their scrutiny from state to global society. Their argument is not that international organizations should govern Tanzanians, but that people need to look beyond "the national" and recognize themselves within a larger, global order. Such visions suggest that editorials not only reflect, in the post-Enlightenment sense, an ideal of a civil society—an ideal that places private citizens at the center of their own reform—but that citizenship in the late twentieth century is understood in connection with global markets and that global citizenship abounds with an ideal of civility. To those who advocate curl kits, hairstyling speaks of "progressive," "new," "young," and "fresh" ways of configuring female Tanzanian selfhood. It reflects cultural transformations in ideas about health, beauty, and personal self-determination and offers a way for educated people to champion the cosmopolitan cultural practices that, to them, construct modern personhood.

In this regard, notions of civility are implicit in Tanzanian notions of citizenship, even if, as Karlström notes in chapter 4, the civil society concept as it is often used by political scientists today distinguishes political debate from upbringing and good manners. Editorial discussions about hair curling and luxury imports appeal constantly to readers' tastes. They refer to standards of personal conduct (good manners and morality) and to modes of citizenship and governance (human rights and access to resources). Schooled reasoning and breeding are as much a positive factor in Jaqueline and Lucy's letter as they are a stroke against Sr. Arna's audience and a mark, to critics, of incivility and social endangerment. It is not that writers refer directly to the "incivility" of their foreign adversaries, nor even, for the proponents of curl kits, to the championing causes of international regulatory and donor agencies, but that the entire debate, on both sides, is cast in terms of what is best for civil citizens. Civility here is directly connected to citizenship and civil polity; it is not about mutual tolerance and aloof respect, as is often minimally assumed in conventional discussions of civil society, but about virtue and civic right-mindedness among a moral community grappling with a privatizing economy.

Civil Society and Politics in 1993

However, if hair fashion raised generalized concern about biological reproduction and health in the late 1980s, and if it threatened to dissolve and "corrupt" the body politic, it also raised specific concerns about the integrity of families and communities. Nearly five years after the editor of the *Sunday News* tried to end the hair curling controversy by declaring "This debate is now closed," Dr. Rajabu I. Putta addressed the issue again in an article titled "Unwanted Effects of Hair Curling and Dyeing."

> . . . [W]omen, beware! I want to give a medical deprecate for the nowadays desired common beautifying methods.
>
> These cosmetics have got harmful medical effects to a number of users. . . . The most common unwanted effect is *hypersensitivity.* This is an allergy which makes a harmful reaction to the body. The whole body develops painful skin rashes accompanied by itching, fever and blurred vision. . . . (17 January 1993, 6)

Dr. Putta's article was followed a few weeks later by an article in the Saturday Chat column. In it, John Waluye focused on the dangers of hair curling for pregnant women and unborn children.

> . . . Yes, curling or any other form of hair dressing that uses hair chemicals is dangerous to pregnant women. . . .
>
> . . . [A] pregnant woman who dyes, bleaches, curls or relaxes her hair with the hair chemicals puts the unborn child at risk of deformity, unexplained sudden death and other strange diseases. . . . (*Daily News*, 6 March 1993, 12)

Time had moved on, but the images of curling persisted. Tropes like "painful skin rashes accompanied by itching, fever and blurred vision" and "sudden death and other strange diseases" described the potential risks of hairstyling in 1993, just as they had done nearly five years earlier.

But if these cultural idioms persisted, the social problems and political ills debated among citizens had not. The political and economic climate in 1993 was different from what it had been late in 1988. The Economic Recovery Program, first implemented in 1986, was now in its second phase, and the national economy was showing signs of improvement. A $600 million Integrated Roads Project, supported by foreign donors (Rösch 1992, 43), was approximately half completed, and the roads of Dar es Salaam almost completely repaved. To many, the city looked more glamorous and clean than ever. The government had reprivatized several parastatal organizations, and social institutions such as schools and hospitals were being turned over in increasing numbers to religious and nongovernmental organizations. A multiparty political system was officially approved in April 1992, and campaigning was in full swing by 1993.

Women's hair salons had become lively places for participating in the "winds of change"—the political and economic reforms that many described as "sweeping the nation" in the early 1990s. Salons had been targeted in 1991 as worthy enterprises for receiving small business loans, and in contrast to the negative tenor of government views expressed in the national media, lending agencies viewed hair curling favorably—at least for its profitability (Women in Small Business 1991, 5–7). Financing strategies promoted by the National Bank of Commerce—and its Department of Women in Development (WID)—fostered networks of friendship and mutual aid that built upon, and in some cases cross-cut, neighborhoods, schools, and churches (see Tripp 1994). Increasingly, women in rural areas were setting up ad hoc shops in their homes—sometimes using the hot sun, rather than electricity, to dry the curls.

These specially funded associations constitute a "civil domain" in the sense that the civil society concept has been intimately linked to aid programs and to privatization assistance. They epitomize what nongovernmental donor agencies might point to as evidence of recently founded democracy. Indeed, the creation of civil society by external intervention is precisely what many donors hope to found. Yet research into nongovernmental organizations in Tanzania indicates that such is rarely ever fully realized on the ground (see Mercer 1998). If readers' editorials provide any insight into the workings of an emergent democracy, it is clear that such specially funded associations are as *generative of* debates about civil society as they are connective tissue in the democratic process. As the editorials suggest, citizens' questions of governance go beyond associations and organizations. They take place in communications media and direct their gaze to the very institutions that have been designed to develop "the civil."

What is more, citizens' letters speak to and reflect the substance of reports presented in the government media. By January 1993, national politics was near breaking point. National news sources reported that Zanzibari officials had agreed to join the Organization of Islamic Countries. Some opposition party leaders accused President Ali Hassan Mwinyi of conspiring to bring secular Tanzania under Muslim law. These accusations were later retracted, but such outspoken criticism against the government underscored the political power of a legitimate opposition and, more generally, of a multiparty political system. Several organizations and groups were targeted for this unrest, among them a collective category of women: women who "curled" and otherwise fashioned themselves in ways that some thought were foreign and degrading. They were, from one official view, the *un*civil populace, unfit for civil society. Political cartoons portrayed this group as a cadre of women selling out to foreign interests. Reminiscent of the older editorial debate, they emphasized the theme of undesirable, foreign intervention and made a mockery of some styles of women's fashion. In one cartoon, a government worker pointed to two women wearing short skirts and salon-styled hair: "Look at those girls there! What kind of clothes are they wearing, or is this 'multi-party politics'?" One of his friends proclaimed, in the following frame, "If they are robbed or accosted they run to the police!"—suggesting that women dressed this way really ought not be protected by the law. To these two men, a middle-aged woman exclaimed, "Their dress is a bold display of lust! We should scold them so they behave well! What kind of 'political change' is this?" Her full-length skirt reflected her conservative politics; her untreated hair signified her purity (*Mfanyakazi*, 31 March 1993, 13).

Competing understandings of subjecthood and citizenship are reflected in such cartoons. The women under scrutiny are, like their opponents, drawn into restricted channels of political and economic participation. The "new curled Tanzanian woman," from the dominant media view, is an atomistic subject, increasingly responsible for her own needs. Her "new" ideas about politics and citizenship communicate a novel, alternative vision of power—and, as the ongoing debate in the press suggests, of women's roles in civil society.

Conclusion

The rich debate that arises in Tanzania around the value of women's hair curling provides unusual insight into a moment of changing gender, class, religious, and civil identities. Unlike more conventional accounts of state politics that interpret social change in terms of social and economic restructuring (Rösch 1992; Stein 1992), I have emphasized here how concepts of civil society bear upon people's personal lives—and vice versa. The privatization of the national economy, beginning in 1986, provided the opportunity for personal displays of wealth in commodity forms like curl kits. It also led to discrepancies in wealth that were starkly revealed in women's fashion. Conversely, too, Tanzanians' personal lives and decisions both reflected and aggressively reconfigured civil society. Women's decisions to curl their hair challenged dominant views about the contributions of ordinary citizens to the operations of the state. Editorial debate such as that surrounding hair curling suggests that liberal individualism is finding a place in this East African context, but it does not indicate that globalization is inimical to the persistence of cultural difference (see Hann 1996, 20). For some Tanzanians, curled hair foreshadowed a shift in personal allegiance from "traditional" families toward *inter*national organizations, and the "dangerous" act of exposing oneself to heat-producing curling chemicals condensed a novel set of sociocultural assumptions associated with the aspirations of an urban, educated elite.

As national debate continues to focus on the constituencies and powers of a multiparty state, and as religious difference serves increasingly to characterize Tanzanian politics, personal attire—including but not limited to hair—is becoming an ever more charged symbol of civil society. Riots by "militant" Muslims opposed to the intrusion of Western styles in Tanzania in the late 1990s may signal that civil contentions are framed increasingly in terms of religion rather than multiparty politics (Reuters 1998; see also *Family Mirror*, May 1993, 1). And Tanzanians' responses to the bombings of U.S. embassies may indicate that civil society must work even further at policing the projects of international and donor organizations themselves. Whether or not violence continues, certain basic signs have become ever more politically charged. Editorials—and political cartoons that draw on popular images to evoke civil (and uncivil) citizens—provide evidence of a "civil" domain of public debate that scrutinizes everything from state governance, to globalization, to the moral conduct of citizens themselves. Hair fashion, in this context, remains highly controversial. Any impulse to view curling as merely an innocent act overlooks the polarized—and overtly politicized—context in which Tanzanians debate their own responsibilities as citizens.

Notes

1. Colloquially, these products are called "curl kits." They are usually assemblages of creams and lotions that are packaged in a single box.

2. "Hair curling" in Tanzanian English refers to the chemical process of straightening and then perming—or "curling"—one's hair. I use the conventional Tanzanian term—curling—throughout this chapter to refer to what North Americans frequently describe as "hair straightening" and "retexturing."

3. Anthropological interest in hair has been something of a fashion itself, though here I focus less on the symbolic meaning of hair than on the power of the editorial debate to reflect emergent threads of civil society. Leach's essay "Magical Hair" (1958) marked the beginning of an interpretive trend to view hair as a medium for the expression of personal and social identity. Attempting to merge theoretical differences between psychology (Berg 1951) and anthropology, Leach bridged what he considered an artificial distinction between the individual and collectivity. Like Malinowski, Durkheim, and Frazer before him, Leach regarded hair as a symbolic register that marked social transformations and ritual transitions. Hallpike (1969) challenged Leach to explain the significance of hair in terms of specific cultural evidence, not universal symbolic principles; and Synnott (1987) followed suit with a functional analysis of hair symbolism in North America and Britain. Obeyesekere, who maintained that Leach never adequately resolved the distinction between psychological emotion and ritual symbolism, argued in *Medusa's Hair* that the symbolic manipulation of hair is a universal manifestation of libidinous energy (1981, 9). More recently, Jeannette Mageo (1994) returned to a more specific contextual approach, arguing that changing hairstyles in Samoa reflect a history of female sex roles from the time of European contact to the present.

4. The following excerpts are from the *Tanzanian Daily* and *Sunday News*. To re-

tain writers' original arguments, I have not edited excerpts or articles except to correct typographical errors.

5. "Sr." most likely refers to Sister.

6. Ironically, old images of a helpless Africa live on in this debate about civil society. Women's attraction to curl kits and foreign imports are portrayed as another manifestation of "feminine impulse," and women are depicted as the weak underbelly of a developing nation. Like market women who traffic in illegal goods and who are held responsible for corruption in the "informal" economy (Kerner and Cook 1991), or women who wantonly subject themselves to deadly disease for the sake of money or bodily pleasures (Weiss 1993), women who curl their hair are represented here as being consumed by matters that do not concern them. As the *Sunday News* editor communicated through the titles of two letters, women should stop "This Hair Curling Fever!" (25 December 1988, 4) and say "Bye-bye Curl Kits" (12 February 1989, 4).

7. To illustrate the relative expense of curl kits: monthly salaries for secondary-school teachers at the time were about 500/=.

8. The *Sunday News,* run by the *Chama cha Mapinduzi* (Revolutionary Party), reflected a history of caution against political opposition (Mytton 1983, 137).

References

Abrahams, Ray. 1987. "Sungusungu: Village Vigilante Groups in Tanzania." *African Affairs* 87:179–96.

Anderson, David G. 1996. "Bringing Civil Society to an Uncivilised Place: Citizenship Regimes in Russia's Arctic Frontier." In *Civil Society: Challenging Western Models,* ed. Chris Hann and Elizabeth Dunn. New York: Routledge, 99–120.

Barthes, Roland. [1967] 1983. *The Fashion System.* Translated by M. Ward and R. Howard. Reprint, New York: Hill and Wang.

Berg, Charles. 1951. *The Unconscious Significance of Hair.* London: George Allen and Unwin.

Cohen, Jean, and Andrew Arato. *Civil Society and Political Theory.* Cambridge: MIT Press.

Fox-Genovese, Elizabeth. 1987. "The Empress's New Clothes: The Politics of Fashion." *Socialist Review* 17 (1): 7–30.

Habermas, Jurgen. 1989. *The Structural Transformation of the Public Sphere: An Inquiry into a Category of Bourgeois Society.* Translated by Thomas Burger in association with Frederick Lawrence. Cambridge: MIT Press.

Hallpike, C. R. 1969. "Social Hair." *Man* 4 (2): 256–64.

Harbeson, John W., Donald Rothchild, and Naomi Chazan, eds. 1994. *Civil Society and the State in Africa.* Boulder: Lynne Rienner.

Hann, Chris. 1996. Introduction to *Civil Society: Challenging Western Models,* ed. Chris Hann and Elizabeth Dunn. New York: Routledge, 1–26.

Heath, Deborah. 1992. "Fashion, Anti-fashion, and Heteroglossia in Urban Senegal." *American Ethnologist* 19 (1): 19–33.

Kaminski, Bartlomeij. 1995. "The Legacy of Communism." In *East-Central European Economies in Transition,* ed. John P. Hardt and Richard F. Kaufman for the Joint Economic Committee, Congress of the United States. Armonk, N.Y.: M. E. Sharpe, 1–24.

Kerner, Donna O., and Kristy Cook. 1991. "Gender, Hunger, and Crisis in Tanzania." In *The Political Economy of African Famine,* ed. R. E. Downs, D. O. Kerner, and S. Reyna. Philadelphia: Gordon and Breach Science Publishers.

Leach, E. R. 1958. "Magical Hair." *Journal of the Royal Anthropological Institute* 88 (no. 2, July–December): 147–64.

Loizos, Peter. 1996. "How Ernest Gellner Got Mugged on the Streets of London, or: Civil Society, the Media and the Quality of Life." In *Civil Society: Challenging Western Models,* ed. Chris Hann and Elizabeth Dunn. New York: Routledge, 50–63.

Mageo, Jeannette Marie. 1994. Hairdos and Don'ts: Hair Symbolism and Sexual History in Samoa. *Man* 29 (June): 40732.

Mercer, Claire. 1998. "Access to Power and Resources: The Non-Governmental Sector and the State in Tanzania." Paper presented at the African Studies Association annual meeting, Chicago.

Mytton, Graham. 1983. *Mass Communication in Africa.* London: Edward Arnold.

Obeyesekere, Gananath. 1981. *Medusa's Hair.* Chicago: University of Chicago Press.

Reuters. 1998. "Two Dead, 135 Arrested in Tanzanian Moslem Riot." 14 February, 6:01 A.M. ET.

Rösch, Paul-Gerhardt. 1992. "Tanzania: The Failure of a Model for Development and the Process of Adjustment." Research paper for Faculty of Economics and Business Administration, University of Bayreuth.

Rubin, Deborah S. 1996. "'Business Story Is Better Than Love': Gender, Economic Development, and Nationalist Ideology in Tanzania." In *Women Out of Place: The Gender of Agency and the Race of Nationality,* ed. Brackette F. Williams. New York: Routledge, 245–69.

Russell, Paitra D. 1996. "The Cultural Construction of Identity: African American Womanhood Produced and Consumed." Master's thesis, Department of Anthropology, University of Chicago.

Spulbeck, Susanne. 1996. "Anti-Semitism and Fear of the Public Sphere in a Post-totalitarian Society: East Germany." In *Civil Society: Challenging Western Models,* ed. Chris Hann and Elizabeth Dunn. New York: Routledge, 64–78.

Stein, Howard. 1992. "Economic Policy and the IMF in Tanzania: Conditionality, Conflict, and Convergence." In *Tanzania and the IMF: The Dynamics of Liberalization,* ed. H. Campbell and H. Stein. Boulder: Westview Press.

Synnott, Anthony. 1987. "Shame and Glory: A Sociology of Hair." *British Journal of Sociology* 38 (3): 381–413.

Tripp, Aili Mari. 1994. "Rethinking Civil Society: Gender Implications in Contemporary Tanzania." In *Civil Society and the State in Africa,* ed. John W. Harbeson, Donald Rothchild, and Naomi Chazan. Boulder: Lynne Rienner.

Turner, Terence. 1980. "The Social Skin." In *Not Work Alone,* ed. J. Cherfas and R. Lewin. Beverly Hills: Sage.

Wedel, Janine R. 1995. "U.S. Aid to Central and Eastern Europe, 1990–1994: An Analysis of Aid Models and Responses." In *East-Central European Economies in Transition,* ed. John Hardt and Richard F. Kaufman for the Joint Economic Committee, Congress of the United States. Armonk, N.Y.: M. E. Sharpe, 299–335.

Weiss, Brad. 1993. "'Buying Her Grave': Money, Movement and AIDS in North-west Tanzania." *Africa* 63 (1): 19–34.

Women in Small Business. 1991. *Sauti ya Siti* 15 (special issue, October–December).

10

IBB = 419: Nigerian Democracy and the Politics of Illusion

Andrew Apter

On June 23, 1993, the day of the annulment of the national presidential election, the military committed the most treasonable act of larceny of all time: it violently robbed the Nigerian people of their nationhood.

—Wole Soyinka

The government has by its own actions legitimized a culture of fraud and corruption.

—Chief Gani Fawehinmi

. . . the postcolonial state stems to a great extent from its own representation.

—Jean-François Bayart

ON 26 AUGUST 1993, Nigeria's self-appointed military "president," General Ibrahim Badamosi Babangida (popularly known as IBB), broke down in tears. At least that is how the popular story goes. It was during his televised farewell address, twice postponed until late evening, when the tired general finally announced that he would "step aside" from office, that he allegedly cried like a baby. Of course the tears were never shown. The momentary breakdown, if it actually occurred, was edited from the final broadcast, in which IBB attempted a graceful exit from the eight years of kleptocracy that brought Nigeria down from a middle-income nation to among the poorest in Africa. IBB had indeed exhausted his country and his options. Democratic return to civilian rule was repeatedly postponed from 1990 until the ill-fated elections of 12 June 1993, which he annulled on vague charges of improprieties that were never formally established. In the following weeks, IBB tried to buy support, disbursing *billions* of naira to governors, senators, even traditional rulers flown to Abuja each week as his guests. But no alliance or coalition formed, and finally, even the military turned against him. By 26 August, the game was up. Were IBB's invisible tears those of a leader betrayed by his nation or of a nation betrayed by its leader? Were they a hidden sign of his personal failure or a collective representation of relief and despair? Did they flow from the dictator's body or from the popular imagination? Or were they a smokescreen, part of a well-crafted vanishing act giving IBB the last laugh?

These questions are not merely rhetorical, but reflect a more general crisis of representation pervading the political and economic condition of Nigeria today. For most external observers, the failure of "June 12" represented the most recent breakdown of Nigerian democracy, undermined by the familiar syndrome of state patronage and rampant corruption unchecked by ineffective courts. As the 1983 elections of Shagari's Second Republic revealed, in a system where wealth and power depend upon political access to state petroleum revenues, no party can afford to lose the vote. Rather it will engage in widespread intimidation and electoral fraud before conceding victory to the opposition (Apter 1987; Hart 1993; Joseph 1987). However, the aborted elections of 12 June 1993 represent not the latest version of a familiar story—the return of electoral tragedy as democratic farce—but a new type of crisis; one that is of a different order of magnitude from mere vote rigging and competition for the national cake. For, unlike the last elections of the Second Republic—which were actually held, even if rules were broken to produce questionable results—the elections of 12 June 1993 never really took place. At least, not in any politically meaningful sense. As subsequent events and information have revealed, IBB's long-awaited elections were a ruse, a confidence trick, an elaborate simulation of the democratic process. A consensus is growing to the effect that, almost from the very start, IBB had no intention of giving up power. However, my argument extends beyond the ambitions of an individual dictator, beyond the personification of corruption and greed, to grasp the *logic* of his dictatorship—a regime of arbitrary truth and pervasive illusion that developed as the oil-economy collapsed.

At issue is the correlation of different forms of value, particularly exchange value and truth-value, as the oil economy boomed and then went bust. During the 1970s, when the petro-naira was stronger than the dollar at an exchange of 1.60 to 1, Nigeria was flush with buying power. Expatriates of all stripes and colors invaded the Nigerian universities and professional workforce as teachers, doctors, agronomists, and architects. Nigeria was a land of third world opportunity. Money could be made from large contracts and experts could find markets for their knowledge. Nigeria's problem was the proverbial fate of all oil economies, which is not how to make money but how to spend it. The national currency may have been fixed at an artificially high rate of exchange, but it was backed by oil, which was globally distributed through OPEC. Under these conditions, Nigeria enjoyed a high degree of international visibility and credibility. As the quality of everyday life improved for increasing proportions of the population, a new fetishism of commodities animated the nation, based less on the objectification of productive relations than on those of consumption and exchange. In the new object-world of imported commodities and rapid growth, seeing was believing. Commodified forms of national development were in the last instance backed by petrodollars, represented by letters of credit, contracts, trademarks, bridges, monuments, museums, highways, traffic jams, and a rising nouveau bourgeoisie. Whatever practical obstacles to finalizing a contract might occur—be they revised estimates, kickbacks, or successive mobilization fees—Nigerian social, political, and economic life was ultimately redeemable in foreign exchange. If the oil-rich state was not exactly democratic, at least it was accountable in dollars and cents.

All of this created an image of modernity that was backed by hard evidence. Or so it appeared. The infusion of oil money into the economy did not generate the alienated, impersonal, rational calculus of the modern industrial economy as variously portrayed by Marx, Simmel, and Weber. After all, oil capitalism is not industrial capitalism, wherever petroleum's final destination may be. Rather, the monetization of an oil-rich Nigeria gave rise to a celebration of visible "naira power," a national measure of value that could hold its own in international markets while attracting considerable foreign investment.[1] If money remained "magical"—powerful in its capacity to buy influence, erotic in its ability to buy love, with its hidden source beneath the ground a state-owned secret—its consequences were tangible. They signified "objective" growth in the universal language of the dollar. The naira was a credible currency not because of its internal semantic properties, such as denominational units or engraved designs, but due to its favorable relation to the dollar and the pound.[2] In the object-world of imports and exports, it bolstered the authority of the state by presiding, with its imprimatur, over a regime of national renewal. For, whatever Nigeria's boasts or demands, the buck stopped with the Nigerian National Petroleum Corporation (NNPC). Oil thus underwrote the veracity of a range of discourses, from the technical and scientific to the national and even racial, as the redeemable and redemptive wealth of the black and African world. The state emerged as the locus of truth, not because it wielded arbitrary power but because it was the locus of distribution. It pumped oil revenues into the expanding public sector while diverting dividends—such as import licenses, contracts, and jobs—to political clients and even potential opponents of the regime.

By 1983, however, the oil economy had entered its downward spiral. Things began to fall apart. The credibility of the nation and the naira began to wane as the civilian chaos of the Second Republic gave way to a succession of military takeovers. After IBB toppled the Buhari-Idiagbon regime in the bloodless coup of 27 August 1985, one of his explicit goals was to restore Nigeria's credibility by floating the naira to establish its "free" market value. The new regime sought to attract foreign investment and eliminate illegal traffic in foreign exchange. The result, coupled with a stringent Structural Adjustment Program designed to stimulate domestic production, was massive inflation, devaluation, and extensive deterioration of public institutions and infrastructures (Anyanwu 1992). As the world price in oil dropped, Nigeria's dependence upon petroleum increased, creating a political economy of dwindling resources and intensified competition to appropriate them. By the late 1980s, in an atmosphere of frustrated expectations, broken contracts, and unfulfilled national development plans, a new kind of crime began gaining momentum—less violent than the roving gangs of armed robbers who took over at night, but more pervasive within the dramaturgy of Nigerian business culture and everyday life. Referred to colloquially as the "419," after the relevant section of the Nigerian criminal code, it covered a range of confidence tricks involving impersonation and forgery for fraudulent gain. The "419" has continued to grow as a major industry in Nigeria, second only to oil (or in some accounts, third, after narcotics) as the nation's major export earner of foreign currency.[3] In what follows, I will expand the equation "IBB = 419" to illuminate not just the failure of the 1993 elections but their broader significance within the crisis of representation that developed after the dollar dropped out of the naira—when the mysterious "substance" of monetary value literally disappeared.

The Art of the Deal

On 4 September 1991, the Singapore International Chamber of Commerce issued a warning against fraudulent deals with Nigerians. In an article titled "Singapore Weary of Nigerian Businessmen," the 5 September 1991 *Daily Times* reported that according to the executive secretary, at least thirty of its members received letters from Nigerians promising to pay several million dollars in return for help in transferring large sums of money from Nigeria into Singapore bank accounts.

In a related incident, one Singapore computer company lost $23,000 worth of computers over a shipping deal made on a false bank draft. By the time the forgery was discovered, the computers were on their way to Nigeria.

The story is a ripple on a tidal wave of financial fraud that is sweeping across the globe, "from South Dakota to Ulan Bator" according to Cindy Shiner's recent (30 August 1994) *Washington Post* exposé, "Scamming Gullible Americans in a Well-Oiled Industry in Nigeria." It belongs to a hybrid narrative genre—combining low tragicomedy with high moral parable—about greed, corruption, and ruinous deception perpetrated by crafty Nigerians on their credulous marks. The *Economist* calls it "The Great Nigerian Scam," otherwise known as "advanced fee-fraud" or, more simply, "419" after the Nigerian criminal code enacted to prosecute such cases. Its basic features involve all the trappings of advanced parastatal oil-capitalism, replete with faxes, forms, stamps, insignia, letters of credit, invoices, corporate logos, and bank accounts, which figure as props in a well-staged illusion. The *Economist* explains:

> A typical "419" letter is written—supposedly—on the headed writing paper of the NNPC or some other state enterprise. A supposed official cheerfully admits to some scheme to rip off his employers, and offers the foreign recipient a 30% share of the $40–60 [million] or so which, he says, he needs to send urgently overseas. The recipient, normally a company, simply has to send details of its bank account, invoices for its fictitious services rendered to the state corporation—and some sheets of its own headed writing paper, blank but signed. Absolute secrecy is requested for a "highly classified" transaction. (1995, 36)

To set the proposed money-laundering operation in motion, the mark typically greases a few palms, with $5,000 in "fees" and a few more thousand in "taxes," with some Rolex watches and airplane tickets thrown in to soften senior gatekeepers and bank managers, not unlike ordinary kickbacks of business as usual. In the meantime, the signed letterhead, purportedly used to make the transaction look legitimate, is sent to the victim's bank manager with instructions to transfer thousands or even millions into a dummy account held by the scamster. In most cases, the credibility of the scam rests on references to excess funds accumulated through inflated contracts negotiated during the oil boom. Many foreigners, including businesspeople from the heartland of America, have some sense of Nigeria's prominence as a major oil-producing nation, even if they cannot locate the country on a map. This awareness, coupled with the misguided sense that the "third world" plays by flexible rules, generates considerable gullibility. An editorial in Nigeria's *Daily Times*, appropriately titled "Much Ado about 419" to play upon the "nothingness" behind the elaborate decoys (and more obliquely, upon the foreigner's shared responsibility for the crimes), elaborates on the techniques of *faire croire:*

> The foreign victims are taken in by fake circular letters or unauthenticated fax or telex messages relating to purported approved transfer of funds running into millions of US dollars arising from excess claims on some alleged foreign contracts awarded between 1979 and 1983. These purportedly authorized letters lend support to enable the transfer of funds from Nigeria to off-shore bank accounts with a promise to share in the illegal proceeds. To make the deals look authentic, the fraudsters infiltrate public places like the Nigerian National Petroleum Corporation (NNPC), the Central Bank of Nigeria, Merchant Banks and strategic government departments. The crooks use government facilities and impersonate public functionaries and in the end leave large sums of unpaid telephone and postal bills. In many of the "successful" cases, the tricksters disappear after receiving substantial deposits as advance payments which are supposedly meant to "soften the ground" and bribe "officials" who might be sitting in on the "deal." (27 February 1992, 18)

Here we can see how the oil boom, specifically during the last contracting heyday of Shagari's Second Republic from 1979–83, establishes the backdrop of such financial dissimulation. It provided a historical context of considerable fiscal accumulation and gave rise to the corporate forms and monetary instruments that marked Nigeria's participation in global market transactions. Two remarkable dimensions of the "419" deserve special consideration: the range and scale of operations; and the performance art of the con games themselves, which involve stagecraft, impersonation, and those collusive fabrications that Goffman (1974, 83–123) unpacks with such acute sensitivity in his phenomenology of social interaction.

The global scale of the "419" erupted rather suddenly in 1990, when, after several years of deliberation, IBB deregulated the banking system and foreign-exchange market, sending the naira into its downward spiral. As the naira dropped against international currencies, the "419" took shape, following the circuits of global capital that had developed in the era of flexible accumulation (Harvey 1989, 141–200) throughout Europe, Asia, and the Americas. Financial scams reported in Thailand, Canada, Scandinavia, Austria, the United Kingdom, and the United States engaged the energies of Scotland Yard, the FBI, Interpol, the Royal Canadian Mounted Police, and a variety of private and subsidiary agencies like the Better Business Bureau and the Financial Crimes Enforcement Network (FINCEN) of the U.S. Treasury Department. In an article titled "Nigerian Scam Lures Companies," published in the *New York Times*, 21 May 1992, Steve Lohr reported that according to the managing director of Kroll Associates, a large financial-investigation company based in New York, "You almost never see a net spread this wide in white-collar fraud" (D1). The State Department's Office of Public Affairs even published a pamphlet of "Tips for Business Travellers to Nigeria." Its list of "scam indicators" includes large financial deposit transfers in exchange for a substantial percentage with discretion, letters claiming the soliciting party has personal ties to high government officials, and "any deal that seems too good to be true" (Shiner). Estimates of the annual income earned by this "well-oiled" Nigerian industry range from Scotland Yard's $250 million to more than $1 billion according to Terry Sorgi, who worked as a commercial attaché for the U.S. embassy in Lagos and handled 474 Nigerian fraud cases in 1992 alone.[4]

Sorgi claims that the average money-laundering sting nets $150,000, although amounts exceeding $1 million have been received from forged real estate purchases and merchandise orders. Among newsworthy Canadian victims, Corrine Baker lost $470,000 (which her sales and promotion company raised for charities) when she diverted it to Nigerian bank accounts in Germany and England in anticipation of a 30 percent share of $20 million promised to her by her Nigerian correspondents. They convinced her to forward a percentage of the total to get the money released and pay for legal fees; as a result, she was charged with defrauding her Canadian clients. In another case, a Toronto investment broker lost $690,000 after traveling to Nigeria several times in one month to seal a deal. In an article titled "Beware of Scam, Hotel Owner Says," the *Montreal Gazette* reported a related incident, in which two Calgary oil and gas companies lost a combined total of $625,000 to Nigerians who said they wanted to launder millions by issuing fake invoices to the government for supplies of the firms' oil-field equipment (20 February 1994, A6).

Lured by the prospect of windfall profits, overseas businesses have paid dearly for their mistakes. Among the counterfeit purchase order victims, a New Zealand businessman lost $200,000 worth of computers and supplies when he shipped the equipment against a forged letter of credit. In the United States, George Davis, a retired Texas oil engineer, also received a fake purchase order from a Nigerian company for $15 million in industrial hardware from his business, International Equipment. After sending more than $70,000 in processing "fees," Davis had to file for bankruptcy. On a more sanctified register, Houston evangelist Jerry Smith (pastor of Woodland Trails Baptist Church and author of religious books distributed in Nigeria) and the Reverend Don Kettler (of St. Joseph's Cathedral, Sioux Falls, S.D.) lost $32,000 and $90,000 respectively in their efforts to release bogus legacies bequeathed to them in Nigeria. In both cases, the beneficiaries were convinced to pay inheritance taxes and legal fees up front, only to discover that the anticipated bequest did not exist.

In one of the most spectacular cons, EER Systems, a private aerospace engineering firm that has worked for NASA and the U.S. Department of Defense, lost $4.4 million in a simulated deal with the Nigerian Ministry of Aviation. After the firm's president met with his "partners" in Nigeria, they convinced him to use wire transfers to deposit $4.4 million into Nigerian accounts to expedite a $28.5 million deal that, of course, never materialized. Instead, the three Nigerian associates have been charged with wire fraud by a federal grand jury, but the Nigerian government is in no hurry to extradite the confidence men. For, despite official disclaimers and the establishment of a Nigerian Task Force on Trade Malpractices in 1992, evidence is growing that the Nigerian government's complicity in the international "419" goes all the way to the top. Although the Justice Ministry published a wanted list of 1,200 suspects, and investigators have made a few arrests, no convictions to date have been carried by the courts. Perhaps the most delightful "419," and one that directly implicates the Babangida regime, was the fleecing of South Africa's foreign minister, Pik Botha, in a deal that combined political tactics with financial injury. According to Chris McGreal in a 4 September 1993 *Guardian* feature story titled "Victims Caught in a Web of Corruption," Arthur Nzeribe, one of Nigeria's most controversial politicians, approached Botha to underwrite a new African magazine that would provide sympathetic coverage for Pretoria, on condition that the South African connection was kept secret. According to the deal that was struck, Nzeribe's and Botha's foreign ministries were each to put 320,000 pounds sterling into a British bank account from which either could withdraw. When Botha deposited his money, Nzeribe took it out. Whereas the South African foreign minister never recovered a penny, "the Nigerian politician has since gained further notoriety as the military's front-man in using the courts to cancel Nigeria's presidential election" (Foreign section, 11).

To be sure, there is a certain degree of righteous third world banditry to the Nigerian "419." In a country that has been a dumping ground of surplus (and often defective) commodities, operating under unfavorable terms of trade dating back to a colonial economy that diverted producer profits into British securities (Helleiner 1966, 161–62), the "419" might appear as just deserts. Some Nigerians see it as reparations for colonialism and the slave trade. Fred Ajuda, a "419" hero who traveled with a police escort in Lagos, has called himself "a black man's Robin Hood"("Great Nigerian Scam" 1995). Nigerians are quick to point out the scams could not work without unscrupulous Western dupes seeking illicit profits. Indeed, their techniques—raiding bank accounts, using dummy corporations, banking on trust, building confidence—echo the language of high finance with its corporate raids, hostile takeovers, and most especially its fictitious financing and capital formation (Harvey 1989, 194–95). Of course, the dividing line between legitimate and illegitimate business is permeable, increasingly so as the instruments of financial speculation retreat into virtual reality. Instead of criticizing the perpetrators or the victims of the "419," however, I focus on the underlying conditions of its efflorescence in Nigeria, not only as a phenomenon to be measured in dollars but also as a phenomenology of *transacting* value.

In the spending spree of the oil boom, when economic growth was both visible and credible, there emerged a new Nigerian elite of urbane, cosmopolitan, and studiously bourgeois businessmen, contractors, and professionals. The old elite of first and second generation colonial civil servants and lawyers, with school ties to London and Oxbridge, was not so much displaced as swallowed up by this burgeoning bourgeoisie, inflated by new money and the plethora of degrees and certificates afforded by the oil bonanza.[5] Many students from the boom era studied in second- and third-tier schools overseas—in the United States, India, and the Soviet Union—retaining the prestige of "been to" status while relying less on the cachet of school name. Others entered elite ranks by passing through Nigeria's university system, which built new campuses, expanded postgraduate programs, hired more faculty, and graduated more students. Universal primary education—and, in some states, secondary as well—widened the net of middle-class recruitment by providing schooling opportunities in the cities and in the bush. And the military emerged as a popular career pathway to important friends and powerful patrons.

By 1976, however, economic growth produced a new social anxiety, a credibility crisis within the status system as the old hierarchy was overwhelmed.

The margins of the elite became vulnerable to invasion by a nouveau riche that grew up as quickly as the new houses and hotels it built. At this moment, a flurry of certificate racketeering scandals emerged, as fraudulent examination results were discovered among high school graduates seeking jobs or admission to training colleges and universities. Whatever its scale might have been—and there is no doubt that documents were forged, examinations were leaked, and results were bought—the discourse to which it gave rise indicated a nation, as Chinua Achebe put it (in his novel of the same title), "no longer at ease." Thus an editorial titled "Do Something about Certificate Racketeering" in the 11 January 1976 issue of the *Nigerian Observer* warned the public to beware of false graduates; maintaining that the few cases of certificate racketeering actually probed were but "the tip of the iceberg," it declared the whole country at risk. The problem was said to have developed in the remote "townships and rural areas" where "amongst the teeming teenagers will be found pushers and hawkers doing their dirty trade, hustling the young, easily gullible idle student to find a criminal way out of the difficulties of exams" (3). In language reminiscent of nineteenth-century American advice manuals that "protected" country youth from city "seducers" (Halttunen 1982, 1–32), but rerouting the flow of evil from city to country, the editorial remonstrated against false representations—not just credentials but also the social identities that they purportedly reflect. In almost prophetic anticipation of the "419," the editorial focused on the social conditions of all official documentation: the "receipts, licenses, currency, cheques," that, like certificates, must be "security printing jobs"—that is, "distinctive enough for all to see and identity, yet defy easy reproduction and so improper mass circulation." Read as social allegory, the "improper mass circulation" of bourgeois credentials and identities, propelled by a booming economy, threatened the social basis of a more genuine distinction, which was visible but *not* mechanically reproducible. If seeing was believing during the oil boom, being seen could also mean passing and deceiving.

The social dislocations precipitated by the influx of petrodollars were different from those resulting from the oil bust; but they shared connections beyond money. The anxiety generated by an expanding middle class in Nigeria was not confined to the isolated acts of technical forgery that it may have encouraged. It grew out of the processes of bourgeois self-fashioning, bordering on the impersonation of social standing, produced by the sudden circulation of cash and commodities. Fortunes *were* made during the boom, and the art of the business deal was negotiated with tremendous style and lavish celebration. "You got the contract? Great! Join me for a Gulder!" exclaims the sophisticated executive to his associate on the telephone in one contemporary television beer commercial. Magazine advertisements reveal modern Nigerians dressed for success, with chic couples using Western deodorants and proud mothers cooking with vegetable (not palm) oil for their nuclear families.

As the petroleum economy internationalized the state (Watts 1992, 35), the nation followed suit, embellishing cosmopolitan modernity with Nigerian hospitality. Obviously the fruits of the boom were not evenly distributed; most Nigerians could only aspire to the lofty heights of the new elite, even if money flowed into the informal economy through patronage networks and the parasitic service sector. Nonetheless, the hotels, nightclubs, business offices, and banks of Lagos and Ibadan were bustling with deals, and it is from the culture of contracting that developed at this time that the elaborate cons of the Babangida era derived.

To appreciate the more dramaturgical arts of the "419," I shall focus on two cases profiled at some length in the press: the first involves Canadian real estate broker Ben Vanderburg; the second, Charlie Pascale, an American businessman who tried to outsmart those who duped him.

One of the remarkable aspects of the Vanderburg con is that, despite losing $60,000, the victim was so taken in by his Nigerian associates that part of him still believes them to have been sincere in their efforts to protect $32 million against government theft. In an article titled "Nigeria Bank Scam Dupes Broker" in the 31 December 1994 issue of the *Toronto Star*, Rick Haliechuk reported that Vanderburg received a call from a man identifying himself as Dr. Shoga Elias from the Ministry of Finance, requesting help on behalf of a group of Nigerians who wanted to get their money out of the country and invest it in real estate. Included in the proposal was a $10 million cut to Vanderburg for his role in keeping the money "out of the hands of corrupt rulers." All he had to do was fly to Lagos with three Rolex watches, for the Nigerian bankers they would be meeting, and $15,000 for "processing fees." When he arrived in Lagos, Vandenburg was met at the airport and driven to the home of another high-ranking official in the Ministry of Finance, where he saw a parked red Porsche. That evening, he was introduced to the "group" trying to get its money out. According to Vanderburg, "I felt very, very comfortable, very much at home. . . . They were cultured, well-to-do people, educated, fluent in English." The following day, more meetings took place to work out the transfer of funds to Canada. Vanderburg was puzzled that the Canadian-educated, Nigerian lawyer working for the group was named Mike Anderson. But he explained that he had changed his name in Canada. More disturbing was his statement that, according to a new government decree, the group would have to come up with an $800,000 cash fee. At another staged meeting with bankers, government bureaucrats, and the investment group—"many of them wearing Nigerian ceremonial dress and 'looking like a million dollars'"—Vanderburg was praised for the wonderful job he was doing for patriotic Nigerians. He was then asked to raise $170,000 as his part of the processing fee, whereafter the Canadian embassy in Lagos contacted him and informed him of the scam. Two weeks after his return home, the principals were still contacting him, as if the deal were going through. Even after losing $60,000 in fees, plane tickets, and gifts of watches and cellular phones, Vanderburg maintained, "I would be happy to meet them and give them a hug; that's the kind of people they are. . . . They're so convincing, it's beyond belief"(A1).

Like any well-planned con, Vanderburg's story illustrates the "collusive fabrications" whereby one party is "contained" by the activities of a "net" or team (Goffman 1974, 84). Exploiting the difference between social appearances and realities, the con artists simulate a business opportunity in which the mark invests, getting in deeper and deeper until the illusion pops and the game is up. The primary frameworks deployed in the "419" include the instruments of international finance, institutional offices and venues like the Nigerian National Petroleum Corporation (NNPC) and the Central Bank, and, most importantly, the staged class habitus of a privileged elite that saturates the mark with subtle cues of shared affinities. The Porsche in the compound convinced Vanderburg that his Nigerian associates were serious, that they were for real. The business meetings and parties constructed a credible social reality of "cultured, well-to-do people," a representation from which material consequences would follow as long as the mark's credulity was sustained. And unlike the constructions of "primary" social reality (Goffman's "keyings"), the truth-value of the appearances is not shared—what is "true" for the mark is "false" for the fabricators. Such unequal terms of social interaction create unequal terms of financial exchange: money changes hands in one direction only, despite the expectations of a return. Vanderburg's case was really quite simple, illustrating how deeply he invested in the "reality principle" of his associates.

The case of Charlie Pascale is more complex, because it adds an extra level of framing to the interaction, rather like the logic of counterespionage that his story resembles. According to "Charlie's Hustle," an article by Tom Dunkel in the 27 February 1994 *Washington Post,* Pascale's invitation came directly from Mr. Dodo Oto of the NNPC's accounting department, offering a 25 percent cut of $35 million in excess revenues that needed to be spent before a year-end audit. In exchange for the use of his Alpha Electronics company account, Pascale would keep $8 million for himself. Recognizing the deal as a money-laundering scheme, he played along, putatively planning an exposé if the deal fell through or proved illegal. Employing his own cloak and dagger tactics, including code words, mail drops, and hidden cameras, Pascale traveled to Nigeria where a meeting with a man named Alhaji from the Central Bank was arranged:

> The meeting took place in a parlor filled with tasteful bamboo furniture. Alhaji seemed someone of substance. He was "impressive," Charlie later faxed to [his business associate] Johnson. Things were looking up! The missus served cold drinks and hot tea on a silver tray. Then a man named Julius, who identified himself as a representative of the bank, asked Pas-

> cale for . . . $750,000. The money, he explained, was needed to cover the "transfer tax" levied on the $35 million before it left the country. (F1)

The stage thus set in a convincing bourgeois interior, the plot thickened. The man called Alhaji appeared taken aback by Julius's sudden demand, and turned on Mr. Oto from the NNPC accounting office, threatening to kill him for apparently bungling the negotiations. According to Pascale, "Oto essentially crawled over on his hand and knees and squatted." Pascale pulled out in time, although he continued to fax his partners from the United States, losing another $5,500 in airplane tickets that he sent to Julius. What makes this particular case so interesting, beyond the dramatic stagecraft, is the secondary playing of the fool against the fool. The con combined elements of bourgeois respectability with bungling slapstick, playing ever so delicately upon third world "mimicry" (Bhabha 1994, 85–92) and mimesis (Taussig 1993) of the West to reinforce the mark's sense of confidence and superiority. Pascale was taken in by his superiors in the game because they allowed him to feel that he was their superior. A history of colonial stereotypes and paternalistic conceits were thus brought into play—of the evolué who tries too hard, and of the enterprising liberal who thinks he knows better. In some scams, the advance fee is called "an economic recovery tax," playing on the possible meanings of economic recovery as "getting better" and "getting back."

As the dialectical laminations of the "419" deals increase in complexity, the foundations of social interaction begin to crumble. Unstable identities are represented by shifting names, like the Nigerian lawyer Mike Anderson who had changed his name in Canada; by general names like Alhaji, which refers widely to any Muslim who has been to Mecca, and can be used even more liberally to denote bigmanship; by first names like Julius, which are untraceable, and by false ones like that of Dan Musa, who, according to one "419" report, did not exist, yet managed to transfer 13,000 pounds sterling through the Central Bank and into a fake company account (this story is also reported in McGreal, "Victims Caught in a Web of Corruption," *Guardian*, 4 September 1993, Foreign section, 11). As Scotland Yard's fraud investigator explained, "the victim is left facing bogus people with bogus documents. . . . Identifying the people behind one of these . . . is a big problem" (Lohr, "Nigerian Scam Lures Companies," D1). In many stories involving elaborate venues (e.g., "There was a plaque and a doorman in a hat, and the office had lots of NNPC documents"), the dupe returns to find an empty office, a dead telephone line, and no trace of his business associates. Michelle Faul of the *Chicago Tribune* described how one Houston businessman who was offered four million barrels of crude oil at $2.50 below the market price became convinced that the deal was straight "because he was taken to meetings at the state-owned oil company, shown paperwork at the Central Bank, introduced to military officers in government offices and shown the tanker said to be loaded with oil" ("Dangerous Fraud in Nigeria," 1 June 1992, 8). These examples illustrate how the "seeing is believing" of the oil boom has given way to the visual deceptions of the oil bust, a social world not of objects and things but of smoke and mirrors, a business culture of worthless currency, false facades, and empty value forms. Oil, the "underlying" substance of economic value, might lend credibility to Nigerian business ventures and to the "glib and oily art" of the deal. But its pathways—from public institutions into private coffers—have become uncertain. Many "419s" simulate oil's direct purchase and sale, while others invoke the revenues that it has generated. If its presence or absence makes a real difference in transacting value, its decreasing availability as a national resource has undermined Nigeria's credibility, both at home and abroad. The instabilities of social identity produced at the margins of the rising middle class, when the state expanded the public sector with oil revenues during the 1970s, have now reached into the center. In a *Toronto Star* article titled "Crooks and Con Men Stain a National Image," Bill Schiller recounted the words of Alhaji Aliyu Atta, Nigeria's inspector general of police: "Con men are threatening to submerge the nation's economic well-being into one despicable abyss of fraud and corruption" (10 May 1992, F3). To understand how democracy was thrown into this abyss, when the "419" entered into politics, we can turn to the Big Con of 12 June 1993.

The 1993 Elections

Addressing the nation during his 1992 budget speech, General Babangida proclaimed: "We must hold ourselves collectively responsible for the negative image which our nation projects" (Schiller, "Crooks and Con Men"). Speaking for himself, and his inner circle of syndicate bosses, he knew what he was talking about. IBB's personal fortune, estimated between $5 and $7 billion (Useh 1993, 13), places him among world-class kleptocrats like the late Ferdinand Marcos of the Philippines and the late Mobutu Sese Seko of Zaire. Using the military regime to make deals and issue decrees, IBB constructed a labyrinthine business empire that he controlled directly, through the NNPC and the Central Bank of Nigeria (which he moved from the Ministry of Finance to the presidency), and indirectly, through front companies like Foundation Mira, white elephant projects like the Ajaokuta steel mill, and military-industrial contracts that provided a constant stream of kickbacks. Dubbed "Babangida Unlimited" by the popular press, this financial imperium emerged from the infamous Bank of Credit and Commerce International (BCCI), with which IBB became involved just months after coming to power. The BCCI link pinpoints with almost topological precision how international finance and fraud were coordinated with national banking and petroleum revenues by the Northern-based bloc of old power and new wealth known as the Kaduna Mafia.[6] The chairman of BCCI's Nigerian affiliate, BCCI (Nigeria) Ltd., was none other than IBB's godfather, Alhaji Ibrahim Dasuki, whom IBB appointed as sultan of Sokoto in 1991. That same year, he installed his finance minister, Alhaji Abubakar, as the sardauna of Sokoto, thereby clinching Northern dynastic control over Nigeria's political and financial affairs.

In the early days of the Babangida era, after the bloodless palace coup, the regime appeared less venal. Return to civilian rule, not Northern politico-economic hegemony, was the order of the day. Turning over a new political leaf, IBB banned all former senior-ranking politicians—going back to the First Republic—from seeking elected office; this in order to produce a "new breed" of honest politicians and to break old party alliances and patronage networks. In the upshot, it was said, a new "political class" would emerge with a more contemporary and sophisticated political culture.[7] Thus started the official "transition programme" referred to as "directed democracy," a return to civilian rule, stage-managed by the military, which would organize grass-roots participation, mass mobilization, and a new constitution, and would arrange a series of elections beginning at the local level and ascending to the presidency by 1992. Thus was a bottom-up democratic process imposed from the top down, defining the rules of engagement and dictating the institutional blueprint "represented" by the new republic. The military government formed a new Directorate of Social Mobilization (MAMSER) to inculcate democratic values and produce an enlightened citizenry, a Constitutional Review Committee to help write a new constitution, and a National Electoral Commission (NEC) to oversee the political process. As we shall see, the Armed Forces Ruling Council, the NEC, high courts, and two political parties that ultimately emerged became the leading actors in an electoral charade that was fabricated, screened, revised, postponed, and choreographed by the regime's inner circle, only to be canceled at the final curtain.

To understand the false starts and stops of democracy under IBB, we might follow two orders of political action: the first, strategic and tactical, illuminates the tricks deployed by the dictator to sabotage the ballot and remain in power; the second, less conscious and more profound, concerns the epistemology of political representation that developed as the democratic process and its forms of governmentality degenerated into shifting claims and truth conditions.[8] From this latter perspective, the question of what went on in IBB's mind, his secret agenda and vested interests, becomes less important than the conditions of structural adjustment and the categories of accountability that established the official fictions of a new politics of illusion, a "liberal" variant of what Mbembe (1992, 11–18) calls a *simulacral regime.*

The first elections of the Babangida era took place as early as 12 December 1987, in (what were then) the 301 local government areas of Nigeria's twenty-one states. IBB had already created two new states from Kaduna State and Cross River State; this was justified as a reform to bring government closer to the people, but actually sought to spread the national cake (in this case, into his wife Maryam's home area) to increase federal penetration at the grass roots. As we shall see, this strategy was repeated on 27 August 1991, when IBB purportedly yielded to popular demand by establishing nine additional states—which entailed new local government areas and, hence, new elections. The 1987 nonparty ballot for councilors in the 301 constituencies was annulled by the NEC due to a shortage of ballot boxes and alleged electoral malpractice. Angry protestors rioted in Lagos, burning vehicles and beating two police officers among those stationed to stop people moving between local government areas to cast multiple votes. On 11 December 1987, the *Reuter Library Report* related that in Ondo State, a candidate was arrested with 2,415 voting cards hidden under his bed. While the shortage of ballot boxes and even polling booths prevented many people from voting at all, the net figure of 72 million registered voters was clearly inflated, implying a total population of 150–200 million! IBB's transition program was not off to a good start, with grassroots elections at the local government area repeated on 26 March 1988, and again on 8 December 1990, when Nigeria's two political parties finally emerged.

The lifting of the ban on party politics and the creation of the Social Democratic Party (SDP) and the National Republican Convention (NRC) marked a turning point in the reality principle of Nigerian democracy: a shift from the populist mechanism of a general will represented from below to that of a military general, or leviathan, establishing the conditions of representation from above. Not only did the rules of the game change; so did the game itself—away from the participatory model that IBB avowed and toward the carefully staged con of a political "419" in which elections were more simulated than real. Called "democracy by fiat" by one Nigerian journalist (Ofeimun 1989), Nigeria's "two-partyism" (Oyediran and Agbaje 1991) was promulgated in the new draft constitution of May 1989, a document that voiced the recommendations of the civilian Political Bureau and Constituent Assembly but gave the last word to the Armed Forces Ruling Council (AFRC). The idea of stipulating two parties, given Nigeria's troubled electoral history, was to break the formation of ethnic blocs that characterized the First (1960–66) and Second (1979–83) Republics by a simple limitation of alternatives that would cut across ethnic affiliations, and by wiping the slate clear of all past parties and politicians. To prevent religious (Muslim versus Christian) and regional (North versus South) divisions from forming, the constitution required that both parties have their headquarters in Abuja, the new federal capital, and that their names, emblems, and mottoes contain no ethnic, religious or geographical connotations (Oyediran and Agbaje 1991, 222).

Thus the stage was set on 3 May 1989, when the six-year ban on party politics was lifted and all eligible citizens were allowed to form political associations that might qualify as one of the two recognized political parties, subject to the NEC's approval. In a two-month flurry of political activity to meet the

15 July submission deadline set by the NEC, forty-nine associations emerged around powerful patrons of the Babangida administration, factions within the Constituent Assembly, "geo-ethnic and religious caucuses" (Oyediran and Agbaje 1991, 224), and former politicians hiding behind clients. Given the short amount of time provided for such associations to organize, raise funds, and develop constituencies, many fell by the wayside, and only thirteen presented themselves to the NEC for registration.[9] According to the NEC, the new generation of "transparent" politicians failed to meet the standards of transparency. In its report to the government, the commission endorsed none of the aspiring associations, charging that:

> All the associations made deliberate false claims. . . from the inclusion of false, including ghost names and addresses on membership lists, to the affixture of somebody else's picture on the membership card belonging to another person; to the padding of names from voters' register; and to the offering of various forms of corrupt inducements to people so that they can pose as members of associations for verification purposes. (quoted in Oyediran and Agbaje 1991, 225)

Here we can see how the distinctive features of the "419"—unstable identities, misleading images, false numbers, and official registration forms—entered into politics, attributed at this stage to grassroots politicians but playing into the hands of the dictator. Whatever truth there was to the accusations, the incipient system of political representation was nipped in the bud. According to a Reuters 7 December 1989 Money Report titled "Nigerian Elections Put Back to End 1990," IBB disbanded all thirteen associations, claiming that "none of the groups had broken decisively with a history marked by tribal politics, religious bigotry, electoral fraud and violence." In their place (and outside the options outlined in the NEC report), he established two entirely new political parties ex nihilo: the Social Democratic Party (SDP)—which according to Kenneth Noble in the 8 November 1990 *New York Times,* he called "a little to the left," and the National Republican Convention (NRC), "a little to the right of center" ("Cynicism Clouds Nigerian Election," A17).

At this stage, the big con of the "transition programme" began in earnest. The federal government, operating through the Directorate for Social Mobilisation, wrote and published the manifestos of both parties, each of which mirrored the regime's basic social and economic policies, including its commitment to structural adjustment (figure 10.1). If the SDP had a progressive, populist tinge, sometimes characterized as welfarist and even socialist by the opposition, the NRC saw itself as conservative, even ruggedly free market. Echoing the most general qualities of the American Democratic and Republican Parties, Nigeria's new parties were short on content, long on rhetoric, and considered essentially the same. In his 8 November 1990 *New York Times* article, Kenneth Noble quoted Pini Johnson, a Nigerian journalist and editor:

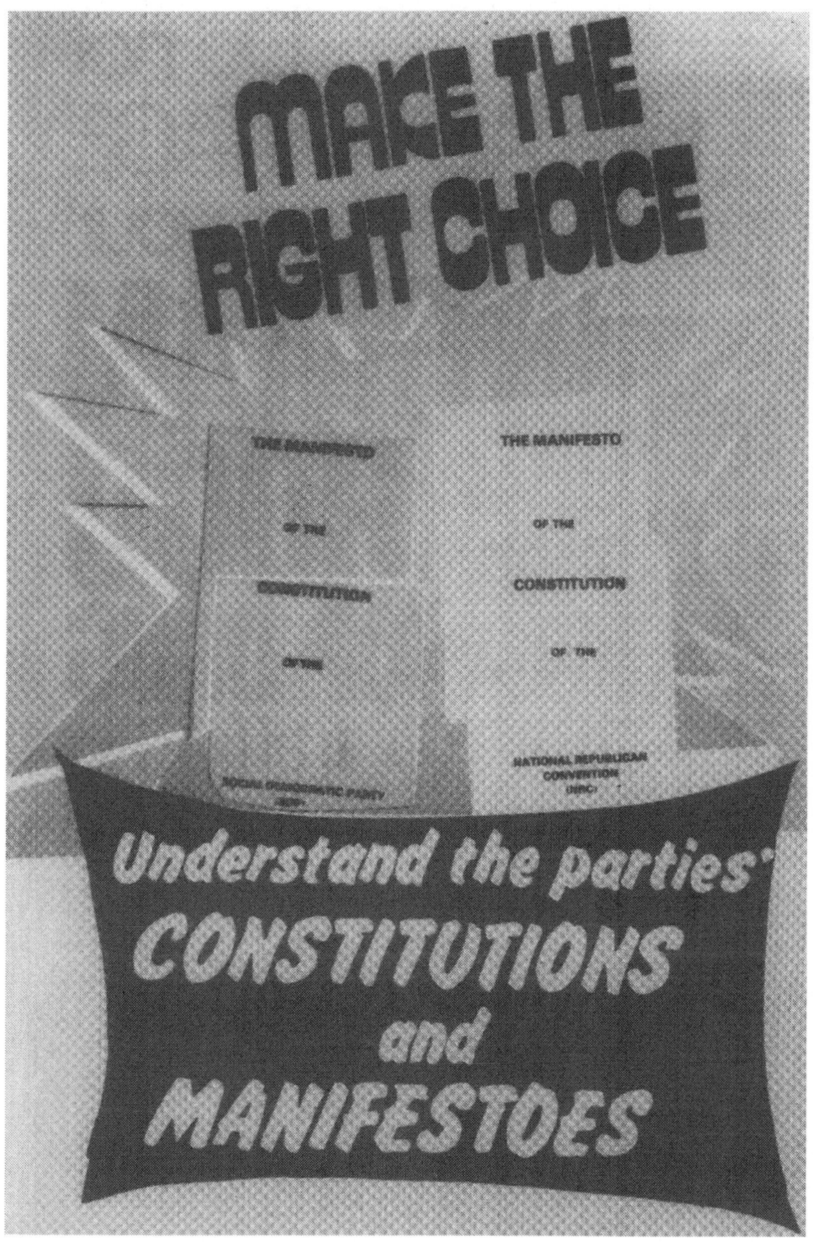

Fig. 10.1. The regime's mirror-image political parties (SDP and NRC), Federal Ministry of Information (Lagos). From the *Nigerian Interpreter* 5, no. 4 (July–August 1991).

"These new parties have no message. They're just parroting what they've been told to say. . . . The problem is that the military is constantly looking over their shoulders, so they can't say or do anything out of line" (A17). Political rallies for the rescheduled local government elections were notoriously vacuous. The parties lacked ideology and social base. But IBB called them "expressive symbols of the new political order"; even if their platforms were drafted by a committee of the AFRC, had they not been "debated" in party conventions at state and national levels to refine the final manifestos? The imputation of populist involvement was common with IBB. He employed it in the national constitutional conference, in the IMF and structural adjustment debates, with the national census, and in changing election dates; it allowed him to rule unilaterally while pretending to follow the advice of civilians. Like a liberal version of democratic centralism, IBB's new democratic order empowered the military to represent "the people" to themselves. In the name of "directed democracy," a "grassroots democratic" two-party solution permitted the state to design and stage-manage the entire political process, forestalling any real mass participation. This was accomplished by funding both organizations; by building party offices in all local government headquarters, state capitals, and in Abuja, at tremendous expense; by appointing party secretaries at all of these levels (later supervising their replacement by elected officials); by holding training programs for party officials at the regime's Centre for Democratic Studies, while issuing a number of draconian decrees that detained critics, banned professional associations, passed retroactive legislation, and prohibited judicial review (Oyediran and Agbaje 1991, 228–29). With such an overarching political infrastructure administered from above, IBB could recommence the long electoral march to Nigeria's Third Republic.

In the last three years of his misrule, IBB lived up to his nickname "Maradona," after the Argentine soccer player known for his deft dribbling and zigzagging on the playing field. Nigerian's electoral experience from 1991 to 1993 was marked by sudden election annulments, disqualifications, and rescheduling, and by reversals of bans and balloting procedures dictated from Abuja. In December 1991, the NRC won a small majority in the gubernatorial elections, which had been postponed to accommodate the nine newly created states, while the SDP gained a majority in the thirty state assemblies. To prevent ballot stuffing and stealing, the government developed an "open queue" voting system, whereby registered voters would line up and be counted behind the poster image of their candidate. The method was controversial, subjecting people to intimidation and influence from patrons and employers—and drawing criticism from middle-class professionals who complained of lining up for hours under the hot sun or in drenching rain. In the meantime, IBB lifted his earlier ban against all former politicians and public officials from entering the race; as Kenneth Noble reported in the 20 December 1991 *New York Times*, after meeting with the AFRC in Abuja, IBB announced that "the time has come for the old and new to mix, to cooperate and compete"("Nigeria Ends Ban for Ex-Officials," A7). A floodgate of power brokerage and influence peddling was suddenly opened, releasing not only the old political guard but also leading members of the military government into the political fray, adding to the collective sense of uncertainty and doubt. But, despite the growing cynicism and apathy among Nigerians, many of whom suspected IBB of a secret agenda to stay in power, elections to the National Assembly on 4 July 1992 were successfully held, with the SDP winning a majority of seats in both the Senate and the House of Representatives.[10] At this point, IBB's house of political cards began to look real, with a bid for the national presidency a significant challenge. The duties of the National Assembly were not yet specified, and IBB would later dictate that its members could officiate on matters cultural but not political! But with a substantial amount of political machinery in place, the keystone of an elected presidency would establish the reality of the Third Republic. And it was this reality that IBB simulated, projected, and hijacked in the final stages of his political "419."

The presidential party primaries had already been postponed several times: 4 August 1991 to 7 September; then to 19 October, after the creation of new states and local government areas; finally, to 1 August 1992, whereafter the AFRC stopped the fledgling vote, citing vote rigging and widespread malpractice, and commanded the NEC to repudiate the results. One notorious figure to emerge at this time was SDP multimillionaire and presidential aspirant Arthur Nzeribe, who boasted of 25 million (some said 32 million) pounds sterling in his campaign "war chest." As Karl Maier reported in an *Independent* article titled "Nigerians Contemplate the Price of Democracy," General Olusegun Obasanjo (the former head of state) warned of an emergent "moneytocracy . . . a government of moneymen for more money for themselves and for those who paid their initial bill for the elections"(1 August 1992, 11). Bills indeed ran high, as both parties imposed levies of 10,000–13,000 pounds on each candidate, ostensibly to reduce their number. By the second round of voting on 19 September 1992, the SDP frontrunners were Major-General Shehu Yar'Adua and Olu Falae, while Adamu Ciroma, Bamanga Tukur, and Umaru Shinkafi led the NRC. All important officials in previous military and civilian regimes, these candidates and their campaign finances were investigated by the dreaded State Security Service (SSS), in a catch-22 arrangement whereby the NEC announced its right to ban candidates without explanation after the primaries.

For many, the writing was already on the wall. In October, the military government suspended the primaries and banned the frontrunners from further participation because of their "money-politics." Another round of primaries was scheduled, and the handover date to civilian rule was pushed back to 27 August 1993. By this time, few illusions remained for Nigeria's enervated electorate. If any enthusiasm could be mustered it was less for a valid democratic process and more for a way of removing the dictator. Kole Babalola of the Inter Press Service reported another surprise twist in a 21 December 1992 electronic bulletin titled "Nigeria: Voting System Needed 'Nigerian-Factor' Proof": the NEC announced that the secret ballot would be reintroduced to avoid influence peddling—but this time in a modified form, called an "open secret ballot," as it was openly displayed but gave voters some measure of secrecy. An appropriate name indeed for the open secret, publicly voiced, that IBB had no real intention of leaving office; also an appropriate figure for the oxymoron "Nigerian democracy." With a low voter turnout, the Southern business tycoon Chief Moshood Abiola emerged as leader of the SDP, and his Northern opponent, the wealthy but relatively unknown Bashir Tofa, captured the NRC. The potential for a North-South split presented by the candidates was softened by the fact that both were Muslim, with Abiola's influence extending well into the North, given that he was the vice president of the Organization of the Islamic Conference (OIC), second only to the sultan of Sokoto, who was its president.

The final act that followed is now known as "June 12," the date of the long-awaited presidential elections that the AFRC and the NEC kept promising and postponing. Days before the ballot, in a televised debate between the candidates, Abiola's popularity soared when he proposed specific plans for rehauling the national economy and for initiating a rational petroleum policy; Tofa presented no vision or leadership qualities, announcing that he would work out solutions after assuming the presidency. In the meantime, the federal government decreed that no court order could stop the elections from proceeding, thereby according the NEC exclusive regulative powers. This made the regime appear sincere. It seemed even more so when a conservative organization of former politicians and wealthy merchants, called the Association for a Better Nigeria (ABN) and representing Northern oligarchic interests, won an order from the Abuja high court to ban the polls on 10 June, arguing that IBB should remain in power for four more years due to "religious" tensions in the country; in response, NEC president Humphrey Nwosu invoked his constitutional powers to overrule the order so that the elections could proceed.[11] Again, voter turnout was low (30–40 percent), given the frustrations and disappointments of the past. But an international team of observers invited by the military government and led by British High Commissioner Sir Christopher MacRae judged the elections to be the most free and fair in Nigeria's postcolonial history.

Despite a ban on the release of early results—which included a presidential decree to imprison any journalist or editor who published returns prematurely—votes tallied from fourteen states at the NEC headquarters in Abuja (and publicly displayed on an electric billboard) showed Abiola leading Tofa by 4.3 million to 2.3 million; estimates had it that he was winning nineteen states to eleven.[12] With a presidential victory so close at hand, the Northern-based Association for a Better Nigeria (ABN) struck again, together with the NRC, declaring the election results "unofficial and unauthentic." This time it won and sustained a court injunction (from the same Abuja high court) against the release of the final results. Despite the military decree barring judicial intervention, and two counterrulings against the nullification from high courts in Lagos and Benin City, on 23 June the federal military government sealed the returns. It also suspended the NEC, ordered yet another round of primaries, and invented new rules that disqualified Abiola and Tofa from the race. According to popular testimony, NEC president Nwosu was visited by the State Security Service (SSS), which coerced him into accepting the ruling and forced him to confess that he had taken bribes. Civil unrest in Lagos and Ibadan erupted as protestors took to the streets (figure 10.2), shouting "IBB must go!" and declaring, at least on one demonstrator's placard, that "IBB = 419."[13]

IBB had lost all credibility by wasting the nation's money and trying its patience in an electoral charade of "pro forma democracy" (Ibrahim 1993, 137) that he himself directed and choreographed. He invented the parties and set the stage; he changed the rules, the dates, the ballots, and the candidates by pulling the strings of his puppet court at Abuja; he reversed his own decrees and subjected the populace to a prolonged series of false initiatives and empty motions in order to maintain himself in power. Ballot fraud there was, but it was stage-managed from Abuja. The equivalence between IBB and the art of the con was not just metaphorical. It was literal. One of the principal actors in the electoral illusion was Arthur Nzeribe, a model mercenary who had made a killing by selling arms to both sides during the Biafran war and had sought the SDP presidency for himself; but also, as we have seen, he had distinguished himself as an international con artist in the propaganda scam pulled on Pik Botha. On 17 July 1993, *Newsday* reported in "Nigeria Election Scam" that Abimbola Davis, the ABN's number-two official, confessed—at a news conference held in hiding forty minutes before he fled the country—that the annulment of June 12 was engineered through "an organized confusion by just a few of us to prolong the lifespan of the present military administration" (Nassau and Suffolk edition, 8). From this account, Nigeria's politics of illusion emerges as the deliberate work of a professional team of confidence men, whose expertise was matched by the enthusiasm of security forces in jailing civilian groups like the Campaign for Democracy and union leaders.

But a more pervasive condition of verisimilitude and dissimulation was also sabotaging the nation. Epitomized by the "open secret" ballot that produced "unauthentic" electoral results, this condition eroded the distinction between truth and falsehood—and with it, the very existence of truth-value. For example, when Abimbola Davis's confession was first published, government newspapers like the *Nigerian Times* proclaimed it a fabrication by enemies to discredit the ABN. But who was the ABN? And who was the government?

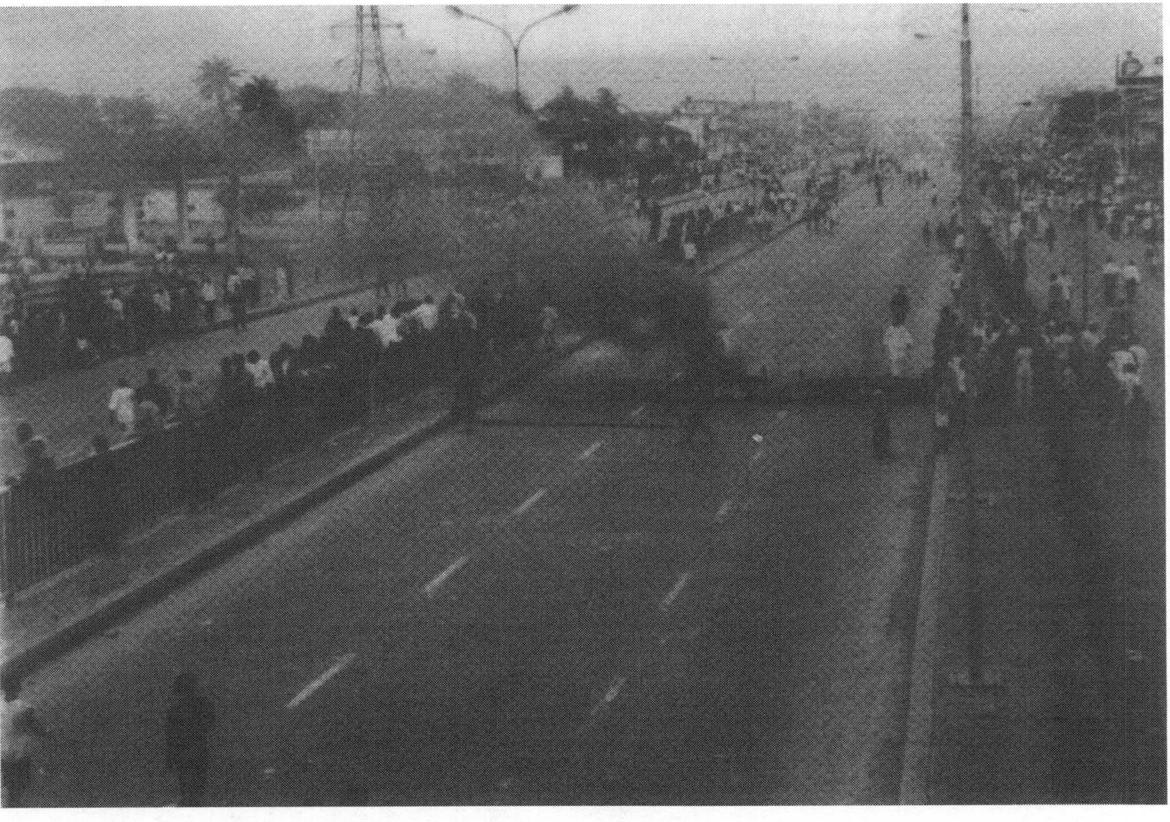

Fig. 10.2. Protesters on Ikorodu Road, Lagos, 23 June 1993. Photograph by Andrew Apter.

With senior generals defecting from the military in protest against the annulment of June 12, with courts overturned, with governors and incumbents of the national and state assemblies lost in a legal-rational twilight zone, the state itself began to dissolve.

Not that the battle was over. IBB remained the enemy, and his eventual resignation on 26 August was a brilliant victory for his political opponents, who blocked his every move to buy support. But the very instruments of opposition, the largely symbolic warfare on the streets and in the press, reflect the epistemological uncertainties and unrealities of the time. In addition to general strikes and "stay at homes" that brought public life to a standstill (and in which more than a hundred lost their lives), the techniques of "419" were turned against IBB to discredit him further. Plans and secret photographs of his hideout mansions in Minna and around the world were published, with drawings and sketches providing "evidence" of his embezzlements (figure 10.3). One photocopied letter that circulated throughout Lagos "documented," in near-perfect officialese, a British banker's inability to transfer 66,500,000 pounds of First Lady Maryam Babangida's ill-gotten gains into a Swiss account. The only blatant error was the positioning of his letterhead on the bottom of the page. That these tools of resistance were "forged" had little to do with their ultimate truth-value, because IBB and Maryam *did* build mansions and embezzle millions. This simulacral quality of political protest, *no less true for its falsity*, or *real* for its *unreality*, reflected a general quality of the Nigerian state and its imputed forms of governmentality. Take the census, for example, that administrative instrument of bureaucratic rationality that once documented, quantified, and categorized the citizenry—and that, under IBB, proved to be worth its weight in words. "We attach great importance," he proclaimed, "to the 1991 census as a way of laying a solid foundation for a stable third republic." What the 1991 census did provide, in addition to evidence that the population was 25 million less than supposed (down to 85 million), was an opportunity for the state to harass its population, to close all borders, to prohibit all movement, and to command people to stay home from work while officers counted heads. Or consider Nigerian maps, no longer adequate to the nation's shifting territories, local government areas, and dilapidated roads; or its national museums and monuments, once proud harbingers of a new Nigeria and now bankrupt, plundered, and poorly maintained, devoid even of visitors. The forms of governmentality that flourished under colonialism were gradually emptied during the Babangida era, deployed not as means of rational administration and taxation to impose order and control but as technologies of obstruction and interference.

Nowhere is the breakdown of governance more clearly manifest than in the civil service reforms associated with structural adjustment. Like the twisted logic of "directed democracy," IBB's version of administrative perestroika was designed to streamline the service and protect its leaders from

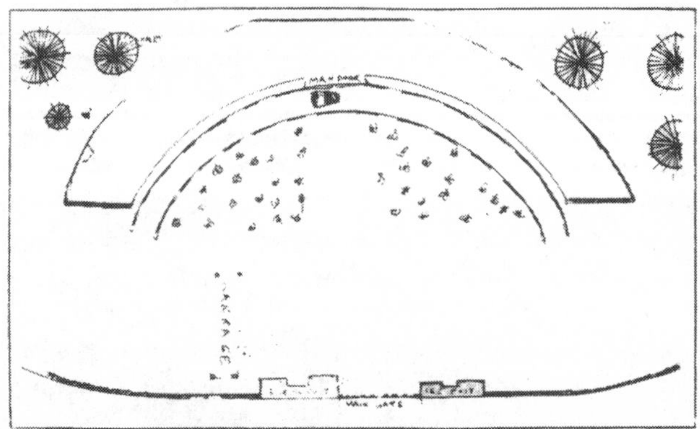

Aerial view of the paradise of IBB in Minna

Artist's impressions by Sanya Ojikutu

Front view of the Minna wonder which reportedly cost N500 million.

On the left, inside the compound, are exotic cars - Benz, BMW-Jeep etc.

Fig. 10.3. "Graphic evidence" of IBB's Minna mansion. Sketches by Sanya Ojikutu. From *Fame,* 21–27 Sept. 1992, 5.

those "mischievous civil servants" who "deliberately misled their ministers" into making decisions "inimical to government interest" (Imoko 1991, 7). To protect his loyal ministers from undisciplined and unpatriotic subordinates—according to the official line—IBB decided to make the minister of each ministry its chief executive and its accounting officer as well. Somehow the "reform" was supposed to emphasize "professionalism" in the service. But, in practical terms, it allowed each minister to authorize his own embezzlements without cutting the Accounting Office in on the deal. Unilateral powers of plunder and patronage were thus accorded to a restricted inner circle, less expensive to maintain than multiple lines of misappropriation and more loyal to the center. The old 50 percent rule still applied; it obliged a subordinate to send half his loot "upstairs" or face the sack. The men at the top, however, no longer had any strings attached, no potential exposés or incriminating documents that could not be contained.[14] When Ernest Shonekan—head of the ephemeral interim government—probed the NNPC after IBB "stepped aside," the petroleum ministers could not account for nearly *$12.4 billion* of missing revenues that had accrued from Nigeria's Gulf War windfall (Ukim 1994, 9).

In an era of planned privatization, a new line of directorates and programs, designed to mobilize the grass roots into sustainable development, provided unchecked access to the national cake in the name of the interests they were supposed to serve. In 1987, IBB launched MAMSER (the Mass Mobilization for Economic Recovery, Self-Reliance and Social Justice program) to raise political consciousness and lift the masses out of poverty. He then set up the Directorate of Foods, Roads and Rural Infrastructures (DFFRI), with its associated Community Development Associations, Direct Participation Scheme, and Integrated Rural Development Scheme. Some funds *did* trickle down into fertilizer subsidies and irrigation projects in selected showcase projects. Usually in remote corners of Bauchi and Borno States, these projects had their "launchings" broadcast by the National Television Authority. And in several southern states, local rice cultivation resumed after the price of imported Uncle Ben's skyrocketed. But, in general, the regime's directed development, like directed democracy, was an illusion, providing money for the powerful in the name of the masses. During a videotaped interview in Ayede Ekiti, 8 September 1990, when I asked market woman Mama Juwe to comment on IBB's regime, she replied repeatedly, "Aiyé ti bàjé!" ("Our life is spoiled!"). What about conditions for women? It appeared that Maryam Babangida's "Better Life for Rural Women" program, designed to organize and empower women in the countryside, lived up to its more popular appellation, "Better Life for Rich Wives." The first lady, together with the wives of governors, launched their projects in state capitals, sporting the finest lace and fanciest headties, forever out of reach and out of touch.[15]

But, to appreciate more fully the conditions of simulated governance that dominated and infiltrated everyday life in Nigeria, creating an entire world as misrepresentation, let us return to oil, the mysterious and elusive substance of value itself.

The Crisis of Value

In 1991, after finishing a degree at the London School of Design, Bisi returned to Lagos where she set up a small interior decoration business. In a 29 November 1993 interview in Ibadan, Bisi told me that among her first clients was a young woman like herself, seeking advice on how to design the office space of her own new business. Bisi visited her client's unfurnished workplace to discuss preliminary ideas and plans. While she was there, a man named Alhaji suddenly rushed through the door in an extreme state of agitation. "The deal is off!" he exclaimed to the woman. "The chemicals and paper arrived safely, but the *Ọ́ọ̀ni* [of Ife] is pulling out." He then proceeded to unpack his load, and demonstrate the efficacy of the paper and chemicals by taking blank sheets of paper from a roll, dipping them in a tray of black liquid, and pulling out crisp new fifty naira notes. He had barrels of the liquid chemical, but the problem was finding another partner to take the *Ọ́ọ̀ni*'s place. Only then did he notice Bisi, off to the side, a witness to the demonstration. He was furious. "Who is this woman? She has seen everything! How can we trust her?" At this point, Bisi felt mesmerized and dull, the effect, she later concluded, of the juju medicine that Alhaji was using to make her gullible. Combining threats with propositions, Alhaji and the woman reluctantly agreed to cut Bisi in on the deal at a bargain price. All she needed to do was return quickly with 20,000 naira and they would "release" her with a share of the money-making supplies. Bisi recalls returning to her office, getting the cash, and calling her sister at the last minute for advice. Her sister brought her back to her senses, and Bisi went home. Days later, she ventured past her "client's" office and saw that it was vacant.

Bisi's story represents a species of "419" known as the "neon money" scam, perpetrated mainly against fellow Nigerians, although Westerners have fallen for it as well. In this case, the con artist invoked the celebrated traditional ruler and business millionaire, the *Ọ́ọ̀ni* of Ife, to provide "recognition" and hence credibility to the ruse. Craig Spraggins of the U.S. Secret Service, who specializes in uncovering "419" operations in Nigeria, described to me during a 16 August 1995 telephone conversation other versions of this con, in which the "neon" money supplies are said to have been put up as "collateral" by the CIA during their covert operations. In both examples, secret sources of wealth and power are associated with mysterious, if not illicit, forms of procurement and profit. In cultural terms, the roots of this belief in money-magic go back to traditional idioms of money-fetishism and illegitimate wealth in southern Nigeria. One story I collected in Ayede-Ekiti during fieldwork in 1984 related how a rich man kidnapped children by stunning them with juju medicines and led them to his house, where he had a large calabash that he would fill with human blood and bring to a room with no windows. After he uttered incantations, the blood would turn into money, which the man spent whenever he needed it.[16] This notion of effortless gain at the expense or even "consumption" of others is echoed in various witchcraft beliefs as well, but the underlying template that motivates it is the conversion of blood into money; bad money, to be sure, sometimes referred to as "hot" or "soaked," curiously "infertile" in its capacity to be spent frivolously, without reciprocal advantage or gain. What is so interesting about Bisi's story, and the genre of neon money in general, is how it transposes this template into the oil economy, in that a black chemical that, like oil, comes in barrels, possesses the money-producing valences of human blood.[17] As Barber (1982) and Watts (1994) have so vividly demonstrated, Nigerian oil money has always generated a certain malaise, a negative moral tinge if not connotations of evil.

It is this negative valence, the unreal quality of the nation's effortless oil wealth, that is reflected in ideas of neon money, the ethereal precipitate of the money form that took over after the monetary value of oil declined and detached itself from the national currency. This is not to suggest that oil has become worthless in Nigeria; rather, that the decline in world prices and mismanagement by the state has radically diminished its contribution to the national economy. The downward trend, exacerbated by the deregulative measures of structural adjustment, produced a general crisis of value, of runaway inflation, distressing depreciation, defaulting banks, and, above all, the impoverishment of everyday life. As Anyanwu has argued, "Unless it is brought under control inflation will destroy the very fabric of Nigerian society"(1992, 7). His prediction may be near at hand. As I have suggested, IBB's regime of fraud and deception gave rise to a national culture of "419," in which illusion has become the very basis of survival.

Macroeconomic indicators reveal a precipitous drop in real wealth under General Babangida, with increased proportions of foreign exchange being committed to debt servicing. Just as significant as a net decline in real income and GDP are the sociocultural indicators of privatization and deregulation, particularly in the banking system and foreign exchange market. In an effort to stimulate domestic investment, the Central Bank floated interest rates and authorized merchant banks and investment houses to engage in high-risk speculation.[18] The result was a flurry of uninsured investment companies offering outrageous returns on substantial deposits, such as 30 percent interest on "Midas Gold Notes" for a minimum deposit of 50,000 naira advertised by the Midas Merchant Bank Ltd. in the *Financial Post,* 19 June 1993 (4) (figure 10.4). Like the legendary Midas touch, these deals seemed to work like magic, with fast profits and turnovers whetting the appetites of the young professionals. The new managers sported fancy cars and even patronized the arts, but

Fig. 10.4. Advertisement for Midas Gold Notes. From the *Financial Post* 5, no. 22 (6–19 June 1993), 5.

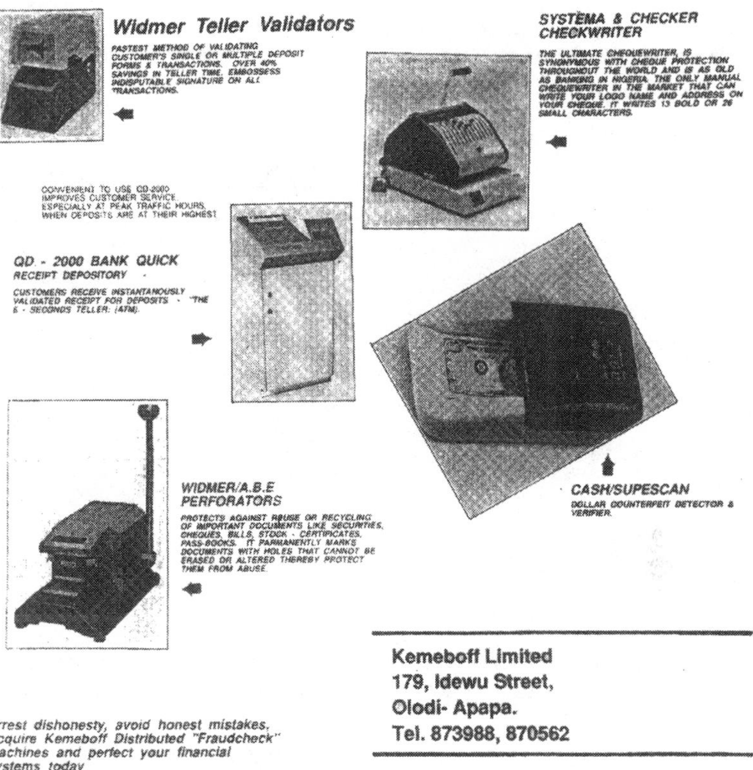

Fig. 10.5. Advertisement for counterfeit money detectors. From the *Financial Post* 5, no. 22 (6–19 June 1993), 10.

their wealth was insecure and ephemeral, invested in nothing more than the future returns on high-risk Ponzi schemes. Soon, the commercial banks and finance houses began to fall like dominoes with no government treasury to bail them out, and reports of more generalized bank fraud and counterfeit currency trafficking began to circulate in the press, together with advertisements for "fraudcheck" machines (figure 10.5). At the same time, the government raised the domestic price of gasoline, increasing transport costs of food commodities that were passed on to consumers, adding to inflation. With characteristically inverted logic, the government then blamed market women for greedy and unpatriotic pricing—as if they were responsible for the rising costs—and periodically mowed down their stalls with armored vehicles. As staples like cassava, beans, rice, and yams soared in price, even middle-class Nigerians began to go hungry, leading to popular expressions of hardship such as "1-0-0," " 0-1-0," "0-0-1," and even "0-0-0," where "1" refers to a meal consumed during the day and "0" to meals skipped for lack of funds. As costs rose and quantities diminished, the basic quality seemed to decline, in that people would describe the same foods as less "filling" than before.[19] A new "style" of clothing called "air-condition wear" flourished in markets like Aswani in Lagos that specialize in secondhand clothes, making a jest of penury and necessity. The austerity of the 1980s has given way to desperation in the 1990s. In another manifestation of the "419," a rash of born-again Christian prophets has swept the country, promising profit through prayer while extracting from their followers what little surplus they can muster. On a more professional register, business centers with photocopy machines, computers, faxes, and international telephone lines proliferated into bustling sites of activity as job seekers constructed professional CVs, printed up authentic-looking contracts, and purveyed the instruments of finance capital with the tools of the international "419."

As the cost of living rose and real incomes fell, and the professional middle class gradually withered away, oil was transformed from the lifeblood of the nation into the bad blood of corrupt government; or as Watts (1994) has so elegantly put it, from black gold into the devil's excrement. In the process, the rich have become criminalized, their wealth associated with expensive cars and the mansions of "Cocaine Alley" in Ikeja, Lagos; with theft of government revenues from the NNPC and its subsidiaries; with oil bunkering, black marketeering, and the moral bankruptcy of the daily "419." As medical supplies ran out in state hospitals, Nigeria became the number-one exporter of Asian heroin to the United States. In the popular imagination, oil money and drug money began to converge at the top, with IBB's family and inner circle directly implicated in trafficking; so much so, it is said, that he arranged the parcel bomb murder of journalist Dele Giwa in 1986 to prevent him from breaking the story (Olorunyomi 1993). In gendered terms, the inverse qualities of the new Nigerian woman, so conspicuously championed by Maryam Babangida, emerged in the witchlike counterpart of the female courier who used her "womanhood" to smuggle drugs (figure 10.6). Oil, furthermore, has come to represent a scourge against the natural and social environment, as the Ogoni fight for survival against the pollution that ruined their fishing waters, and against a regime that has waged a near-genocidal campaign in response to their demands for compensation (Saro-Wiwa 1990, 1992; Welch 1995). Fighting for their civil rights, and for all Nigerians who have experienced the erosion of civil society, the Ogoni—led by the late Ken Saro-Wiwa—have been portrayed as subversives and saboteurs, as unpatriotic vermin on the national body, and as a backward and subhuman minority "tribe." In his *Similia: Essays on Anomic Nigeria,* Saro-Wiwa (1991) wrote with brutal wit about "Babangidance," referring to government by cheating, a national culture of fraud, and

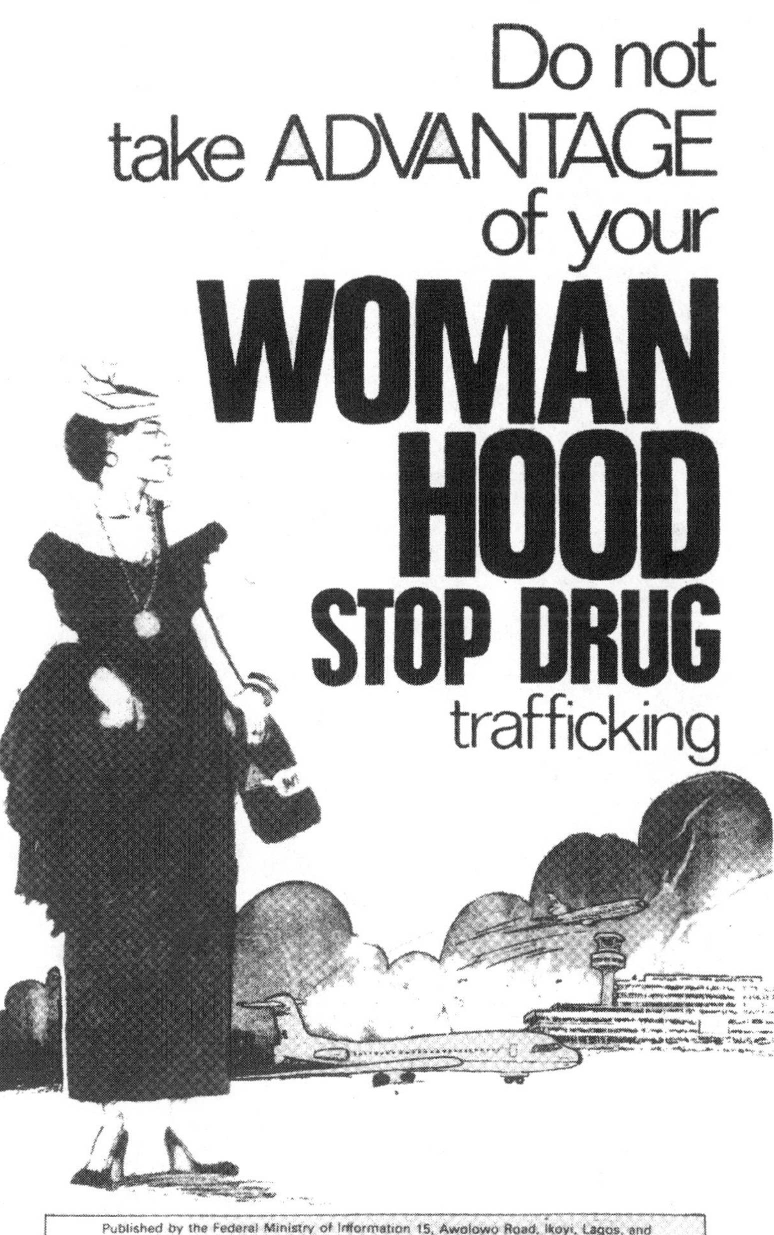

Fig. 10.6. Female courier as figure of illicit wealth (poster), Federal Ministry of Information (Lagos). From the *Nigerian Interpreter* 5, no. 4 (July–August 1991).

the resultant devaluation of life for all Nigerians as both individual and collective loss.

Significant here in Saro-Wiwa's political diagnoses are the cultural corollaries of inflation and devaluation, less anomic than *anemic*. When the substance or fetish of original value, oil, mutated from lifeblood to bad blood, Nigeria's nation form, once proudly modeled on the money form, grew weak and lost its shine. As the state privatized the oil industry—first by diverting revenues into private accounts, and second, by auctioning block allocations to private concessions that in many cases simply lifted and hawked the oil, without any new investment or exploration—the public sector virtually collapsed into mimetic representations of itself. Bureaucrats and civil servants still went to work dressed in threadbare suits dutifully starched and pressed: but, by the end of the Babangida era, they were earning about $20 per month, and spending up to a third of their salaries on transportation. Unlike the oil boom, when social distinctions were redrawn to accommodate a growing middle class, the bust set off a great leveling wave of rampant inflation that, as one contemporary report put it, "is better imagined today than quantified" (Ogbonna and Udo 1993, 6). What sort of instabilities has such hyperinflation created? Reflecting on Weimar Germany, Elias Canetti has argued:

> An inflation can be called a witches' sabbath of devaluation where men and the units of their money have the strongest effects on each other. The one stands for the other, men feeling themselves as "bad" as their money; and this becomes worse and worse. . . . It is a double devaluation originating in a double identification. The *individual* feels depreciated because the unit on which he relied, and with which he had equated himself, starts sliding; and the *crowd* feels depreciated because the *million* is. As the millions mount up, a whole people, numbered in millions, becomes nothing. (1984, 186)

Witches' Sabbath indeed. For all the historical and cultural differences between Weimar Germany and IBB's Nigeria—and the different magnitude of the inflation rates involved—this passage illuminates a fundamental transformation that occurred during the Babangida regime; namely, the unhinging of individual and collective identities from fixed social coordinates into the everyday arts of the "419."

Canetti continues to argue that the devaluation of the German mark was displaced onto the progressive devaluation of the enemy within, the Jew, whose destruction would restore the nation's vitality. Following this line, it is possible that the persecution of the Ogoni people will intensify as the economy continues to collapse, given how they have agitated against oil and state terror, and have been racially "othered" in distinctive ways. However, even if the state continues its pogrom, and General Sani Abacha's hanging of Ken Saro-Wiwa on 10 November 1995 could be portentous, it is unlikely that the nation will follow its lead, since the Ogoni are generally "remote" and, unlike Jews in Germany, do not live among the population at large. More likely, the lumpen armed robbers and common thieves among them will be publicly executed on Bar Beach, as occurred under Buhari in 1984, to provide spectacular relief for the masses, while intellectuals, journalists, and activists continue to be jailed. In a recent government "419," forty alleged coup plotters, including former Head of State Olusegun Obasanjo and Chief of Staff (and SDP presidential aspirant) Shehu Yar'Adua, await uncertain fates in prison, having been tried by a secret military tribunal that has extended its jurisdiction to sundry critics of the regime. I call this a "419" because no evidence of a plot was ever publicly established, although the illusion of a trial has been sustained. But, whatever political traumas may lie ahead, a return to civilian rule seems less likely than ever. The decline of the oil economy under IBB, and the politics of illusion that he fostered, formed the nation's real transition program to a simulacral regime, a new Nigeria that is, quite literally, a shadow of its former self.[20]

Conclusion

In expanding the equation "IBB = 419," I have suggested that there is more to the relationship between cash and politics than mere influence peddling or vote buying. More, also, than the truism that "money is power." Inasmuch as "IBB = 419" ties electoral fraud to economic fraud, as indicated on the placard of the outraged protestor, the equivalence flows from an underlying cultural logic that developed under specific historical conditions; these range from the colonial antecedents of the postcolonial state and its inherited forms of governmentality to the political economy of the 1970s oil boom that went bust in the decade that followed. In short, "419" was not just a "culture of fraud and corruption." It was embedded, from the first, in wider webs of implicit meaning, embodied knowledge, and historical consciousness. I have tried here to penetrate the tissue of illusion that characterizes the everyday practice of "419" in order to grasp a more fundamental transformation of value that occurred during IBB's dictatorship, a transformation that produced a national crisis of representation with thoroughgoing political and theoretical implications.

In this connection, the lessons to be learned from the international "419" are not about fraud and dissimulation as such. They are about a symbolic transformation whereby the value forms that emerged during the boom years have become detached from the value of oil itself, to become forms of value and sources of illicit profit unto themselves. The letters of credit, bank drafts, official signatures, and corporate logos that previously legitimated and authorized the international instruments of purchase and sale began to circulate like "floating signifiers," devoid of any real monetary or institutional referent—

until, quite literally, they hit their mark, a credulous dupe who went for the bait, losing his or her shirt by giving something for nothing. This truly dialectical transformation from value form to form of value, conflating the economic signifier (monetary instruments, purchase orders, bills of exchange, etc.) with the economic signified (money, commodities) has not, moreover, been limited to the pure realm of economics. It has extended into politics via such authoritative institutions as the NNPC and the CBN, which, as we have seen, participated in many ways. Some "bad eggs" working on the inside furnished their partners with the information, forms, letterheads, and even offices needed to work the scams. Others played key roles in siphoning off foreign exchange or petroleum into private, "dedicated" accounts, both for themselves and for others. The inability of the NNPC and the CBN to account for their expenditures and foreign exchange over the last seven years is itself endemic to the international "419," because fictitious forms and ghost accounts have undermined the very principle of accountability itself. By breaking its promise to back up its currency (Watts 1994, 441), the state has further inflated and devalued the naira, passing the cost of its fraudulent practices onto its citizens, while undermining its own credibility and violating the public trust.

Within this nation of masquerading value forms, democracy could not and cannot take root. If President Babangida remained unaccountable, making a mockery of the civil courts and even overruling his own decrees, the citizens themselves could not be counted, and did not count. Like the counterfeit value form of the business "419," IBB directed his "pro forma" democracy, producing manifestos, building hundreds of local government party headquarters, and printing registration forms and ballots—none of which bore any substantive relationship to collective concerns or preferences. The 1993 elections took place in a political vacuum, as if projected on a screen, and were thereby detached from a much abused electorate that had no way of registering its final judgment. There was, in effect, no political representation, because the ballot never really took place. True, the actual presidential vote was judged free and fair by international observers. But, because it was nullified, there was no need to trouble rigging it! Throughout the prolonged succession of aborted elections, banking on the cultivated expectation of a return to civilian rule, IBB was able to neutralize his opponents; first within the army, because a countercoup could hardly gain popular support with the Third Republic so near at hand; and second within the political class, many of whom revealed themselves during the primaries and ruined themselves by spending lavishly for ineffectual support. In this respect, it was almost overdetermined that Arthur Nzeribe, infamous perpetrator of the international "419," would play a critical role with the Association for a Better Nigeria in derailing the June 12 elections. This last point warrants further consideration, because it is precisely in the middle ground between structural determination and individual agency that the culture of "419" writ large assumes theoretical significance for our understanding of the state and civil society in this part of Africa.

Two familiar analytical extremes frame current debate about postcolonial Africa. One, consistent with historical materialism, explains contemporary economic problems, and the so-called crisis of the state, in terms of colonialism and underdevelopment: it is a perspective that is sometimes too easily dismissed as blaming the West for everything that has gone wrong. The other, more consistent with methodological individualism, identifies the root causes as corrupt leadership, nepotism, and the plundering of public spoils by a privileged few. The politics of illusion in contemporary Nigeria, and the culture of "419" to which it belongs, however, are themselves a product of *both:* a history of global economic articulation, radically transformed by an oil boom gone bust; and a pernicious cycle of "feeding at the trough" (Bayart 1993) that, with a few exceptional regimes, has gone from bad to worse. Following the utilitarian principle of rational choice, we have seen how the fraudulent deal, as a conscious dissimulation by individuals and teams, has been refined almost to an art form in Nigeria. But, underlying and motivating the "419" we have discerned a structural transformation of value forms, whereby the public sector (the state) and the public sphere (civil society) have dissolved, leaving only traces of their former existence. The naira is still the naira, but it is now worthless. The same holds for the state, the civil service, and, most important of all, even oil. The lifeblood of the nation has become anemic, undermining its credibility at home and abroad.

In more cultural terms, the anemia of the oil economy, and of the body politic through which it circulates, is expressed by a number of idioms that contrast significantly with those that predominated during the oil boom. When oil was king, it informed the nation with the fetish of intrinsic value and the luster of gold—expressed racially in terms of blackness; culturally, in terms of a glorified national heritage celebrated extravagantly during the Second World Black and African Festival of Arts and Culture (FESTAC '77) and explicitly represented by the gold rectangle of the festival flag; and economically, in a strong exchange relation to the U.S. dollar. Today, oil scarcely circulates. The Warri and Kaduna refineries operate at fractional capacities, chronic fuel shortages lead to endless gasoline queues, and frequently the petrol itself is *diluted with water*, causing engine failure. But, if Nigeria today is no longer on the move, its devalued and inflated economy suffers from more than just anemia. We have seen how the Ogoni minority has recast oil as pollution, how wealth itself has lost its legitimacy, now associated with cocaine and theft, and how the degradation of the money form has destabilized social identity and diminished the quality of everyday life. Indeed, Ogoni ecopolitics reveals how the state has destroyed the very "ground" of civil society itself.[21]

But what is this sphere of civil society that functions rhetorically in the language of liberal political economy as the "natural" ground of effective democracy through a free market of interests and preferences? In a larger sense, the era of the "419" in Nigeria sheds light on the location of civil society in postcolonial Africa, where, following Kunz (1995), two dominant perspectives compete. The more Lockean viewpoint "posits [civil] society as a self-regulating realm, the ultimate repository of individual rights and liberties, and a body that must be protected against incursions of the state" (181–82). This vision concurs with the American constitutional separation of powers and protection of civil rights and liberties, such as free speech, assembly, et cetera that are ultimately "grounded" in a market mechanism with its own assumptions of natural law. It also presupposes norms of sincerity, trust, and accountability in the representation of individual and collective interests. A second, more "Hegelian" understanding of civil society, presents "an integrationist or holistic picture of civil society and the state" (182) where the former functions more as a sphere of communication and interaction within the nation-state as a whole. There is no question that as African states have liberalized in the late 1980s and early 1990s, pursuing uneven paths of structural adjustment and democratization, the liberal model has reestablished itself in Africanist scholarship, particularly among political scientists focusing on "weak states" and predatory regimes. The rise of the Nigerian "419" appears to support this perspective, in that pervasive fraud and deception have so clearly eroded the normative fabric of civil society. Indeed, the very appearance of "IBB = 419" on a protestor's placard in Ikorodu Road reflected this vision of civil society in the streets.

The dialectics of Nigerian rentier-capitalism, however, and the forms of objectification that it has entailed, suggest a Hegelian or even Marxian approach to civil society in Africa, not as a natural and autonomous domain to be protected and reclaimed, but as *a fetishized sphere of circulation within the national economy.* As oil accelerated the circulation of money and commodities through what were primarily political relations of distribution, the nation was naturalized as one blood and soil beneath a benevolent state rising above. But as the oil economy burned down and the dollar dropped out of the Nigerian naira, the illusory basis of the country's wealth became apparent, draining the very blood of the nation and its citizens. Within the sphere of circulation, the arteries of the nation were blocked by irrational shortages until even oil disappeared from the gas stations. And, as we have argued, when inflation soared, arbitrary exchange values destabilized the very phenomenology of exchange itself, giving rise to the era of the "419"—of fraud, con artistry, deception, and desperate survival. From this perspective, the breakdown of civil society and the norms of intersubjectivity governing accountable interaction and political representation in Nigeria can be attributed not only to the rapacious appetites of predatory rulers and multinational companies, but to the collapse of a sphere of circulation whose previously obscure relation to "the hidden abode of production" (Marx 1976, 279) has almost literally disappeared.

Notes

1. See, for example, Buchi Emecheta's *Naira Power* (1982), a novel that captures the spirit of the era. For a discussion of this and other novels and plays dealing with the dubious and deadly powers of oil wealth, see Watts 1994 (425–27).

2. In keeping with our semantic perspective, we could say that this truth-functional "meaning" of the naira denotes its "extension" rather than its "intension," its reference in dollars and commodities rather than its "sense" as constituted by a formal code.

3. See, for example, Cindy Shiner, "Scamming Gullible Americans in a Well-Oiled Industry in Nigeria," *Washington Post,* 30 August 1994, A15; and Bill Schiller, "Crooks and Con Men Stain a National Image," *Toronto Star,* 10 May 1992, F3.

4. See "Charlie's Hustle," Tom Dunkel, *Washington Post,* 27 February 1994, F1.

5. For a marvelous window into the world of this first elite, see Bola Ige's autobiographical *Kaduna Boy* (1991).

6. For the BCCI scandal, see Truell and Gurwin 1992; Beaty and Gwynne 1993; for the Kaduna Mafia, see Takaya and Tyoden 1987.

7. Decree No. 25 of 1987 banned all former and current public office holders from campaigning in party politics.

8. For a general definition of governmentality, see Foucault 1991; for discussion of colonial governmentality, see Thomas 1994 (105–42) and Scott 1995; also Bayart 1993 (249) for its relevance to the postcolonial state in Africa.

9. These were the All Nigeria People's Party (ANPP), Ideal People's Party (IPP), Liberal Convention (LC), National Unity Party (NUP), Nigerian Labour Party (NLP), Nigerian National Congress (NNC), Nigerian People's Welfare Party (NPWP), Patriotic Nigerian Party (PNP), People's Front of Nigeria (PFN). People's Patriotic Party (PPP), People's Solidarity Party (PSP), Republican Party of Nigeria (RPN), and United Nigeria Democratic Party (UNDP) (Oyediran and Agbaje 1991, 225).

10. Of 89 senatorial seats, 52 went SDP and 37 NRC; of 589 seats in the House, 314 went SDP, 275 went NRC. Two outstanding senate and four outstanding house seats were held in later by-elections. "Nigerian Elections: SDP Wins Majorities in Senate and House of Representatives," British Broadcasting Corporation, Summary of World Broadcasts, 13 July 1992. West Africa; ME/1431/B/1.

11. Tensions ran so high during these days of suspense that when the director of USIS-Lagos, Michael O'Brien, declared any further postponement of the elections to be "unacceptable to the United States government," he was expelled from the country for his "blatant interference" with Nigeria's internal affairs. "Nigerian Election Still Set for Today," *San Diego Tribune,* 12 June 1993, A13.

12. The constitution stipulated that the winning candidate needed one-third of the vote in at least twenty of the thirty states. Sources for voting figures are from "Complaint Delays Release of Vote Results," Agence France Press, 15 June 1993; and

Michelle Faul, "Candidate Declares Victory in Nigerian Election," Associated Press, 18 June 1993.

13. At this time, noted singer and critic Gbenga Adewusi produced an underground recording in the Yoruba *Oro* chanting mode that circulated widely in shops and on the airwaves. The artist, who was jailed and released, is credited for bringing IBB down with the song "Babangida Must Go!" and for influencing events with the power of his curse.

14. It would be interesting to see if the old method of covering one's misappropriation—burning down the government buildings where the records were kept—decreased after the "reforms."

15. This popular revision of an official appellation or acronym provides an example of what Mbembe (1992, 8), no doubt following de Certeau (1988, 168), calls the "poaching" of meanings, as when Cameroonians renamed the Rassemblement Démocratique du Peuple Camerounais (RDPC) "redépécer," as a gloss for "cut it up and dole it out!" Nigerians sometimes jokingly refer to NEPA, the National Electric Power Authority, as "Never Expect Power Again" because of its long and frequent power failures.

16. See Barber 1982; Bastian 1991; Fagunwa 1961; and Matory 1994 (123–24) for discussions of money-making magic. When Major General Muhammadu Buhari changed the currency notes after his 1983 coup (in an effort to regulate the money supply and to determine the amount that the Shagari government printed to buy votes), a rash of kidnappings were reported because—like everybody else—rich wizards *(oso)* using money-magic also needed new bills.

17. Haynes describes a scene in Baba Sala's first film, *Orun Mooru/The Oven Is Hot* (1982), in which Baba Sala is defrauded by an herbalist who "tricks him into believing he could magically fill oil drums with money, casting the magic of oil wealth in the idiom of 'traditional' money-magic" (1994, 3).

18. As part of SAP, the Central Bank abolished all controls on interest rates on 31 July 1987, which pushed prime lending rates up to more than 40 percent in some banks (Anyanwu 1992, 13).

19. I thank Robin Derby for this firsthand observation.

20. Since the time of writing, General Sani Abacha died in the arms of two prostitutes and Olusegun Obasanjo was released from detention to win the presidential elections of 27 February 1999. Yar'Adua died in prison.

21. I have developed this argument more fully in Apter 1998, where the concluding discussion of civil society as a sphere of circulation first appeared.

References

Anyanwu, John C. 1992. "President Babangida's Structural Adjustment Programme and Inflation in Nigeria." *Journal of Social Development in Africa* 7 (1): 5–24.

Apter, Andrew. 1987. "Things Fell Apart? Yoruba Responses to the 1983 Elections in Ondo State, Nigeria." *Journal of Modern African Studies* 25 (3): 489–503.

———. 1998. "Death and the King's Henchmen: Ken Saro-Wiwa and the Political Ecology of Citizenship in Nigeria." In *Ogoni's Agonies: Ken Saro-Wiwa and the Crisis in Nigeria,* ed. Abdul-Rasheed Na'Allah. Trenton and Asmara: Africa World Press, 121–60.

Balibar, Etienne. 1991. "The Nation Form: History and Ideology." In *Race, Nation, Class: Ambiguous Identities,* ed. E. Balibar and I. Wallerstein. London: Verso, 86–106.

Bastian, Misty. 1991. "My Head Was Too Strong: Body Parts and Money Magic in Nigerian Popular Discourse." Paper presented at the Committee of African and African American Studies' conference on "Meaningful Currencies and Monetary Imaginations: Money: Commodities and Symbolic Process in Africa," University of Chicago.

Barber, Karin. 1982. "Popular Reactions to the Petro-Naira." *Journal of Modern African Studies* 20 (3): 431–50.

Bayart, Jean-François. 1993. *The State in Africa: The Politics of the Belly.* Translated by Mary Harper. London: Longman.

Beaty, Jonathan, and S. C. Gwynne. 1993. *The Outlaw Bank: A Wild Ride into the Secret Heart of BCCI.* New York: Random House.

Benjamin, Walter. 1983. *Charles Baudelaire: A Lyric Poet in the Era of High Capitalism.* London: Verso.

Bhabha, Homi. 1994. *The Location of Culture.* London: Routledge.

Canetti, Elias. [1962] 1984. *Crowds and Power.* Translated by Carol Stewart. Reprint, New York: Farrar, Straus and Giroux.

Certeau, Michel de. 1988. *The Practice of Everyday Life.* Translated by Steven Rendall. Berkeley: University of California Press.

Emecheta, Buchi. 1982. *Naira Power.* London: Macmillan.

Fadahunsi, Akin. 1993. "Devaluation: Implications for Employment, Inflation, Growth and Development." In *The Politics of Structural Adjustment in Nigeria,* ed. A. O. Olukoshi. London: James Curry, 33–53.

Fagunwa, D. O. 1961. *Aditu Olodumare.* Lagos: Nelson.

Foucault, Michel. 1991. "Governmentality." In *The Foucault Effect: Studies in Governmentality,* ed. G. Burchell et al. Chicago: University of Chicago Press, 87–104.

Geisler, Gisela. 1993. "Fair? What Has Fairness Got to Do with It? Vagaries of Election Observations and Democratic Standards." *Journal of Modern African Studies* 31 (4): 613–37.

Goffman, Erving. 1974. *Frame Analysis: An Essay on the Organization of Experience.* New York: Harper and Row.

Gordon, Colin. 1991. "Governmental Rationality: An Introduction." In *The Foucault Effect: Studies in Governmentality,* ed. G. Burchell et al. Chicago: University of Chicago Press, 1–51.

Halttunen, Karen. 1982. *Confidence Men and Painted Women: A Study of Middle-Class Culture in America, 1830–1870.* New Haven: Yale University Press.

Hart, Christopher. 1993. "The Nigerian Elections of 1983." *Africa* 63 (3) 397–418.

Harvey, David. 1989. *The Condition of Postmodernity: An Enquiry into the Origins of Cultural Change.* Oxford: Blackwell.

Haynes, Jonathan. 1994. "Structural Adjustments of Nigerian Comedy: Baba Sala." Paper presented at conference, Media, Popular Culture and "the Public" in Africa. Institute for Advanced Study and Research in the African Humanities, Northwestern University, 30 April.

Helleiner, G. 1966. *Peasant Agriculture, Government, and Economic Growth in Nigeria.* Homewood, Ill.: Richard D. Irwin.

Ibrahim, Jibrin. 1993. "The Transition to Civilian Rule: Sapping Democracy." In *The Politics of Structural Adjustment in Nigeria,* ed. A. O. Olukoshi. London: James Currey, 129–39.

Ige, Bola. 1991. *Kaduna Boy.* Ibadan: NPS Educational.

Imoko, Dave. 1991. "An Overview of Structural Adjustments in Nigeria." *Nigerian Interpreter* 5 (4): 4–7.

Joseph, Richard. 1987. *Democracy and Prebendal Politics in Nigeria: The Rise and Fall of the Second Republic.* Cambridge: Cambridge University Press.

Kunz, Frank. 1995. "Civil Society in Africa." *Journal of Modern African Studies* 33 (1): 181–87.

Marx, Karl. 1976. *Capital: A Critique of Political Economy,* vol. 1. Translated by Ben Fowkes. Harmondsworth, Eng.: Penguin. Quoted in Moishe Postone, *Time, Labor, and Social Domination: A Reinterpretation of Marx's Critical Theory* (Cambridge: Cambridge University Press, 1993).

Matory, J. Lorand. 1994. *Sex and the Empire That Is No More: Gender and the Politics of Metaphor in Oyo Yoruba Religion.* Minneapolis: University of Minnesota Press.

Mbembe, Achille. 1992. "The Banality of Power and the Aesthetics of Vulgarity in the Postcolony." *Public Culture* 4 (2): 1–30.

National Electoral Commission (NEC). 1989. *Report and Recommendations on Party Formation* (Lagos, 1989), 8–9; quoted in Oyediran and Agbaje (1991, 225).

Ofeimun, Odia. 1989. "Democracy by Fiat." *West Africa,* 18–24 December, 2091–93.

Ogbonna, A., and E. Udo. 1993. "Face to Face with Failure." *Financial Post* 5 (22), 6–19 June, 1, 6.

Olorunyomi, Dapo. 1993. "The Giwa Affair." *The News,* 25 October, 13–18.

O'Malley, Michael. 1994. "Specie and Species: Race and the Money Question in Nineteenth-Century America." *American Historical Review* 99 (2): 369–95.

Oyediran, O., and A. Agbaje. 1991. "Two-Partyism and Democratic Transition in Nigeria." *Journal of Modern African Studies* 29 (2): 213–35.

Riddell, J. Barry. 1992. "Things Fall Apart Again: Structural Adjustment Programmes in Sub-Saharan Africa." *Journal of Modern African Studies* 30 (1): 53–68.

Saro-Wiwa, Ken. 1992. *Genocide in Nigeria: The Ogoni Tragedy.* London: Saros International Publishers.

———. 1991. *Similia: Essays on Anomic Nigeria.* London: Saros International Publishers

———. 1990. Introduction to *Ogoni Bill of Rights: Presented to the Government and*

People of Nigeria. Published by the Movement for the Survival of Ogoni People (MOSOP).

Scott, David. 1995. "Colonial Governmentality." *Social Text* 43:191–220.

Takaya, Bala, and S. G. Tyoden, eds. 1987. *The Kaduna Mafia: A Study of the Rise, Development and Consolidation of a Nigerian Power Elite.* Jos: Jos University Press.

Taussig, Michael. 1993. *Mimesis and Alterity: A Particular History of the Senses.* New York and London: Routledge.

Thomas, Nicholas. 1994. *Colonialism's Culture: Anthropology, Travel and Government.* Princeton: Princeton University Press.

Truell, Peter, and Larry Gurwin. 1992. *BCCI: The Inside Story of the World's Most Corrupt Financial Empire.* London: Bloomsbury.

Ukim, Utibe. 1994. "Where Is the Money?" *Newswatch,* 24 October, 9–14.

Useh, Abraham. 1993. "Babangida (Nigeria) Unlimited." *Tell* 41, October 18, 7–13.

Watts, Michael. 1992. "The Shock of Modernity: Petroleum, Protest, and Fast Capitalism in an Industrializing Society." In *Reworking Modernity: Capitalisms and Symbolic Discontent,* A. Pred and M. Watts. New Brunswick: Rutgers University Press, 21–63.

———. 1994. "Oil as Money: The Devil's Excrement and the Spectacle of Black Gold." In *Money, Power and Space,* ed. Ron Martin. Oxford: Blackwell, 406–45.

Welch, Claude, Jr. 1995. "The Ogoni and Self-Determination: Increasing Violence in Nigeria." *Journal of Modern African Studies* 33 (4): 635–49.

CONTRIBUTORS

Andrew Apter is an associate professor of anthropology at the University of Chicago. Author of *Black Critics and Kings* (1992), he writes on politics, ritual, and representation in Nigeria and the Caribbean.

William Cunningham Bissell is currently completing his Ph.D. in anthropology at the University of Chicago. His primary research interests lie in colonial cities and the politics of space and place; he conducted his doctoral study in Stone Town, Zanzibar.

Jean Comaroff is the Bernard E. and Ellen C. Sunny Distinguished Service Professor of Anthropology at the University of Chicago. Her books include *Body of Power, Spirit of Resistance* (1985) and, with John Comaroff, *Of Revelation and Revolution,* vols. 1 and 2 (1991, 1997).

John L. Comaroff is the Harold H. Swift Distinguished Service Professor of Anthropology at the University of Chicago. His books include, with Simon Roberts, *Rules and Processes* (1981) and, with Jean Comaroff, *Ethnography and the Historical Imagination* (1992).

Deborah Durham is an assistant professor of anthropology at Sweet Briar College. Her research has been centered on Botswana; she has written about ethnicity, democratic liberalism, the place of youth in society, and Herero identities in southern Africa.

Mariane Ferme is an assistant professor of anthropology at the University of California, Berkeley. She has written on the politics of religious change, the aesthetics of secrecy, gendered practices, and personhood in Sierra Leone.

Elizabeth Garland is a Ph.D. student in anthropology at the University of Chicago. Earlier interested in development work in Namibia, she has done research on gorilla tourism in Uganda and is currently working on her doctoral study.

Mikael Karlström is currently a Harper-Schmidt Instructor in the College at the University of Chicago. His doctoral research in Uganda concerns the politics of Ganda kingship, past and present; he has also written on processes of democratization in East Africa.

Adeline Masquelier is an associate professor of anthropology at Tulane University. She has worked in Niger, focusing on the Bori cult, spirit possession, and, more generally, the connections between modernity and mystical practices.

Amy Stambach is an assistant professor in the Department of Education and Policy Studies at the University of Wisconsin, Madison. She has worked in Tanzania, studying schooling among the Chagga peoples of Kilimanjaro.

Gary Wilder is an assistant professor of history at Pomona College. His doctoral work focuses on colonial government and cultural nationalism within the French imperial nation-state during the interwar period; his research intersects political history, historical anthropology, and social theory.

Index